IAN HEALY

Hands & Heals

Best Wishes

Ian Healy

IAN HEALY

Hands & Heals

THE AUTOBIOGRAPHY

HarperSports
An imprint of HarperCollinsPublishers

Harper*Sports*
An imprint of HarperCollins*Publishers*, Australia

First published in Australia in 2000
Reprinted in 2000
by HarperCollins*Publishers* Pty Limited
ABN 36 009 913 517
A member of the HarperCollins*Publishers* (Australia) Pty Limited Group
http://www.harpercollins.com.au

Copyright © Ian Healy 2000

HarperCollins*Publishers*
25 Ryde Road, Pymble, Sydney, NSW 2073, Australia
31 View Road, Glenfield, Auckland 10, New Zealand
77-85 Fulham Palace Road, London W6 8JB, United Kingdom
Hazelton Lanes, 55 Avenue Road, Suite 2900, Toronto, Ontario M5R 3L2
and 1995 Markham Road, Scarborough, Ontario M1B 5M8, Canada
10 East 53rd Street, New York, NY 10022, USA

A CIP record of this title is available from the National Library of Australia.

ISBN 0 7322 6758 7.

Front cover design: Bluecork
Design and finished art: Brevier Design
Printed and bound in Australia by Griffin Press on 100gsm Publishers Offset

7 6 5 4 3 2
03 02 01 00

CONTENTS

FOREWORD *by Ian McDonald*   vii

INTRODUCTION *by Geoff Armstrong*   ix

FROM BILOELA TO THE BAGGY GREEN   1

1   **A LUCKY COUNTRY KID**   5

2   **HOW GOOD IS THIS!**   17

3   **THE ONLY ONE**   28

4   **STICKING IT UP 'EM**   42

5   **THE ASHES 1989**   53

6   **THE GAME GOES ON**   67

7   **THE TOUGHEST TEST**   78

8   **FOR TEAM AND COUNTRY**   89

9   **IS IT WORTH IT?**   98

10   **A GREAT DAY IN MY LIFE**   108

11   **THAT'S FOR YOU, GRANDPA**   120

12   **BAD BREAKS IN PAKISTAN**   130

13   **ASHES PAIN, SHIELD GLORY**   139

14   **WAUGHSOME!**   153

15   **UNDER THE SOUTHERN CROSS**   164

16   **CAPTAIN DIPLOMACY**   178

17   **KEEPING THE FAITH**   187

18   **KARACHI'S GONE, MATE!**   197

19   **SACKED AS VICE-CAPTAIN**   208

20   **BOWLED WARNEY**   218

21   **A NEW WORLD RECORD**   230

22   **THE FINAL STRAIGHT**   245

23   **A GOOD LIFE**   254

STATISTICS *by Ian Russell*   265

INDEX   282

PHOTOGRAPHY CREDITS

The authors and publishers are very grateful for the support of the following photographic sources.

ACP Sport: page 129.

Allsport Australia: pages 35, 52, 60, 63, 72, 90, 113, 115 (both), 118, 121, 126, 134 (both), 143 (all), 144, 155, 159, 161, 163, 168 (both), 174 (both), 176, 180, 185, 190, 194, 199, 201, 205, 210, 219, 228, 231, 233 (bottom), 235 (top), 238, 241, 247, 249, 253, 257, 259.

Courier-Mail: 18 (photographer Glenn Barnes), 21, 88 (right), 165, 207 (right).

Patrick Eagar: pages 2, 55, 65.

Empics Sports Photo Agency: pages 110, 212 (both).

News Limited: pages 29, 50, 70, 76, 79, 85, 87, 88 (left), 94, 100, 103, 106, 123, 124, 132, 136, 149, 182, 189, 207 (left), 225, 235 (bottom), 262.

Queensland Cricket (photographer Bob Jones): page 257.

Reuters: page 39.

Sport. The Library: pages 220.

Steve Waugh: pages 237, 251 (both).

The still of the run out of Curtly Ambrose on page 196 appears with the kind permission of Channel Nine.

Colour

Section 1

ACP Sport: page 3 (bottom).
Allsport Australia: pages 2 (both), 6 (both), 7 (all).
Patrick Eagar: pages 1, 3 (top), 4 (top).
News Limited: page 8 (bottom).
Sport. The Library: pages 4 (bottom), 5, 8 (top).

Section 2

ACP Sport: page 2 (top).
Agence France-Presse: page 6 (bottom).
Allsport Australia: pages 2 (bottom), 3 (all), 6 (top), 7 (both), 8 (both).
Jamie Hanson (Sunday Mail): page 5 (top).
Patrick Eagar: pages 1, 5 (bottom).
Empics Sports Photo Agency: page 4 (top).

All other photographs in *Hands & Heals* are from private collections.

GEOFF ARMSTRONG

Geoff Armstrong, who worked with Ian Healy in the development of *Hands & Heals*, is also the author of the official centenary book of the Sheffield Shield, *A Century of Summers* (published in 1992). As well, he co-wrote *The People's Game* (1994), a history of Australia in international one-day cricket, with Mark Gately. He was the compiler and editor of *The Greatest Game* (1990), the first anthology ever produced on Australian rugby league, and the co-author of Mike Whitney's book, *Whiticisms* (1995).

Armstrong has worked with Steve Waugh on each of the Australian captain's eight best-selling books, and is the co-author, with Peter Thompson, of *Phar Lap* (published October 2000) and co-editor, with Ian Heads, of *Winning Attitudes* (June 2000).

He has also worked as editor or publisher with a number of Australian sporting personalities, including Mal Meninga, David Boon, Peter Brock, Merv Hughes, Bob Simpson, Laurie Lawrence, Michael Slater, Geoff Lawson, and Wayne Pearce, and with writers and commentators such as Bruce McAvaney, Ian Heads, Peter FitzSimons, Gordon Bray, Phil Cleary, Phil Tresidder, Larry Writer, Mark Ray, Neil Marks, David Middleton and Alan Aitken.

FOREWORD

by Ian McDonald
Australian team manager, 1986–1998

IN AUSTRALIAN DRESSING ROOM folklore, the player chosen by his teammates to jump on a table and lead the victory chant after an Aussie win, by reciting *Under the Southern Cross*, always typifies the tough, never-give-in image that is the traditional hallmark of Australian teams … a man who wears the famous 'baggy green' with intense pride.

Such a man is Ian Healy. It is a tribute to his character as a player that he was chosen to follow his boyhood hero, Rod Marsh, Australia's most famous 'little Aussie battler' Allan Border, and the rock-like Tasmanian David Boon in filling this role. When Boon named him as his successor in January 1996, Ian Healy took over with tremendous pride and fulfilled the role with passion and gusto.

That's the way he was behind the wickets and that's the way he played his cricket. He was a tough, uncompromising team man with a fierce determination to win. Of course, wicketkeepers are tough nuts anyway — they're a special breed, an integral part of the team with play revolving around them, always cajoling their teammates, the sort of blokes you would like beside you if you were fighting in the trenches. Australia has a proud tradition of producing great keepers, stretching back to Jack Blackham in the 19th century. The toughness of the fraternity was typified by Bert Oldfield during the 1932–33 Bodyline series, when he had his skull cracked standing up to the English bumper barrage. In more modern times, there have been Don Tallon, who was in Don Bradman's famous 1948 team, Wally Grout, who was with Richie Benaud's teams in the late 1950s and early 1960s, Rod Marsh, who was in Ian and Greg Chappell's teams, and then Heals. There have been other good keepers, but when it comes to the best ever, the argument inevitably narrows down to the three Queenslanders — Tallon, Grout and Healy — and the West Australian, Marsh. I've been fortunate to see all four in action and each brought his own individuality, flair and touch of class to the toughest role in cricket.

Comparing players from different eras is difficult, but there are two indicators that place Healy at the top of the field. Statistically, he is Australia's greatest keeper, having passed Rod Marsh's record of 355 dismissals, and in 1999–2000 he was selected as wicketkeeper in the ACB–ACA Team of the Century. He was in elite company in that team, alongside Sir Donald Bradman, Arthur Morris, Bill Ponsford, Neil Harvey, Greg Chappell, Keith Miller, Shane Warne, Bill O'Reilly, Ray Lindwall, Dennis Lillee and Allan Border. It was apt that Warne was selected in that team with Healy, because television viewers throughout the world had become used to hearing Heals yelling out through the stump microphone, 'Bowled Warney!' The combination of the great legspinner and the astute Healy became the most lethal in world cricket, a combination that ranks with that of Rod Marsh and Dennis Lillee, because like Healy bettering Marsh's record, Warne also broke Lillee's Australian Test wicket-taking record.

Healy's ability to keep so well to the prodigious spin of Warne was a pleasure to witness, but so too were his performances keeping to pacemen such as his mate Craig McDermott, who rose from the ranks of Queensland junior cricket with him, the volatile Merv Hughes, and then Glenn McGrath, who is well on the way to breaking a few records himself.

There Heals crouched behind the stumps, sleeves rolled down, shirt collar turned up most of the time, and the baggy green pulled very firmly on his blonde head. Always well prepared, because that's the nature of the man, he was also always well organised and very fussy about neatness. It must have something to do with the sun in Queensland, because in my 13 years as Australian Team Manager, Heals, Craig McDermott and Allan Border stood out as the neatest and best organised players in the dressing room. Away from these players' places, it often looked as if a cyclone had scattered gear everywhere.

If ever there was a role model for kids, Heals was it. The country boy from Biloela got to the top and stayed there through sheer hard work, aided by a fierce determination to succeed and the courage to overcome and play with painful injuries. Earlier in his career I used to wonder where he'd disappeared to in the morning before breakfast. Some players jog, swim or go to the gym but Heals wasn't to be seen, until one morning I went to the basement carpark at our Melbourne hotel and found him with his inner gloves on throwing and catching a golf ball as it rebounded from the wall, making sure his footwork and glovework were right — all to ensure that when he took the field he would be able to move his feet into position quickly, ready to take the ball on the inside of his body. Like Grout and Marsh, he worked on the principle that you should be in position to take the ball on your feet and only dive if you have to.

Popular with his teammates, he was always one of the boys — geeing them up on the field and celebrating with them when they won. His popularity didn't always extend to officialdom, because sometimes he over-celebrated, and he was a strong advocate for players' rights, was at the forefront of the push for a Players Association and was involved in the 1997–98 players' dispute with the ACB. Heals is as honest as they come, but sometimes his forthright attitude ruffled a few official feathers. Despite this he had their respect, because he was doing it the only way he knows — fighting to get the best for his team.

After the Allan Border era ended in 1994, Healy, Mark Taylor, Steve and Mark Waugh and David Boon became the experienced backbone of a team that rose to No. 1 in the world. This book takes you on that trip with him. His career ended at the Gabba in 1999, his family were all there — his wife Helen and their three kids, his mother and the rest of the Healy tribe — and as he was driven around the ground in an open car the crowd gave him a standing ovation.

It was a fitting farewell for a great Australian keeper ... and a great bloke.

by Geoff Armstrong

I FIRST SAT DOWN to talk to Ian Healy about his autobiography on January 19, 2000, the day after he'd been named as the wicketkeeper in Australia's Team of the Century. I asked him straight away what it was like to be thought of so highly, above all the other keepers who'd dreamed of appearing in grade cricket, never mind playing for Australia. As a boy playing with his brothers in the backyard, against the men on Saturday afternoons, or even in his sleep, he wouldn't have dared imagine, surely, that his cricket life would end with such an achievement, being part of a team as renowned as this.

'Mate, it's kind of surreal,' was his response. He was extremely honoured, and clearly at least a little overawed to have his name included in such exalted company. More than any other high-profile cricketer I have met, I was struck by what an unaffected bloke he was. Nothing in the six months that followed, as we trawled through his life and cricket experiences and built the chapters that make up this book, changed that impression.

Later, his wife Helen told me the story of a very excited and emotional husband, standing behind a curtain at that Team of the Century function and on his mobile phone as he waited to have his photo taken with his new teammates. 'If I'd known this was going to happen,' he told her, 'I'd have got you and Mum down here.' It was a simple wish — one he has emphasised whenever he's talked to me about that day — which genuinely reflects the gratitude he feels for his family's support, from the early days, the best part of 30 years ago, when his parents began to help shape his cricket life, to the long tours through the 1990s when Helen stayed behind to keep house, offer support and for long periods raise their three children on her own.

Helen is clearly very proud of her husband's achievements, and can philosophically look back on his extended leave from family life. It was, she concedes, part of the game. It is almost as if she taught herself to enjoy them.

> **Helen Healy:** I got used to the absences, even to the point where there was one tour and he was away for about eight weeks, but came home early. It threw things here into total disarray. I was far better off knowing what day he was leaving and what day he was coming home; I'd be fine with that. Normally, about a week after he'd gone, I'd have a day of thinking, 'Oh, God this is going to be a long time', but then I'd pick myself up and get on with it.
>
> To this day, I don't know how I managed to watch him, weekend after weekend, playing grade cricket for Norths before we were married. And it wasn't just for an hour. I sat in his mum's little white Torana for the whole day,

and when play finally finished they'd get changed, have a beer and he'd roll up to me at 7.30pm. I didn't know what I was getting into, but I was happy to go along for the ride. It was a case of like it or lump it. I am by nature a very independent person and was happy to run everything here, and then go away on tours when I could.

Ian Healy's original Test selection, for the Australians' difficult 1988 tour of Pakistan, came from nowhere. For the first two years of his international career he routinely kept his place without ever really convincing the cricket community that he was truly Test class. However, from around the start of the 1990–91 Australian summer until 1996 he was an automatic selection, and from 1994 his country's vice-captain, as he built an imposing record and reputation. But then, with captain Mark Taylor's extended batting slump, the development of the concept of separate Australian Test and one-day sides, and the emergence of Adam Gilchrist, a lesser gloveman but superior batsman, Healy's status was suddenly questioned, first in the media and then around selection tables. First, before the 1997 Ashes tour, he lost the vice-captaincy; then, straight after that tour, the one-day keeping job. Two years later came retirement, after 231 first-class matches, 119 Tests, 168 one-day internationals, 395 Test dismissals, 4356 Test runs, four Test centuries …

It is generally acknowledged that Greg Chappell played a key role in first getting Healy into the Australian team. In the four seasons since Rod Marsh had retired in 1984, no one had been able to lock themselves into the keeping role, and Chappell, back in 1988 a member of the Australian selection committee, saw in Healy the kind of qualities he felt the position, and the side, needed.

'We were searching for guys who had strength of character as well as talent,' he told the *Sydney Morning Herald*'s Philip Derriman in 1996. 'Healy wasn't the best keeper, the best gloveman, in the country then, but he was uncompromising in his determination to succeed, which is what Australia needed.'

In the pages that follow, Healy tells the story of Chappell coming up to him in the dressing room during the lunch break of a Shield game against Tasmania in Launceston. It is Healy's belief that their brief chat was what first put the idea that Healy might be a Test player of the future in Chappell's head. Healy was 58 not out at the time, and playing just his fourth first-class game, as a substitute for the injured Peter Anderson, the highly rated regular Queensland wicketkeeper. Chappell remembers that dressing room conversation with Healy, too, but recalls also a discussion he observed between Healy and the other not out batsman, Glenn Trimble, who was well past his hundred. The match was delicately poised, and Trimble wasn't quite sure what to do. Greg Chappell's memory is that the talk went like this:

Glenn Trimble: 'What do we do?'

Ian Healy: 'Mate, we just go back out there and keep doing what we're doing. We got to try to get the team into a position to win the game.'

That Queensland side was in a bit of turmoil, with a clear split between captain Allan Border and star import Ian Botham. Chappell watched Healy over that week at the ground and in and around the team hotel, and saw that Healy was smart enough to back his own judgment, make his own decisions and keep away from where the trouble was.

Greg Chappell: In doing this, he reminded me very much of Rodney Marsh. He had the same attributes that stood Rodney in good stead. He also had a lot of talent, a terrific temperament and a great desire to succeed.

For Healy's first Australian captain, Allan Border, who was also his state captain through much of the 1980s (though often required on the international stage when Healy was taking his first steps in first-class cricket), the early memories of the wicketkeeper are not as strong as Greg Chappell's.

Allan Border: He was just another young bloke in the nets. In the latter stages of his career, Heals' keeping was just phenomenal, but back when he started, I reckon Peter Anderson probably had a little bit more flair. But whether that made Anderson a better keeper or not ...

Pakistan was probably a good first-up education for Heals, because it was hard work keeping over there, with the heat, the low bounce and the varying conditions. I think he came back from that tour saying, 'Well, I've got a bit of work to do if I'm going to keep at this level.'

He had a tough initiation, but then you realise that he'd only played half a dozen first-class games and had never, ever experienced two and a half days in the field with gloves on [before that first Test]. I think it would take a special type of person not to make mistakes in those circumstances. So it was straight into the cauldron for I. Healy, and I think he came out of it pretty well.

One person who was stunned by that initial selection was Steve Waugh, a NSW teammate of the previous Australian keeper, Greg Dyer. Waugh had played against Healy in the Under 19s, and the two had been opposing captains in a rained-out NSW–Queensland Colts match in 1984, but otherwise he knew little about him.

Steve Waugh: At that time most of the guys, including myself, were more concerned trying to establish themselves in the team. But we had heard good reports about Heals, that he was an excellent team man and potentially a very good keeper and batsman.

What he brought to the team initially was his tough attitude. He didn't really care who he was playing against and their reputations. He just got in there and did the hard work, did the dirty stuff, got stuck in. We learned over his first couple of seasons that he wasn't afraid to say things on the field, whereas others might have protected their reputations a little. He was always there at the forefront, putting himself in tough situations and backing himself to get out of them.

Healy's long-time friend and cricket comrade, Craig McDermott, has spoken of Healy's 'presence' on the field, a constant threat — not physical, but psychological — behind the batsman's back. That Healy was sometimes sharply criticised for his on-field belligerence was almost an inevitable by-product. In most cases, he accepted that criticism, and his captain wasn't too concerned.

Allan Border: With the advent of stump microphones you hear a lot more of the wicketkeeper than you ever did in the past. Every wicketkeeper I've played with or against, they all tend to be the focus for the fielding side. You need to have someone in the field yakking it up and most keepers take it upon themselves to keep the vibe going out in the field.

Heals was one of those blokes who thought, if I think that this bloke deserves a bit of a rocket I'm going to give it to him. If the West Indies or anyone else didn't like it … tough. The Windies had run roughshod over everyone for the previous 10 years and it was about time some of us threw the anchor out and dug our heels in.

I think Heals has to take a lot of credit for the way Australian cricket is at the moment, as far as the steely toughness that's in the side, the work ethic and the resolve to win. That's Ian Healy. He was a real focal point for the players in the side. Even from his very early days he was a very strong character within the team.

Occasionally for Healy, though, the public scrutiny did wear thin; never more so than in 1992–93, when TV replays showed over and over again that the West Indies' Brian Lara had been wrongly given out stumped after Healy's gloves had broken the stumps without having control of the ball. Healy admits that the endless analysis, barbs from spectators, a disclaimer from the umpire and bitter recriminations from his opponents brought him to the verge of a premature retirement. Australian team manger Ian McDonald's view is that Healy got himself more upset than he needed to, but perhaps that response shows something about the man that has in the main been kept from the public view.

Errol Alcott (long-time Australian team physiotherapist): Heals always wanted to be out there. And he's shown me, too, that he's a man of emotion. I've seen him cry, and I've seen him belly laugh. He had a determination, a fierce competitiveness and a tunnel vision in regard to his expectations of perfection for himself. Sure, he had his ups and downs, but he is human …

From our many conversations over the past six months, I have learned that, despite his 'tough guy' image, Healy is a bloke who suffers the same human frailties as all of us. He does want to be liked, while conceding that his hard-nosed approach to his sport inevitably made him unpopular with some opponents and occasionally with opposition supporters, too. This is a potentially dangerous emotional mix, and from time to time the stresses that came with this conflict affected the Healy mood. His personal diaries — which became such a fantastic resource for us as we went back over his cricket life — sometimes reveal a man not quite as confident and comfortable as those around him may have thought.

When I suggested to Steve Waugh that his long-time teammate and friend could not always have been as self-assured as his cricket face indicated, he thought for a moment …

Steve Waugh: That's an interesting call. People think Heals is very confident, which he can be, but I think everyone at the top level has their doubts …

I don't think we realised until his last year of cricket that in some ways Heals was a bit insecure. It all surfaced towards the end of his career, when he made a few of us aware of certain things that we had all taken for granted. We thought he could play every game and was indestructible; that he didn't need to be talked to a lot, didn't need a lot of praise. We just thought he was so good at his job that he'd keep going, that we didn't need to pep him up. But towards the end it became increasingly obvious that he did need a bit more support than he'd got over the years.

His role in the team was such a demanding one — keeping, batting, being one of the leading players in all discussions during team meetings and on social committees. He was never far from the action on the field, all the time. He was regularly being described in the papers as being a 'sledger'. We saw him as being so mentally tough that we could leave him alone with all that. But eventually, I guess, it all took a toll.

There is no doubt that Healy was hurt by three selectors' decisions, made between April 1997 and October 1999: the first cost him the vice-captaincy, the second his place in the one-day team and the last hastened his retirement. As he constantly stressed to me as we worked on this book, he can see the thinking behind all three — though he might not agree with such logic — and recognises entirely the right and duty of selectors to make such decisions. What grates with him, though, is that the manner in which he was treated suggested a lack of respect from the decision-makers for what he had achieved and the pain and effort that had gone into this work. Are high achievers entitled to such esteem?

Steve Waugh: I think he did sometimes get treated harshly. Particularly in the case of the vice captaincy — he didn't deserve to lose it. He was sacrificed because of the situation that was going on at the time. It was a decision I didn't believe was right. If you tend to make a fuss, carry on and seem to be vulnerable, people tend to take a bit more notice and take care of you a bit more. But if you're tough and look as if you don't need help, then people are more likely to cast you aside.

When I got the vice-captaincy [before the 1997 Ashes tour], it was unexpected. I was actually shopping at Grace Bros when I got the phone call from Trevor Hohns [the chairman of selectors] and was pretty shocked that Heals had been dropped as vice-captain and I'd replaced him. It was a tough situation, because he's a good mate and I respect him as a player and a person. I knew it meant a lot to him, being vice-captain.

In the final instance, his retirement, the angst came not over whether he should retire but when. For more than six months, Healy wrestled with a range of conflicting emotions, and then, with his mind made up, he came up with what he thought was the perfect retirement plan. Unfortunately, things went awry, which — as he explains in Chapter 22 — left him again feeling let down by the selectors. It does seem clear that all three situations could have been handled better.

Helen Healy: Ian was so ready to retire. I could sense that in the 12 months before it finally happened. His whole demeanour changed. Whereas once he would always give 150 per cent to keep the team together, in that last season he'd ring me at night and I'd ask, 'Why aren't you out with the boys?' Early days, he was very much for keeping the guys together, working behind the scenes to get team camaraderie up and running. But towards the end I could see how that had become too big a role for him. I think the constant travel, the day in, day out monotony of the routine, wore him down.

I know the life of an Australian cricketer always looks very glamorous to everybody else. But I could understand how you'd get that burnt-out feeling. And then everything becomes a struggle.

Healy left the game with more dismissals and more appearances than any other keeper in Test history. In fact, his array of records — across Test and one-day international cricket — is remarkable. A trawl through Ian Russell's exhaustive statistics at the end of this book will find any number of laurels and landmarks. Did you know, for example, that Healy was the 100th person to score a Test century for Australia? That his 161 not out against the West Indians in Brisbane in late 1996 is the highest score ever made by an Australian keeper in Tests? That he is the only wicketkeeper to play 100 Tests? That he completed more Test dismissals off Glenn McGrath and Craig McDermott than off Shane Warne?

But records and milestones aside, just how good was he? Allan Border describes him as a 'keeper of substance, probably our best ever …'.

Steve Waugh: The sign of a really good wicketkeeper is if you don't notice him. We never noticed Heals making too much fuss, making any errors or taking unnecessarily spectacular catches. Once again, we took him for granted. He took some magnificent catches, but his standards were so high that in the end you didn't even realise that he was performing so well because, for Heals, it was just run of the mill, everyday stuff. Now, I look back and think that there were very few chances that he missed throughout his whole career.

He was an outstanding keeper, who got better as the years went by. His keeping to Shane Warne was phenomenal. Warney would quite often bowl into the rough well outside leg stump, pitching in a place where the keeper couldn't have got a sight of the ball. But Heals' reflexes and instincts were such that he always knew where the ball was going to be, which is a skill you can't coach or learn. Heals was also a deceptively good mover, with a great technique, which was something he always worked on. He was always in the right position and had a unique knack for sniffing out a half chance. When I was fielding in the slips or in the gully, every time I heard a nick I knew it was going to be out. If it was anywhere near Heals, for the batsman it was good evening.

And as a batsman? Healy and Steve Waugh had a highly successful time batting together in Test cricket. Their average per partnership was not much below 50, and three of Healy's four Test centuries involved long stands with Waugh. Inevitably, given that Steve usually batted at No. 5 or 6 and Healy at No. 7 for many seasons, the pair would have had many opportunities, but still their continued success together was impressive.

Steve Waugh: It was something about his personality, the way he played. Whenever he came in to bat, straight away I felt more relaxed and started to play more shots. For some reason, before he came in I really felt like I had to dig in and get a big score. Then Heals came out and I knew that he would take the pressure off me. He'd play his shots and I could relax more. His presence seemed to bring out the best in my game. We did run together well. There was never much said about it, but I thought we were very good between wickets.

The rearguard stuff was what we really enjoyed, rather than coming together in a good situation; we probably played better when we knew the team depended on us. Yeah, it was always enjoyable batting with Heals. Good conversation ... he was pretty relaxing, but at the same time he was always focused on the job at hand. He was dedicated to doing well.

Off the field, it seems he was the ultimate team man. 'He gave it everything on the field, and off the field he'd celebrate real hard, as hard as anyone's ever celebrated,' is how Allan Border remembers him. 'I enjoyed that the most.'

Allan Border: When Heals used to get up on the table and do *Underneath the Southern Cross* ... he'd do it with such passion, he'd add little lines to it every now and then, he'd go through what happened in the match and take the piss or rev the troops up to a bit of a frenzy and then off into the verse. They're the endearing memories I've got of Heals, in the baggy green cap and a jock strap or whatever he had on at the time, singing our song with such passion ...

Helen Healy reckons her husband's greatest virtues are 'his honesty, integrity, work ethic, his devotion and passion to what he thinks are good things, and most of all, his loyalty'. His mother, Mrs Rae Healy, appreciates the fact that 'he's never been spoilt by his success'. As she puts it, 'Ian is always just an ordinary fellow.'

And that, for me, is the key to the autobiography that follows. Ian Healy is in so many ways simply a good, ordinary Australian bloke, albeit one who found himself in many unusual, very public and sometimes difficult situations. When he was attacked by an English fan after the last Ashes Test in 1994–95, he wrote in his diary, 'I am no longer a normal person.' In writing this, he was acknowledging the reality of a high-profile Australian cricketer's life. But despite such stresses, he was able to retain his earthiness, his humour and his humility throughout his career and beyond.

He's made good in the most highly regarded of Australia's sporting schools. One of the great joys of Australian cricket over the decades is that all young boys, rich or poor, from the city or the bush, can dream of playing for Australia. As Ian Healy's story demonstrates, all you need is plenty of talent, a penchant for hard work, a little luck, good instincts, team spirit and a bit of fire, passion and character, and you're a chance.

You might even make the Team of the Century.

—¤—

AT EVERY STAGE IN the development of Hands & Heals, I have been heartened by the support Heals and I have received from some very good people. Personally, I am very grateful for the backing and confidence of Ian's manager, Paul Smith, who has been such a strong supporter of this project from day one.

..And we have needed and appreciated the support and especially the patience of Barrie Hitchon and Shona Martyn from HarperCollins.

During the making of the book, so many people have put up with me squeezing deadlines and asking for the impossible, but they have all managed to deliver. I'm thinking especially of Jake Causby, Kylie Prats, Sarah Shrubb and Ian Russell — classy people without whom the book could never have happened. Mr Russell, or 'Mr Cricket' as we like to call him, has produced yet another astonishingly comprehensive statistics section. He also quickly but thoroughly read through the manuscript, finding the most minuscule of statistical errors as he went, and helping immensely in the process. Thanks, too, must go to Ian McDonald, for his help and prompt action with the Foreword.

In writing *Hands & Heals*, one excellent resource was Heals' first book, *Playing For Keeps*, which was published by Swan Publishing in 1996 and written with the help of Robert 'Crash' Craddock. Crash and Heals did an outstanding job with that book, and often as we flicked though its pages I had to accept that our job this time was not to try to outdo its paragraphs, but to match them.

The photographs in *Hands & Heals* come from a variety of sources. We are extremely grateful to the people at Allsport Australia, especially my good mate Mark 'Snoop' Skarschewski and their star wicketkeeper and boss, James Nicholls. Michelle Bailey at the *Courier-Mail* in Brisbane and Julian Zakaris and Cynthia Watts at News Limited in Sydney were also magnificent, and thanks, too, to Jeff Crow at Sport. The Library, Jen Little at Empics Sports Photo Agency in Nottingham, Norm Tasker and Darren Hadland at ACP Sport, Patrick Eagar and Steve Waugh.

Of course, there is no one to whom I am more grateful than the man himself. Before this project, I knew Heals was a good fella and a champion cricketer. Now, I know he's a champion bloke. He has a knack for saying the right thing at the right time, and I appreciated the way I always came away from talking to him feeling better about the book, the deadlines, about almost everything. His family — mother Rae, wife Helen and three kids, Emma, Laura and Tom — all made me feel welcome and were very helpful. In all, it has been a project I am very proud to have been a part of.

Geoff Armstrong
August 2000

FROM BILOELA TO THE BAGGY GREEN

THE LATE RAY LINDWALL is one of the greatest cricketers I have ever met. I don't mean 'great' in respect of his ability, which I'm sure was extraordinary if his record and the way people who saw him in his prime talk of him is any indication. But I never saw him play, so how can I truly judge? No, I mean 'great' purely in terms of the man — larger than life, a person whose aura in cricket circles was such that as soon as he moved into the group that you were in, joined your conversation or sat at your table, you knew you were in for an enjoyable and rewarding time.

In Hobart in November 1995, I found myself in the Bellerive Oval dressing room with Ray Lindwall and one of his Queensland and Australian teammates from the 1950s, Ron Archer. Outside, as a cold wind whipped off the Derwent River, it was chilly. However, in here the atmosphere was warm and hearty, even if, we three apart, the room was empty because the party that followed our victory over Pakistan in the second Test of that summer had moved on to the team hotel. We stayed behind, Queenslanders and Australians, and sat there with just our chat, a bottle of Bundaberg rum and my baggy green cap for company. We were toasting an Australian Test victory, but in fact the celebration, from my perspective at least, was for much more than that. As we slowly polished off the 'Bundy', Ray and Ron took turns, half an hour at a time, to wear my baggy green cap and reminisce about the good old days and compare those times with what I enjoyed today. In so doing they reminded me, never directly but simply and gently by who they were and what they said, how incredibly fortunate I was to be a part of their cricket family and to have the opportunity to wear that baggy green.

This was one of the most rewarding afternoons of my cricketing life. Sadly, Ray Lindwall passed away soon after, but the memory of our time together that day will stay with me forever.

—✻—

THE WAY AUSTRALIAN CRICKET maintains a link with its past, through traditions such as the baggy green, is one of its greatest features. When I went out to keep wicket for Australia, I was often reminded that I walked the same path as men such as Rod Marsh, Wally Grout, Don Tallon, Bert Oldfield and Jack Blackham. I would be pretending, however, if I said I was aware of this when I was first

First Test, Australia v the West Indies, Kingston, Jamaica, 1991.

selected for the national team, or that I quickly saw myself in their league. That didn't happen for a long time, maybe not even until that bottle of Bundy in Hobart. When I was first selected to wear that baggy green I had played just six first-class games — I went straight from being a club player to a Test cricketer — so I never had a chance to draw breath and appreciate what had gone before me. At that point I probably knew more about the story of my club, Norths, than I did about the history of the Australian team. Before that, playing and practising in the Queensland country town of Biloela, I'd lived only for the cricket moment. However, as I grew as a person and sportsman with the Australian XI, so too did my rapport with the traditions of the game grow. Consequently, when I was named in the Australian cricket Team of the Century on January 18, 2000 — alongside Ray Lindwall, among others — I rated my selection as the biggest thrill of my cricket career, the ultimate accolade.

The day of the announcement was in many ways a strange one. First up, I wasn't even aware that the team was being picked. At pre-function drinks, just before we moved in for the luncheon where the team would be revealed, the former Queensland and Australian wicketkeeper John Maclean came up to me and said, 'Heals, good luck ... you're short odds to make this team.'

'What team?'

'The Team of the Century.'

I don't know where I'd been. Maybe I'd had my head down, concentrating on my new role as a cricket commentator with Channel Nine. Perhaps there hadn't been sufficient publicity. More likely, I had been reading snippets, hearing whispers, but it just hadn't gelled that I was a contender. As John walked away, I started thinking ... maybe I am a show.

I was the world record holder for number of Test dismissals, although in my mind that didn't prove a whole lot — it just meant I'd played more matches than my predecessors. A second thing in my favour was that I had just retired, which meant I might receive a small 'sympathy' vote. The selection panel was dominated by former cricketers, all of whom know how hard it is to finally call it quits. Thirdly, I had the good fortune to keep to the greatest legspin bowler of all time, Shane Warne, which advertised a part of my ability in a way no other keeper ever could.

And, I imagined, the selectors would have looked through their alternatives at every position and thought, subconsciously, 'We'd better put a modern guy or two in.' If players such as Steve Waugh and Glenn McGrath were missing out, I might be getting in.

When the announcement finally came, I was very nervous. I kept thinking, 'Gee, I wish Mum was here.' My thoughts were with my family, which told me that this was a big thing for me. If I had known earlier that this team was going to be selected, I would have definitely flown my mum and my wife Helen to the function. I remembered back to when I was first chosen for Australia, staring at my name among the other players and thinking, 'What will people think of this?' My name just didn't look right: 'Ian Healy' was hardly the right stage name for a top-liner. Same with the first Queensland first-class side I played for, and the Australian Under 19s.

The announcement itself was strangely low key. First there was an introduction by the master of ceremonies, Andrew Denton, then an entertainer did a skit on the 'Big Ship' — Warwick Armstrong, famous captain of the great Australian team of 1921. Then came the obligatory auction. Finally, at a moment when it seemed everyone was in the toilets, Australian Cricket Board chairman Denis Rogers was on his feet, telling us that the big moment had arrived.

'Could everyone please resume their seats ... please ... ladies and gentlemen ... please, everyone ... if you don't mind ... quickly ...'

And then he was off. First name was Arthur Morris ... then Bill Ponsford ... Sir Donald Bradman ... captain ...

Afterwards, there were six of us on the stage — Arthur Morris, Neil Harvey, Greg Chappell, Shane Warne, Allan Border and me. Sir Donald Bradman, Dennis Lillee and Keith Miller were unable to attend. Bill Ponsford, Bill O'Reilly and Ray Lindwall have passed on.

I rang Mum straight after the press conference. I get a lot of my traits from my mum: my organisation, neatness, the way I try to be loyal and straight with people. My late father emphasised that straightness, too, and instilled in me an ability to stand up to people and situations, to play a straight bat and have confidence in myself. They both taught me the advantages of having a sense of fun. I recalled immediately the expense and the time both my parents put into my sport, the work they did raising money for country teams I was a part of, the local competitions I was raised in. As kids, we thought we were good players, and we *were* good players, but we never stopped to realise that talent on the field didn't automatically mean it was easy for our parents and supporters to gather money off it. We never appreciated the amount of effort that people such as my parents and other children's parents put in, week in, week out, so that the local Biloela team (and then the Callide-Dawson regional team) could play.

— ⌑ —

ALLAN BORDER ONCE DESCRIBED me as 'one of the great celebrators', and I'd have to agree with him. I love winning and enjoy immensely being passionate about what I do. Getting up on a table or a bench in the Australian dressing room and leading the team in our victory song, *Under the Southern Cross,* was always one of the great experiences of my life. We'd played hard, fought hard, so let's party hard was my philosophy. And yet I have always tried to be practical about the situations I find myself in, to take such situations and the people in them as I find them. In the days and months since that Team of the Century was announced I haven't spent any time dreaming about keeping to O'Reilly, or having Keith Miller standing next to me at first slip. Greg Chappell at second slip, Ponsford in the gully, Morris at short leg, captain Bradman in the covers.

I have, though, occasionally gone back to that Bellerive Oval dressing room, and that afternoon I spent with Ray Lindwall and Ron Archer. That was real and special. I've never thought of myself as being anything other than an ordinary bloke who's lived an extraordinary cricket life. I know that I had talent, and I know that I worked extremely hard to get where I ended up. But I also know I was lucky — brilliant parents, great family, perfect environment to learn the game, right place at the right time in the selection stakes, wonderful friends, superb teammates ...

From Biloela to the baggy green, it's been an amazing ride.

CHAPTER 1

A LUCKY COUNTRY KID

ONE DAY, SOMETIME IN the middle of winter 1972 in a Queensland country town called Biloela, a man in his early forties was standing at the bar. He was the town's new ANZ Bank manager and he was drinking alone, as he had for the past few weeks, ever since he and his young family had driven up from Brisbane to their new posting. Unfortunately, two previous ANZ managers had left town under the same angry cloud, after money from the local bowling club, then the golf club, went missing, so there was no chance the new appointee would be receiving a warm welcome. But one as cold as this? Finally, a bloke came over, a big man, a pig-truck driver, maybe to have a chat ... no, just to put his hand firmly on the wall the bank manager was leaning on, the truckie's arm coming menacingly back over the manager's left shoulder.

'And how long do you think you'll last up here?' was all the truck driver said. It was not a question so much as a statement. You city types are not wanted here.

The bank manager looked up at him, stopped for a moment, then sipped on his beer. 'Mate,' he replied slowly, 'I'm here to ask the questions, not answer 'em.'

The truckie stopped abruptly, affronted, like a famous West Indian cricketer confronted on his home turf. But slowly they started talking. And ended up friends. That bank manager was my father, Neville Healy, and soon Biloela became his town, and though I'd been born in Brisbane it became my town, too, for the next nine years of my life. Dad would end up a distinguished Biloela citizen, treasurer of this, on the committee of that, and even help in the creation of junior cricket in the district, while I'd play sport every spare minute of my life, and get the grounding that eventually helped make me an Australian Test cricketer.

— ⊠ —

WHILE ON CHRISTMAS HOLIDAYS in 1971–72, Dad had learned he'd been transferred to the bush. 'To where?' he did a double take when the phone call came. 'Uh-huh ... [long pause] ... And where exactly is that?' My mother was aghast; it sounded so far from everything she knew. Biloela was the largest town and administrative centre in the 'Banana' Shire (so named after a legendary working bullock named Banana that was buried with great ceremony after dying in 1880), 600 kilometres north-west of Brisbane, around 150k from the coast, between Bundaberg and Rockhampton.

Until our big move, we'd been living in the Brisbane suburb of St Johns Wood and Dad had been manager at the ANZ's Rode Road branch in the Brisbane

A day out at Sea World on Queensland's Gold Coast, on a break from a school sporting adventure, in 1970.

suburbs. When, in March 1972, he and his family — wife Rae and children Kim, Ken, Greg and Ian — jumped into the family Kingswood to head north I was a few weeks short of my eighth birthday. We arrived seven hours later to discover that our new house was a couple of doors from Biloela High's playing fields and cricket nets, right opposite the primary school's footy ground and a short pedal on the pushbike to the town's main sports ovals.

Back in Brisbane I'd played soccer for the local The Gap under-7s team, the youngest age group, when I was four and in kindergarten, and after we steamrolled through the season scoring 120 goals and conceding two, I'd set off on my first tour, on the train all the way to Sydney. My biggest memories of that adventure are of a couple of clinics where we were tutored by some of the game's best players and a slightly sour recollection of a match played on a ground without sideline markings and with a shonky referee. It seemed they played to different rules in Sydney, and I, upfront from day one, threw a four-year-old's dummy spit over the injustice of it all. Mum came as my chaperone on that trip, which was lucky, because on the way home I broke out in German measles.

I kept playing soccer until we headed to Biloela, which was a rugby league town, we discovered. But that was okay, it was all sport. In my last year in Brisbane, 1971, I'd played in the Ashgrove Primary School B team in cricket. I was seven — many of my teammates were 11 — which I guess made me something of a prodigy, but I just knew I loved playing sport and was confident enough to survive in any company. I doubt that this would even be allowed today, as participation rather than competition is seen as being more important.

That last year in the city I was coached for a little while by one of the leading coaches in Queensland soccer, and apparently impressed him so much that he wanted Mum and Dad to leave me in Brisbane when we left for the bush. 'He'll be playing senior soccer by the time he's 15,' he explained, but my parents' attitude was that a lot of things can happen between the age of 7 and beyond, so they didn't even consider it. Three or four years later, they finally started up a soccer comp in Biloela, and I found myself playing league *and* soccer in the winter. I even managed to make the regional rep soccer team, and at the carnival ran into that same coach, who later told my parents that I'd 'lost that edge' I had when I was younger.

It was as part of the Ashgrove cricket XI that I smashed my first six, a mighty blow over midwicket at the home ground of the Ashgrove Marist Brothers school. Geez, that hit went a long way. Or so I thought at the time. One day, around 15 years later, I went back to the scene of that famous swipe and learned, somewhat sadly, that the boundary was around 35 metres from the pitch. I could have sworn the ground was as big as the Melbourne Cricket Ground.

Before we left for Biloela I had my first taste of Test cricket, when Dad took us out to the first Ashes Test of the 1970–71 season. I can't say that the occasion fired any huge ambitions in me, but I can still remember parts of the day vividly,

All rugby league teams need a good goalkicker, and I wasn't the worst in Biloela's junior footy competitions of the 1970s.

This was one of three photos of Biloela Primary School's cricket nets that was taken in September 1999 and given to me at a Year 10 school reunion in May 2000. On the back of one was the message, 'I remember playing on the pitch in the middle of the school ground, too. I still remember you belting that PE teacher, Ritchie Rich, around that ground.'

especially the atmosphere and the Gabba crowd, and the fact that I was part of the huge invasion onto the field when Australian opener Keith Stackpole reached his century. The next day he went on to 207. This was Rod Marsh's first Test, but I never saw him, because Australia only lost three wickets during the entire first day.

I wasn't a keeper in those days. That didn't happen for another three years.

—◻—

I ONCE HEARD GREG Chappell, former Australian captain and selector, one of the biggest influences on my cricket career and a product of the well-heeled Prince Alfred College in Adelaide, state that 'country kids are tougher'. I'm not sure if he's right, but I do know that country kids in the 1970s, from a sporting perspective at least, were luckier. I never stopped to think, as my sporting life evolved, how fortunate I was to be growing up in Biloela, but with hindsight I know I was.

Between weekends I never tired of having another hit, whether at the High School or the even-better nets at the primary school, from where we'd often aim our biggest hits at the Biloela Hospital windows across the road. These larrikin moments aside, I can remember often reminding myself that I was not just playing sport, I was practising my sport as well. I think that made a difference.

No one taught me that, it was just what I thought. I'd go to the footy field and practise kicking goals, or into the nets to rehearse my defensive technique. It was fun to play properly. I was also more than happy to spend an hour hitting a cricket ball that was hung in a stocking tied to the clothes line in the backyard.

The sporting opportunities available to me in Biloela were things I assumed people my age everywhere had. I know now they didn't; in fact I was able to practise much more than the city kids. When we lived in Brisbane, Mum and Dad had told us kids that we wouldn't be allowed bikes until we were 11. In the bush, however, where the pace was half a step slower and traffic hold-ups nonexistent, we had them straightaway. So, from when I was as young as I can remember, I was in the nets with my mates or kicking a footy between the posts, and on Saturday afternoons in summer, after finishing my junior cricket, I'd park my bike behind the dressing rooms and watch the seniors, playing for them whenever they were short, or sub-fielding if someone needed a break. Not only were the nets within such a short distance, but so were my mates, my practice partners. I never got tired. Perhaps some of my colleagues might not have been as keen as I was, but I never acknowledged that at the time.

Today, if I want to take any of my three children to a cricket net, or a netball court, or a ground with football posts, we have to jump in the car. The city has plenty of excellent sporting facilities, but compared to Biloela they are far flung. As I grew up and my sporting prowess and hunger developed, my parents didn't have to drive me to practice, or restrain me because they needed to be fair and drop one child in one suburb, another child in the next suburb, a third further away again.

I was nine when they decided to start junior cricket in Biloela. How lucky was I that this wasn't put off a few years! I believe my father played a part in this initiative, but the chief catalyst was a gentleman by the name of Kevin McSweeney, who invited all the prospective young cricketers from the town and surrounding districts to gather at the main oval on a Saturday morning in September 1973. When he came to talk to we Under 10s who had assembled, Mr McSweeney hushed everyone up and asked, 'Okay, who of you can bat?'

My arm shot up. So did a lot of others.

'And who can bowl?' Mr McSweeney asked.

Up went my arm once more, again with most of the others.

'And who can wicketkeep?'

This time, I was the only one who said yes, so I was the wicketkeeper for the Under 10s.

It was more than simply a youthful desire to be everything that had me nominating for the keeping job in addition to seeking batting and bowling opportunities. My determination to be a gloveman had first been fired at the trials for the Callide-Dawson Under 11s rep team six months earlier. These try-outs took place when the only organised cricket I was involved in was with the Biloela Primary School or the occasional cameo as a very young substitute fieldsman in the men's comp on Saturday afternoons. I can still recall, clear as you like, the 10-year-old keeper of that Callide-Dawson team. I was taken by the extra work he was getting, how everything revolved around him, as if he was somehow special. That's when I resolved to try to be a wicketkeeper, so when Mr McSweeney asked if there were any keepers about, I was quick to show my hand.

—◻—

WHILE BILOELA ITSELF IS a town of around 5000 to 6000 people, its sports people included local townsfolk, farmers and graziers and men who lived in and around town but worked at the nearby Callide coal mine and power station, or even further away at the big Moura mine. It was not unusual for men from towns such as Theodore, Baralaba and Moura, all more than 50 kilometres away, to come to play in Biloela. Many were tough characters, and tough cricketers, who gave little away, even to spirited 11 year olds.

The men's cricket competition involved eight teams, four games every Saturday afternoon, three of them in town on turf pitches and the other on a concrete pitch in the little town of Jambin, around 30 kilometres north. Biloela's main oval was a well-kept field surrounded by a picket fence, and the other two pitches were on neighbouring grounds. Every Saturday afternoon, and Sundays, senior matches were played on these three fields, so it was possible to scout around the six teams trying to find out which of them might be short. Of course I was not the only youngster after a hit, so there was some nous needed to be consistently in the right place at the right time. Then there was the pressure to do a good job so they'd want to use you as a fill-in again. The men seemed like giants. I'd arrive nice and early, with my small kitbag over my shoulder and my brother Greg's hand-me-down spikes tied to my handlebars by their laces, and wait for an egalitarian mix of graziers, coal miners, farmers and power station workers to join their mates from the town centre. If I got a game, I'd bat No. 11 and sprint from fine leg to fine leg. On such days, there was nowhere I would rather be.

Those bushmen were cricket savvy in a way many Test cricketers long to be. I loved playing with them and for them, and learned plenty. The matches were full of characters, men such as Charlee Marshall and Merv Bidgood.

Every year, Mr Marshall captained a local schoolboy team in an open-age competition. He was a lovely bloke, around 50, who was a schoolteacher, poet, farmer, hobby breeder of Shetland ponies and local legend. He was also one of the craftiest cricketers I've met, never beyond trying to get one over the umpires for the sake of his schoolboy teammates. More than once he'd cut short an lbw appeal with a sincere apology for his rudeness, then not even appeal for the next one before explaining that his excitable proteges had a habit of shouting for things that clearly weren't out. But then would come a tremendous shout, 'Now, *that's* out!', which always won the ump's approval. After all, no way would Mr Marshall be appealing for something that wasn't out.

Mr Bidgood's claim to fame, he keeps reminding people, is that he once bowled a bumper at the future Test cricketer, Ian Healy. He was a grazier from

Early days, moving down the legside during a national junior carnival.

out at Baralaba, north-west of Biloela. I was 11 years old at the time, but was also 26 not out, and the team I was filling in for that day were edging towards an unlikely victory. Even back then, winning was important to me. I might have been filling in, batting No. 11 and fielding at fine leg, but I still wanted to win the game as much as any of my teammates did, and sought to be the best that I could be and do the best I could for the team. I remember that ball flying harmlessly over my head, and being genuinely excited that I'd survived my first ever bouncer. This was real cricket! Years later, Mr Bidgood told journalist Robert Craddock, who helped me with my first book, 'What was I supposed to do ... we were trying to win the game.' He also pointed out that there was no way he was trying to hit me, as Dad was his bank manager.

—¤—

I DON'T THINK YOU can ever get luckier than to be born into a loving and caring family; I know I missed out on nothing from my parents and received plenty. When I look back now, I realise with great pride the key role my dad played in my development, teaching me the basics and backing my natural confidence and love of sport. More than once in later years, I'd hear Dad proudly say of me, 'You know, when he was 18 months old he could actually step out to a cricket ball with the right style.' I can vaguely recall, too, the big plastic cricket bat I'd lumber around way back then. There were many who thought that Greg might have been the best cricketer in the family, and Dad might have been among

In 1978–79, the Australian Under 16s carnival came to Rockhampton. This photo was taken during our game against Tasmania, with me, the Queensland keeper and captain, standing up behind Tassie batsman Wayne Squires. My habit of sticking my tongue out was one I took a long while to lose.

them, but one thing I'm sure of is that I had a better temperament for the game than my brothers. While Greg and Ken were prone to spit it whenever they were dismissed in controversial circumstances in the backyard, Mum reckons the only time I ever threw the bat was in South Africa when I was 32 years old. More of that later.

Mum was as keen a supporter as Dad. By the time I was 10, leading into the 1974–75 season, I was desperate to own my own bat, and started saving by stockpiling empty soft drink bottles that I could later get a five-cent refund on. Though I pestered spectators and exhausted players throughout the '74 rugby league season, I was still short of funds when October came around. So Mum put me on an incentive scheme: five cents for every run I scored after I reached 50, and 10 cents for every run past 100. As I'd never scored a century in my life, she probably thought she was on pretty safe ground …

A lot of cricketers keep count of their runs when they're batting. Early in the season that summer, against a team from Monto, I was counting cash. I finished with 179, and was soon the proud owner of a brand new blade that became my closest friend.

Mum was always telling me, 'If you can't be a good cricketer you can at least look like one', and I listened to her. I was an organised person from day one, and was aware that whenever I was billeted out as a kid, I used to amaze my hosts with the way I'd look after all my things, clean my shoes and gear, fold my clothes. I knew a lot of my teammates were ignoring the same advice they'd been given by their mothers, but I didn't care. Even in the Test teams years later, surrounded by cricketers such as Steve Waugh who couldn't live unless their corner of the dressing room was in chaos, I kept everything neat, clean and tidy. My time management back at Biloela must have also been pretty good. I always found time for homework, without ever letting the study impinge on my sport. Another advantage of living in a country town … both primary and high school were only a few doors away, so it was finish school, get home, food or homework, then down to the nets, then back to finish homework. Easy.

Like young sons all around Australia, the three Healy boys were forever playing Australia v England Test matches in the backyard and filling out the blank scorecards in the back of the ABC Cricket Books. Those games we played then remain so clear; in our eyes they *were* Test matches. I can even remember the pair of shorts I wore throughout the 1974–75 season, when we wanted to be like Lillee and Thommo, the Chappells, Rod Marsh and Dougie Walters. However, for me it wasn't a case of dreaming of or wanting to play for Australia. It was just fun, take it as it comes. I was happy doing what I was doing, all the time. And I wanted to be good.

We frequently played with a hard ball, despite what Mum said, which led to the odd bump and bruise, and the occasional broken window when the ball flew over the batsman's head after kicking off the edge of the concrete path that was our crease or the willow tree root that jutted up through the path. Because we bowled away from our house, that window was part of the residence behind us, which belonged to Mr Gesler, manager of the local Bank of New South Wales. Mum and Dad were quick to offer to pay for the damage — we three boys had run a mile — but Mr Gesler said no, the insurance would cover it. Nowadays, he's quick to tell people that Ian Healy broke his window, which may or may not be true because I can't remember who was bowling at the time. My memory is that we broke more windows of our house with the footy than we did other people's with a cricket ball, but what I can't understand is how parents can look back laughingly on things such as broken windows in next-door neighbours' houses. They didn't seem so happy at the time.

As my cricket developed I didn't think my parents were especially involved, but when I look back on my life now, they were doing plenty to allow me to be as good as I could be. The amount of time that Dad put into junior cricket in Biloela — umpiring, fund-raising, helping to get the Junior Cricket Association up and running, urging other parents to be involved — allowed my cricket to be as organised and interesting as it was. Right through my time there we had six competitive junior teams in my age division — three junior games every Saturday — in a town of around 5000 people. Mum was the one who would discipline me, keep me on track. Neither parent pushed me, but they didn't really have to. They could see me going to the nets every day and playing my sport the way I did.

If I had a local role model it was my older brother Greg, who played a lot of junior rep cricket for Central Queensland and Queensland before he moved down to Brisbane to play grade cricket for Norths. We worked together on things and I learnt to play cricket by watching him when I was very young and he was just starting to flourish. In fact, all three of us Healy boys ended up playing for the Queensland Under 19 side, Greg as a batsman and Ken as a batsman and part-time keeper. To be honest, though, I can't remember any of us receiving too much formal training as youngsters, except for all the support we received from Dad, watching the experts on television, and reading the books devoured by so many young cricketers in the 1970s — the Rothmans coaching manuals, Jack Pollard's *Cricket the Australian Way*, Greg Chappell's *Successful Cricket* and Ian Chappell's *My World of Cricket*. However, as I grew older, and began to play more representative cricket, I did start to come into contact with more qualified coaches. And when I made the Queensland and Australian junior sides, I was being helped by the best coaches in the land. I remember one year being told that I 'snatched' at the ball a bit, and being excited at how the coach then took me through a series of drills to fix me up.

Was I a 'natural' wicketkeeper? I don't know. I know I was the gun in the local district, and perhaps I had a greater ability than others to absorb things when I was watching the keepers in the Biloela senior cricket and also the elite keepers on TV. And then I was able to practise and apply these lessons I'd absorbed. If you can call that natural ability then, yes, I was a natural. My guess is that in almost all cases keepers are born, not made, but what you need to be born with are pretty good instincts, a lot of energy and a desire *from the jump* to be behind the stumps. As a nine-year-old, I wanted to be a keeper; I could catch, was agile and was able to learn quickly about technique. If a naturally brilliant fieldsman such as Ricky Ponting had set out to be a wicketkeeper as I did, I think he could have become a good one, but if he started now, in his late twenties, he wouldn't have a chance.

—◻—

CRICKET IN THE SUMMER, footy in the winter. I enjoyed playing rugby league, and every season I can remember feeling disappointed when the league competition ended (as I did when every cricket summer came to a close), but it never quite 'got' me as cricket did. Some of the footy could be tough, especially against teams made up of sons as rugged as their coal-mining fathers, but even so, in 1976 I was lucky enough to be selected as a halfback for the Queensland Primary Schools Under 12s league team, alongside future internationals Peter Jackson, Dan Stains and Mark Hohn, for a three-match series against NSW which we lost two games to one. I'm not quite sure why, but I felt a little intimidated by my rugby league rivals from the city in a way that I never did on the cricket field. The fact I was playing cricket with the men must have played a part. Perhaps I just wasn't a good enough footballer, but I really felt that talented young league players had to move to the city very early in their careers, or they'd

A photograph from the weekend the Queensland Sheffield Shield team hit Biloela in 1974. Queensland and Australian champion Greg Chappell is facing the camera, back right, with Queensland keeper John Maclean, to Chappell's right, looking down as he signs an autograph. I'm standing in front of Maclean, with my cap visible, but my face obscured by the guys in front.

get left behind. I imagine, as the sport in Australia has got more and more city-centric, it's even worse for young country footballers now.

Every sporting schoolboy needs his heroes, and mine were the Australian wicketkeeper Rod Marsh and his Queensland counterpart John Maclean. The television was important, as it allowed us to watch the stars in action — Marsh in the Test matches and Maclean on the ABC during the final session of Sheffield Shield games. My allegiance to Maclean was complete after the Queensland Sheffield Shield squad came to Biloela, pre-season, for a weekend in October 1974. Greg Chappell, Jeff Thomson, everyone. The players, the biggest thing to ever hit town in my eyes (and many others', too), took part in some coaching clinics on both mornings and then played a two-day selection trial. I was supposed to be a scoreboard attendant for the entire weekend, but had to go home on the first night with hives after something dropped out of a tree and nailed me. Sadly, I was wheezing and sneezing, and couldn't back up on the Sunday. Still, I had a field day on the Saturday. At one point I went up to the Sri Lankan-born leggie, Malcolm Francke, and asked for the ball he was spinning, but he replied, 'I'm sorry, it's not my ball to give you.' That's exactly the same answer I always gave to young kids during my career. Earlier in the day, Mum had grabbed my arm and introduced me to Maclean, who kindly talked to me about keeping and showed me his gloves. That was enough. Where can I get some? Maclean recommended Mick Matula's sports warehouse in Brisbane, Dad got in touch with them, and I had a brand new pair of John Maclean gauntlets. I really wish I'd kept those gloves, but eventually they were tossed onto the rubbish pile out the back of the house, rotten to the core from my sweat and the rubbing of wet inners that came with constant work. Seasons later, John became something of a mentor for me, not so much on the technical side of the game, but simply by the way he was always totally supportive. He took me to lunch when I first made the Queensland and Australian sides, which was something I believe the late Wally Grout had done for him, and since then, especially in recent years, he has helped introduce me to the workings of the business world. It's a good brotherhood, the keeping fraternity.

Looking back, it was a real credit to the people of Biloela that they were able to put on the game successfully. It's astonishing, in many ways, to think about how superbly organised the town was as far as its sport was concerned, how important sport was when we arrived there and how this passion for sport appeared to grow in the years we were there. The Queensland Cricket Association wouldn't have backed the venture unless they knew the wicket, the facilities and the local administrators were capable of handling such an event. The Junior Cricket Associations from the region, not just from Biloela but from surrounding towns as well, worked remarkably hard to get the ground right, paid for the charter plane that brought the state players to us, and lured youngsters from far and wide to be part of an experience they would long remember.

The success of this venture reflected the quality of the junior cricket system in Queensland, which allowed a country boy such as me to work right through the grades without ever being penalised for being from the bush. The annual state carnivals gave me, a country kid, a gauge by which I could compare myself with the slickers from the city, and these events became a major target for me. From when I made the Queensland primary school team in 1975–76 right through to 1983 when I made the Australian Under 19 team that toured England, I was always pursuing a place in the Queensland representative teams, and relished the chance to not just play in these teams but captain them too. There was never a chance I'd lose interest in the sport or the competition. My objective, always, was to be good at what I enjoyed doing. This representative cricket was something to work for, and I revelled in the satisfaction of knowing, to this point at least, that I was doing it all right.

CHAPTER 2

How Good is This!

MY JOURNEY FROM PROMISING country junior cricketer to potential Test keeper took a major turn when we returned to Brisbane at the end of 1980. Older brother Greg and sister Kim were already back there, staying at our grandmother's, and Greg was playing grade cricket for Norths. I had been half-planning to go down as well, after we all agreed that it wouldn't hurt me as a person and would definitely help me as a cricketer. Maybe I'd have stayed another year, but Dad put another transfer application in and soon after a move was approved ... to the ANZ's branch in the suburb of Woolloongabba, a lofted on-drive from the famous Gabba ground, the spiritual home of Queensland cricket. With that locked in, I was enrolled at Brisbane State High, or 'State High' as it was universally known, to complete Year 12, and my life as a bush cricketer was over.

The family settled on the south side of Brisbane, but I still went and played for Norths, where my brother was playing. However, Ken joined a junior team that was affiliated to the Souths grade club and ended up playing with Souths, and a few seasons later Greg and I played against Ken on his first-grade debut. At State High, I also tried my hand at rugby union — their major football code — and won a place in the first XV for the GPS season and a tour of New Zealand. Cricket-wise, it was one game in thirds for Norths, then the GPS cricket through February–March (from where I won a spot in the Queensland Under 19 team), and with the '81 winter finally over, my first full season of grade cricket.

I started as a batsman in first grade, the keeping job being held down by a club stalwart, Bryan Phelan, but didn't fare too well and was dropped to the seconds. I missed out on the gloves there, too, because the incumbent was also the Queensland Under 19s keeper, and remained in the twos for most of the season. The firsts had a poor year while we went on to win the premiership. Again, I made the Under 19s interstate carnival, where I probably received more attention for my batting than my keeping, but not enough to get the nod for the Australian Under 19s three-Test series against Pakistan. NSW's Bronko Djura was the keeper for those matches, and remained the first-choice gloveman throughout my time in the Under 19s.

I was fortunate in that my last year in the Under 19s coincided with the second tour to England by an Australian team in that age group. The first, six years earlier, had helped launch the careers of such notables as Geoff Marsh, David Boon and two future Test wicketkeepers, Greg Dyer and Wayne Phillips. The squad I was a part of, as a batsman and second keeper, included future top-

Queensland stars Carl Rackemann (centre) and Greg Ritchie present me with my Queensland Secondary Schools team cap in December 1980. Both had been part of the same side three years earlier, and would both go on to play with distinction for Australia and captain Queensland teams that I was a part of.

liners Mike Veletta (our captain), Tony Dodemaide and Craig McDermott. Also in the team was the future Carlton Australian Football champion, and our vice-captain, Craig Bradley, who stunned us with his stories about the money he was being offered by a variety of Victorian Football League clubs. Bronko Djura was also an outstanding footballer and when he made South Sydney's first-grade rugby league team the following year he decided to concentrate on his football.

I'll never forget one vigorous debate five of us had in a London café one day late in the tour, where we argued as to who would be the first of us to play first-class cricket. The majority feeling among the group was that Queensland's Harley Hammelmann, a tall fast-medium bowler of some ability, was the correct answer, but I pushed strongly for 'Billy' McDermott, whom I'd known since we played together for 'Possibles' against 'Probables' in a State Primary Schools selection trial in 1976. This would not be the first time I'd be backing Billy's talent when others weren't so sure; for a bloke who finished up with 291 Test wickets, I still don't think he's received the plaudits he's entitled to. He was playing first-class cricket within months of us arriving back in Australia, as were Veletta (the first of us to do so), Bradley, Dodemaide and the Western Australian spinner Brett Mulder, and by December 1984 he was facing the great West Indians in a Test match at the MCG.

From a cricket point of view, my England tour was slightly frustrating because Bronko was entrenched as our top keeper, but I scored enough runs to force my way into the 'Test' team as a batsman for the final two internationals, after being 12th man for the first game, at Lord's. I averaged 40 with the bat on tour, but hardly kept at all. However, the experience of being an Australian cricket representative in England was magnificent, even though I found the way in which we played a lot and practised little a bit off-putting. It wasn't the way I'd approached the game in the past, but our six-week, 14-match itinerary was extremely tight, and there was precious little time for the nets.

I actually went to England as a representative of Easts grade club. This had come about after Bryan Phelan decided before the 1982–83 season that he wanted one more summer in first grade. He and I both knew that I needed a top-grade spot if I wanted to make the Under 19 tour, so he arranged for me to move to Easts, whose No. 1 keeper, Peter Anderson, had been seconded to the Colts team. Throughout my career, Bryan was a trusted mentor and friend. Colts was a club captained by a seasoned pro but otherwise made up of promising young cricketers chosen from all the grade clubs, who played together in the grade competition and practised together at the Gabba. I made my first first-grade century at Easts, and when Anderson came back for the '83–84 season I replaced him at Colts, where I stayed for two years. Only then did I return to Norths, where I happily remained for the rest of my career.

— ✠ —

EVEN BEFORE MY YEAR at State High had begun I had been practising with their cricket squad, and it was while I was training that I first noticed the girl who was to become my wife. Helen Perkins was about to start Year 12 and was chaperoning

Harley Hammelmann, Craig McDermott and me, Queensland's three representatives on the Australian Under 19s tour to the UK in 1983.

a cluster of Year 8 students past the nets. For me it was the classic, 'I want to meet this girl.' What I remember as our first 'date' was really no such thing — I simply escorted her in my mum's Torana to a hockey match she was playing in. However, from that less-than-romantic start our relationship blossomed, even for the three years when Helen was studying nursing in Gympie, around 150 kilometres north of Brisbane, while I was studying at Kelvin Grove College of Advanced Education.

I wasn't the first sports-mad teenager to opt for a career in high school physical education teaching when that awful decision as to what to do after high school needed to be made. Following my year at State High I headed to teachers' college, where I gained my diploma: a passport, I thought, into the real world. If I had my time over, I'd have gone for a more business-orientated qualification, but at the time the concept of teaching sport to keen, well-behaved young citizens appealed to me.

My debut teaching appointment was at Kingston High School, 20 minutes south of Brisbane. The children were the sons and daughters of working-class parents, who made it their business to make life as difficult as possible for newcomers. The teacher I was replacing was on stress leave, and I soon discovered why.

Put simply, too many of them, especially many of those aged between 13 and 15, didn't want to learn. I couldn't teach them physical education — or even basic manners. I'd spend hours preparing lessons, devise strategies from inside and outside the teacher's coaching manual, but I quickly became an angry, frustrated wreck. After six months, I could've thrown it in. I vividly recall one occasion when I shed a tear telling Helen that they were treating me like dirt.

Fortunately, things came around, but it took a while. I gradually learned that these kids were rebels and rascals, rather than scoundrels and villains, and the process taught me the value of patience and persistence. They saw it as their right to test me out, to find a weakness. Once a kid swore at me, and I swore straight back. When he mumbled, 'You can't say that', I replied, 'Well, I just did.' I gambled that he wouldn't dob me in, because that would make him look weak, and that's what happened. Whether my approach was the right one, I don't know, but I never had another problem with him.

While I enjoyed teaching, I never really thought I'd be a teacher forever. By the beginning of 1988, after three years in the classroom, I was looking for an out, and grabbed the chance to take a position with my future in-laws' clothing company, Associated Fashion Distributors, selling women's clothing.

— ¤ —

THERE WAS A STAGE in the mid 1980s when I wondered whether my cricket career was going the same way as my teaching eventually did. I dreamed of wicketkeeping for Australia, but wasn't quite sure how that was going to happen. Even when Ray Phillips retired, Peter Anderson was quickly entrenched in the Shield side. For three years I had been captain of the Queensland Colts team —

not to be confused with the Colts grade team — for their annual clash against NSW (in 1984–85 purely as a batsman, with Anderson keeping; in 1985–86 and 1986–87 as captain, middle-order batsman and keeper) but after that third year I was too old to retain that job. At least one senior Queensland official told me to throw away the gloves and try to make the Shield team as a specialist batsman. Which I didn't want to do but nearly did. However, some wiser heads — including my parents, Greg Chappell and Queensland chairman of selectors Ernie Toovey — advised me differently. Still, when I heard rumours before the start of the 1987–88 that South Australia were going to make me an offer to move interstate, I resolved to accept their offer as soon as it came. I would have gone for sure.

I had first made the Shield squad, as the third keeper, in 1984–85. I had to get to practice very early to get a bat, or bat in the dark after the good players were finished. Fortunately, I was still studying at Teachers' College when I first made the squad, and even as a teacher I could still get there by 4pm, which meant I could have a long early net, chase balls or do some catching, then follow up with a hard fitness session, and a couple of beers before heading off home. Queensland training used to be so big and — I know now — so physiologically unsound. Nowadays, the guys do their fitness work by themselves in the morning, and then have shorter net sessions as a squad in the afternoons, but back in the dark old days of the mid '80s state team practice was more like your typical club training session, only grander. The bowlers might go for a 15-minute run, then do a sprint test, then work for two hours non-stop in the nets. But it was really special for a young bloke like me just to be there, watching the biggest names in the sport at work, learning from the best of them, and sometimes sharing jokes and shouts with them afterwards.

State practice was Tuesday and Thursday. In between, I'd go to club practice at

At state practice in September 1986, just prior to the start of the season in which I made my first-class debut.

Norths, and work on my game with a group of close friends and first-graders — Brad Inwood, Steve Monty, Nev Jelich and more — on Mondays and Fridays.

At State training and at Easts in 1982–83, Peter Anderson quickly became a huge influence by encouraging my work ethic, more so by his deeds than words, and making me think about the art of wicketkeeping. He used to practise endlessly. Ray Phillips, in contrast, wouldn't do anything like that amount of glovework. To be honest, when I first saw 'Ando', having heard a great deal about his talent, my immediate reaction was, 'Gee, I thought this bloke'd be a bit better than that.' I learned that he was very definite on how he should keep, what his style was, and had modelled himself on the famous English keepers, such as Alan Knott or Bob Taylor, who were his heroes. I'd come from the bush, and was more like a rough and raw Rod Marsh or John Maclean, just doing what came naturally. I know I'd adopted many of their keeping traits, simply by mimicking them. If I had a style it was to rely on quick movement of the feet. I never dived unless I had to and always tried to take the ball on the inside of my body, so the snick off the outside edge came straight to me. That is, if you like, the 'Australian' way. Ando, like Knott and Taylor, took the ball in front of his body, and dived a lot more. He looked flashy, more likely to be noticed. He was also, I soon learned, very effective.

Ando made me realise that, whatever your individual style, there is a technique to wicketkeeping that needs to be constantly worked on. His dedication to practice made me stop and think about what *my* technique was, about where the gloves needed to be to catch balls coming at different heights, about where the feet should be, watching the ball, staying down to the spinners. And once I became aware of what I was doing, I asked myself, 'Can I do it better?' One day, Ando mentioned the need to watch the ball right into your gloves. I never used to do that, but once I learned how much more consistent a catcher I became when I did it I kept my eye on the ball as closely as I could. Ando was also the first keeper I came into contact with who made a soft thud when the ball went into his gloves. Until then, I didn't care what the ball felt like, as long as I caught it and I was moving okay. Ando taught me that soft hands was a skill that required the right technique.

Without Ando's influence, I'm sure my natural keeping ability wouldn't have been enough for me to last in first-class cricket. Fortunately, I didn't just copy his technique and try to totally revamp my keeping style; absorbing what he taught me and applying it to my own game was a crucial factor in my development as a keeper.

Most importantly, Ando also taught me what I quickly called the 'golf ball'. It involved finding a wall and, while wearing keeping inners, throwing catches off the wall to yourself with the golf ball. At state squad practice at the Gabba, Ando and I would walk from the nets which were situated on the ground itself, over the old dog track that used to surround the field, and do our golf ball on a wall at the base of The Clem Jones Stand.

We never sought to throw difficult catches; the intention was to not throw it hard but to concentrate on catching the golf ball as you would correctly catch a cricket ball as a keeper in a game. We bounced the ball before the wall so it would come back to us on the full, all the while rehearsing our sideways movement, studying our catching techniques, watching the ball into the hands, practising balance and rhythm. Then we'd move closer to the wall, to imitate keeping to the spinners. As I came into contact with different bowlers I'd develop different drills with the ball and wall. For example, in the mid '90s, specifically to mimic keeping to Michael Bevan's bouncy wrist-spinners, I started moving up close to the wall to throw the ball overarm into the wall so it kicked up from the cement surface so I was catching it, high and fast, up around my shoulders. Because you're not throwing it too hard, you can't really get hurt with the golf ball, while getting your gloves and feet moving in all the right directions, so it's a magnificent exercise. Its other benefit is that, unlike almost every other keeping drill, you don't need someone else to help you. You can go away by yourself and work on everything you'll need, and are limited by nothing more than the extent of your imagination.

The golf ball picked up my form a dozen times in my career. I'd just go away, work on my fundamentals and get my technique back in order. This was always quality time, when I could focus on what I wanted to achieve rather than worrying about whether the bloke who was hitting me catches would rather be somewhere else. He might have hit me 200 catches, more than I originally asked for, but I still wasn't quite right. The golf ball never complained.

Peter Anderson was a workaholic, and he found in me a willing partner, but I just wonder whether he gained as much from our partnership as I did. Even near the end of my career, whether I was working with my Test understudy, Adam Gilchrist, or state deputy, Wade Seccombe, I always ensured that I was getting as much out of a practice session as they were. Otherwise, I figured, they were getting closer to me. I think my working relationship with Ando taught me this. Never blasé, I was watching what Adam and Wade were doing and making sure I had them covered in everything. That helped me; helping your understudy should help you. Back when I was the understudy, Ando's injuries — the first a fractured finger in 1986–87 and then a more severe break to his thumb in 1987–88 — gave me a chance to show how much 'sneaking up' on him I'd done.

— ✠ —

MY FIRST-CLASS DEBUT CAME in a three-dayer against the touring West Indies in Townsville in January 1987: January 11 to 13 to be precise. The Windies were in Australia as the third team, with England and Australia, in the World Series Cup, while I'd been playing in a Fourex Country Cup game in Gladstone and spending most of my time greeting friendly faces from Biloela who'd made the short journey east to watch the game. When the call came that I was needed in Townsville, I immediately thought one of the locals was winding me up, but it was true, so I dashed back to Brisbane to collect the rest of my gear and then flew north. I scored 21 and took one catch, Richie Richardson — not a bad way to start — off Billy McDermott and kept my spot for a Shield game in Launceston, where I didn't make a dismissal but scored 40, adding 60 for the seventh wicket with my best mate, Brad Inwood. Then Ando came back for the rest of the season.

My chance in 1987–88 came after Ando badly broke his thumb keeping up to the stumps to Ian Botham in Perth. I was immediately into the team for a home game against South Australia, a thrilling draw that went down to the final over. On that last day I stumped David Hookes and again heard whispers that Hookes or someone from the South Australian Cricket Association was going to approach me about a move. But this never happened.

I played every one of my first six first-class games for Queensland — two in 1986–87 and four in 1987–88 — as if it was my last. Brad and I used to have a few drinks most nights, then get out to warm-ups the next morning, shake out the cobwebs, and off we'd go again. I loved every part of what we were doing: the sport, the camaraderie, the fun, the adventure. And if I got another game, I'd think, 'Geez, how good is this!' In those days, the best way I found to learn was to listen. If I spotted an Ian Botham or a Dennis Lillee in a group, I'd get in there. If I saw David Hookes, Allan Border and Carl Rackemann together after a Shield match, I'd join their conversation. When 'Beefy' Botham played for Queensland in 1987–88 I always listened to what he was saying and involved myself in the whole atmosphere of it all. I'd go home and tell Mum and Dad about Greg Chappell and Botham and Border in tones of reverence, but face to face I'd try to just take it all in.

I always found Greg Chappell very approachable. Greg was, of course, something of a legend in Queensland cricket, having come north from South Australia before the 1973–74 season and immediately turned the state's Shield team from easybeats into contenders. He was also Queensland representative on the Australian selection panel. I'd been told that some fringe players had struggled to mix with him, but I'd also heard Greg say once in a pre-season group session, 'I'm not going to come to you and tell you what to do. But if you ever want to ask me anything, please ask.' That stuck in my mind, so I did approach him and found him very open with his information and his knowledge and grateful that someone had come to him.

Botham was a total contrast to Greg. One boisterous, the other impeccably business-like. Beefy was an extraordinary figure who polarised opinions in Brisbane when he was our star import and was a mass of contradictions. He lived for the moment, always lavishly, often rude, while being as generous a character as I have met. As a teammate, I found him inspiring, even if I rarely saw him involved in serious practice. Unless you call slogging the ball out of the net serious practice. However, during a match he was remarkable, never believing a match or cause was lost. Just about my biggest memory of that season is watching Botham play at the Gabba, where I'd go every Sunday after playing club cricket on the Saturday. They used to get decent crowds, too, when Beefy was the main event.

Do you think I was enjoying myself? An unsuccessful shout for a stumping on the thrilling final day of my first Shield game of the 1987–88 season, against South Australia in Brisbane. This would be the only first-class game I would play at the Gabba before my Test debut.

Allan Border was different again. He was the Queensland captain in those days, but we didn't see him that often because of his international commitments. I quickly learned that he was a bloke who expected first-class cricketers to be able to look after themselves, which initially I interpreted as him being a bit removed. I often wondered what he was thinking, but then, just after I'd decided he was unapproachable he'd come out with a tremendous comment that would pump you up. I remember during the first Shield game I played in 1987–88, he said to me, after I'd been caught at mid-on after trying to hit the South Australian leggie, Peter Sleep, against the spin, 'You just need to play those a little straighter and wait for the bad one a bit longer, then you'll get through.' It was hardly earth-shattering, but it was helpful, constructive advice. And it was from him.

The first time 'AB' really had an impact on my cricket was in an indirect but major way. It had come earlier in that 1987–88 summer, not long after the Australian team had arrived home after winning the World Cup, Craig

McDermott came up to me at State practice and said, 'AB wants you in.'

To which I replied, 'What, in the Queensland side?' At the time I was very much the second-string Queensland keeper.

'No,' Billy continued, 'the Australian side.'

I didn't know what to make of it, but it still acted as a spur and a confidence boost for me. I still don't know whether that comment was actually made — AB can't remember saying it, but Billy is adamant that he did. A few months later, my career took an amazing turn, and I wondered whether the Australian captain might well have been in my corner.

Unfortunately, the Queensland Shield team in those days was not the tight unit it would become in later years. When I was first on tour with the Australian Test side, I'd occasionally look at whom I was with in a restaurant, and I might have been with the New South Welshmen. Or it might be the NSW blokes, Dean Jones and me. The next night, there might be three West Australians and me. The Queenslanders and the Victorians never seemed to have that let's-stick-together mentality, and I believe as a consequence were not as successful in the Shield. This said, the West Aussies, while they were close-knit, didn't have the aura or the confidence that the NSW guys possessed. This changed through the '90s, as many of the key Bluebags in the Test team lost some interest and enthusiasm for Shield cricket. In contrast, Queensland has gone the other way, which is one reason the Bulls are winning Sheffield Shields these days and NSW are not.

When I became captain of Queensland, in 1992–93, I set out to break down the senior player/junior player mentality that was a part of the Queensland set-up. We had to get everyone communicating, and mixing very freely. John Buchanan, who became the state coach for the 1994-95 season, played a key part in this process, after his predecessor, Jeff Thomson, developed a good list of talent. Now we have a very strong, confident Queensland side that doesn't back off against NSW, whether the NSW team is full of Test players or not. That didn't always happen in the late '80s.

Then, Queensland was full of an old school/new school mentality, which had the senior players sometimes intimidating the less experienced. When the Test players came back, the younger guys seemed to step back and wait for the more seasoned men to take over. Treating the 12th man with no respect was a team joke, and there didn't seem to be a game plan beyond everyone going out and doing his best. This all came to a head in Launceston in February 1988, where we lost and AB and Greg Chappell found themselves firmly in one camp and Ian Botham just as firmly in another. The fact that AB, in trying to get some discipline on board, put a curfew and a drinks ban on the team didn't soothe things.

After that game against Tasmania, Beefy and Dennis Lillee, who was playing for Tassie that season, stayed behind for some apparently not-so-quiet drinks. The grog ban wasn't in place yet: AB had announced in the dressing room after the game that once we got to Melbourne the drinks were off. Most of the rest of us gathered in the courtyard of our hotel, ready to set off for Launceston Casino, while AB was delayed in his room. Then Beefy, Lillee and two of the Tassie players arrived, brakes screeching out the front of the hotel, and asked, in a slightly menacing tone, 'Where's Border?'

And off they stormed to see the captain. Beefy, we found later, simply wanted to explain to AB that he'd never gone a day without a drink in his life. Meanwhile, a few of our blokes weren't sure what to make of it, but someone said — people who were there reckon it was me but I can't remember saying it — 'Let's leave them to it.' And off we went.

From Melbourne, where we were beaten outright, we went on to the Shield final in Perth, which was also lost but became more infamous for our flight to the match. AB and Greg Ritchie had an argument somewhere over central Australia and then Beefy got involved, first in the argument and then in a blue with a passenger. After we landed, Dennis Lillee was required to bail him out of the lockup so he could play. The end result was that Beefy's contract with the QCA was terminated, and we still hadn't won a Sheffield Shield. From my perspective, the incidents had little impact — I found them entertaining if anything. I was disappointed that we lost, but happy with the way I'd gone about my cricket, especially at the Melbourne Cricket Ground where I'd taken eight catches and even opened the batting when regular opener Trevor Barsby had a problem with a tooth. I'd confirmed in my own mind that I could hack it at this level, but wondered exactly where and when my next opportunity might come.

CHAPTER 3

THE ONLY ONE

THE THOUGHT OF BEING selected for Australia for the 1988 tour of Pakistan hadn't occurred to me at all. Who might and might not get selected had been a subject of some — but not much — dressing-room banter during the week of the Sheffield Shield final, but I can't recall the name 'I. Healy' being thrown vigorously into the discussion. I certainly didn't know when the Pakistan tour was going to occur, or even when the squad was going to be announced. What I did know was that the Queensland team was going to the country town of Kingaroy on the weekend after Easter, to help open a new field there, and that I was going to be part of that experience. With Peter Anderson fully recovered from the injury that had cost him the last four first-class games of the season — and given me my chance — that trip had not been guaranteed. I was thrilled to have won THAT job!

At around 3.15pm on March 31, 1988, I took a call at work from Lorraine Whitney, who was secretary to the Secretary of the Queensland Cricket Association. 'Have you,' she laughed down the line, 'heard any good news today?'

'No,' I replied, not quite sure why Lorraine would ask such a question.

'Oh … okay then. Umm … I'd better let you talk to Grantley.'

As in Grantley Evans, the Secretary of the QCA. After a quick 'G'day, How are you,' he said …

'Mate, you're in!'

'Yeah, I know,' I replied. 'They told me in Perth. I'm going to Kingaroy. Should be ...'

'No, no, no,' he cut me off. 'You're IN! You're in the Australian team.'

'What?' I blurted out.

'You're in the Australian team …'

Grantley read out the team, but I wasn't listening. When he finished going through it a second time, I asked, 'Who's the other keeper?'

'You're it, mate. You're the only one.'

So I asked him to read out all the names again. Then I sat down. Sandy Ferguson, the office secretary, rushed over and asked, most concerned, 'What's the matter, you've gone white.'

The naming of the team had been embargoed until 3 o'clock, and Lorraine was ringing to wish me luck. But in that 15 minutes between 3pm and that call I hadn't heard a thing from the media or the ACB. Nothing. At the QCA, they thought 15 minutes would be plenty. If only they knew.

I braced myself for the flood of media calls, but absolutely no one rang. These days, if a bloke was picked out of the blue like that, it would be straight into the QCA offices or the Gabba for a packed media conference. Back then, I had no idea what was supposed to happen. But surely, I thought, this was news. Or was it a prank? If it was, it wasn't very funny.

Still white, I sheepishly told my workmates, among them my soon-to-be brother-in-law, Ian 'Perko' Perkins. Every time, I added quickly that the handshake might be premature; this could be a wind-up. Then I rang my father. 'Are you sitting down?' I asked quietly. A few seconds later, straight to the point, he cried, 'No way!' Then he thought for a second …

'You couldn't have, could ya?'

'Could ya?' he whispered again.

'I don't know … I think so … Maybe.'

'Let me make a couple of calls.'

And with that he hung up. Thanks, Dad.

My mum was equally confused. My best mate, Brad Inwood, was the same. 'Bullshit,' was his verdict. 'Wouldn't be the first time someone's pulled that stunt. Mate, we've done this before ourselves.'

With Helen and our bags, packed for an Easter holiday at Moreton Island, on April Fool's Day, 1988, the day after I learned I'd been picked out of the blue to play for Australia.

Finally, soon after, the phone rang. It was Trevor Hohns, whom I'd grown close to in my time in the Queensland side. 'Cracker' had heard from somewhere. *Now* this was getting serious. Then Dad rang back. He'd rung the ABC, who'd confirmed that the news was fair dinkum. But why, Dad, I countered, hasn't anyone from the papers or the TV called? 'Dunno, son, all I know is I'm bloody proud.'

Let's go to the golf club, Perko suggested, which we did, leaving a trail of messages so that if anyone was looking for me, they'd know where to find me. After nine holes, having decided on about the second fairway that yes, it was true, I bounced up to the barman to discover which prominent reporters had called.

'Sorry mate,' he said. 'Nothing at all.'

So there I was, head down on the bar, contemplating what I'd probably become. Perko lived not far from the club, and we'd told the people we left at work that if anyone called and they couldn't get us at the club then to try Perko's home number. But no one had tried to make contact there either. Except for Dad, who had confirmed the news again from Ian Sturgess at the QCA. That was probably good enough. I think.

It wasn't until the next day, Good Friday, that the media calls started coming. Because there were no papers published on that Friday, the reporters had been in no hurry. My fiancée Helen and I had intended to leave first thing for Moreton Island, to spend the Easter holiday camping with Craig and Jodie McDermott, but our departure was delayed when the press converged the next morning. A photo of both of us was snapped for the *Sun*, and I had my first experience of doing a succession of one-on-one interviews, one after the other, each involving the same questions and pretty much the same answers. By the time I got on the ferry to Moreton Island, I was just about over this celebrity business.

When Billy and Jodie met us at the wharf, I quickly told my new Australian teammate, 'I'm picked, I'm in the Australian team.'

'Course you are, Heals,' he grinned. 'How come you're so late.'

'But AB said …'

Billy looked at me. Maybe I was telling the truth. 'No way,' he said quietly. 'That's great … yeah. You're in! … Are you?'

Then it started raining. Rained the whole four days. I didn't care.

— ¤ —

WAS I LUCKY? ABSOLUTELY. When Ray Phillips hung up his Queensland keeping gloves after the 1985–86 season, Peter Anderson was a natural to take over. Ando could have settled in for a long run; in just about everyone's eyes I wasn't even a challenger to him for the gloves, merely his standby. I couldn't help thinking — and still do — had he not broken that finger and thumb, would he have been given the Test opportunity I received?

About four things had to fall into place for me to get into the Australian team. One, Ando had to get injured. And he was hurt twice. His first injury created an opening that gave me a taste, which was important; the timing of the second —

and the fact that it was a severe injury which gave me an extended run — was crucial. Two, I had to be in good form when the chance arrived. As I've said, my form in those games for Queensland in the second half of the 1987–88 season was excellent. Three, there had to be a pre-season tour coming up. Had there been no Test matches scheduled before the 1988–89 season, the Queensland selectors might well have gone back to Ando, which would have left me out in the cold when a potential keeping change at national level was being discussed. As well, it would have been less likely that the selectors would have put such a raw rookie under the microscope of the local media by picking him out of the blue for a home Test. And four, the incumbent Australian keeper had to be under that microscope, which Greg Dyer certainly was at that time.

Underlining it all is the fact that if someone else had got that opportunity, there may never have been another right time and place. I might have played as many Test matches as Peter Anderson, Michael Dimattina and Richard Soule, the Queensland, Victorian and Tasmanian keepers of the time. However, in the four years since Rod Marsh had retired from international cricket, Wayne Phillips, Roger Woolley, Steve Rixon, Tim Zoehrer and Greg Dyer had all kept for Australia (and Ray Phillips had toured England without winning a Test cap) — hardly the ideal scenario for a position that is the focus of so much the team does. Greg Chappell apparently saw in me some of the traits that characterised men such as Allan Border, Geoff Marsh, Steve Waugh, Dean Jones and David Boon, around whom the selectors were developing their long-term plans.

Greg has tried to deflect the responsibility for my selection onto the entire selection panel, but he had to be the catalyst behind my inclusion. He was the one selector who knew me. Bob Simpson, Australian coach and another selector, admitted that he had never seen me play when I was first chosen, and later wrote that Greg 'really went into bat for me'. Laurie Sawle would have scrutinised me in the Shield final in Perth. The others? I don't know.

One key, I have always believed, was a brief conversation I had with Greg during our Shield match in Launceston in February 1988. At lunch on the third day, I was 58 not out, having batted for a long while with Glenn Trimble, who'd smashed a hundred in the session before lunch. Greg came into the dressing room, having just spoken to AB, who'd told him we were about to declare in the hope of setting up an outright result. We were still 118 behind on the first innings and I knew nothing of the impending declaration. Greg said to me, "What do you reckon? If you put your head down you can make a hundred here.'

'Aw, I don't want to think too far ahead,' I replied. 'I'll just play it one ball at a time. That's the only way I can play.'

Good answer.

Six months later, I had another brief chat with Greg before I left for Pakistan, and during it he offered me this bit of advice: 'Think beyond Pakistan.' This confirmed the 'long-term' thinking of the selectors. I would remember that line after we arrived there; more than once I needed an incentive to remind me that my personal battles were worth it.

Our wedding day, two weeks after we'd learned our lives were going to change forever. Left to right: Sister-in-law Sandra, Dad, the bride and groom, Mum, brother Ken and sister Kim. In front is my grandmother on Mum's side. I can only assume my elder brother, Greg, is already at the bar.

For me, of course, life between my selection and the start of the tour was a buzz. Not so, understandably, for Peter Anderson. He admitted soon after my selection that he was thinking of giving the game away. Then an offer to move to South Australia was made, which he accepted. It's astonishing to think that all this could have been reversed, but for that broken finger.

— ¤ —

I HAD FIVE MONTHS to prepare for the tour, which was probably fortunate, because it gave me time to come to grips with the concept of being an Australian cricketer. In early April, when I was picked, I'd just started a new job with my father-in-law's clothing company. Two weekends after Easter I was a married man. Now I was an international cricketer. Suddenly, the papers wanted a happy snap from the wedding. I played winter cricket that winter and was terrible. I kept thinking, 'I'm an Australian player and I should be belting these attacks around.' That was not the way I'd been thinking when I'd been impressing Greg Chappell and company in those four Sheffield Shield matches. I'd never been in a curry house in my life before I was selected, but during those five months before the tour my father-in-law, Don Perkins, Helen and I decided to try them out. Ironically, in Pakistan we would usually head for the 'western-style buffets' at the hotels.

Of course, I knew the Queensland guys in the team — Allan Border and Craig McDermott — and Tony Dodemaide and Mike Veletta were teammates from the 1983 Under 19 tour. The rest were opponents I'd shared a beer with in a dressing room or a stoush on the field, either at Under 19s, Colts or Shield level. I knew my new teammates through their reputations better than they would have known me. At a team dinner in late August, AB quietly asked me if I'd met everyone. 'Yeah, I think so,' I replied. I mixed okay, but it was one thing to mix and another to really feel a part of it.

I found the biggest pressure in the step up from Shield to Test cricket was the internal agony of worrying if your teammates rated you. The fact that your method is now under the microscope — not just from the opposition but also from the media — can be difficult to counter. In contrast, in Shield cricket you can peel off a run of productive performances without ever having your technique truly analysed. Queensland's Matthew Hayden in 1993 is a classic example of the problems this spotlight can cause. When he made the Test team his batting came under severe scrutiny, people started saying he had a weakness here and a weakness there, and quickly everything changed for him. But while that examination is very hard, even harder for me was peer pressure. I wanted to feel worthy. I needed my new teammates to believe that my selection was justified.

There was no reason for me to feel this way. No one set out to make me feel like that. But I didn't know the players very well, and they didn't know me. I was trying to show them my cricket skills, at the same time as I was meeting and learning about them and getting to know them. To make matters worse, from very soon after we landed in Pakistan it was clear that some of the guys didn't want to be in the country at all. The atmosphere within the team was terrible, many miles from what it is today. Pakistan was in turmoil following the assassination of its leader, General Zia, and memories of previous Australian tours of Pakistan had been vividly recalled. Reporters kept pressing Allan Border about England captain Mike Gatting's battles with the local umpires on their tour 12 months earlier, which had ended with Gatting and umpire Shakoor Rana pointing angry fingers at each other while the world looked on, while AB was quick to recall crowd troubles from the 1982 Australian tour, when a one-day international had been abandoned.

Following our pre-tour camp, I wrote in my diary:

> September 1, 1988: 1. Enjoyment of working needs to
> improve; 2. Got to be tougher mentally; 3. Relax, concentrate
> and enjoy. The ball is the only thing that can get you out ...

Most of the time we were in Pakistan, it was uncomfortably hot. Besides that heat, my most vivid first impression was setting foot on the Karachi tarmac and seeing a tent-filled shanty town on the airport's fringe. Lurking in the air was something of a stench. We had arrived early in the morning and went straight to an airport hotel, where we were assigned two to a room, for a wash and a clean-up followed by breakfast, then back on the plane to fly to Lahore. My roomie was 'Simmo', coach with raw rookie. Coincidence? In the hotel room there was one bed with a mosquito net, plus a canvas stretcher. The carpet was way past its use-by date. In the bathroom, the basin was rusty and the water — which we'd been strongly advised not to go near — didn't come out of the taps too well.

And Simmo exclaimed, 'Gee, hasn't this improved!!!'

And I thought, 'Oh no!' Welcome to Pakistan. Everything I had heard on the plane on the way over was true. But in fact the hotels throughout the tour were excellent. In my view, Pakistan wasn't nearly as bad as many of the blokes had made out — and continued to make out throughout the tour. But not everyone agreed and after a while I began to be influenced by that attitude.

Unfortunately, I couldn't find the team spirit that was probably there. If an outsider entered the Australian dressing room today and heard all the piss-taking and sarcastic taunts that fire across the room, that observer would have to conclude that at least some of the blokes really don't like each other. Back in 1988, it was probably worse and I was that outsider looking in. It seemed to me that there wasn't a whole lot of ticker or verve in the side, my form wasn't coming good and too quickly I started to think, 'This a shit place.' Off the field it could get boring, as there was no TV, no nightlife and no socialising other than in the team room drinking the two cartons a day the side received from the Australian Embassy. I had too much time to think, but no way to relax.

As the tour progressed, the Western Australians developed a practice where every day was named after a famous footballer, the number of days left on tour matching the player's number. 'It's "Alex Jesaulenko Day" … 25 days to go,' one of the WACAs told us one morning. We all got involved. Six days out, it was 'Wally Lewis Day'. That was the sort of atmosphere that built up and never let go. I remember, too, being tagged by the fines committee after the first Test. My crime was to innocently clap Javed Miandad after he reached 200. Not one other Australian did, in protest at the umpires' refusal to give him out lbw. Steve Waugh got me for that one — US$20.

There were a couple of games before that first Test, first in Lahore and then in Quetta. Lahore was terrible, stinking hot. Back then, I used to wear a singlet, to absorb the sweat. Allan Border looked at me, collar up, singlet visible through the shirt, and said flatly, 'You've got to be kidding.' What AB said went and so did the singlet. From memory, I hit the first ball I faced for four, then a left-arm orthodox spinner got me out, and I didn't keep too badly. The 'field' in Quetta remained throughout my cricket life the worst surface I ever played on and I know I kept badly on it. I could sense my teammates asking questions. I knew that I was watching the bat rather than concentrating on the ball, and I was coming up too early on a wicket much slower than anything I was used to. Almost immediately, I worried about dropping every ball. With such negative emotions about me, inevitably I became tense in everything I did. In the years that followed I learned that the days I kept really well were the days when I didn't care if they nicked them or not. I'd simply watch the ball. It's amazing how well you keep in such circumstances.

I had no idea about that back then. This was the first time my technique had come under scrutiny. I was coming up from the crouch too early, too tense, gloves hard. I remember missing a full toss from Peter Sleep's bowling. Out of

At our pre-tour camp in Brisbane, August 1988.

'Sounda's' hand I thought, 'Where's he [the batsman] going to smash this?' But the batsman missed it and so did I. I hardly moved at all. It must have looked ugly and the following morning Simmo casually mentioned that one of the team had said to him, 'That full toss, how did Heals miss that?'

'But don't worry, I understand,' the coach said quietly, 'you expect the batsman to hit a full toss.'

All I knew was that someone had said something to Simmo.

Further depressing me was the fact that the body language of some of my teammates did little for my self-confidence. David Boon would stare at me from short leg, but never grin or say much. 'Another one who hates me,' I concluded. Similarly, I thought off-spinner Tim May was over the top with his cynicism. I could never get a serious answer out of him, and I took some of his smart-alec comments a bit personally. He had me worried in Pakistan, but I finally worked him out on the 1989 Ashes tour and he became one of my strongest cricket and personal allies.

This was just their way. I was learning that to enjoy international cricket and prosper at the highest level you need to be tough. Same, as I continue to learn, as just about any vocation in life.

As a group, we approached the first Test, in Karachi, in a dreadful frame of mind. There was a genuine belief that we were about to be stitched up, and as the Test panned out perhaps there was some truth in that. The track was made to order for their three spinners, spearheaded by the great leggie, Abdul Qadir, and we couldn't get an lbw to save our tour. The contrast between this wicket and the magnificent batting tracks we played the final two Tests on was stark. So was the contrast between the wicket in Karachi and the surrounds, which were lush and green. We lost the toss and were bowling, but it wouldn't have mattered if we had won that toss. Had we batted first, they would have spun us out just as quickly.

My first Test catch was a good one. Bruce Reid, the ultra-tall left-arm West Australian quick, was bowling and, having first knocked over Mudassar Nazar's leg stump, he then got one to 'stop' on the fragile pitch. Ramiz Raja jabbed at it and edged it, a dying nick, which I caught, two-handed, in front of first slip. Steve Waugh remembers that everyone was thinking, 'Gee what have we got here,' but then things went awry. I put Javed Miandad down off Stephen's bowling (he went on to make 211) and then missed Salim Malik off Reid. Quickly, they concluded, 'We've got a dud.'

The miss off 'Tugga' Waugh came about when Javed was on 128. He slashed at a wide one, and the ball flew through to me at shoulder height, difficult but far from impossible. The Bruce Reid spill, I confess, I can't remember at all. When someone gently ribbed me years later for costing the big fella a 'five for', I honestly couldn't picture it. But it happened; all the reports mention it. Some pressmen reckoned I missed another as well.

This Test cricket was an intimidating experience. For this Karachi Test especially the mental intensity was as demanding as the physical stress. Our spinners being on so early was totally new for me, as was the need to keep through an innings that lasted more than two days. I'd enjoyed supporting the spinners I'd kept to for Queensland, men such as Trevor Hohns and Brett Henschell, but that had been on much more reliable wickets. I thought I'd always kept well to the spinners, and reckoned that might have played a part in my Test selection. Now I let 16 byes through, all of them quite early in the innings. Looking back today over 119 Tests, I don't think I ever saw another Test wicket as ready to turn on day one as that one.

I can tell you that no Australian wanted to be out there. You'd come off for lunch and blokes would moan, 'We'll never get 'em out.' Maybe they had the confidence to mutter such a comment as a throwaway line. I didn't. In many ways it was unbelievable. There was no one revving us up. On the contrary, all about was a constant groan about the umpires and the pitch. On the Friday, day two, for religious reasons, we had an hour-and-a-half lunch break. Start a bit early, long lunch-break, then a normal middle session, with the last session a bit longer. For those 90 minutes everyone lay about trying to sneak some rest, with no positive talk at all. I'll never forget that Karachi dressing room.

After two days in the field, I got pretty crook and every time I rolled over in bed throughout the night, it was, 'Geeeeez ...' and I'd have to rush to the toilet. The next morning, I staggered downstairs and reported my problem to the coach. But I got little sympathy. 'You're just tense,' he muttered. 'A lot of blokes have been through what you're going through. Better get used to it.'

He was right.

Some of the umpiring was very ordinary. But our complaints fell on deaf ears — there was no referee, no neutral anything. There was no feeling of respect for the team. We were nobodies; it was nothing like how the team is feted these days. Manager Col Egar, a former respected Test umpire himself — became very frustrated with all of it. Sour memories of the Mike Gatting incident from the previous year, often recalled in the Australian dressing room and by the travelling media, was fuel on the fire.

'C. Egar' was in a difficult position: representative of the Australian Cricket Board — the same ACB that had stressed to us and to the media pre-tour how important it was that we act in a patient, diplomatic way whatever fiascoes might be put in front of us — but also a representative of the players. He came down very firmly on our side, which we fully appreciated. On the third day, not long after Steve Waugh had copped a dreadful lbw decision from the same ump, Mahboob Shah, who had quickly knocked us back on a couple of plumb Javed Miandad shouts, Col and Bob Simpson officially protested to the Pakistani officials about the umpiring and the pitch. Then they called an impromptu press conference at the tea interval, to let the world know just how filthy we were. Needless to say, this action caused a furore. Mahboob Shah was one of the nation's most respected umpires, and had officiated in the World Cup Final the previous year. Years later, we had him as a neutral umpire in a series in South Africa and he was excellent. However, our complaints about him in 1988 led inevitably to the locals firing off furious accusations about sour grapes, while the touring press was split, with some thinking we'd overreacted big time and others being extremely sympathetic.

> *September 20, 1988 (fifth day, first Test): Concentration was good in hard conditions. Was very positive but only hitting bad balls. Until dismissal. All of a sudden I wanted to hit Qadir! Idiot. Lost purpose and patience, it was not my job to score. Task was difficult; to bat all day but lost sight of it for that one ball!*
>
> *Team encouragement was nil. Players virtually thought we couldn't do it. Obviously, I also believed that.*

We were beaten outright early on the fifth morning, and later that day a team meeting was called back at the Pearl Continental Hotel. On the agenda was a ballot to decide whether we wanted the tour to continue. AB had already said at the post-match press conference that the team would prefer that the rest of the tour be abandoned. We gathered in the manager's room, with Col Egar perched precariously on a little footstool and the rest of us gathered around him on the floor. When the vote was called, only two players — neither of them experienced — wanted to stay. I wasn't one of them, a fact that disappoints me today. With hindsight, I should have looked at the consequences, both personally and for cricket, more carefully. Even at the time I knew that my hand shouldn't have gone up, but voting with the other guys was simpler. I remember how I was thinking: my form's not too flash, but if I go home now I'll still get the series at home against the West Indies. If we're outta here, then I can't do any further damage to my career.

I'd like to think that taking the easy way out is not usually my style. Nor have I ever seen myself as a conformist. That I voted 'yes' says a lot for the frazzled state of my mind at this stage of my fledgling international career.

Although AB had alluded to the vote during his press conference, we agreed to keep our decision private while cricket politics came into play. In the end, slightly calmer minds prevailed and it was resolved that a walkout was not the appropriate thing to do. Eventually a public statement from the team was drafted, which the ACB agreed to support.

That statement was released not long after we arrived in Faisalabad for the second Test, which was due to begin just three days after the first Test was completed. It read:

> *The Australian cricket team is aware of its responsibilities to the game and to future generations of international cricketers. For that reason, we will fulfil our commitments on the tour as agreed by the cricket boards of Australia and Pakistan. But we fully support Allan Border and our tour management in their comments on playing conditions here in Pakistan. We are not alone in our dissatisfaction with the circumstances which surround Test cricket in Pakistan. Other visiting teams have drawn attention to pitches and umpiring decisions which are clearly unsatisfactory and contrary to the spirit of the game. The situation is unacceptable and damaging to international cricket, yet nothing seems to be done.*
>
> *We appeal to the Pakistan board and International Cricket Conference to take a long and honest look at the situation confronting visiting teams, for the sake of their own reputations, as well as that of the players, whose careers are put at risk. We hope the rest of the tour will be completed as a fair contest between international cricketers and we will be doing our utmost to play and win our matches in the proper spirit.*

These views, coming on top of the confirmation of the rumours that we had wanted to go home, did little for our popularity throughout Pakistan. We were told it was lucky we couldn't read Urdu, because the local press was giving us a hiding. At this point, Pakistan was a long, long way from Biloela. And then, bursting through the doors of the breakfast cafeteria of our Faisalabad hotel, came none other than ace reporter Mike Munro and his camera crew from the Australian version of *Sixty Minutes* ...

Unfortunately, the ACB had told us that we weren't to talk to the media, which meant that Munro's foot-in-the-door technique made Simmo look evasive. All our beleaguered coach could do, after a brief sparring session, was walk forlornly away from the cameras. Then, during the Faisalabad Test, there was

BCCP Patron's XI opening bat Moin-ul-Atiq pads up to the Australian spinners early on the second day of our game in Lahore. Steve Waugh is appealing from slip. This was the Australians' first game of the 1988 tour, and my first day in the field wearing the baggy green cap.

Munro among the crowd, right in front of the visitors' dressing room. 'What do you think of the Australians calling your umpires cheats?' he'd ask of a local fan. He got what he needed.

I learned a few valuable things about my batting in that series. For one, I reckon my goals were too low. I reached the twenties in both innings in my first Test, and both times I subconsciously thought, 'Beauty, that'll keep me in the team.' However, when I looked back about how long I'd survived out there against the spinners, I was dirty. Maybe I could have done better.

To be honest, I didn't know much about batting. I was just a natural batsman in club cricket, making 30s and 40s, and now I found myself in Test matches doing the same thing. I had discovered very quickly that I could do in Sheffield

Shield matches what I had been able to do in grade and Colts matches, and by the end of my first Test tour I was confident I could do the same at the highest level. My natural ability could adapt to any standard. But I quickly realised that I needed to learn how to make big Test-match scores, how to knuckle down. Two hours of just doing nothing can be very valuable in a Test match, but I'd never had to bat like that before.

My first three digs in Test cricket were 20s. Natural talent and my adrenalin got me through. But I had no concentration skills whatsoever. As soon as I became a little satisfied, a little happy ... I was gone. It took ages, about three or four years, for that lesson to truly sink in.

I recall two examples that hammered this message home. In my first Test innings, I came in at 6-60 and immediately hit the offie, Tausef Ahmed, over mid-wicket for four. Then I had a swing at another one, which went nowhere. At the end of the over, Peter Taylor came down and said in his scholarly way, 'Whoa, Ian, we've got a Test match to save here.'

'Yeah, mate,' I replied, my club thinking coming to the fore, 'my best way is to try to hit them.'

'No,' he countered, 'just try to kick them away.'

Maybe he was right. I did hang around for a while, until I was out for 26, caught bat-pad trying to be a little cute against the innocent medium pace of Mudassar Nazar. PT batted through to the end of the innings, making 54 not out.

In the second Test I was going well with AB. We added 52, of which I made 27, but AB was boring me. He was doing it tough, and my instincts nagged me, 'I'd better play some shots, otherwise we're going nowhere.' Then I nicked one into the slips of another medium pacer, Saleem Jaffer, which was stupid. AB went on to 113 not out. I remember sitting in the dressing room that night, thinking over and over, 'He's made a Test hundred ...boring obviously works!'

Throughout the tour, no one went out of their way to help me as a new recruit, but they weren't trying to hinder me either. 'Come along for the ride' was the unstated welcome. Certainly, no one took me under his wing. I worked really hard with coach Bob Simpson on this tour, doing everything he asked, but while I appreciated the way he encouraged my work ethic, I learned from Rod Marsh during the following Australian summer that his methods weren't exactly what a keeper needed. Simmo was a 'catch hitter' who liked to wrong foot catchers during practice. He loved it when he was whacking them too fast and wrong footing me all over the place, and I worked hard not to get beaten. However, as Rod would stress to me, what a keeper wants is rhythm, which means you don't need balls belted so fast that you're reacting rather than rehearsing correct hand and foot movements. Sure, a portion of practice can be the reflex, diving stuff involving bullets from the catch-hitter's blade, but not all of it.

The thing that got me back on track was my golf ball drill. In Faisalabad, seeking an escape from what had been a trying time, I discovered an old squash court not too far from the team hotel. That old court had a crusty cement floor, but I used to disappear every morning, half an hour at a time, to bounce the ball in there. Without even realising it, going back to my basic drills got me back on track. On the field, I rallied. I still feathered a catch which sped between first slip and me. But I snared a good one, too, off the edge of Ijaz Ahmed's bat, diving across in front of the slip cordon in the second innings, and could feel my form and confidence coming back. AB gave me a big hug after that catch, which meant more to me that he could have realised. I sensed, too, that some of my teammates noticed his reaction. In retrospect, that was one of the most important dismissals of my life.

What had happened was that I had begun to visualise my movements and glovework, which got my technique back into a groove. Unfortunately, Simmo's scattergun methods weren't helping my rhythm; nor was the stumping practice at the nets on wickets that were far too slow to offer realistic game-like situations. As well, for too long I was too worried about what others were thinking.

My form improvement coincided with something of a revival in the team's fortunes. In Faisalabad we managed to fashion a small first-innings lead in a drawn game, then in the final Test, in Lahore, we had Pakistan down and almost out at 8-153 when the series ended. Bruce Reid, our most potent weapon, was injured on that final day, which probably cost us, but even then an lbw appeal that was turned down near the end might have made a difference had it gone our way. In fact, if you take all the rubbish connected with the first Test out, the tour wasn't the disaster many think it was. After the first Test we held our own, but then we should have, because our opponents, Javed, Salim Malik and Abdul Qadir apart, were pretty ordinary. Imran had cried off, saying it was too hot to play in Pakistan at that time of year, and Wasim Akram was out because of a groin injury.

We finished the tour much better than we started it. And I felt a lot better about this Test cricket caper than I had after the opening Test in Karachi. Simmo seemed to agree with me, too, which was reassuring. Then, on the way back to the team hotel after the final Test, my captain pulled me to one side and quietly offered me some praise I appreciated and needed.

'Heals,' he said, 'you've done alright, hang in there.'

CHAPTER 4

STICKING IT UP 'EM

LATE ON THE SECOND-LAST evening of the third Test of my first home series, our big fast bowler, Merv Hughes, really got under the skin of the big West Indian fast bowler, Patrick Patterson. The Windies quicks had been bouncing us relentlessly all series, and we were sick of it. Their onslaught was so unrelenting that we'd come to the conclusion that whatever we did, the barrage couldn't get any worse. Geoff Lawson, batting at No. 9 without a visor on his helmet in the previous Test in Perth, had been flattened by the newest addition to their strikeforce, Curtly Ambrose. In this Melbourne Test, played on a pitch more 'ridgy' than flat, our physio Errol Alcott had been out in the middle to rehabilitate our batsmen more often than he needed to remember. Now, here was Patterson batting No. 11, with the Windies miles in front and all of us fully aware that the following day the Windies pacemen were going to bounce us mercilessly once more.

Patto was batting with the often-cranky Gordon Greenidge, who was in much lower than usual because of an eye injury. Steve Waugh was on a bit of a roll, in the middle of a spell that would get him four wickets. Merv, who was bowling from the other end, was wearing a baggy green (which was rare for him) and fielding in the covers for Steve, prancing around like a Greg Chappell or a Ricky Ponting. Steve bounced Patterson.

'Steeck it up 'im, Tugga,' Merv shouted out in his best Caribbean accent, ''e don't like it, maan!'

Patto stared at him, hardly believing what he was hearing. And then Merv charged in from the other end, with Stephen at square leg, mumbling away. This, for Patrick Patterson, was too much. When Stephen kept going with it right until Merv reached the top of his run, the Windies quick jumped up out of his batting stance and walked away.

In the slips, Allan Border had been preoccupied. He'd missed most of the banter between Merv and Patto, and hadn't heard Stephen offering his encouragement either. But he could see Patterson carrying on.

'What's your problem?' he bellowed at the tailender.

Patterson looked up, then around at our captain. 'You talk to me?' he replied.

'What's your problem?' AB repeated, 'Just face up, will ya.'

From the bowler's end, Merv added, 'Good on ya, skipper, steeck it up 'im.'

Patterson was not amused. Soon after, when stumps were drawn with the Windies still nine wickets down and a run short of 400 in front, he stormed off the MCG, up the stairs, through his dressing room and on towards our room.

Ignoring the room attendant and bashing on our door, he demanded to be heard. 'Border,' he roared, pointing to the middle of the MCG, 'tomorrow, we sort it out ... out there.'

Patrick Patterson hadn't been bowling too well in that series. But the next day he took 5-39 as we disintegrated for 114. During a seventh-wicket partnership between AB and Peter Taylor, which started after I was out at 6-75, both guys were battered from head to thigh by a constant stream of short-pitched bowling aimed straight at the body. Soon after the Windies were three up in the five-Test series, with two to play.

At first glance, this new, belligerent approach we showed to Patterson must look pretty stupid, or at least naive: Aussies fire up big fast bowler, who responds with five-for. But I think it, or the change of attitude it symbolised, was a significant point in the evolution of the Australian cricket team. Previous sides, which included many of the guys who were part of that XI, had been copping it for so long from these blokes. We'd all had a gutful, of getting beaten and getting beaten up.

Three times on that final day, Errol rushed out to see me during my short innings of 8, after I copped one ... two ... three rockets straight into my groin. It might have looked funny from the stands. After we'd been beaten, I could see, from where I was sitting with piles of ice from my waist to my thighs, Steve Waugh nursing a nicked finger and a nicked chin. He'd suffered both nicks from the same delivery, which climbed on him, caught the finger and then went up into the jaw. Peter Taylor was looking at his fingers, then the bruises on his arms, shoulder and chest. We all had bruises. Geoff Lawson's jaw was wired. We'd spent much of the Test counting the bouncers and wondering why the umpires didn't find them intimidatory. That night, Ian McDonald, our long-serving team manager, put a message under each of our doors. His objective was to confirm departure and flight times, but he added a message along the lines of 'See you in Sydney, where we're going to beat these blokes.'

Actually Macca didn't put it quite that nicely. He, like the rest of us, knew we couldn't bowl as fast as they could. We all accepted that we didn't have as much God-given talent as they had. But we knew, too, that we couldn't allow ourselves to be intimidated by them. And for the rest of the summer we were at least their equal, taking a game from them in the World Series Cup finals, winning the Sydney Test and then having the better of a drawn final Test in Adelaide.

— ✠ —

WHEN I ARRIVED BACK in Australia after my first tour as an international cricketer I believed that while my spot in the side was not locked in concrete, I would get selected for the first Test of the new summer. As I've explained, the tour didn't end too badly for me. Still vivid in my mind was the memory of Greg Chappell's pre-tour comments that the selectors wanted to be patient and give me an extended run. I remembered, too, Bob Simpson's philosophy: 'The last person you want to change in any cricket team is the wicketkeeper.'

A hook shot off Western Australian pace bowler Chris Matthews during a brief ninth-wicket partnership with Craig McDermott in the 1987–88 Sheffield Shield final at the WACA. Batting No. 9, I made 14 in this first innings, and a duck when promoted one spot in the order in the second, as we lost by five wickets. The next time I played in Perth was eight months later … for Australia in a Test match against the West Indies.

Although some observers had been critical of my performance in Pakistan, it was not as if I was the only player not to have a five-star tour. Dean Jones had averaged less than 10 in the Test series, David Boon and Steve Waugh less than 20. The fact that Ando had moved to South Australia took away the potential for a Healy v Anderson battle for the Queensland keeping spot. Still, I was prepared to accept whatever happened.

This was an attitude I adopted throughout my career. If I got dropped, so be it. So long as I did everything I could while I was there, in my own mind I'd be okay. I hoped for respect from the selectors, and later in my career believed that I had earned it. Throughout my career, I was never complacent and it wasn't until many years into my international cricket life that I felt that if I missed a game because of injury I'd get back in as soon as I recovered.

Back in Australia in late 1988, before the Windies series, I felt the expectations of all those keenly watching this new Australian keeper. There was no TV coverage of the matches from Pakistan in those days, so for all but the regulars attending Shield matches Australian cricket followers had never seen me play. Perhaps this new-found pressure was the reason my early-season Shield form was not as good as it had been the year before. Then, I had been treating every game as my last. Now, I felt as if every spectator at the ground was taking notes. I wasn't as confident and natural with my gloves as I had been.

But while my keeping was struggling, I felt my batting was on the improve. I started with two unbeaten efforts, 44 not out and 26 not out, batting No. 8 against NSW at the Gabba. The second innings was a beauty, as I was in at the death with Dirk Tazelaar as we put together a 24-run partnership that gave us a last-over two-wicket victory. And then against Tasmania I was unbeaten again, this time on 14, when we secured first-innings points. The fact that I kept my head in these circumstances, with many of my Australian teammates watching (and in the NSW game, with the man I replaced as Aussie keeper, Greg Dyer, behind the stumps) was good for my self-confidence. A duck against Victoria, made well after we'd taken first-inning points and were looking for quick runs, left me going into the first Test with a first-class batting average for the season of 80.

The first Test of the series, at the Gabba, was a big occasion for me, a bigger deal for family, but was hardly turned into a huge local celebration by the Brisbane media or the QCA. I think many locals were a little confused by the ongoing Healy/Anderson debate, and perhaps were a little hesitant to support me in case it turned out that they were backing the wrong horse. More than one ex-player told me that they couldn't believe I'd been picked after just six games. 'Mate, I've got to be honest with you …' they'd begin. The late, great Ray Lindwall was one who sidled up at the Queensland Cricketers' Club and whispered, 'Congratulations, son, good luck. You've been lucky, I reckon. I really rate that Peter Anderson …'

Unfortunately, the Gabba crowd didn't have a lot to cheer about in the first Test, as we crashed to defeat in two days and a session on a beautiful wicket. Just as I'd done in my first overseas Test, I was out in the twenties in both innings, which brought me some praise in the press from the Windies captain, Viv Richards, but frustrated me because it indicated I hadn't learned anything from watching AB in Pakistan. As a team, we were battered and demoralised by the superb West Indian attack of Patterson, Ambrose, Malcolm Marshall and Courtney Walsh. Steve Waugh did manage a brave 90 in the second innings, but the only other batsmen to get past 50 in the match were West Indian.

The West Indies had a physical presence without needing to talk on the field. One thing I was learning quickly was that there was a lot less chat on a Test-match ground than there was back in Brisbane grade cricket. When you were out in the middle, you could look around, and there'd be little Gus Logie under your nose at short leg, maybe a cover and a fine leg, the big fast bowler at the end of his run and the slips cordon miles back. Not much talk, but then the slip fielders were so far away they could have been having a party and you wouldn't have heard them. And the ball was always hitting the bat hard. Nothing was over-pitched; there were hardly any shots to be played.

I was happy with the way I kept. I was helped in a slightly bizarre way by the fact that Chris Matthews, the West Australian and later Tasmanian left-arm swing bowler had been recalled to the Aussie line-up. Chris' previous international appearances had been two years earlier, when he bowled poorly against England. This time, the poor bloke couldn't get his line right at all, and sprayed them all over the place. I was diving everywhere to stop them, which I did with one exception. He made me look good, without ever showing the cricket world what an excellent bowler he could be.

If the Gabba offered a good cricket wicket, the WACA, venue for the second Test, did not. It was outrageously cracked, going in all directions, and I feared for my life as I made 52 on the final day. Marshall bowled one that hit the deck just short of a length and then speared over my head. The conditions definitely made you concentrate. As 'Henry' Lawson so cruelly demonstrated — take your eye off the ball and you might be gone. I made my 50 by taking advantage of all the fieldsmen being up as the Windies tried to close out the game. Anything down the ground or off the legs was four.

Despite this innings, the Test was not a happy experience for me. The WACA crowd clearly thought Tim Zoehrer was a better keeper than I was, and weren't shy about letting me know. Sadly, they had plenty to shout about, especially in the second innings when I let 14 byes slip through. Keeping wasn't easy on that track, but the crowd didn't seem to care and frankly, neither did I. I should have done better. But I wasn't on my own. Tim May was belted around, especially by Viv, and Tony Dodemaide finished with match figures of 1-180. Afterwards, the three of us walked miserably back to our hotel together and although none of us actually came out and said it, I think deep down we all thought the three of us were gone. This was nearly right, too; I was the only one who played in the next Test in Melbourne.

The crowd was not the only thing that got to me. I was worried, too, about how Rod Marsh, the great former Australian and West Australian wicketkeeper who was up in the commentary box, was rating me. I desperately wanted him to think I was okay. Later in the season, back in Perth for the one-day internationals there, I introduced myself. Any thoughts, Rod? His initial reply was frustratingly crude: 'If it's in your half have a swing, if it's in their half duck.' But then he gave some excellent advice on how to concentrate while keeping. To his expert eye, I was working feverishly for every minute we were in the field. What he had done throughout his career was work into the session, set it up, and then relax and work naturally. Work hard for the first 20 minutes, he argued, and from there, if your preparation has been right, you should be okay.

Rod Marsh is a bloke who, like everyone from that era, you have to earn your spurs with before they will open up to you. After that, he was fine. He kept an eye on me and ended up helping me. At one point not much later in the summer, he came up and mildly castigated me for the way I was practising. He'd seen me doing catches with Simmo, jumping everywhere, too often on the wrong foot. He emphasised the need for keepers to practise rhythm, and getting the feet and gloves moving. But at this point I wasn't game to tell the Australian coach that I didn't think he was helping me. Then, after we won a thrilling one-dayer in Melbourne in late January, I saw Rod at the bar. It was a good win, I'd had a good game, but Rod was into me. 'If you're going to waste my time, I won't talk to you.'

'Whatddya mean?'

'You haven't listened to me. I saw you warming up with Simmo on the field today. You've got to slow him down.'

Fortunately, we did talk further and by the time we parted we'd organised a time, when I'd be in Perth for the WA–Queensland Shield game in late February, where we'd have a practice together and he'd show me how he used to do it. Which we did. After that, first on the '89 Ashes tour and then for many season after, I'd always remind Simmo how I wanted to go about things. And he was always excellent. He listened to my opinion, took it in and eventually, I'm pretty sure, agreed with it. To be honest, I didn't care what he thought as long as he helped me; I knew that's what I needed. Simmo would grab a bat and some balls, I'd put on the gloves, and he'd ask with a smile, 'What is today Heals, technique or reflex?' And off we'd go, though every so often I'd have to stop and say, 'Just take a bit off them please, Simmo.'

Back in January 1989, as soon as Rod got up me that night, I knew he rated me, cared about what I did and how I performed. I felt I'd climbed a big step up the credibility ladder.

— ¤ —

THIS SEASON WAS, OF course, my first experience of one-day international cricket. I had played one game in Pakistan, a nail-biter that went down to the final ball of the 50th over. But this was different, and outrageously exciting. I loved it, valued it, but quickly found it easier than Test cricket. I had a set time to keep, on a wicket that was never going to deteriorate. As a late-order batsman, not only could I do something stupid and not get out for it, but I might easily get a run for the indiscretion and get off strike.

That was then. For batsmen today, I don't think batting in one-dayers is much easier than Test cricket. In some ways it's just as difficult. The amount of pressure the batsmen are starting to put on their techniques and the way they play is different from what they did in 'my' day. We used to pace ourselves through the middle of the innings, save wickets and then have a bash at the end, whereas in the 21st century batsmen are putting the 'bash pressure' on their techniques all the way through the innings. This was something we should have been doing and I often argued that way in the mid 1990s. Rather than pace ourselves, why not use all our wickets, including the tailenders. My strategy was that you bat someone such as me, Paul Reiffel or Shane Warne, during the middle overs. I could have gone in, at say 2-60 after 15 overs, chipped the ones and twos, and maintained a rate of six an over, a run a ball. What teams used to do was have their third and fourth-wicket partnerships slip back to three or three-and-a-half an over. The cricket in this period could get boring, as the batting team took their singles and the fielding team, usually using their weaker bowlers, were happy to give the singles away. The batting team was not so much protecting wickets as protecting *top-order* wickets. That was when you'd see the Mexican waves appear. My idea was to get Warne, Reiffel or me in that during this period.

If the fielding captain responded by bringing his field in to attack the 'tailender', we could have a bash over the top. If we got out, then bring the batsman in to take the three or four an over.

Bob Simpson and Mark Taylor wouldn't have a bar of it. I still maintain — and I think it's starting to happen now — that each batsman should play a role in a 50-over innings, rather than simply bat in the same place in the order.

Back in 1988–89, the 'Simon O'Donnell' years if you like (O'Donnell was a dynamic one-day cricketer, capable of taking wickets with his fast-medium bowling and of slamming quick runs late in the innings), we tried to score 160 runs in the first 40 overs. Thirty off 10, 80 off 20, 160 off 40, then bash for the last 10. A total of 220 was very defendable, anything more was an excellent result. On a good day we'd get up to 240 or 250 and on most nights defend that easily. Using two white balls during the innings made that defence easier.

When I compare today's one-day cricket with how it was back in 1988–89, the one facet of the game that hasn't really improved much, if at all, is the batting. As I said, that evolution is just beginning. The bowling today is much smarter, featuring yorkers, slower balls and the like. Because the quicker guys can't bowl bumpers they've been obliged to conceive other deliveries and strategies. The great bowlers have adapted. The fielding today is astonishing.

> *December 15, 1988: No use playing if I'm not going to learn from past experiences. Must stay relaxed in ALL situations. Can't let umpiring, teammates' attitudes affect aggression either. Enjoy the game immensely. Enjoy the challenge of playing such good opposition …*

My first one-day summer was full of highlights. In Sydney, we lost a game under lights against the West Indies by one run, after Craig McDermott was caught off the last ball of the last possible over. I was batting with him at the time. 'Geez Billy, we could have been heroes!' I said to him as we walked slowly off. He didn't say anything. Earlier in the game I'd stumped Viv Richards off Peter Taylor's bowling, a beauty, as good as any one thing I'd done in international cricket. There was our first win over the Windies, in Melbourne by 8 runs after Tugga took a wonderful catch behind the sightscreen in the third-last over to dismiss a rampaging Roger Harper. And the first final, also at the MCG, which we won by two runs and where I had the then novel experience of having the late Malcolm Marshall calling me a cheat.

I have no doubt Malcolm was out, run out, after PT threw the ball in from midwicket. The ball wasn't cleanly in my gloves, but it was in there. Then, as I took it to the stumps, it slipped out and hit the stumps. *Then* my gloves smashed into the wicket. As I dashed off to celebrate, the ball stayed on the ground. I thought sweet, no problems at all. The replay, though, was inconclusive.

We heard that Malcolm went right off in the dressing room and his manager, Clive Lloyd, later reprimanded him. And that was the last I heard of it from the West Indians.

When the media guys approached me afterwards, I simply explained what had happened. I remembered the hullabaloo that surrounded an incident involving Greg Dyer during the previous summer, when he claimed a catch that the video showed shouldn't have been allowed. He wasn't permitted to speak to the media, which accentuated the belief that he had cheated, when in all likelihood he simply wasn't sure and was happy to take the umpire's word for it. The morning after the Marshall run out, the backpage headline in one paper roared: 'I'M NO CHEAT'. The article wasn't that bad, but the headline sure was provocative. This was my first controversy.

—¤—

THE FOURTH TEST IN Sydney was Trevor Hohns' initial Test match, 16 summers after his first-class debut. At the time, he'd played more Shield games than any other player going round in interstate cricket. Cracker and I had always enjoyed a good relationship as state-squad and then Shield teammates. He was naturally quite anxious about his debut, and I found it quite funny, me playing the experienced Test cricketer, and Cracker being the nervous rookie. The day before the match started, after practice, we went up to have a couple of quiet beers at a Kings Cross hotel and I discovered he was looking for as much support as he could get.

It was a big match for me as well. The Sydney Test would always take a lot out of me. It usually featured continuous spin bowling, so you needed to be on the ball. In this game, Peter Taylor was on very early, by the ninth over, and I remember he spun one down the leg side to a right hander and I took it cleanly. And the crowd went, 'Ooooh …', acknowledging the take and the amount of turn evident so early — I knew then I was in for a big day!! I had no real reputation as a keeper to slow bowling at this stage, and it was rewarding to get that sort of reaction, so different from Perth.

Terry Alderman had returned to the Australian XI in Melbourne after serving time for going on the rebel tours to South Africa in the mid '80s and immediately was our best bowler. He was tremendously accurate, and his swing and seam gave our attack a new, significant weapon. At the end of the first day in Sydney, most of which he spent at first slip for the spinners rather than leading the attack as he would have done elsewhere, he chased me, patted me on the back and said, 'Great day, you kept your bowler up, you were happy, great job.' That sort of feedback was terrific.

I was starting to feel like a genuine Test cricketer. But only for a minute. At the end of the day, having been bending down behind the stumps all day, I decided to stretch the body out and go for a run around the ground. I got right around to the scoreboard, no more than a slow jog, when a security guy, who was standing facing out towards where the Hill had once been turned to me and shouted, 'C'mon you, off the ground, off you go.'

'Mate, I'm a player,' I responded.

'Course you are. Get off, will ya. We don't want any trouble, do we?'

Desmond Haynes, caught by Mark Taylor at slip to end a masterly innings of 143 in Sydney in 1988–89. Haynes had nicked the ball onto my pad, before it lobbed to Tubby, who took his first Test catch.

'Mate, I'm Ian Healy.'

'Oh … fair dinkum?'

I kept running.

'Sorry ...'

Maybe that experience was a reflection of the profile the Australian team commanded back then. But even in 1999–2000, in my first season of commentary, a super-officious gatekeeper insisted on checking all my bags as I was walking into the SCG.

'No, no, he's alright,' another official said quickly. But that made my bloke go even harder.

'No, he's not,' the gatekeeper advised. 'He's just like everyone else.'

Finally, he said I was okay. No, I insisted, there was still one pocket in my computer bag that he hadn't looked at. 'That's where I usually hide the bomb,' I told him.

'No, sir,' he said flatly, 'I DID check that.'

'Mate, you didn't.'

'Yes, sir, I did.'

One of my jobs that day was to be the guest speaker at the SCG Trust's official lunch. At least the bloke had given me something to talk about. I started by telling the audience how happy I was to be back.

Though the Windies lost that Test in '88–89, a couple of their players put in sterling performances on a pitch that didn't suit them at all. Malcolm Marshall fired up and bowled long spells superbly, while Desmond Haynes batted magnificently. I don't think the Windies thought they were stitched up by the umps, but maybe by the pitch. AB, of all people, finished the match with 11 wickets, which didn't happen in Test cricket all that often and might have fuelled their suspicions a bit. But the Sydney wicket had been turning heaps for years, and they had been beaten there four years earlier, when 'Dutchy' Holland and Murray Bennett spun them out. They were extremely disappointed, as all good sides are after they get beaten, especially because they didn't play very well at all. Bar Haynes, the rest self-destructed against the ball turning away from the bat. This might have been the first sign that they were getting tired. In Adelaide a week later, for the final Test, they *were* cranky.

Sydney was my first Test win and we partied hard afterwards. George Negus, then of the Channel Nine *Today* show and formerly a Queensland rep cricketer, came into the dressing room and I had more than one drink with him. After a couple of beers, George was offering his guidance, suggesting I didn't give enough with my gloves. And as we got more drink into us he got more game. 'You're good,' he'd state firmly, 'but you could do this and you should do that.' I loved it!

For a while in Adelaide we thought we'd win again. Dean Jones batted magnificently for 216, while Merv stunned us all by making 72 not out. Then Mike Whitney, in for the injured Alderman, took seven wickets and we had a first-innings lead of 146. But we weren't confident enough to declare during the last session on the fourth evening, so we left ourselves only the fifth day to knock the Windies over again, while setting them an impossible target of 370. They were happy to bat the day out, Viv Richards making 68 not out in his last appearance in Australia.

But even though the match was a draw, our performance gave us additional confidence by proving that the Sydney win wasn't a fluke. The atmosphere in the camp was so different from what it had been back in Melbourne after that third Test shellacking. We felt tougher, more resilient and had more faith in ourselves and each other.

> *February 7, 1989: Relax — let natural ability flourish. Be a ball cushion not a wall. I'm still allowing myself to get distracted. Watch ball, move, stay down. Must get tougher. Relax, enjoy, be confident. GET WHAT I WANT FROM THIS GAME.*

After the Adelaide Test, in their dressing room, I had a long and fruitful conversation with my keeping counterpart, Jeffrey Dujon, who'd been the Windies gloveman throughout the 1980s. 'How are you enjoying it?' was the first thing he asked, before moving on with some very gentle, helpful criticism which I'll never forget.

'Ian, you need softer hands, your hands can get too hard,' he told me. 'The gloves should be like cushions, like this ...'

A run out shout against Gus Logie during the final Test of the 1988–89 summer.

I had always thought my hands were pretty soft, despite what George Negus might have reckoned. But 'Duje' was much more persuasive. I listened to his advice and was a better keeper for it. Wicketkeepers tend to stick together. Even our teammates don't appreciate what goes into our job, what we're working on. When we're taking catches at practice, they don't realise we're working on different things — the position of our feet in various situations, movement, how we're feeling, how it's going into the gloves. In a game they don't appreciate the concentration level required. But in the opposition dressing room, I know there is always one guy who is on the same train.

I did not go into that Windies dressing room seeking Duje's counsel, but I would have grabbed any morsel of advice he gave me. I'm usually not one to try to discover what other people think about me. My first Colts coach, now Australian coach, John Buchanan, picked this up in the early 1980s. He reckoned then that I needed to talk more when things weren't going well, rather than trying to always deal with my problems myself. This was still a fault of mine on my first Test tour in Pakistan, when I struggled so much through the first half of the trip. But I would always think: why should I annoy other people with my dilemmas? After all they've got their own situations to worry about and, more importantly, they'll be saying, 'He's a Test cricketer, he should be able to either do or fix the things he's not doing right.'

It's funny looking back at old press clippings. When I was first picked for Australia, everyone spoke of my 'maturity' and 'composure'. 'He showed instant maturity, which obviously the selectors picked up,' said Allan Border in August 1988, 'He's a pretty level-headed sort of fellow.' And Bob Simpson around the same time: 'He's very mature and keen to improve.' But underneath that facade was a lack of confidence I needed to fight and conquer. I learned quickly that there's nothing wrong with wanting to improve, being curious or not knowing how to do everything yourself. None of us is perfect.

CHAPTER 5

THE ASHES 1989

AT LUNCH ON THE final day of the first Ashes Test of 1989, at Headingley, England were 1-66. Earlier in the day, Allan Border had declared our second innings, leaving the Poms 402 to win. A more likely ambition for them was the 83 overs they needed to bat to see out the day. As our meals were being served, we were cock-a-hoop … because we knew we couldn't lose. Even better, after the way AB and Dean Jones had smashed and taunted the English bowling first thing that morning, it was just about impossible for us not to come out of the game with something of a psychological advantage. Sure, we mightn't win, but you must remember that we weren't used to winning or even having a significant advantage in Test matches. Australia had a lost a few series in recent seasons and hadn't won a Test series in England since 1975. Some keen historians had been reminding us that Australia hadn't regained the Ashes away from home since 1934. A few critics had quietly told us we were the worst Australian team they'd seen.

After lunch we went out, most of us totally relaxed, and bowled them out. We could hardly believe it. Terry Alderman was magnificent, Geoff Lawson and Merv Hughes not far behind Suddenly we were unbeatable.

—✠—

ONE OF THE MOST remarkable statistics of my Test cricket career is that, after being on the losing end in four of my first six Tests, we lost only three of my next 36. In next to no time, we went from being a side too used to losing to one that was supremely confident. AB had decided, apparently after talking to Ian Chappell, that he wasn't going to give the Poms anything and we followed him into battle armed with that philosophy. For his loyal lieutenants, Geoff Marsh and David Boon, such a tough approach was perfect. The memory of our comeback against the West Indies was still fresh in our minds. Into our squad had come a few seasoned professionals — Alderman, Lawson, Carl Rackemann and Trevor Hohns — while Steve Waugh, Dean Jones and Merv Hughes had matured into genuine Test cricketers. With hindsight, the speed of our ascendancy and the extent of our Ashes triumph is not so surprising.

Before the Ashes squad was announced I was reasonably certain I was going to be picked. Overall, I had been happy with my keeping form against the Windies, though dissatisfied with my batting. But I knew that on tour nothing was guaranteed — if my form dropped even a fraction, and Tim Zoehrer, the other keeper selected, was going well then he could very easily grab my spot — so I approached the trip in a slightly apprehensive frame of mind. Throughout the four months I had my head down, working hard, never stopping to smell the roses, never taking anything for granted. When I returned to England four years later, I was astonished that so many things were new for me. I hadn't noticed them, or at least appreciated them, in 1989. On my first Ashes tour I was totally focused on my job at hand. And thus too tense, a bit like Pakistan the year before.

We were such big underdogs that the English press and our own expectations allowed us to ease into the tour. In the buzz of early-tour functions and sponsor obligations, no one stopped to consider that we might be a chance. An early loss on a horror wicket at Worcester, in a three-day match that didn't last even two, confirmed the worst, and when we were beaten decisively in the first Texaco Trophy one-dayer, the British players and press seemed frighteningly optimistic.

The first signs that an Australian revival might be on the cards came in the second one-dayer, at Trent Bridge, which ended in highly dramatic circumstances. We weren't perfect, sure, but we did keep fighting all the way to the final ball. In many ways it was unfortunate that our efforts were camouflaged by a farcical incident that took place late in the match, in which I. Healy was very much the central player. First up, though, came an unfortunate mix-up which probably cost us the game and definitely left me with a crook knee. I was batting with Steve Waugh and we were going along comfortably, needing 53 to win off 10 overs. I turned one down to widish fine leg; we took one, two and he wanted three ...

I didn't run for three. I was watching the ball, as the fieldsman from fine leg gathered it in. Stephen has a habit of running a few steps before he decides whether there's another run to be had. This time it was those few steps and then a frantic, 'C'mon, c'mon.' I heard him, but instead of taking off I slipped. My leg went from under me and I ended up on my face while he was run out trying to make back the three-quarters of the pitch he'd raced down before realising I wasn't going anywhere.

Immediately, I knew the knee wasn't right, but I continued unassisted for around three overs, thinking it would come good. It didn't, so after a brief consultation involving the umps and England's captain, David Gower, Dean Jones rushed out to run for me. Almost immediately, in the second-last scheduled over, I hit my best shot of the innings, right off the middle of the bat, and in the excitement of the moment took off, totally forgetting about the knee or the runner. I sprinted through for two (as did 'Deano' and the other batsman, 'Henry' Lawson), slid my bat at the end of it ... and then realised that the crowd was going right off. I looked around and saw Deano looking at me, Geoff Lawson, looking at me, Gower looking at me, umpire Dickie Bird looking daggers at me and I thought, 'Oh, shit.'

Gower came over and said that the runner would have to go. I argued strongly that everyone knew I could run when Deano came out; I'd asked for the runner as a precaution against me causing further damage to the leg. I knew, though, that the way in which I'd hared up and down the track made my case look pretty

The final ball of the second Texaco Trophy match in 1989. Needing one to tie, two to win, I (far right) charged through for a bye to the keeper, Steve Rhodes, after Carl Rackemann had swung and missed. It might appear that I'm running freely, but the knee that I damaged earlier in this innings would cost me the third one-dayer of the series, at Lord's, and almost the first Test as well.

skinny. Gower, clearly amused by all of this, was very clever about the way he asked Deano to leave. 'Thanks for popping in', was his farewell, to which Dean replied with something a little less civil. Afterwards, Gower told reporters I'd run 'faster than Ben Johnson', which everyone chuckled at, while AB went off big time in the post-match press conference. It was unfair, he argued, for the umpires and the English captain to put the well-being of his first-choice wicketkeeper at risk. Certainly, we all felt the Poms had played it very tough and I think the incident hardened our resolve to give the home team absolutely nothing during the Test series. In the years since, whenever I read about what bastards we were on the field during that series, I think back to the cocky way they approached that situation with the runner. It seemed they thought they were better than us at that stage of the tour.

Eventually, the game came down to the last over, which began with us needing 9 to win, 8 to tie. Phil DeFreitas began with a wide and then two full tosses, which was good of him, but when Tim May was bowled off the second-last ball we still needed 2 more runs. Carl Rackemann swung and missed, and as Steve Rhodes, the wicketkeeper, underarmed wide of the batsman's stumps, I ran through to tie the game.

Once I knew I was safe I punched the sky in celebration, which annoyed Ian Chappell, up in the commentary box, who thought I got too excited, considering it was only a tie. 'It's as if he's won the game,' he complained. (Later, we discovered that because England had lost fewer wickets they had won the series, whatever happened in the third and final game at Lord's.) But this was where the team was at that point in its evolution. The tie was a positive for us; we were just making some moves forward. We'd been humbled in the first game, and even when we won at Lord's, after Geoff Marsh made a hundred and Stephen played a great slogging knock, few observers rated us very highly at all.

If I was too excited on the field, back in the dressing room I was very emotional after I received an early prognosis on the knee. 'It's the medial ligament,' physio Errol Alcott told me, 'you're definitely out of the next game, could be out for a while.' I was just about in tears, not because of the pain — there wasn't much really — but just because I was going to miss a match. Looking back, I took the thought of missing even one game very seriously.

> *May 29, 1989: Selectors rest me for third ODI [one-day international] and Warwickshire at Birmingham. Six days to get right. Ten days till Test.*
>
> *Really think about your game. Improve concentration and enjoyment while keeping, especially in tight situations. Keep developing that relaxation to allow the best possible job to the done.*
>
> *Love your job.*

I was told that it was a 'two-week' injury. That was okay, I pondered, the Test starts on June 8. The one-dayer had been on May 27. But then came an ultimatum: if you want to be considered for Test selection you need to be available for the game at Derby, which begins five days before the first Test. Ouch! No way were they going into the first Test with an unfit wicketkeeper, I was informed. Fair enough, too. Fortunately, I managed to get myself right for Derby ... just. Even the night before, I wasn't sure. But I knew that if I gave Tim Zoehrer a chance I mightn't ever get back in. That's how I was thinking. Every night, I was up on the hour, icing it; every day I was doing the exercises Errol had prescribed, wearing the knee brace he'd shown me how to take on and off. I learned about painkillers in a hurry, too.

The demands of 'Hooter' Alcott's job are such that he's on call 24 hours a day whenever he's with the team. This was just the first instance of him devoting many a long night on tour to treating my ailments, working as hard as I was to get the knee, or hamstring, or finger, whatever right so I'd be at my best when needed. He was a crucial part of the squad throughout my career, never one to

Celebrations all round after I caught David Gower down the legside off Geoff Lawson during our final-day demolition of England's batting line-up at Headingley in 1989.

get carried away but always willing to do anything to help the team and any individual in it. I found him to be a master at giving sensible advice and being able to pick up a guy when that player was down, or keeping the same guy's feet on the ground when things might be going a bit too well.

First morning of the Derbyshire encounter, AB won the toss. Beauty! Another day to rest the knee. Then their pace attack — Ian Bishop, Devon Malcolm, Ole Mortensen and Simon Base — ripped through our middle order. From 1-74 we crashed to 5-93. I was due in at No. 7, but was still being strapped up when the fifth wicket fell. This, I thought as our No. 8, Cracker Hohns, walked out to bat ahead of me, is not the cleverest way to remind everyone that the knee is not 100 per cent. Finally, Hooter had my leg strapped from high up the thigh to the lower calf to give me maximum support when I moved sideways. I was able to bend it up under my butt, but couldn't straighten it. That bandage was cruel. Every night when we took it off, some skin came with it. But it worked, even though, if you watch a video of the first Test you can see that my crouch is ridiculous. I'm trying to get down low but that bloody cast won't bend.

Considering my ailment I did all right in that Derbyshire game, scoring 30 and 39 (batting seven) and taking five catches to book my Test spot. But it was a game that did little for our confidence going into the first Test, as we sneaked home by 11 runs after setting them just 153 to win. Derbyshire had never beaten an Australian touring team, bar the Services team of 1919, but they would have defeated us except for a dramatic spell by Terry Alderman, who reduced them to 5-35 on the final day after they'd reached 31 without loss.

We desperately wanted to avoid a defeat so close to the start of the Test series, so the relief in the side was enormous. Personally, I was delighted to have made it through the game and was excited about the prospect of my first Test on English soil. But almost immediately after we arrived in Leeds to begin our preparations for the Test, I was caught out big time by our intrepid coach. Upon arrival at our hotel, after a bus trip up from the ground at Derby, we checked in and then headed for our rooms. On the way down from reception to my room I ran into Tom Moody, who smiled at me and asked, 'Heals, what are you up to tonight?'

'Dunno yet Moods,' I shot back with a smile from ear to ear, 'but it's gonna be a big one.'

Just as I said that, who should walk UP the stairs but Simmo. For some reason, he'd decided to use another entrance, from the basement up, to get to reception.

'Oh, Ian, is that right, is it?' he said flatly.

After spending an hour with Hooter working on the knee I finally arrived at the pub where the boys had gathered. Wherever I went, the conversation quickly turned to how Simmo had been hammering the point that players should not be drinking when they're treating injuries.

'Heals, you want a drink?'

'Just another soda, thanks, mate.'

I suppose I should have been grateful for the coach's abiding interest in my health and well-being.

— ✠ —

MANY CRITICS RECKONED ALLAN Border's 66 on the opening day of the first Test set the tone for all our performances in the 1989 Ashes series. England had gone with an all-pace attack, and Gower won the toss and sent us in under cloudy skies. Mark Taylor had been in shaky form, but it was Marsh and Boon who fell, leaving us 2-57. What another wicket would have done to the Englishmen's confidence is anyone's guess, but our captain came out and attacked from the start, even square cutting a six, as he and 'Tubby' added 117 and changed the mood.

As for Tubby, it's amazing what a difference a day makes. I'm sure the selectors wanted our batting line-up to begin with Mark Taylor and Geoff Marsh, left hander and right hander, with David Boon at No. 3, but Tubby's early-tour form was ordinary at best, and strong consideration was given to opening with Boonie, with Dean Jones at first wicket and either Tom Moody or Mike Veletta in the middle order. Tubby had first come into the Test XI for the fourth Windies Test the previous summer, and was now very fearful that his Test career was going to be a lot shorter than he'd originally planned. At the bottom of his form slump, in late May, he told a group of us during a quiet drink at a bar in London one night that when he next went to the wicket he was just going to go out and hit them. 'I don't think I'm good enough to make runs at this level,' he lamented, 'I'll just belt 'em.' Tubby knew he was at rock bottom, but from that moment, his tour turned around. He made a strong half century at Warwickshire and then, at stumps on day one of the first Test, we were 3-207 and he was 96 not out. By the end of August he'd scored more runs in an Ashes series than any Australian bar Bradman in 1930. It's no coincidence that when you've got a clear plan, however haphazardly it might be instigated, things can work out for you.

After that first day, we were a long way from being in total control, for we could easily have been bowled out the next day for 300, but instead we batted right through, with Tubs going onto 136, Steve Waugh smashing a brilliant hundred, and Merv and Deano getting big scores, too. At close of play on day two we were 6-580, and we even continued on the next morning to 600 — to 'turn the screw' as AB put it — before declaring. I think AB might have learned that one from the West Indies, who seemed to like delaying their declarations. During the previous Australian summer, Viv Richards had delayed making second-innings declarations in Perth and Melbourne, something our shellshocked batsmen hated. He was only delaying the inevitable.

We certainly respected this English batting line-up we were up against, given that it included proven Test campaigners such as Gower, Graham Gooch, Chris Broad and Allan Lamb. Add to that Robin Smith, a rising star. So we were happy to get a significant first-innings lead (171) and happier still to smash them around in the second innings, to set up that conservative, last day declaration. Then, after that somewhat buoyant lunch of ours, we came out and went right through them, stunning everyone — ourselves included. The wickets tumbled, the key ones being Gooch, lbw Hughes, for 68, and Gower, caught by Healy down the legside off Lawson for 34. It wasn't a really tough catch but it was important in many different ways. As well as getting rid of arguably their most dangerous batsman, caught by what looked like a simple set-piece to bowl at and outside his legs, it also gave the papers a chance to bag their captain unmercifully the next day for what they called a silly, lazy shot. In all, six wickets fell in the middle session, and not too long after tea the game was over, with an astonishing 28 overs to spare.

It wasn't until after our win in the first Test that it first dawned on me just how special these Ashes might be. I saw the reactions of the senior guys, how much it meant to them. I saw this again, multiplied many times over, after we won the series and regained the Ashes at Old Trafford. AB, Clem and Henry — they'd been there in 1981 when Ian Botham won three Tests just about on his own —

A laugh with my mate Jack Russell during his gallant century in the fourth Test, at Old Trafford, in 1989. If you have a good look, you can see how in one way we're an odd couple. While my equipment is relatively new, Jack's pads seem well 'worn in'. I remember in 1993, he was keeping in gloves that, he proudly told me, were 11 years old. It was not unusual for me to go through three pairs of gloves in a single Australian summer.

and their emotional response eight years later underlined the little urn's importance, and the way lost Ashes battles burned at their cricket pride. Until then, I probably hadn't given enough thought to the historical significance of what I was involved in.

— ⬧ —

AS I'VE SAID, THROUGHOUT that first Test I couldn't crouch properly and wasn't moving too well, but I still felt I had an okay match. Except, perhaps, near the end, when I reckon I started to think too much about getting through without a major hiccup. Don't blow it now, was the thought in the back of my mind and, inevitably, I started fumbling a few. No matter how many times I drummed into myself, 'let the outcome look after itself', I could still be guilty of letting my concentration wander.

I actually fumbled quite a few throughout the series, mainly because I couldn't loosen up. It wasn't a lack of concentration, rather a lack of relaxation. I kept reminding myself to relax and to watch the ball, which only made me tighten up more. Fortunately, I didn't miss much during the Test series, maybe nothing at all, although I didn't get many either — 14 dismissals, all catches. On the positive side, I was very happy with my preparation for each Test, which was always thorough. Throughout my career, I loved those last two lead-up days. Being organised was never a problem for me.

Back during the 1988–89 season, the Queensland team had a weekend away at Kooralbyn, for some bonding, some practice and some chats with a few guest speakers and coaches. One of those who spoke to the team was Greg Chappell. I remember noticing during his address that I was the only bloke taking notes — maybe that says something about me. And those notes today remind me that the thing Greg stressed during the session was the importance of concentration skills. Around the same time, my brother Greg and I went to see Greg Chappell one afternoon after big brother had volunteered to 'manage' me, in the sense that if any business or sponsorship opportunities came up, he would look after them. To be honest, we had no idea what might be out there. Greg Chappell's advice was that I'd struggle to make any money outside the game. In this regard, he proved to be wrong, as the times were a'changin'. Greg Chappell argued then that I'd be better off concentrating totally on my cricket. That's what you are good at, he told us, that's what you do for a living. He stressed, too, the value of being organised. That was a virtue I'd inherited from my parents; it was something Greg Chappell liked about my batting. I was a batsman, he explained, who went forward to 'forward' balls and back to the 'back' ones. Simple really, but not everybody does that.

Organised? Definitely. Concentrating? As hard as I could. Why then, couldn't I relax? I think I just wasn't used to being an Australian cricketer on tour. I felt as if I was caught on a famous stage, playing with the very best, but I was just a plodder not entitled to be among them. I desperately wanted to be good, but it wasn't happening yet. I had enjoyed the experience of being an Australian cricketer on home soil, keeping on wickets I was familiar with, in front of crowds who were on our side. On tour, however, there was another keeper always challenging my spot, and I was an Australian cricketer 24 hours a day, seven days a week. And around me always, in the bar, at breakfast, sharing my room, was one or more teammates analysing my game and remembering my mistakes. Unless you have total faith in your ability, such a scenario preys on your mind.

It was a strange situation. On a personal level, I was struggling, yet at the same time I was completely enveloped by the extraordinary team spirit that built up over these four months. I knew I was part of something special and loved the camaraderie, the winning, the glory. But in the county games between the Tests I missed quite a few chances, especially to the spinners. Because the fielders in those county games took a casual approach to the matches, so did I. Hell, I wanted and needed to be one of the boys. But then a nick came and I put it down. I looked like a goose and had let a bowler down. I learned that a keeper cannot afford to lose concentration in any tour game, even if all the other blokes can. In 1993, I kept really well in all the matches, internationals and county games, because of what I went through in '89.

While my keeping in those games was ordinary, my batting was okay — unlike in the Tests, where my performances with the blade were terrible. No Australian, not even proven No. 11 Terry Alderman, finished with a lower Test batting average than I did in that series. I made just 103 runs, 44 of them in the last Test when I just went out and smashed them. Fortunately, I didn't need to make any runs during the series because the top six were going so well. Otherwise my poor batting might have become a selection issue.

THE SECOND TEST WAS a great Australian occasion from the moment we bowled them out on the first day for 286. At 6-265 in reply we held only a very small advantage, but then Steve Waugh took absolute charge. With support from Hohns, Hughes and especially Lawson, Stephen won us a lead of 242, the key to our six-wicket victory.

To get that victory we still had to bowl very well to dismiss England again. Merv was tremendous, as was Gower, who made a dramatic hundred. Despite our opposing captain's efforts, they set us just 118 to win, but getting this proved a bit more tricky than we originally anticipated. On the final day, Geoff Marsh lost his off stump immediately, and then a thunderstorm threatened briefly to wash away the rest of the match. When we got back on, after losing an hour, we tumbled to 4-67, before Boonie and Tugga steered us home.

In two Tests, Steve Waugh had gone from being potentially a good Test cricketer to being definitely an outstanding one. I can still picture him, at one point on this tour, padded up in the dressing room and commenting, 'You know, Heals, I feel great again today.' He wasn't being cocky, just displaying that supreme confidence that comes when you are totally on top of your game. I reckon he eagerly looked forward to every innings on that tour. Back at Headingley, I was out in the middle with Stephen when he reached what was his maiden Test hundred, after three and a half years of trying. The relief and joy were palpable. But unlike many cricketers who might have been satisfied with the three figures and lost concentration for a second, Stephen put his head down, determined to get as many as he could. That was his way of savouring the moment. When he reached 137, he looked up at the players' balcony and waved at Tubby Taylor, who had made 136. 'Gotcha!' he signalled.

It seemed England's only hope was Ian Botham, who was rushed back for the third Test, at Edgbaston. The English papers and the team's supporters hoped Beefy's bravado and reputation would turn things around. Things got worse for them, however, as we totally dominated a match ruined by rain and had it not been for the weather I'm sure we would have won. From there, Botham's contribution was negligible. At Old Trafford in the fourth Test, he played a horrid shot against Trevor Hohns, mirroring his team's frustrations in the process, and was bowled. And then in the fifth Test, at Trent Bridge, he badly dislocated a finger and couldn't bat in the second innings. And that was Ian Botham's summer. All up, he scored 62 runs in his three Tests and captured just three wickets.

The Old Trafford victory that won us the series was clearcut, even though we were held up by Jack Russell's brave hundred on the final day. When we finally ended England's second innings, the requirement on our part was 78, which we knocked off for the loss of only one wicket. David Boon had the honour of hitting the winning runs, sparking pandemonium on the away team's balcony, and the beginnings of a party that would last long into the night.

Before the celebrations could really get into gear, we had to wait for our captain to return from talking to the media. When he did, he gave a brief, very

No. 11 Nick Cook is caught Healy bowled Hughes at Old Trafford, to end England's second innings. Soon after, we'd knocked off the 78 runs needed to win, and were celebrating the return of the Ashes. Also in this photo are the two other members of our highly successful pace attack — Terry Alderman at slip and Geoff Lawson at short cover.

emotional, unrehearsed speech during which his composure nearly cracked more than once. 'This means a lot to me ...' he said quietly. 'I want to thank you ... you blokes deserve all the accolades you get ...' I'm sure there was a tear in his eye but, within seconds of him finishing, any tears would have been washed away by the flood of grog that was sprayed like an exploding fire hydrant in his direction. We chanted 'Border ... Border ... Border' as everything and everyone in the room was deluged. That was the first big Australian 'beer celebration' and it started something of a tradition, something the team still cops criticism for today.

Midway through the night after our Old Trafford win, when both of us had more alcohol in our systems than we needed, a call came through to the hotel from a Melbourne radio station for Steve Waugh and Ian Healy. Passed on to me, the station's listeners got an exclusive interview. Or did they? In fact, we played each other, never missing a chance to put the boot in. First 'Heals', played by Steve Waugh, explained how he was happy to be a part of it but 'was looking forward to scoring a run or taking a catch'. Then 'Tugga', as in me, shot back with a comment about wanting to bowl more, 'but the trouble is I'm always getting injured'. And so it went on. To this day, we're not sure if the people back in Melbourne knew what was going on. Or whether we did either.

Early on, though, I had been a touch withdrawn from the celebrations. I remained frustrated with the way I was playing. Instead of jumping into the party, I began by watching from the sidelines, with a contented grin on my face that I was a part of it, if not a major reason for it. Slowly, though, I was lured into the mayhem. But my dissatisfaction with my performances was still bugging me at the end of the tour. I can remember, at one end-of-trip function, sitting down with Trevor Hohns and saying that, on a personal level, the tour had frustrated me, because I knew I could play a lot better than I had.

The only problem with our celebrations was that we had a game to play the next day. Now this didn't create a serious problem for me, because like our captain and Terry Alderman, our leading bowler, I, as wicketkeeper, always got the game immediately after the Test off, on the basis that we were the ones that the Test just gone had taken the most out of. Apparently, in this game against Nottinghamshire, 'Swampy' Marsh won the toss and batted on a greentop. He had to — all his bowlers were lying flat on the dressing room floor, fast asleep. When I met the guys after the first day's play of that game, around 7pm in the hotel reception area, I felt terrific. A few of the guys who batted didn't feel quite so flash.

While we were recuperating, there would be no recovery for the Poms. Morale, if their body language was any guide, was at rock bottom. Gower and his team were lampooned by tabloids, and then ruined totally by the South African rebel tour controversy which hit the headlines during the fourth Test. Then Graham Gooch asked to be excused back to county cricket, to try to find some form. Meanwhile, after the glory of Old Trafford, we continued on our merry way, to Nottingham, where we won again — this time by an innings and 180 runs — to go 4-up in the series.

While the rest of the boys were out on the field mopping up the English second innings in that fifth Test, I watched the end of the game from the dressing room, after I wore a wide one from Trevor Hohns that jumped out of the bowler's footmarks. Hooter said I had to come off, and I was off the field when I heard the last wicket fall. Within seconds, I was on the Trent Bridge balcony to help cheer the players in. This was a Test notable for the first-innings effort of Taylor and Marsh, who batted throughout the first day, and for the fact that our eventual winning margin of an innings and 180 runs was the largest ever inflicted by an Australian team on England in England.

> *August 14, 1989: Cracker pitched in the footholes and cut my face — four stitches. Taylor kept! Border pooed his pants thinking he'd have to do it …*
>
> *Very quiet celebration early. I went to hospital to be stitched. Wives allowed in pub! Very good late night …*

The series concluded with a rained-out draw at The Oval. Deano hit his second Test hundred of the summer, and Alderman had time to take seven more wickets, giving him 41 for the series. Having taken 42 wickets in the 1981 Ashes

A hook shot at The Oval in 1989 during my only significant Test innings of the series.

series, Clem followed up in remarkable style this time. He is a hard, resolute individual, quite prepared to back himself, his opinions and his comrades. I loved playing and touring with him. He killed the Poms, always attacking the stumps with either his stock ball, the outswinger, or a slight inswinger, off-cutter or straight one that might as well have been an inswinger so on guard were batsmen against the one that dived away. Geoff Lawson and Merv Hughes, each in his own way, offered terrific support. Between the three of them, they took 89 of the 103 English wickets that fell during the series.

Clem can be very opinionated and very stubborn if you want to argue with him, but he also has a fantastic sense of fun, which I always appreciated. I will never forget a sponsor's night in Canterbury, when we made the mistake of stopping to discuss the cricket with a group of Poms on a street corner, and then had to make our escape in a shopping trolley. I hung on while Clem did the driving but, inevitably, it ended with a big spill and a few bruises we couldn't explain to management the following morning. All we could do was front up for play and battle on through, which we did … with the occasional chuckle between overs as we recalled what had happened.

After the series was over, we all partied for two days solid, the highlight being a very fashionable evening on Park Lane, funded by those great supporters of

Australian cricket, Austin Robertson and John Cornell. To ready ourselves for the occasion, we had to head into London's fashion centre to buy the right clobber, but it was all worth it, for this tour needed a final celebratory exclamation point. The next day, the tour sponsors put on a lunchtime rooftop garden party, which went long into the night, and by the third morning I couldn't lift my head a centimetre off the pillow. I was gone, ready to come home.

—✠—

ALLAN BORDER WAS AN excellent leader on this tour, in many ways. As the members of the side grew in confidence, he could do so much more with them — such as set the legside traps that worked so well as we attacked Graham Gooch and David Gower. As a result, he finally looked like the good tactician he probably always had been. He was committed to the tour sponsor, Fourex, and knew what they wanted out of the tour. He didn't stress how much winning back the Ashes meant to him, but you could see that he was ready to win. He was adamant that there would be no wives and partners on tour, until the last two weeks, or at least no wives and partners staying in the same hotel as us. 'Tell 'em to blame me,' he said gruffly when a couple of the guys complained at one stage on behalf of their spouses.

The Fourex sponsorship never impinged on the cricket. They used our time very well, and we loved it. Shrewdly, most of the photo opportunities and appearances were squeezed into a hectic period at the beginning of the tour. After that, we just had to attend a Fourex function on the night before the rest day of each Test. The touring party would split up, three or four of us together, and journey to different locations, usually clubs or pubs in the neighbourhood. Rather than being a grind, I found these functions gave me an escape from the 'what are we going to do tonight?' routine of the tour.

All in all, this was a historic trip, for our part almost totally free of controversy. The British papers were happy to spend their time bagging their own team. Meanwhile, Australia achieved something we could not have imagined we were going to do when the tour started.

The spirit in the team was as good as anything I have ever been involved in. We all went through something we didn't think we could do together and when that happens, teams invariably get and stay close. The input by the reserves was excellent. If I wasn't happy with my own form on tour, I was at the very least fired up with a desire to be good enough to play at the highest level for as long as I possibly could. It was a landmark tour, and a benchmark for future Ashes tours. In this era, things will always get compared to '89. We had to be careful in 1993 not to talk about '89 too much, and then in 1997 we made sure we didn't get caught reminiscing about '89 *and* '93 too much. Sooner or later, there's going to be an Ashes tour in which the expectations will just be too high. We need to remember that, in terms of success on the field, it can't always be as good as this tour was.

If only it could.

CHAPTER 6

THE GAME
GOES ON

IT'S AMAZING WHAT A difference a winter makes. We'd gone to England as rank outsiders but come home as the best team since Bradman's, to be greeted by tickertape, keys to cities and universal acclaim. Within weeks, the cricket caravan moved to India for the Nehru Cup, a one-off tournament involving six Test-playing nations and staged to commemorate the centenary of the birth of India's first Prime Minister. That done, we returned to Australia for the 1989–90 season, which involved six Tests and the World Series Cup, then a short tour to New Zealand. Then, after a five-month break — my first let-up since I left for Pakistan in early September 1988 — we faced an Ashes defence at home, another World Series and finally, a three-month tour to the Caribbean.

In India, we won only two of our five matches, losing to England, Pakistan and India (in Bangalore, in front of 50,000 screaming fans). But the main talking point to come out of that tour didn't involve the on-field action; rather the issue of player contracts was put back on the agenda.

I was very much on the periphery of this debate. Though many of the senior players would have hated to hear me say it, I would happily have played for match payments, and didn't care at all, at that point in my career, what my 'retainer' was. My first contract guaranteed me $3000 and I was rapt to sign it. If my memory's right, Geoff Lawson chaired the meeting, held at the Indian seaside resort of Goa, where the issue was strongly debated, and it was resolved that AB would go back the Australian Cricket Board with a series of demands.

In the mid 1980s, in part in response to the threat of rebel tours to South Africa, the Board had given a number of players four-year contracts for decent money. Unfortunately, in many cases the administrators didn't get value for their money, so they changed tack and introduced shorter-term, incentive-based contracts with lower guarantees. Some players, with Henry definitely the most vehement, were not happy. His argument was that the Board was doing this at a time when the game was bringing in big dollars through the gate and the TV. As I said, at that moment in my career, I didn't really care what I earned so long as I played, but looking back, I'm sure he had a point.

This was a players-only gathering. Simmo wasn't invited. But within hours, he knew something had happened. Simmo really should have been a detective, not a cricket coach. 'What were you doing yesterday?' he grilled me at one point. In my view, we should have either invited Simmo to that meeting, and thus given him some ownership of our campaign, or at least kept him abreast of what was going on. I'm sure he would have enjoyed supporting the players in the negotiations that followed. However, some saw him as an ACB man so he was kept on the outside, which I don't think was right.

Eventually, my retainer was boosted to $9000. Six years later, when we decided to have a real go at forming a players' association, we invited Simmo to contribute from the outset. And his input was helpful and productive.

I have some standout memories from the Nehru Cup. In Bombay, it was decided our team photo would be taken at the imposing Gateway to India, which meant that the traffic would need to be stopped for a little while. This the police did, beating back the crowd who, while unconcerned about the traffic hold-up, were desperate to get a glimpse of international cricketers. In Bangalore, I was stunned by the crowd, the noise, the firecrackers and the passion of the locals. The crackers were so loud, you swore they'd been fired right behind you. But, no, they'd been exploded in among the fans, who were jammed in tight in the stands. Their tailender, Chetan Sharma, won that game with a six, the first time I learned that cricketers from the Indian Subcontinent and Sri Lanka can be extraordinarily long hitters. Against England, in Hyderabad, AB did some long-hitting of his own, smashing five sixes in making 84 off 44 balls, but we still lost, with Gooch and Wayne Larkins getting the Poms home.

Back in Australia, we faced one Test against New Zealand, then two against Sri Lanka and three against Pakistan. While some of our team might have been looking at the first three as something of a lead-up to the major series against the well-credentialled Pakistanis, for me all six were big games. Having started the domestic season in good touch, I was at a stage of my career where my concerns were with maintaining and improving my own form, while enjoying the roll the team was on. Cricket, every minute of it, was exciting for me.

The Ashes success had definitely altered the way the Australian team was treated at home. In my first home season, few recognised the Australian cricket team. We'd go to a bar or a club and look after ourselves. Similarly, most of the corporate world didn't want to know us. Sponsorships outside specific cricket gear deals were rare. After the Ashes tour, however, things began to change, and by the mid 1990s, with the advent of Shane Warne, we were genuine celebrities. I was there, in the background, when this started. I watched it all happen and saw how the way people responded to us changed, and how we evolved, too.

I started taking more Test catches in 1989–90 — 19 in all, compared to 12 the previous year against the Windies and 14 in England — which was more a reflection of the team's rising confidence than any grand improvement on my part. I hadn't been missing many, even though my numbers weren't great, but now our bowlers were finding more edges. My first 'five-for' came in the fifth home Test of the summer, against Pakistan in Adelaide, and included two really good diving catches, one straight after the other, off Carl Rackemann and then Big Merv. The victims were good ones, too — Salim Malik and Imran Khan — which added to my satisfaction.

The six Tests brought us two wins and four draws. Rain played a part in two of the draws, and only in the Adelaide match were we in any real danger of defeat. We'd now gone 14 Tests without a loss, the longest unbeaten sequence by Australia in Test cricket for almost 30 years. Unfortunately, our run was about to end.

Having played New Zealand in Perth at the start of our home season, we now faced them again in mid March at the Basin Reserve in Wellington. It poured with rain for days leading up to the Test, and when it dawned grey and bleak on what was supposed to be the first day, there was a genuine concern as to whether the Test would be staged at all. We hadn't had a fair dinkum practice for three days. Bob Simpson wasn't with us in the lead-up and we'd quickly spied a chance to ease up a bit. The day before the Test, we did no more than muck around at an indoor centre, using white and orange balls. At the team meeting the night before the scheduled start, as the sound of raindrops hitting footpaths echoed outside, the talk was all about whether we'd be playing a couple of one-dayers instead of the Test, if and when the clouds cleared.

The sun did eventually come out late on that first-day morning, and we sauntered down to the ground around 2pm. As we approached the ground we could hear the helicopters, hovering above the playing surface, trying to dry the ground. Some chance, we thought, but when the covers were dragged off the pitch was bone dry, if underprepared (although not as underprepared as us). By stumps, New Zealand were 0-18, after we'd been spreadeagled for just 110. The rain came back on day two, we battled on to day four, but the final margin was nine wickets after their tough opening bat, John Wright, hit a gritty century. It was our first Test-match loss in 15 months.

One personal memory I have of that Test is being given a colossal sledge by their offie, John Bracewell, after he dismissed me in the second innings. He gave me a huge send-off. To the best of my knowledge, I hadn't bagged anyone or invited such an outburst but he didn't miss me. Bracewell was bowling very well that day, better than I thought he could, and he finished that innings with six wickets, including the last four for just 3 runs. That, I reckon, was the worst I was ever sledged in a Test match.

Peter Taylor topscored for us in both innings — 29, batting No. 8 in the first and 87, as a nightwatchman in at No. 4 in the second. He also took 3-44 off 33 overs in the home team's first innings, but couldn't break through, while bowling tightly again, in the second. A week later, PT was stunned to be made 12th man for NSW in the Shield final against us at the SCG. The Blues selectors preferred Greg Matthews and the young leggie, Adrian Tucker, who'd impressed in a couple of late-season Shield matches while PT was wearing the baggy green in New Zealand.

In that Shield final I broke a finger trying to glove the fourth ball of the match. I caught a ball that had been ignored by the NSW opener, Steve 'Jack' Small, awkwardly and knew immediately I was in a bit of trouble. I treated it like a sore finger and had a shocker, letting 13 byes through in the second innings, as

Carl Rackemann seems pretty excited about dismissing Pakistani opener Shoaib Mohammad, caught Healy, at the MCG in early January 1990. Also celebrating are Merv Hughes (running in from mid-on), Terry Alderman and Geoff Marsh. We went on to win by seven wickets.

NSW piled up a huge advantage. Mark Taylor, captaining NSW for the first time in place of the injured Geoff Lawson, scored a century in each innings, Matthews took eight wickets, and the final margin was 345 runs.

> *March 24, 1990: Things to cope with in Shield final:*
> - *Crowd bias and noise effect — no noise when we do well.*
> - *Bad/ugly comments.*
> - *NSW smart-alec confident — pressure in field, sledging, etc.*
> - *Pressure from ourselves, not to mention officials, supporters, etc.*

'Moey' Matthews played his mind games throughout that game, which didn't worry me but did rile some of my colleagues, including our captain, Greg Ritchie. There is no doubt that NSW had a dominance over us back in the '80s, especially in Sydney where they were very comfortable. While I didn't relish this game, I did enjoy the battles between the two states, which were invariably fierce. Later on, when the cricket program became so crowded that there were precious few opportunities for the international players to appear at Shield level, I missed them. And I think the Shield competition as a whole lost an edge, which it needs to rediscover.

It is a weird scenario, sharing a dressing room with some of your best friends for weeks on end and then suddenly finding yourself opposing them, and giving them nothing. In these circumstances, when you're playing against a mate, you know him better than the rest of your team does. You know how he reacts, what he likes … and dislikes. If you can say something on the field that will get his mind ticking, then you have an obligation to go for it. 'Is Heals serious?' he might start thinking, when he should be concentrating on the job at hand. If he doesn't have the mental strength to ignore me, that's his problem. It's part of the game. More than once, later in my Queensland career, I was given the job of talking to an up-and-coming opponent who reputedly had a strong respect for the high-profile Test players. Sometimes it works, sometimes it doesn't.

If a state's Test players come back and are quiet on the field, they are not having any impact on the game. In the late '80s, the Bluebags in the Test team came back and worked hard for their team. Nowadays, if the international players come back to the Queensland team but don't slot in, they get left behind. Queensland's Shield players never had the confidence to do that in the '80s; instead, they'd let the Test players, who were looking for a break rather than seeking a major role, drag everyone down. Hence the regular late-season collapses. In my view, John Buchanan's greatest achievement as Queensland coach was to increase the confidence of the whole squad and reassure them that they can — and must — do the job themselves, rather than wait for the return of the Test players. Once that happened, the Test players enjoyed coming back more, and were more productive as a result.

After the Shield final, we flew to Sharjah for the Austral-Asia Cup. After defeating New Zealand, still cocky after their recent Test victory, first up, we reached the final, largely on the back of an amazing innings from Simon O'Donnell in the semi-final against Sri Lanka. He smashed 50 off 18 balls and finished with 74 off 29. Pakistan were much too good for us in the final, winning by 90 runs and it was amazing afterwards to see huge sums of money changing hands, as supporters rewarded players from the successful team for their matchwinning performances. At the time I thought naively that these people just had too much money for their own good; today, I wonder whether there might have been more to it.

During our Sharjah experience, AB was approached by Imran Khan, who wanted to know if we were interested in playing a couple of exhibitions in the USA straight afterwards. India had pulled out and the organisers were desperately seeking a replacement. Simmo opposed it. 'This,' he said, 'is the last junket you'll be going on.' He could probably see that the team was beginning to get a bit comfortable with its new-found fame. Still, the team wanted to go, we got the ACB involved (a shrewd move as it turned out), and eventually spent five days in New York and five in Los Angeles. The original money being proposed was pretty good, with business-class travel and flash hotels thrown in, but in the end we only received half of what we'd been guaranteed. Mind you, we had a brilliant time, and I remember saying, on the flight home, that I would have gladly done it again for half the money we'd received.

We'd started to worry about whether we'd get paid when we arrived in LA and still hadn't seen any cash yet. The game there was played at the Coliseum, and while play was continuing out on the field our manager, the ACB-appointed Col

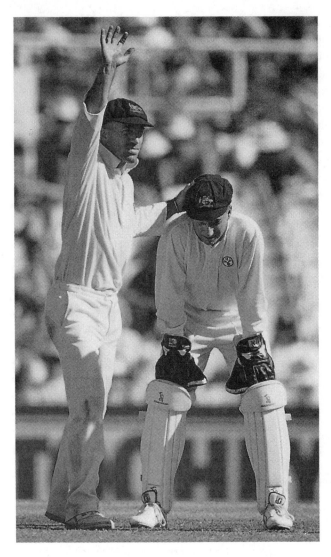

Greg Matthews calls for help after I was clipped above the eye by a ball that flicked up off David Gower's pad during the third Ashes Test of 1990–91. The cut needed five stitches and I was off the field for nearly half an hour.

Egar, was downstairs in an office, counting the takings and making sure it all went in *his* bag.

In New York, we'd drawn around 6000 to a game that was played on a mown strip of grass covered by matting and featured shorter bowling run-ups, a slogged 80-odd from Dean Jones, a hat-trick from Wasim Akram and a last-over Australian victory. In LA, the attendance was much smaller, maybe 2000, the pitch just as makeshift and Pakistan won with about three overs to spare. The next day, while C. Egar and Clem Alderman were busy in negotiations with the organisers trying to scrounge the rest of our money, we headed off to Disneyland and Universal Studios. Soon after, we were on the plane home. The 1988–1990 cricket season was over

WHAT TO DO WITH my time off? I was always a hard trainer, and kept working on my fitness while staying right away from my bat and my gloves. Workwise, I returned to Associated Fashion Distributors, but not for long. Initially, I knocked back a string of invitations to make personal appearances, arguing that I owed it to my in-laws to put some time in at the office, but finally temptation got the better of me. The former Queensland keeper, Ray Phillips, then working for Fourex, invited me up to the Whitsunday Islands, on the Great Barrier Reef, for three tough days. 'Heals,' he said, 'it's race week. We'll be on a yacht for a day, then Hamilton (Island) for two days, then sail to the start of the next race.'

'I can't, mate,' I replied sheepishly. 'I've got to work. I want to, but I can't.'

Next day, I summoned up the courage to tell my father-in-law I was leaving. Don looked at me and quipped. 'Son, I thought you would have gone months ago.'

Soon after this I accepted an offer to do some work with the Queensland brewery, Powers, and set about preparing for the upcoming series against the Poms.

This season was the first time we had defended anything, and I think we all saw it as a tremendous opportunity. Not just the Ashes series either. If we could prove the 1989 series was no fluke, we figured, and go to the Caribbean and beat the Windies straight afterwards, then no one could dispute that we belonged right up there with the best teams in the world.

> *November 19, 1990 (pre Ashes series discussion): As the keeper, I want to take a more positive role for the bowlers and fielders — be aware of their actions, seam, line and length, etc. Be on 'em.*
>
> *This is to be done while my glovework is up and running. I know I can do it!*

YOU MUST ALWAYS MOVE FORWARDS.

I went into this Australian summer feeling more settled as my country's keeper than I had felt in the past. In previous years I had hardly dared to think more than one game ahead. This time, in the lead-up to the series, I drew a simple pencil sketch of the Ashes urn on a page in my diary, with the question underneath: 'Who's it to be?' After each Test, I would write the innings scores and result of the match just completed around that drawing. And at series end I was able to proudly add 'It is us!!' under that original question. Back before a ball was bowled, I had held no reservations about thinking ahead.

This was the first summer that I copped criticism for appealing too much. I'm not sure if it was a fair accusation, and certainly wasn't something I consciously set out to do. I think it reflected two things: the ever-increasing TV presence of the stump microphones and my rising confidence. Whereas previously I had been more concerned with getting my own game right, now I wanted to support my bowlers as much as I could. If I was appealing, they must be doing something good. Terry Alderman, when he was fielding at first slip, had always drummed this into me. He hated going up for an appeal on his own when he was bowling, and during the following over, between balls, he'd let me know if I hadn't. I resolved never to let him or any of the bowlers down. And my support went further than just appealing. Whereas previously I'd waited until asked before giving bowlers advice, now I went to them with feedback. Not all of it was accepted, of course, but they welcomed my input. It was good to be so involved.

In the years that followed I did become a little agitated at being branded over-exuberant, and deliberately toned it down a bit. Occasionally, if a bowler had a go at me, à la Clem, for not supporting him, instead of apologising and promising to do better next time, I might have replied, 'Mate it was missing leg.' But I never stopped backing my teammates. It was the least I could do.

If you look purely at the results column in the history books it seems clear that we dominated the opening two Tests, but that was hardly the case. At the Gabba, England led by 42 runs on the first innings, 194 to 152, but then collapsed totally in the second dig, leaving us just 157 to win, which we got in 46 overs without losing a wicket. Then in Melbourne, the Poms led again at the halfway mark, 352 to 306, and were 1-103 in the second innings when Bruce Reid began an extraordinary burst of wicket-taking. Gooch, England's captain on this tour, fell for 58, and the last eight wickets tumbled for 35, leaving us 197 to win. At tea they had been 4-147. Reid, who finished with 7-51, to go with his 6-97 from the first innings, was world-class, right up in the top bracket of international bowlers. Had he stayed fit, instead of having his career ruined by a succession of injuries, he could have been anything. He's something of a forgotten man today, but then it is so easy to forget, to move on to the next generation. That's the way modern sport works. I reckon Merv Hughes is something of a forgotten man, too, and he took 212 wickets in 52 Tests and was the folk hero of his day.

We truly thought that target was going to be difficult, especially when Mark Taylor and I, as nightwatchman, were dismissed before stumps. We began the final day at 2-28, with Geoff Marsh and David Boon at the wicket, on a pitch in which eight wickets had fallen for 31 runs in the tea-to-stumps session on the previous day, and didn't lose another wicket. Boonie tells the story of Swamp coming up to him mid-pitch and threatening to kill him if he got out. Knowing how serious Geoff Marsh takes his cricket, he might have meant it. The pair, best mates off the field, were magnificent on it that day. Now we led 2-0 with three to play.

I have always felt that this was an important win for us, a key stage in our development. It proved that we weren't just front runners; that we could recover even in adverse circumstances. We forced that collapse and then knocked off the runs in clinical fashion. There were cracks in the wicket, everyone thought it would turn big time, but by the end the English bowlers had nothing.

We were a tough team.

That unsuccessful effort as nightwatchman was my first time in that role in a

Test — hardly an auspicious start, but I was given another go in the following game and did much better. My batting wasn't coming along as well as I might have wanted it to at this point in my career. The fact that I was being used as a nightwatchman pointed to this, though admittedly, with Greg Matthews (who averaged 41 in Test cricket) in our team for this series, I was batting behind him at No.8 and thus was a stronger candidate for the emergency role. I welcomed the opportunity to go in early, as it gave me a great chance to make some runs, but with hindsight, perhaps I wasn't concentrating on my batting as much as I could have.

At the same time, our bowling attack was evolving into an extremely professional unit. The combined resources of Reid, Hughes, Craig McDermott, Terry Alderman and Carl Rackemann, all of whom bowled in this series, made for as impressive and deep a line-up as Australia had possessed for years. Unfortunately, though, a combination of injuries and old age meant we rarely had all five at our disposal.

Big Carl could have taken 200 Test wickets, but he was hampered by injuries at different stages of his career, and probably didn't have the sheer professionalism that we demand of our cricketers nowadays. Neither Carl's nor Bruce Reid's body was suitable for a long career as a fast bowler, but today I'm sure the professionals associated with the team would have worked to remedy that. Bruce was too fragile; for some reason, despite his best efforts, incapable of putting bulk on his stringbean frame. Carl, or 'Mocca' as he was known, struggled to back up after a long day. If, for example, we had a day in the field that left the opposition 5-280 at stumps, he often struggled to come back the following morning and knock them over. His relatively skinny legs were no match for his huge upper body.

> *January 6, 1991: Kept really well — positive, bubbly and worked hard. At 5.10pm was hit in head from Mo — ball flicked Gower's pad — cut me, five stitches. Twenty-eight minutes, back on field ...*

In Sydney, needing just a draw to retain the Ashes, I had what I considered to be my best Test to date. Keeping at the SCG always took it out of me, but I thought I handled things excellently, and I batted well in both innings. In the first I made 35, while adding 95 with Moey Matthews, and then in the second, most of it on the final day, I played what to then was the longest knock of my Test career. Again in as a nightwatchman I survived until stumps and then batted on the following day while higher-profile wickets fell around me. I finished with 69, having batted for nearly three hours, while Mocca had the distinction of batting 107 balls for 9, the first 79 of them for no runs at all. Later he admitted he'd been caught bat-pad twice before he scored but been given not out both times. 'A pair in one innings' he called it. When we were finally all out, England needed 255 in just 28 overs. Although Gooch and Gower had a spectacular swing that made things interesting for a little while, the Ashes were safe.

Allan Border leans forward to congratulate Mark Waugh, as 'Junior' returns to the Adelaide Oval dressing room after scoring 138 in his debut Test innings. Others seen applauding here are (left to right): Craig McDermott, me, Merv Hughes, David Boon and Geoff Marsh.

During this summer, I had the rare distinction for a wicketkeeper of winning a man-of-the-match award in a one-day international. It was a game at the MCG, which came down to the final ball. We had batted first and slipped to 6-127 before Steve Waugh and I added an unbroken 95. My contribution was 50 from 33 balls. England's reply collapsed to 8-146, before Fraser and Martin Bicknell, and then Fraser and Phil Tufnell got them within a boundary off the final ball of winning. But Tufnell swung and missed. I took two catches to go with my half century, which the judges said was enough to get the prize. Mark Waugh took 4-37 and scored 36, and argued in the dressing room that he should have won the award. 'Let him whinge,' I laughed.

Two weeks later, at the Adelaide Oval, the 'Junior' Waugh had his moment of glory when he scored a brilliant hundred on Test debut. He had taken his brother's place in the line-up, Steve having been dropped after playing in Australia's previous 42 Tests.

Did we feel sorry for Stephen? Yes and no. As a close friend I felt for him; as an Australian cricketer my first thought was, 'If it's happened to Steve Waugh it could happen to anyone.' It made me more determined than ever to make sure that *my* position could only be lost through injury. The Australian team is a hard, harsh unit. If someone gets dropped, or left behind because of injury, the guys still in the team have to move on. You can learn from your ex-teammate's misfortune, sure, but you mustn't mope about it. Your energies need to be on making the newcomer feel welcome and comfortable.

This occurred when my international career ended. The players were still thinking about me, but it wasn't for them to get up and criticise the selectors or to constantly call me, to make sure I was okay. In terms of the team, I was immediately a piece of history. They needed to stay focused on the job at hand and look to the future. As did I.

For the first time in my international career, in 1990–91 I had to admit to myself that I got a little bored with the constant stream of cricket. Having New Zealand reach the one-day finals didn't help, as they were a side that bowled defensively and tried to bore their opposition out. I was aware that I had to fight this feeling, which wasn't difficult, really — all I needed to do was think about what I would be doing if I wasn't where I was. I found that during an Australian season, I could get a little stale around mid January, before the one-day finals. I'd have been playing cricket, catching planes, swapping hotel rooms and phoning family since early October, and there was still a fair way to go before the season was through. I would find myself getting a little short with autograph hunters — that was a sure sign. I worked out that I had to go out and train harder, to get back into the 'cricket focus' I'd had pre-season, or alternatively ease off my training a bit, relax more and maybe avoid a few of those room service meals. I just needed a change of routine.

The Adelaide Test was drawn, with honours even, and in Perth we won by nine wickets, with my mate, Craig McDermott, back in the team after Bruce Reid was injured, taking 18 wickets in the two games. I finished with 24 dismissals for the series, all caught, and at the presentation after the final Test, Swampy Marsh sauntered over to me and said he thought I should get the man-of-the-series award. I didn't agree with him, but I was very grateful for his comment. Gaining the acceptance of my peers was always an obsession of mine, and by the end of this series I really felt I was beginning to belong.

CHAPTER 7

THE TOUGHEST TEST

ONE OF MY BIGGEST ambitions in cricket was to be regarded as a bloke who would never be run over by anyone. They might beat me one day, but the next I'll be back out there, as hard to climb over as ever. That was the thought in my mind as I prepared for each season and each match. I was getting tougher by the Test, though some, inevitably, offered more lessons than others. The next experience in my cricket career — a journey to the Caribbean to take on the best team on the planet — would prove to be one of the toughest of them all.

I left for the West Indies under an injury cloud. On the final day of the 1990–91 Ashes series, I had successfully caught Alec Stewart down the leg side off Craig McDermott, but didn't quite nail it. When we came in for tea soon after, with the series almost done, I called Errol Alcott over as I gingerly pulled off my glove. The index finger on my left hand was purple. We iced it during the interval and just before we went back out to wrap up the Test, Errol taped it up extremely tight. Out in the middle, it may have looked as if I was gloving them all right, but I knew something was very wrong. Phil Newport, batting eight, slogged 40 off 55 balls, but that apart the Poms capitulated and I didn't have to stay out there long. Before the presentations, I slipped the glove off, quietly as I could, and though most of the finger was covered in tape I could see little bits of flesh which weren't purple any more. They were black.

I didn't have an x-ray until I returned to Brisbane, but well before I went to the radiologist I knew it was broken, maybe badly broken. The tour to the West Indies was due to depart in less than a week.

Dr John McKnee, one of the best in the business, stared at the x-rays, looked studiously at me as most doctors do just before they deliver the bad news, and said quietly, 'I'm sorry Ian, this isn't good. There's four fractures … two either side of the joint … You won't be able to go the West Indies.'

To which I replied immediately, 'Sorry, doc, I'm going.'

My attitude throughout my career was that broken bones and general joint injuries are a fact of wicketkeeping life. Today, my left index finger won't bend at that middle joint, both little fingers refuse to straighten as well as they used to, and my right index finger is a bit knobbly because of the knock I received in the 1989–90 Shield final. But the fingers are not as mangled as legend might have it, and my hands work almost as well as if I'd never kept wicket in my life.

I always hated the thought of a sore finger costing me a Test match. Every Test match missed was an experience that passed me by. And why give some other bloke a chance on the highest stage; everybody knows that's how I received my

Just another day at the office in the Caribbean, 1991. In this instance, a flier from Courtney Walsh has flicked my glove during our game against Jamaica at Sabina Park in Kingston.

big chance. You don't forget those things. The only thing that would have made me stand down was if the injury would impinge on my performance, but I learned quickly in my career that I could perform at my best despite the odd broken bone or strained ligament.

Dr McKnee did have me worried. He'd referred me to a bone specialist, Dr Peter Myers, but not before he asked with a grin for a copy of my x-rays. 'I'd like to use them in some lectures I've got coming up,' he explained.

I pictured him showing them to his students and then explaining how the fool to whom the hands belonged actually thought he could keep wicket in a Test match. Dr Myers studied those x-rays in the same way Dr McKnee had, then peered at me with that same very concerned look, and commented, 'I can't stop you going ... good luck.'

Fortunately, there was no official fitness test, even though the powers-that-be were aware of my injury. I appreciated this on two fronts: it showed a faith in *my* ability to determine whether I was right and it confirmed that they valued how I was going about my job. Instead of being put under their microscope, I was told I could have the first week off, missing the opening game of the tour, at St Kitts. Near the end of our time there, before we left the island to head to Kingston, Jamaica, I opted to have a net session, just to see how I was travelling. Not too good. I struggled to hold the bat, let alone hit the ball any distance. The slightest jarring quaked up the handle. Pass the painkillers, will you Errol …

I hated taking painkillers at any time, but on rare occasions during my career there was no alternative. This was one such case. I had to play against Jamaica, a four-dayer that preceded the first one-day international and the first Test.

All up, we spent two weeks in Jamaica, a nasty fortnight where the locals made it plain they didn't like us very much. Sabina Park, long the island's home of cricket, was a depressing place with a pitch of rolled clay and an outfield that had more bumps than my broken finger. Courtney Walsh, the star of Jamaica's pace attack, was in a frightening mood, taking aim at our batting line-up and eventually sending Craig McDermott to hospital to have a cut eye stitched. Earlier, Mark Waugh had been hit in the helmet, and I was caught behind trying to avoid one Walsh pinged straight at me. When Billy returned to our dressing room, he was full of aggression, and the whole team was fired up. Whether or not this was Walsh's intention, I don't know, but it did set the scene for an angry Test series.

We won the game against Jamaica — and the one-dayer, too — but I was glad to get out of there. The Test, close and exciting for three days, was ruined by rain. This frustration, plus my nagging finger and the poor conditions — sure, it was my choice to play with the damaged digit, but the lousy wicket meant that balls were constantly taking off, scuttling through or bouncing in front of me — made this a long, depressing fortnight. The duck I got in the first Test, lbw Walsh, didn't help either. I was lbw to Courtney Walsh more than once during my career.

For six weeks from the moment I damaged it, the finger hurt like hell. I'd reached the point where I could anticipate the pain. 'Oh, oh, this is going to sting!' I'd prepare myself as a return fell short or a delivery didn't carry through on the full. And sure enough, it would. Then, in Barbados for another one-day international, Bruce Reid fired in a low return from down near the pavilion, I cringed before I caught it, but felt nothing except that beautiful thud of ball rifling into glove. I never thought about the finger again.

When I returned home, I didn't go to see either of the doctors. But they would both help in the future, especially Peter Myers, who was instrumental in me getting back on the field as rapidly as I needed after I smashed my thumb in Pakistan in 1994. Having seen me get through that broken finger three years earlier, he knew what he was dealing with. He looked at the thumb joint, peered at the x-rays, and asked how long we had.

'Five weeks,' I told him.

'No chance,' he said. And with that he wrote out a schedule for my recovery.' Five weeks later, I was keeping in the first Test of that season's Ashes series.

WE APPROACHED THAT WINDIES series in 1991 knowing that as a team we were going pretty well. We wanted to challenge these West Indians, have a go at them, but after the battle was over we conceded that we just lacked that supreme self-belief we needed in order to prevail. The signs were there that we weren't too far away, but we weren't there yet. We did attack their batsmen, and served it up to their tail a little bit. In contrast, they hammered our tail unmercifully and we were inevitably six out, seven out, all out. In all our last three wickets batted eight times during the Test series, that's 24 partnerships, and scored 181 runs, an average of 7.5 runs per wicket. The Windies' last three averaged nearly 20. We learned from that, and in future series, most notably in 1995, we vowed to assail their late-order batsmen, as they always did ours.

We wanted to get up them, but were held back just a little by their demeanor and reputation. I vividly recall one team meeting at the start of the tour, when the emphasis was very much on staying positive. For too long, Simmo told us, we'd built the Windies up as supermen.

A bit later into the meeting, our coach informed us that the second new ball would be available after 75 overs, rather than 85 as had been the case in Australia. 'Won't that be fun,' I said.

As soon as I said it I wished I could have it back. 'Now that's just the type of statement we don't need, Ian,' Simmo roared. There wasn't any point explaining that I was only trying to be funny. It wasn't funny and Simmo was right.

After the rain-ruined first Test, we won three of the four remaining one-dayers to take the series 4-1. Of course, we were really there for the Tests, but to win the limited-overs game so decisively was satisfying, especially given the Windies' imposing home record in this style of cricket. Going into the series, Richards' team had won 18 home games straight, going back to 1986. They'd never lost a rubber at home. But in one-dayers at least, as a team we weren't scared to lose. It was nice to feel like that in games against the West Indies.

The nature of one-day cricket, with its emphasis on defensive bowling and embargo on bumpers, blunted the West Indies attack — Malcolm Marshall and Courtney Walsh are two bowlers who were much more effective in Test cricket. We enjoyed more than matching them everywhere but in the third match, in Trinidad, when we lost by seven wickets after a rain delay simplified their run chase. We had a number of star performers thoughout this series — McDermott and Marsh were the standouts — while Steve Waugh distinguished himself by immediately bouncing Viv Richards when the King of the Caribbean strode out to bat in game one.

Unfortunately, the Test series was a different matter. In the second Test in Guyana they smashed us, with Richie Richardson slamming a particularly brutal century. It wasn't just that they scored 500, but they got them so quickly. Ironically, this came after they'd bowled their overs at a ridiculous funereal pace on the first day — they were playing games, bowling just 24 overs before lunch and not getting through to their 90th over, the number required to be bowled each day, until around 6.40pm. Stumps was supposed to be at 5.05. Batting for eight hours, bouncer after bouncer with plenty of time to think in between, was so hard.

I made 53 and 47 in that Test — run out in both innings, which was stupid — and was proud of the way I concentrated. I was happy, too, with the way I focused on the moment at hand, without worrying about outcomes at all. This was something I specifically set out to do in this Test and it came off brilliantly. Up to this point, I had been a batsman who got out in the 20s too often, whether in grade, Shield or Test cricket, so to go beyond that in both innings of a Test, especially against this relentless bowling, was a good sign. I was learning.

—¤—

BY THE TIME WE arrived in Barbados for the fourth Test we were one down with two to play, after torrential rain had limited play in the third Test, in Trinidad.

> *April 9, 1991 (Fourth day, third Test — West Indies had recovered from 5-56 to 8-220 in their first innings of the third Test, in reply to our 294): Went flat. No continuous pressure on bats. AB could have called us all together.*
>
> *Almost as if we didn't want to annihilate them. Rather bowl then bat and draw tomorrow — less pressure that way. DO WE WANT TO NAIL THESE BLOKES?*

The grind of the tour was getting to me at this point, though I still loved the actual cricket. Too often, off the field, the locals tried to intimidate us — everywhere we went we copped lines such as 'you're going to get licked tomorrow' or 'wait till Curtly's finished with you'. They were pumping up their team while belittling us, and I found you often couldn't talk to people for any length of time before they'd be tossing in a loudmouth comment or a sly dig. I didn't relish that then, but I coped much better in 1995 and 1999. On those two tours, I just turned my back on them.

I did like the fact that they took their cricket very seriously and passionately. It was the rank partisanship that annoyed me. In Guyana, they were obsessed with betting on the action. They were right in front of us, with wads of notes at the ready. They'd bet on where the next ball was going to be hit, who was going to field it, anything. And the notes change hands every ball. Later, I found the fans in Antigua were excellent, they simply enjoyed good cricket. But in Barbados, after a run-in with local hero Desmond Haynes, my name was poison. I didn't enjoy the place.

In that fourth Test, we won the toss, sent them in, and quickly had them 3-27 — Greenidge and Richardson to McDermott, Carl Hooper to Hughes. At the other end, Haynes was scratching about, making just 10 runs in the game's first 17 overs. He was unhappy, we were on top, and then came the on-field blue that put my name in the next day's headlines and turned the entire island of Barbados against me.

In my experience, Desi Haynes was too often an angry man. We'd previously crossed swords during the final one-day international, in Guyana, when he was given out lbw to Peter Taylor even though the ball struck his front pad, which was a reasonable way down the wicket. I reckoned it was out, but Desi didn't and stood there indignantly, marked where his foot had been in relation to the batting crease, looked daggers at me and finally stormed off. He didn't say anything to me, but as he marched angrily past Mark Waugh, he spat out, 'Tell Healy he's a thief.'

Junior poked his head into our huddle and asked, 'Heals, what did you say to Desi?'

'I didn't say anything,' I replied. I had wanted to mutter something to send him on his way, but something stopped me. Maybe self control, maybe just a sixth sense that a smart-arsed remark at that moment might have provoked something ugly.

'Well Desi said to tell you you're a thief.'

Thanks, Junior.

When we batted, AB annoyed the Windies later in the day by slogging out of the ground a delivery from Phil Simmons that slipped out of the bowler's hand and bounced up nicely on the pitch adjacent to the one we were playing on. They, Desi especially, thought that was against the 'spirit of the game', which we thought was a bit rich given the spirited way they liked to bounce our tailenders. At the presentation after the game Desi was at it again. He sidled up to Junior and whispered, 'Did you pass my message on to Healy.'

'Yeah, Desi, I did,' Junior responded. 'What happened anyway?'

'He should never have appealed,' he explained. 'Healy, he appeals too much.'

A bit later, I took Deano and two beers into the Windies dressing room, but as soon as we arrived the atmosphere turned frosty. Conversation stopped. ''Ello, 'ello, 'ello,' you sense them thinking, 'what have we got here.'

I think it was Gordon Greenidge who asked, with a chuckle, 'Yes, what can we do for you?'

'I've come to talk to Desmond,' I said, as strongly as I could. I felt like Oliver, asking for more.

Desi hardly looked up, I offered him the beer, he ignored it, grabbed one of his own and I asked him what the problem was.

'You're appealing too much,' he began. 'Our umpires are terrible. If you appeal a lot, the decisions will go your way.'

'Don't you think you were out today?' I responded.

'That's not the point, you're doing it all the time.'

Neither of us was listening to what the other had to say. Meanwhile, the rest of them were watching what we were doing. I stayed for the full beer, conversation was muted, and then I said, 'Let's leave it, I'll get out of your way.'

We didn't solve a thing.

It seems my zealous appealing remained a bugbear for him throughout the Test series, and matters came to a head that morning in Barbados. The incident occurred after Haynes edged a Craig McDermott off-cutter onto his leg — I am convinced he nicked it — and I moved forward to catch it on the leg side. For a moment, I thought we had the mighty Windies 4-28. The umpire, however, ruled otherwise, but only after the batsman had indicated that the ball had flicked him near the waist or hip. I know Haynes' gesture had no impact on the umpire at all, but it was still unnecessary and provocative, something cricketers the world over hate to see.

And this was coming from a bloke who a month earlier had complained about me trying to unfairly influence umpires!

'Why don't you,' I shouted with the odd expletive thrown in, 'let the umpire do his job.'

The response was astonishing, especially coming as it was from a cricketer with nearly 15 years' experience at the highest level.

He ripped his helmet off and strode angrily towards me, bat pointed in my direction as if he was ready to jab me in the chest.

'I don't have to take that from you,' he roared.

'You take what you get out here, mate,' I replied. I wasn't backing away a centimetre.

'How about I see you after the game?' he continued.

I blew him a kiss, which, looking back, probably wasn't very clever and I'm sure looked provocative on television. But I hated the 'see you after the game' line, which I thought was crass and juvenile. 'You are a big man, aren't you?' I sneered to him, and walked back to get ready for the next delivery.

Soon after Haynes had a piece of dirt caught in his eye, and he rather theatrically asked short leg David Boon to help him. Boonie, good on 'im, was unmoved, so Desi had to go off to see his batting partner, captain Viv Richards, for some support. On the way off for lunch he was into me again. I just ignored him. In all, Desi batted for more than three-and-a-half hours that day, for 28. Throughout, and for a while after, I didn't like the bloke, but I admired his tenacity. He wasn't in good form or thinking straight, but he still stuck at it.

During the lunch break, Laurie Sawle and Bob Simpson were keen to discover what I'd said. They were okay. 'That's been happening in cricket for 50 years,' was the coach's verdict, a point he underlined when asked for his reaction to the clash by the media after stumps. Meanwhile, I deflected the media approaches, using the old 'what happens on the field stays on the field' defence. Maybe that was a bit naive, but that's how I wanted to play it. Desi wasn't quite so reticent, and in an interview given to the *Barbados Sunday Sun* he said:

> *Healy used abusive language at me and I am sorry if it looked as if I was protesting because he appealed. It was just a matter of showing Healy where the ball hit me on my shirt, but then he started cursing me.*
>
> *It was not that I was trying in any way to make a scene and I apologise to the fans and people of Barbados.*

I have to admit I was shaken by the clash. For the rest of the Test the locals were on my back, shaking fists at me, cheering my errors. I had made the

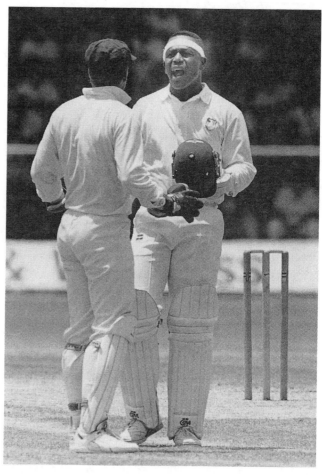

The infamous Haynes-Healy clash in Barbados, April 1991. Though we mightn't look the best of mates in this photograph, I'm truly looking forward to the day when I can sit down and have a few beers with Desi. We may not have seen eye to eye during this series, but he's still a cricketer I have a lot of respect for.

mistake of getting involved in a very public incident with a local hero and in the end the biggest loser out of it was me. The fact that it looked worse than it actually was didn't matter at all. When Channel Nine used video of the blow-up in the on-air promotion for the following Australian summer, I complained to the ACB. Nine argued that they had the right to use the images, which they owned, any way they wanted to. I came to understand their position, but when it was first aired I'd had enough of being asked about the incident and on a personal level didn't like the fact that for many I was now a bad guy.

However, I didn't regret the affair, or my part in it. I think the fact that I stood up to Haynes was significant in the sense that it reflected very publicly the fact that this Australian team was getting a tougher, meaner edge. My biggest regret was that we ended up losing the Test disastrously. I may have been irritating our opponents and perhaps some of the gentlemen in the press box but I wasn't irritating my teammates. We weren't backing away any more, weren't scared of being the bad guys — we were standing up, playing naturally, the style of cricket combat we'd grown up with. Cricket in the modern era is a game where a psychological edge is critical and being able to intimidate and to resist intimidation are crucial parts of a side's make-up. You need to have the strength and confidence to back your ability and judgement, knowing that strong opponents will try to rattle your composure. I'd have stood up to a bloke in club or Shield cricket if he'd reacted as Haynes did, so why not at Test level? I didn't like people off the field bagging me, but in many ways I didn't really understand why they were so quick to do so. I know the answer now, but at that point in my life, I had no training or feel for the intricacies of cricket diplomacy or what it meant to be a role model. I was just a cricketer, trying to win.

Relations between the teams weren't good, and this was nearly the low point. People in both camps pleaded for a return to more civil times, but then Viv Richards came out, after the Windies had easily won the Test (by 343 runs after being bowled out for 149 in their first innings) and retained the Frank Worrell Trophy, and put the boot into Bob Simpson. There were so many other more positive things he could have been talking about.

We recovered a semblance of pride in the final Test, winning by 157 runs on the back of big hundreds from Mark Waugh and Mark Taylor. I had a wild experience during that match, going in as nightwatchman when the fast bowlers were at their nastiest. Fortunately, Tubs got to face most of that fire, as I expertly stayed at the other end. The next day I finished with 32, off 43 balls, and was rapt in the way I batted and manner in which I approached the task. This, like quite a few things to come out of that final Test, were good signs for the future. But the underlying disappointment remained: we hadn't come all this way to lose the series, so this Test win was really little consolation.

> *April 30, 1991: If every ball is watched, intensity is right and mind is not worrying about the outcome, I will score plenty. Note that Tubs' 144 [in second innings of fifth Test] included three dropped catches and a missed stumping ...*

—☒—

BACK ON FEBRUARY 24, 1991, February 25 Australian time, I was in the team room in Kingston, Jamaica, waiting to go out for the evening with a few members of the side. I was rooming with Merv, who wasn't coming out with us; he was staying behind to treat an injury. Mike Veletta, who was with us, was a bit on edge, as his wife, Linda, was very, very pregnant back in Perth. Due to give birth at any minute, in fact, to the point that cigars had been purchased, in readiness for Waggy's transition from husband to parent.

Up in Brisbane, my wife Helen was a couple of weeks behind Linda Veletta. A fortnight from now, I thought, I'll be as edgy as my WACA mate is now. So when I ducked up to my room to grab something before we left and Merv said, as I was rummaging through my suitcase, 'Oh yeah, Heals, Helen rang to tell you she's having contractions,' I simply thought, 'Course she is, Merv.'

I set off to catch the other guys up, with Merv in the background crying out, 'No, no, I'm fair dinkum, She is, she is.'

To my great shame, I didn't call back until the next morning, after Merv reminded me yet again about that call. He convinced me to phone home ... and it WAS true! Helen was heavily in labour by that point and, soon after, tiny Emma Healy introduced herself to the world. My first sighting of her was courtesy of a fax from the *Courier-Mail*, who had dispatched a photographer to the hospital. Gregg Porteous, who was covering the tour for all the News Limited papers, took a photo of the boys partying with me, complete with Waggy's cigars and Dean Jones pouring a bottle of bubbly over my head. That was wired back to the *Courier Mail*, who sent another snapper out to the hospital to photograph Helen and Emma holding a photo of her father on the other side of the world, celebrating her birth.

> *February 25, 1991: EMMA KATE! 4.36pm. 12.36am*
> *(Jamaica). 6lb 9oz. Party in room 5220 — cigars (ordinary!)*
> *Rang all peers and press, etc.*
>
> *Training hot — overdid it. Sick in arvo, then sleep.*
> *Merv's always sleeping, acting annoyed with phone calls ...*
> *Billy, Terry, PT very happy. All boys were ...*
>
> *A nice experience.*

Such is the life of a cricketing dad. I was very focused on my cricket at that time, to the point that I didn't appreciate what Helen had gone through, carrying the baby through a long summer, and now being a single parent. I didn't begin to think how hot it was for her at home, while I was away in the best air-conditioned hotels. I know that looks very uncaring and selfish, but if I was

A toast in Kingston, Jamaica, to the Australian cricket team's newest father. Left to right: Craig McDermott (complete with black eye after being clobbered by a Courtney Walsh bumper), Dean Jones (at back with a nearly empty champagne bottle) Dad, Mark Waugh, Errol Alcott and Peter Taylor.

Left: Helen and nine-week-old Emma at Brisbane Airport, waiting for me to return from the West Indies tour. Below: 'And you must be my father.' Emma introduces herself to her first-time Dad, while I try to look as if I know what I'm doing on my return home in May 1991.

to succeed as an elite cricketer I believed that that was the way it had to be. Helen's support throughout my career was unwavering, and she never complained, even when she was entitled to.

Like all first-time Dads, I had no idea what fatherhood involved. Later I was able to be at the birth of my daughter Laura and son Tom, which was wonderful. If I had been there for Emma's birth, it would have been desperately difficult to be away for either of the others. But the fact is that when Emma arrived I was in Jamaica, and I didn't know what I was missing. I did know that I was in the West Indies doing what I wanted to do, and doing everything I could to be a success at it. Fortunately, I was married to a very strong woman who understood my ambition (I think!!).

Following the Test series and a batch of one-day matches in Bermuda we were on our way home. I knew that waiting for me at Brisbane airport was a nine-week-old daughter I'd never met, which presented something of a two-edged sword. I couldn't wait to see my daughter, and yet I was terrified by the prospect of cradling her in public. Visions of press photographers snapping away and the Australian wicketkeeper dropping the most important catch of his life filled me with dread. I was a bloke who'd never been one to pick up baby nieces and nephews and give them a hug. In my mind, I didn't have a clue how to hold a baby. When I finally picked Emma up the cameras were there to capture it all, and I handled the situation okay. No, better than okay. I was as proud and delighted as any bloke could be.

With that, the press guys left us alone and I thought, 'What do I do now?'

CHAPTER 8

FOR TEAM
AND COUNTRY

FEW MEN I ENCOUNTERED during my cricket career loved the game of cricket more than Allan Border. Perhaps only Bob Simpson outdid AB in terms of the sheer pleasure they got from being heavily involved in cricket. Both could discuss the game interminably, would get excited *every* match day and be an integral part of practice every single day. AB always wanted to be out there, trying as hard as he could, which sounds simple but is actually extremely difficult. And he expected that of others.

I love the way he has never changed in all the time I've known him. There is nothing bogus about him. As a batsman, one of the best of them all, he never cared how he looked out in the middle, as long as the runs came and the team benefited. I never saw a better out-of-form batsman; somehow, he still made runs, especially when they were needed, despite the fact that in those rare dark periods he could never find the middle of his bat.

AB didn't want to impose himself on anyone, and consequently was not what I would call a 'natural' leader. You always felt that he believed that it wasn't his job to motivate or educate Test players, other than through his own example on the field and in the nets. His logic was typically blunt: I never needed this sort of inspiration from others. Yet if asked, his advice was invariably spot-on.

He also hated most of the off-field intrusions and responsibilities that went with the job, and sometimes resented the questions of the media and administrators, who he often felt didn't understand. As captain, AB wore the performance of the team like a badge, taking both success and failure very personally. Especially the failure, which was a problem in the first four years of his captaincy when, except for the 1987 World Cup, the team hardly won at all. Yet he was never selfish. I remember during our tour to Sri Lanka in 1992, a trivia night was organised and during the evening AB was asked the question, 'Who was the last Australian to take three wickets in four balls in a Test match?' The answer was 'Allan Border', but he couldn't remember doing it. He wasn't one for records even though he broke plenty. Wins were what mattered. His biggest fault was that he could get angry, very angry, and lacked the ability to confront people before situations became really difficult. These two attributes together meant that things could build up inside him and then explode spectacularly. Ian McDonald, our long-time team manager, often had to cope with AB threatening not to do this or not turn up to that because things in the

Allan Border has just broken Sunil Gavaskar's world runscoring record, in Christchurch in 1993. I was lucky enough to be at the other end at the time, and thrilled to be the first to shake his hand, but I must confess that immediately after he played the shot that took him past Gavaskar, I thought he still had four runs to go.

captain's eyes weren't right. A better way would have been to talk to the team or the officials who were annoying him, to clarify rules and responsibilities, before things reached that knife-edge, but AB bottled it up instead. When the genie finally got out, it could be ugly. This said, he rarely blew up in front of the players — it was usually management who saw the worst of AB.

Yet AB is a guy who has never, ever held a grudge. If he had a run-in with you one day, the next day he was fine, which was very handy given the way he could explode. I remember during our first tour of South Africa, in early 1994, during the second Test in Cape Town, he and David Boon were involved in a very slow but important partnership, at a time when AB, as captain, was under huge pressure. The Board had fined two of his players for misbehaviour, the team was not playing well and AB's future with the team was being scrutinised by the media. As the two guys came in for tea, the players applauded them heartily, recognising their brave effort. The mood in the room was upbeat, as we were slowly getting ourselves in a position to win the game. During the break, I jokingly grabbed AB's bat and went to put some ice on it, to 'cool' it down. The facetious implication, of course, was that he was on fire! He wasn't, we all knew that. So did he ...

'I hope you're jokin', Heals,' he snapped. 'I am batting my arse off out there ... why don't you go and play with the rest of your schoolboy mates.'

And so the tirade continued. I was filthy, and shoved the bat back in his corner of the dressing room and went and sat in mine. I didn't care that he had been under stress. He'd never complained to anyone, never pulled anyone into line, and now he was into me.

The next day he was fine. I wasn't. I couldn't approach him for a while. Finally, though, we were okay. He was too good a bloke for me to stay angry with him for too long. I thought his blast was unfair and out of line, but he was the captain and that was the way he was.

And he was a tremendous captain, once his team became confident. I saw him grow as a leader in my first two seasons. As blokes such as Steve and Mark Waugh, Mark Taylor, Merv Hughes, Craig McDermott and me, plus 'veterans' such as Terry Alderman and Geoff Lawson, started doing their jobs well for him he became an excellent skipper. By the 1991–92 Australian season, he was outstanding and we were a very efficient side.

The summer of '91–92 was one where cricket talk was dominated by the fifth World Cup, scheduled for late in the season in Australia and New Zealand. During the summer we won four of five Tests against India, and then dominated the World Series against the Indians and the West Indies. This was also the season of AB's most infamous blow-up.

It came late in the Test series, after the selectors decided it was time to drop Geoff Marsh. A dead-set battler, Swamp had had a greater influence on the Australian team than his Test batting average of 33 implies and, I think, a greater impact than the selectors and administrators realised. He was a guy everyone liked and got along with, a strong backer of AB, and an effective 'middle man' when AB was grumpy. As vice-captain, Swamp saw his role as primarily looking after AB's interests and ambitions. He had no pretensions to the captaincy; his sole ambition was for the team to function effectively as a unit and always fall in line behind the captain. AB loved that, and was eternally grateful for Swamp's support.

The first I, or any of the guys who had kept their spots in the side, AB included, knew of Swamp's (and Mark Waugh's) omission was when Bob Simpson informed us during warm-ups before the last day of the fourth Test at the Adelaide Oval. We led the series 2-0 at that point, and were preparing to try to bowl the Indians out for less than 371. They were 0-31 overnight; an exciting day's cricket was in prospect.

On the surface it seemed a ridiculous time to make the announcement, just before an important day's Test cricket, but perhaps the authorities had no choice. The fifth Test was due to start in only three days time, and the new players, Tom Moody and Victorian opener Wayne Phillips, needed to be told. Better, I'm sure the Board thought, to be up front than to have the story leak out during the day.

I don't think AB cared about the timing, but he was ropeable about the decision to sack his vice-captain, who had supported him through thick and thin over the past five years. AB remembered back to the Caribbean, when Swamp (and Junior) had stood so bravely in front of the Windies quicks. Now, with the team dominating this series, they'd been left out. To him it was heartless, disloyal and wrong.

Back in the dressing room, I might have been sitting well away from AB but I could see he was fuming. Swamp and Junior, who had been told of their demise before the rest of us, just stared blankly across the room. Five minutes before the start of play, our captain stood up, looked for 12th man Paul 'Pistol' Reiffel, and snapped, 'Get your bloody whites on.'

Pistol had been towelling down after a shower. 'Yeah, okay,' he mumbled. He was the 12th man, he thought, there was no hurry.

Pistol hadn't played a Test at this stage of his career, just a few one-dayers. He didn't realise AB meant 'get your whites on NOW!' I guess none of us did. But AB, in full blow-up mode, soon set him straight.

'Just get 'em on. You're going out with the team!'

And with that AB stormed out of the room, to find a phone to call Laurie Sawle, chairman of selectors, in Perth. Geoff Marsh, playing what would prove to be his last day of Test cricket, led us out onto the Adelaide Oval.

AB was on fire. He didn't come out on to the field until he'd given Laurie a gobful. On the field he was distracted all day but we won, despite a long partnership between Mohammad Azharuddin and Manoj Prabhakar. After the match had been completed, we had to quickly shower, get dressed and catch a flight to Perth for the final Test. But while the rest of us dashed about, AB sat there in his whites. When Mike Whitney asked him if he was coming, he said, 'I might see you there.'

We *might* see you there?

So, while both teams, Australia and India, caught the flight to the WACA, our captain stayed behind with his sacked teammates. Whether he was just making a one-man protest or pondering his future, no one knew.

Of course, he did make it to Perth, about a day and a half late, amid a flurry of stormy local headlines about the great wrong that had been done to Geoff Marsh, WA's favourite cricket son. Swamp's replacement, 'Rowdy' Phillips, never had a chance.

I roomed with Rowdy through that Test, and though he looked okay on the surface I could sense he was churning up inside. This was his Test debut and his captain didn't want him and the crowd hated him, or so he must have thought. The WACA, notorious for backing their own, didn't miss him at all. We all tried to give him as much support as we could, but it was a terribly hard ask for the bloke, replacing Swamp on Swamp's own turf. Rowdy made 8 and 14 and never played international cricket again.

Geoff Marsh came back for the World Cup, but then missed selection in the side to tour Sri Lanka in August. Mark Taylor was the new vice-captain. AB continued on, still disappointed about the original decision, but that was now in the past. Nothing could change him.

Emma's first Christmas, Melbourne 1991. Other cricketing dads in the photo are (left to right): Allan Border, Craig McDermott, Bruce Reid, David Boon and Geoff Marsh.

THE INDIA SERIES WAS the first home rubber Australia had dominated for many years, probably since 1983–84, the farewell summer of Dennis Lillee, Greg Chappell and Rod Marsh. It was also notable for the international debut of a young Victorian leg-spinner called Shane Warne, who was brought into the team for the Sydney Test.

From the day I first kept to Shane, in an Australian XI v West Indies encounter in Hobart in December 1991 — which was also the first time I captained a team in a first-class game — he reminded me more of an old bush cricketer, rather than a young rookie. He was the bloke who's carrying a bit of weight, would rather be leaning on a fence than fielding in the covers, but can land them on a sixpence when it's his turn to bowl, and has been doing so for years. Shane smoked a lot, was confident, socially streetwise and bowled with a maturity that belied his inexperience at the elite level. From my vantage point behind the stumps, I saw how the ball fizzed out of his hand right from the word go, and how his line and length was superior to just about every leg-spin bowler I'd ever seen.

When he made his Test debut he was a terrible fieldsman. It's a real credit to him that he stopped being a liability in the field in a very short space of time. I'm sure Simmo must have got to him!

In his maiden Test he dropped a catch off his own bowling and had another chance missed at midwicket, but outside of that he was simply unfortunate to

Whenever I had a chance, I'd do my 'golf ball' drill. In this case, I'm in an old laneway at the back of our hotel in The Rocks in Sydney in early 1992, but normally I'd prefer a more even surface to maximise the exercise's value.

make his Test debut on a very flat Sydney deck against a team whose line-up featured some fine players of slow bowling. Although 18-year-old Sachin Tendulkar had produced a couple of promising cameos against us during the first two Tests, this was the first time his talent exploded, as he crafted a very impressive, unbeaten 148. Their opener, Ravi Shastri, as good a player of the spinners as you could find, hit a double ton before becoming Shane's first Test wicket and only scalp of the game. By the end of the series, Shane's Test bowling average was 228, but we all knew he was going to be special.

From the jump, he was big on encouraging others. I saw him clapping and yelling his support and wondered whether that was just a camouflage to hide the insecurities that come with being the new kid on the block. But I soon learned that it was his nature to back his teammates. This never changed, from the day he took his first Test wicket to the day he broke Dennis Lillee's Australian Test wicket-taking record eight summers later.

It's funny to think of it now, but before the arrival of Warney the cricket world didn't have a high opinion of spinners. Everyone reckoned they were something of a dying breed, only to be played on absolute turners such as the SCG in the 1980s. Elsewhere, we'd go with a defensive medium pacer before we'd play a spinner, or maybe a spinner who could bat, such as Peter Sleep, Greg Matthews or Peter Taylor. I know AB thought that and I tended to as well. Between the first Test of the 1988–89 summer and the Sri Lanka tour in August-September 1992, I didn't complete one Test stumping. They just didn't happen.

WE WENT INTO THE World Cup on something of a one-day roll. Defending champions, we'd won the World Series Cup each of the past three years and beaten the West Indies in the Caribbean. The tournament was made even more exciting and historic by the re-emergence of the South Africans after 22 years as cricket outcasts. It was something we'd all been looking forward to for a long time. And we failed to reach the semi-finals.

Our first game was in Auckland against New Zealand, and we fielded very poorly from the word go. The Kiwi captain, Martin Crowe, was in peak form and we dropped him on the way to his hundred. In reply, Boonie made a hundred, but seven of the other 10 failed to reach double figures and we crashed to defeat by 37 runs. In Sydney, we tumbled to a dreadful nine-wicket loss to South Africa, during which I tore a hamstring running between the wickets. With me on the sidelines and Boonie behind the stumps we managed to edge out India at the Gabba, but then we returned to Sydney to be thrashed by England and our tournament was almost shot. I came back for that England game, and played in the rest of our matches, but the leg was never right. We did defeat Sri Lanka, Zimbabwe and the West Indies, but lost to Pakistan in Perth and that was that.

In hindsight, I think we made the mistake of trying too hard to treat the World Cup like any other tournament, as if it was an extension of the World Series rather than something special. Instead of going into camp in the lead-up to the Cup, we went back to the red ball in the Sheffield Shield, and then had just two warm-up one-dayers — one in Sydney against NSW the day before we flew to Auckland for the Cup opener, the other against an Auckland XI the day after we arrived. Twenty-four hours later, the Cup was on! It might have been more than coincidence that our best performance in the World Cup was our last, when we hammered the West Indies at the MCG.

—✠—

I ALWAYS FOUND IT difficult preparing for cricket tours in August, as we did in 1992 when we travelled to Sri Lanka. My catching wasn't flash to start with, and I had to work very hard in the first few days of our pre-tour camp, and in a warm-up game in Darwin, to get my technique up to par. I was still flinching a bit in the early matches on tour, including the first Test. I wasn't the only one struggling, and this, combined with the fact that we underrated our opponents a fraction, made for a tricky tour. We'd left Geoff Marsh, Merv Hughes and Steve Waugh at home, and then in all three Tests batted first on wickets that looked like belters, but every time, having thought we'd make 500, their seamers worked us out. We were 5-109, 5-109 and 5-58 in the first innings of the three Tests and did well from there to come away with a 1-0 series win.

I had my best Test series so far with the bat. Batting at No. 8, I made two half centuries and a 49, and averaged just over 50 for the series. Throughout, I was much more patient. I felt as if I understood more about this batting caper, that I knew how to settle into an innings, and stay focused and composed. Greg

Matthews, one above me in the order, was excellent, making five half centuries from his six innings. I enjoyed batting with him and felt I learned from him. And Dean Jones also had a good Test series. He might have had some luck, but he did score heavily and I appreciated the way he grafted to get his runs, forsaking his usual flamboyant style as soon as he realised that was not the way to succeed against their attack. In contrast, Tom Moody, drafted from the middle order into Swamp's opening bat spot, scored just 71 runs in the Tests, 54 of them in one innings. Mark Waugh had two pairs in a row.

While their seamers were very effective, our bowlers, good operators all of them, couldn't find anything in the wickets, except for one famous afternoon in the first Test. It was very strange; in the end we blamed the balls, which were harder and had a higher seam than the balls we were accustomed to. Of course, they also bowled extremely well and we came away with a much greater respect for Sri Lankan cricket. Among the cricketers who impressed us was an off-spinner, Muttiah Muralitharan, who we saw for the first time in Kandy, in the opening first-class match of the tour. He was turning them a long way. AB thought he was a leggie and kept missing the off spin until Mark Waugh walked down at the end of Murali's first over and said, 'Skipper, I reckon he might be an offie.' Of course we'd see and hear a lot more about Murali in the future.

The first Test was a beauty, one of the most exciting I ever played. Faced with a first-innings deficit of 291, we managed to set them 181 after a strong second innings batting effort. Everyone reached double figures, even Mike Whitney who was 10 not out and shared a critical last-wicket partnership of 40 with Shane Warne. Of the 10 blokes dismissed in that innings, I was lowest scorer with 12. Top score was Boonie with 68, then Moey with 64, Deano 57, Junior 56, Tubsy 43, Billy 40, Warney 35. A real team effort.

The home team then crashed from 2-127 to all out 164. It was a remarkable collapse, brought on by some aggressive captaincy, good catching and excellent bowling. At 2-125, Tubsy at slip had whispered to me, 'What can we do to turn this tour around?' Two runs later, AB took a stunning catch, running backwards from mid-on, to dismiss Aravinda de Silva and the Test began to spin. Billy dismissed their captain, Arjuna Ranatunga, and then our slow bowlers took over.

Moey was excellent, keeping it nice and tight and getting wickets when we needed them. And then AB threw the ball to Warney. I recall thinking, 'Geez, that's a gutsy move.' Shane, at this point, had taken one Test wicket in his life, but he was good enough to land it on the right spot and confident enough to want the ball when AB offered it to him. He came through, taking the last three wickets for just 11 runs. At nine down, I missed a stumping chance when I came up too early and the ball scuffled away from me, but Warney got the crucial final wicket in the following over, for which I will always be grateful. It was a sensational victory, and that night the whole team was seen dancing together at the 'Blue Elephant', one of Colombo's finest nightclubs.

I guess in the great scheme of things this wasn't a major tour in the history of Australian cricket. The final two Tests were both heavily interrupted by rain, so we came home with a series win even though we had rarely played as well as we knew we could. However, the tour was an important one for me. As my batting settled, so my confidence rose, and I can clearly remember one night walking from the lift to my room at the Taj Hotel in Colombo and thinking, 'I'm an important part of this team now.'

At another point, the night after we lost the second one-day international of the tour to lose the three-match series, I cautioned Bob Simpson against blasting the team before the third and final game. Simmo was filthy, 'embarrassed for us' as he put it, and wanted to hammer the team for our lack of hunger. We spoke for ages about the tour, the heat and humidity, the guys' attitudes, many different things. I knew the guys were very disappointed, wanted to set the record straight in game three (which we did, winning by five wickets), and I thought we deserved that opportunity before copping a roasting. I told Bob that and he listened.

I would never have been game to offer our coach such advice even six months before. Nor, I reckon, would Simmo have been ready to discuss his concerns in such depth with me. Clearly, he now saw me as an influential member of the team, rather than just a handy part of it, and I appreciated that.

CHAPTER 9

IS IT WORTH IT?

FOR SOME, I GUESS, there is a very small margin between playing hard and cheating. Between what I call gamesmanship and what everyone knows is cheating. For me, there is a world of difference: the former is acceptable, in cricket at least; the latter is not.

Test cricket, the ultimate form of the sport, is a tough game that sorts out the weak from the strong. Knowing this, throughout my international career, I abhorred giving my opponents anything and always sought to gain any psychological advantage I could. This was something I learned very quickly as a teenager in district cricket. Brisbane grade cricket in those days featured many tough, battle-hardened men renowned for testing out the mettle of opponents whenever it suited them. There are countless examples, some of them unprintable and many seeming pretty trivial when I recall them today, such as when the former Shield opening bat, Max Walters, later a chairman of the Queensland selection committee, shouted, with expletives added, 'Go and wear your schoolboy shirt somewhere else, you superstar', after I was dismissed in a Brisbane grade match. I'd made the mistake of wearing my Australian Under 19 shirt. The old pros thought I was showing off. I probably was.

My senior teammates came from the same school. Once, when I was fielding close-in to Graham Whyte, I inadvertently put my right foot behind the stump line which meant the square-leg umpire called a no-ball because we had three fieldsmen behind square leg. 'Whytey' was into me so severely I felt I didn't have a friend in the world. It was a tough environment.

If cricketers are hungry there will always be occasional fireworks. Steel against steel. A tough cricketer, however, needs to have more than a loud mouth and a propensity for one-liners. A tough cricketer can handle the verbal barbs, maintain concentration, make big runs or take important wickets and devote himself or herself to his or her sport without losing control. It certainly didn't hurt me to face such gamesmanship when I was young. In fact, it strengthened me, as a person and cricketer, and prepared me for the climb to first-class and Test cricket.

These men were not cheats. In fact they were very fair, but very hard. I came to realise very quickly that cricket at the elite level needs gamesmanship, because without it the game would be too easy. I reckon that Test cricket could be as much as 90 per cent mental, the rest physical talent. You need to be making decisions, judging situations, reading what the other guy is thinking, all the time. Why not make that process as difficult as possible for your opponent? I learned there are ways of approaching opponents that might get them thinking in a manner they shouldn't be. Achieve that and you've got an edge.

This is, of course, what many like to call 'sledging'. As I said, I've got no problem with it, so long as it doesn't degenerate into personal abuse. Now that can be a fine line and what some people think is okay is not acceptable to others. I admit that on occasions I've said things that I probably shouldn't have, but there have been many more times when opponents have taken what I or one of my teammates have said and put an entirely new twist on it. The Sri Lankans are good at that and were especially so back in the days when they saw themselves as a 'minnow' cricket nation.

If there was a best way to get to me it was to be quiet when I batted. I love people talking to me, and I grew up in a grade cricket environment where it was normal to be sledged. But elsewhere cricket life is not like that, which is why, I believe, the Australian team gets nailed sometimes for its on-field behaviour. What we consider normal and acceptable other nations do not. When we get dobbed in, we can't say, 'No, we didn't do that,' when we did.

Of course, for every time a piece of gamesmanship works perfectly there's another when the reverse applies. In a Test in Sri Lanka in 1992, my old mate Asanka Gurusinha was continually trying to work Greg Matthews through midwicket, no matter what line Moey bowled. 'Any danger of you playing straight?' I sneered at 'Guru' from behind my glove. Which he promptly did and went on to a big score. Behind me at first slip, Mark Taylor heard my question and asked, 'Any danger of you shutting up?'

Another time, when playing for Queensland against NSW, Stuart Law and Matty Hayden decided one day to niggle Steve Waugh when he started to struggle after making a hundred. Tugga turned around, looked at them, said something along the lines of 'Sorry fellas, I think I'll stay a bit longer now,' and went to 180. You don't talk to Steve Waugh, not when you're a fieldsman and he's batting. The great West Indian, Brian Lara, is the same. If he's scratching around it probably means his concentration is wavering. Better to let him go than to make a comment and risk getting his thought processes and ambition back on track

— ◻ —

BRIAN LARA WAS AT the centre of one of the most controversial incidents in my career, a brief minute which led to me being branded a 'cheat' by spectators and opponents alike. I didn't cheat, never have in my life. But I did make a mistake, one that I regretted for the rest of my cricket career.

It was the first Test of the 1992–93 home series against the West Indies. Day two, the Saturday. We'd been bowled out for 293, after being 6-259 overnight. The Windies in reply were 3-170, having been 3-58. Lara and another left-hander, Keith Arthurton, were slowly getting on top. Greg Matthews was bowling to Lara.

Greg was coming round the wicket, and flighted a ball beyond the leg stump. Lara went forward, but the ball skidded past his bat and pads so wide that, by the

Brian Lara has just got his bat back, the bails are tumbling, the ball's gone free and I, in very ungainly fashion, am still trying to complete a stumping. However, my right glove, hidden here behind my pad, has already broken the stumps before Lara regained his ground. But did the ball hit the stumps first?

time it reached me, my gloves were almost a metre from the stumps; Lara, overbalancing, stumbled forward, but in my haste to complete a stumping the ball hit my wrists and spun to the ground. I saw the ball on the deck and three times tried to scoop it up towards the stumps, Lara turned and dived back to the crease, the stumps were broken, the ball was on the turf, not in my gloves, Moey appealed and umpire Terry Prue gave Lara out.

The television replay up in the stands clearly showed that the decision was wrong. The batsman might have been out of his ground when the stumps were broken, but I never had control of the ball and the ball never hit the stumps. They had been broken by my gloves. Down on the field, however, I had no idea. Mark Taylor at first slip was pretty sure it wasn't out. Moey, highly competitive, thought it was. Brian Lara was adamant it wasn't.

The drama continued. Lara stayed prostrate on the ground, bat outstretched, right hand holding the bat, left hand pleading for mercy. I looked at him and admitted I didn't know what had happened. Moey ran down to congratulate me, I picked up my cap which had fallen off in the flurry to get the bails off, the team gathered around the stumps and umpire Prue walked in from square leg. Lara, still on the ground, appealed to the umpire, but Prue said firmly, 'You're out, Brian.' By this stage, Arthurton had walked down and picked his teammate up, and with Prue clearly not going to change his mind, Lara began a slow, angry meander off the field, brushing the Gabba dirt of his shirt and trousers as he went. Meanwhile, on the TV, the replay was being showed over and over again. Every angle showed the same thing — Lara was robbed.

I was the villain. I had not appealed, unless you took my 'I don't know what happened' gesture to be an appeal. When Prue had got in among us to repair the broken wicket, I explained that my glove had hit the stumps but whether the ball had before the glove, I did not know. Tubby added, 'The glove hit the stumps, but I don't think the ball did.'

However, Prue seemed confident. 'I saw the ball hit the stumps,' he replied. It must have been out, I'd thought when he said that.

My mistake, one I rue to this day, was to let the umpire decide rather than back my instinct, which told me to give the benefit of the doubt to the batsman. Unfortunately I didn't and have had to live with the consequences. Four and a half years later, at Lord's for the second Test of the 1997 Ashes tour, I was faced with a slightly similar situation, on a catch low down which might not have carried. I told umpire David Shepherd that and, on the basis of what I said, he ruled not out. Some of my teammates disagreed with me, arguing that they were sure that I'd caught it cleanly. I didn't care. I backed my instincts

Back in November '92, team manager Ian McDonald, recalling again the Greg Dyer controversy from 1987–88, asked me to front up to a press conference. When I faced the media, the questions flew, but I simply described what happened. I did admit that it hadn't occurred to me — or anyone as far as I knew — to recall Lara. After all, the umpire had given him out and said clearly that the ball had hit the stumps. I was asked if the incident would affect the Australian team and replied, 'I wouldn't think the team would be upset, but this is unsettling to me.'

Then someone asked my opinion on umpires using TV replays to help them. 'I think that would be a very good idea,' I remarked. 'Sooner the better.'

They were actually introduced by the time we went to New Zealand in early 1993, and I was the second man to ever be given out by one in an international match, during a one-dayer in Christchurch. And I gave the third ump plenty to do, by managing to get myself involved in run-out appeals at both ends, after taking off for another run after the stumps were broken the first time.

Back at the Gabba, after leaving the press conference, I headed to the Windies dressing room to have a chat to Lara. I apologised and explained again what had happened from my perspective. We even watched another replay of the incident, which was showing on a TV in their room, on the evening news. When I left him I felt better, because I thought he understood. But that night, in the next few days, whenever, he came to the conclusion that I'd deliberately ripped him off. My relationship with him, and many of the West Indian players, was never the same again.

Maybe that conclusion came about before the start of the next day's play. Brisbane's *Sunday Mail* ran a huge banner headline 'I'M INNOCENT' with 'We told umpires it was with my glove' in smaller, still-bold letters underneath, and then a story featuring my responses at the press conference. Alongside that story was a statement from umpire Prue, which contradicted in part what I had said. I couldn't believe it. Prue's statement read: 'I accept that Australian players stated the stumps were broken by Ian Healy's gloves, however, I would like to stress at no stage did I hear any player inform me of this. I believe it is important this fact is made clear and I now consider the matter closed.'

And that, as far as the ACB was concerned, was where it ended. But not for me. I wanted the Board to take it further, after the Test, but on the final day there were more problems — AB and Merv were reported for disputing umpiring decisions — and amid the turmoil those hearings created, no one got around to asking Prue to confirm his version of the 'stumping'. I was tarred with the cheat brush, and wore it for a long time to come. My next appearance was in Perth for a one-day international and I was hammered by the WACA crowd. Part of this was simply their usual support for the local keeper, Tim Zoehrer, but much of it related to the Lara incident. A lot of West Australians called me a cheat, or things similar, that afternoon and night. The vitriol from the crowd when I came out to bat was dreadfully malicious.

'I'm not the sort of bloke who can brush that aside,' I told reporters afterwards. All sorts of negative thoughts went through my head, and for the first time in a couple of years I feared for my place in the side. Not because of form, but because of a perceived lack of credibility.

It's tough when your honesty is questioned. Suddenly, I had a significant percentage of the cricket community and many casual observers believing I was a cheat. I doubt I will ever be tough enough to cope with that. Even today, I know there are people who reckon I was a cricket cheat. You get little hints here and there, in an article or a conversation related via a third party. As late as 1997, when I had a few drinks with one of Australia's leading cricket writers, he told me I had once had a credibility problem with some of the journos. As I said, I always played hard, but I never cheated. I hate it when people don't believe me, and don't believe in me.

Back then, I was a person who wanted everyone to like me. I loved the drink after stumps were drawn, with teammates and opponents; it was part of the game and had been since I shared a coke with my much-older batting partners and rivals back at Biloela. However, as my Test career evolved, I grew to care less and less about whether or not the opposition liked me. Today, I'm still a bloke who wants to be liked by one and all. On the cricket field, though, I was there to win, to do the right thing by my teammates and the baggy green cap. If my rivals couldn't come to grips with that, that was their problem. This series was the catalyst for me developing that attitude.

Throughout that summer, I sensed that the West Indians disliked me, but they didn't come out and say as much until the SCG Test, the third of the summer. By then we were leading 1-0, after having the better of a draw in Brisbane and then seeing Shane Warne spin them away on the last day in Melbourne. The Sydney Test was where Brian Lara played one of his most famous innings, a stunning 277 that some veteran observers reckoned was the best dig ever played on the ground. The ball flew off his blade so quickly he made the ground look so small, yet his placement was awesome. It was as if we

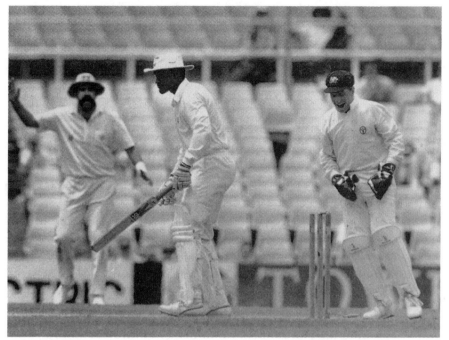

Carl Hooper bowled, as clean as you like, at the SCG. Why did it take the umpires so long to give him out?

didn't have any fieldsmen. At stumps on day four, which came not long after Lara had been run out (just about the only way we were ever going to get him out), we all ducked into their dressing room to say well played.

A few of the West Indian players specifically asked me not to come in. Keith Arthurton, who was standing near the door, spat out, 'Do you want ya arse broken, man?'

I said, 'Pass on my regards to Brian', and left immediately. At least now I knew where I stood. But I wasn't enjoying the cricket. The fans were on my back. People were whispering behind my back. I thought my opponents hated me. Was it worth it? In mid January, during a spell of one-dayers, I actually sat down and wrote out a list of the pros and cons of playing big-time cricket. The pros, of course, won out easily, but it says plenty for my state of mind that I actually went though this process. I think I probably came out of it a stronger cricketer and probably a better person, too. But it shook me, no doubt about it, and on a bloke-to-bloke level I never enjoyed playing against the West Indies again. I loved beating them and facing the challenge their best cricketers presented, but I disliked having to cop their caustic approach to me.

I was especially pissed off with Arthurton, who to me was just an ordinary cricketer with a bad attitude. In Brisbane, he'd made a big hundred, but only after Umpire Prue had missed a big edge through to me when he was on 72. I thought that decision was worse than the Lara one the previous day. That dig aside, Arthurton played quite a few games against us, but rarely had an impact. More than once, he failed to handle the pressure of a big occasion, most notably in the World Cup semi-final at Chandigarh in India in 1996, when he slogged wildly and unsuccessfully when a cool head was needed.

The morning after my 'send off' from Arthurton, Carl Hooper was bowled by Shane Warne, the ball clipping the very top of the off stump, and the umpire (Terry Prue, can you believe!) didn't give him out immediately. Instead, he went over to confer with the other umpire, Darrell Hair. To me it was a straightforward dismissal: a leg-break had spun past the outside edge of Hooper's bat and struck the off stump. I had gloved the ball after it hit the stump, and run towards Shane, before stopping when I realised that Hooper had walked away and Prue hadn't put his finger up.

I took the fact that umpires were consulting as a personal insult. The only possible way it wasn't out was if I had broken the stumps with my gloves. So the umps were discussing whether I had cheated or not. As Prue and Hair met at midwicket, I said to my teammates, who had gathered around Shane and me, 'If this is not out, I'm retiring.' The way I was feeling, I would have. Finally, fortunately, Hooper was sent on his way.

> *January 6, 1993: My integrity was questioned yet again when Hooper was bowled. I've got very serious about what's happening ... near retirement! Must sort the situation out — can't continue to let it worry me, but accept that people are now split. Get on with things.*
>
> *A keeper's lot is IN amongst it and I can't back away from it. I must lighten up about it and accept it as part of my job and contribute to a team victory no matter what.*
>
> *Overall, quite a good match for me. Worked hard. (I now dislike the opposition).*

—✠—

IRONICALLY, IN A SEASON when my honesty and credibility were so severely scrutinised, I had my first regular leadership experience at the first-class level. I was again captain of an Australian XI against the West Indies in Hobart, in mid November, a drawn match most notable for two big innings by Steve Waugh, 95 and 100 not out. This appointment followed my earlier naming as new Queensland captain, the fifth Maroons leader in five years, after Allan Border, Greg Ritchie, Trevor Hohns and Carl Rackemann. I relished the job, though I was aware that while I kept my spot in the national side I was not going to captain as many state games as I would miss. Which is exactly what happened — I was captain of Queensland for seven seasons, but only led the team in 26 of the 84 first-class matches the state played in that time.

When, after my appointment, I was asked by Wayne Smith of the *Courier-Mail* whether I was dreaming of a ticker-tape parade down Brisbane's Queen

Street Mall, with the Sheffield Shield cradled to my chest, I laughed and said, 'I suppose we all do that, and that's okay as long as it remains a fantasy and doesn't start to inhibit your thinking. But we have to develop patience. The public has to be patient and the Shield team has to be patient on the playing arena.'

When asked whether I was now a contender for the Test captaincy, once Allan Border retired, I admitted I thought I was. Of course Mark Taylor's credentials were impressive, I continued, and don't forget Steve Waugh. 'He has one of the best cricketing brains around,' I remarked, 'and he can't be discounted if he can get himself back into the Test side.'

After those two knocks in Hobart, Steve was selected, batting at No. 3 for the first three Tests, from where he scored a gutsy hundred in Sydney, and then moving down the order for the final two. Dean Jones, on the other hand, was left out, despite topping the Test batting averages in Sri Lanka. He'd come back and failed in three Shield innings, and was made 12th man in Brisbane. Western Australia's Damien Martyn was his replacement, with Steve at three and Boonie opening with Tubsy. I thought the decision to leave Deano out was wrong, but he didn't do himself any favours afterwards. He was probably the worst 12th man we ever had, was left out completely for the second Test, and never played Test cricket again. He did stay in the limited-overs side, batting as exuberantly as ever from No. 3, but he hated being tagged a one-day cricketer.

Deano is a fantastic bloke, and was the type of cricketer every team needs. The nickname of 'Legend' suited him perfectly on the cricket field, because he had a confidence, almost arrogance, that served him well. But as I got to know him better I learned that behind that brash exterior was a heart that really is in the right place. One thing I'll never forget is that Deano looked after me very well on my first English tour, when we roomed together for most of the trip. He's an emotional man, and a bloke with a million ideas, some of them crazy, some bizarre, many more than worthwhile.

Mark Waugh, who in contrast to Deano had a terrible time in Sri Lanka, kept his place in the side and rewarded the selectors by making a stirring hundred in Melbourne, when AB also scored a ton. In all the excitement about Warney's brilliant 7-52 on the last day, which included an absolutely fabulous flipper to knock over the Windies' new skipper, Richie Richardson, the skill and courage involved in those two first-innings hundreds was forgotten. People often forget you have to set a match up as well as finish it off. Still, Warney was *the* story. We now had a weapon just as dangerous as the fastest and best of the quicks. Within minutes of the game finishing, it seemed, Shane had assumed 'popstar' status. Even the next day at the airport, the media was everywhere and not just the cricket writers — the interest was much wider than that.

Another new face in the squad was West Australian left-hander Justin Langer, who came into the team for the fourth Test, in Adelaide, and nearly won us the game with a brave dig on the final day. Bowling-wise, Merv Hughes and Craig McDermott were now clearly our frontline pace bowlers, while Tim May was chosen for the fourth Test, on his home ground in Adelaide, and immediately

By the time we journeyed to New Zealand straight after the West Indies series, the video replay was in use, and I managed to get myself run out at both ends during a one-day international. Here I'm waiting for the red light, which I know will be coming at least once.

took 5-9 in the Windies' second innings. Two guys who'd been in and out of the team during my first four seasons, Greg Matthews and Mike Whitney, played their final Tests during the series

Merv and Billy certainly went hard at the West Indies throughout. Without Viv, Gordon Greenidge and Malcolm Marshall, and with Desmond Haynes a shadow of the great batsman he once was, they were not as strong as they had been. But in Ambrose, Walsh, Patterson and Ian Bishop they still had an extremely powerful pace attack, Richardson was an excellent batsman and Lara was in imposing form. And that was just enough to get them home.

Adelaide was awful. We lost by one run but we should have lost by a lot more. I blame Billy for all the heartache we went though. In the second innings, batting at No. 11, he lasted for nearly an hour and a half, faced 57 balls, scored 18 and with Maysie took us to within two runs of winning the series. He was never expected to play that well! The drama was extraordinary, as they edged towards victory. It was Australia Day, and as the match drew to its amazing conclusion, the crowd starting singing *Waltzing Matilda*. Maysie was superb, so sensible and composed. When they got within one, with Billy facing Courtney Walsh, a push to mid-off might have been the single, then Haynes at short leg got in the way of a leg side push that would have been it, then Walsh bounced one, Billy tried to get out of the way, it might have brushed something … and Darrell Hair gave it out. And it probably was out, though Billy said in the dressing room afterwards that he wasn't sure what it hit, if it hit anything at all.

AB took it hard; that was his big chance, and probably his last chance, to beat the Windies, who'd been bouncing him since 1979. Right through that final partnership, probably longer on that tense afternoon, he had an old ball, his 'worry ball' we called it, and he threw it from hand to hand, shined it up, never let it go. When the wicket fell, he stood up and threw it, hard as he could, into the viewing-room floor. Geez, this game can hurt.

I made a pair in that Test, and a quick pair, too. I think I put too much pressure on myself. For four years, I'd been fighting my natural instincts, concentrating on not being over-aggressive; now I wondered if I had become too defensive. I went in there determined to dig in, but got too negative and ended up chopping one from Walsh back onto my stumps. Maysie played it much smarter, having a crack when the chance was there, but otherwise protecting his wicket for all he was worth.

Ironically, I thought my wicketkeeping in that Adelaide Test was excellent. But it didn't matter. A number of us were totally despondent afterwards, and I recall the next morning, at the airport waiting to catch the plane to Perth, Mark Taylor said to me sadly, 'I'll take your game any day over mine.' His point was that at least I had my keeping to justify my place, whereas for that Test at least he had nothing. Tubsy had scored just 1 and 7 in the fourth Test, and would be dropped to 12th man for the final match.

> *January 27, 1993: So depressed about my batting and general persona. Negative, internal and quiet … So what, I've failed with the bat. Get on with it and 'keep throwing punches'. Don't take the easy option of giving it all up …*

Perth came too soon after Adelaide. I think the despondency we carried contributed to our poor effort there. We were crabby, distracted and looking for enemies. At one point umpire Steve Randell warned Jo Angel, playing his first Test, for bowling two bouncers in one over. 'What,' Steve Waugh taunted the ump, 'we're playing that rule today?' We didn't expect to lose in two and a half days, as we did, but we hardly thought we had a chance of winning either. Ambrose was too good, and was smart enough to realise that he didn't need to bounce us — just put them on the spot at good pace and let the pitch, which had too much moisture in it and consequently seamed all over the place, do the rest. At Ambrose's pace, and from the height he delivered the ball, he was nearly unplayable at times on that sort of deck. At one point, after lunch on the first day, he took 7-1, and almost all his victims, me included, were caught behind or in the slip cordon.

Despite the fact we actually lost the series in Perth, it's the fourth Test I always think about when I'm reminded about that summer. Adelaide was the spur. We swore we'd get them when we met them again in the Caribbean in 1995. The next one's ours, I said to myself. We didn't make any pledge as a group, but I'm sure every one of us was thinking as I was.

CHAPTER 10

A GREAT DAY
IN MY LIFE

OUR TRIP TO NEW ZEALAND, which came after the West Indies series, was the third instalment in a 20-month travelogue that began in Sri Lanka in August 1992 and would include two Australian seasons (1992–93 and 1993–94), plus tours to New Zealand (February–March 1993), Britain and Ireland (April–August 1993), South Africa (February–April 1994) and Sharjah (April 1994), with only minor pitstops in between. This, of course, meant you saw little of your home life and little of your family unless they toured with you but I, for one, didn't resent what we were being asked to do. We all knew that if we did complain, the administrators devising these programs could quickly find others who'd happily swap their jobs for ours. Anyway, I soon grew to enjoy the lifestyle, and always loved the cricket.

However, as the demands on the Australian team increased through the 1990s, there were calls in some quarters for a 'squad' approach to be applied to the team, especially in one-day cricket; a fast bowler, even the captain, might be rested from games even when fully fit. The logic was that this would lengthen players' careers. In my view, this approach would be wrong, and demeaning to international cricket. It would see the development of a 'club' mentality for the Australian cricket team. Club sides have spells in a long season where they don't play at their top, then peak for the finals. International cricket teams shouldn't do this; every game needs to be important and cricket officials need to be ultra-conscious of this fact. The Australian cricket team has prided itself on making every game special and preparing thoroughly for them all. Thus in New Zealand in 1993, we might have been a little mentally stale, and a couple of our key guys might have been carrying injuries after a long, rugged season, but we didn't deliberately take the foot off the accelerator, not even a fraction.

— ¤ —

I HAD SPENT PART of 1992–93 genuinely worried about my place in the Australian side. This was a result, mainly, of the attacks on my character. In the previous two years I'd seen Steve Waugh, Merv Hughes, Geoff Marsh, Mark Waugh, Dean Jones and Mark Taylor all get dropped for varying periods, and knew that in my case, as keeper, being left out for one game might actually mean a much longer spell on the outer. Ironically, these self-doubts were coming at a time when I truly believed that, from a playing perspective at least, I had established myself in the cricket community's eyes as the best keeper in the country — and when I'd won recognition within the team as a player with something to contribute to the development and maintenance of the team's game plans.

As I headed in to the 1993 Ashes tour, I knew I still possessed an 'Achilles heel' … my batting. After our short tour to New Zealand which followed the West Indies series, I'd scored 1434 runs in 47 Tests, at 21.73, with a highest score of 71. Such figures might have been acceptable in the days of Oldfield, Tallon and Grout, but these were the 1990s, and men such as Rod Marsh, Alan Knott and Jeffrey Dujon had made their names as better-than-handy batsmen as well as exceptional glovemen. By the time Marsh had played his 48th Test, he'd scored three Test hundreds. At this point of my life, I didn't have a single first-class century to my name.

When the selectors announced the team for the Ashes trip, I read it as significant that they declined to give the second keeping spot to a younger man, such as Victoria's Darren Berry, or NSW's Phil Emery, or even Emery's deputy, Adam Gilchrist, who'd played as a batsman for the Blues in the Shield as early as 1991–92 and was impressing as a keeper in Sydney grade cricket. Instead the selectors turned again to Tim Zoehrer.

My form in New Zealand had been average at best, as was the team's. We could only square the Test rubber and win the five-game one-day series in the final over of the fifth game. I think most of the team were jaded after the Australian season, and had half an eye on the upcoming Ashes tour, too. The exceptions were our lead bowlers, Warne, McDermott and Hughes, who all had productive Test series, although both Billy and Merv needed minor operations before they were right for the England trip.

The highlight of my tour was being at the other end when Allan Border broke Sunil Gavaskar's Test batting aggregate record in Christchurch. I suddenly broke into goose bumps when the moment came. The low point came in the same game, when a spectator put up a banner which read 'Be honest, Mr Healy'. My 'reputation' had gone international. Billy ripped it down before play began. As a close friend, he, more than most, knew how much I'd been hurting from some of the slurs on my integrity.

I actually finished second on the tour batting averages for that Kiwi trip, but scored only 86 runs in the three Tests, 54 of them in the first Test when the team made 485. Three months later, I went into the first Test of the 1993 Ashes series having scored the grand sum of 35 first-class runs since we'd arrived in England. There was no grand change in our first innings either, for after Graham Gooch won the toss and sent us in we were all out for 289 (Taylor 124, new cap Michael Slater 58, Healy 12).

England replied with 210, but on day three we got away, as David Boon and Mark Waugh added 109 for the third wicket, from 2-46, and then Boonie and AB put on a further 76 before stumps. The following morning dawned bright and sunny, but before noon our captain had been dismissed for 31 and Boonie

With Steve Waugh after reaching my first Test hundred, at Old Trafford in 1993.

had missed out on what would have been his first Test hundred in England by just seven runs. I was in at 5-252, a lead of 331. Although there were still more than five scheduled sessions remaining, my feeling was that we had enough runs already, so my attitude was let's get on with it and see what happens. If I get out, I get out; if AB declares, so be it. If I had a target, it was to set the Englishmen a target of 400 — teams never get that many batting last in a Test match.

By lunchtime we'd added 90 runs, but AB told us to keep going. I was 44 by this stage and seeing them well. I had adopted the same philosophy I'd put to Greg Chappell back in that Launceston dressing room in early 1988: I didn't think about the century at all, merely about continuing in the same vein until AB called us in. Tugga and I were running really well between the wickets, the English bowlers were uninspired, and I kept hitting them. Tugga kept farming me the strike — 'It's your day,' he laughed after another boundary. And then I went past 90 and into uncharted waters for me in first-class cricket.

It wouldn't be a bad idea, I pondered, to have a chat to the experienced man at the other end. 'Tugga,' I asked at drinks, 'what do you do when you're in the nineties?'

'I dunno,' he replied, 'I've buggered up five hundreds myself, you know. Why don't you try to do it with a six!'

The laugh was good for me. I wasn't nervous, just terribly excited. Every cricket instinct told me to keep swinging, and I did. A two got me to 95, then I struck two consecutive fours and was there. My clear memory of both those boundaries is that I struck two balls from Phil DeFreitas that were pitched around leg stump, the first hit over towards deep mid-wicket, the second to the right and over mid-on. Afterwards, everyone commented on how relaxed and confident I was in the nineties; then I saw a replay which showed both balls were actually pitched well outside off stump and I'd actually dragged them across, cavalier-like, to the leg side. I was in that 'zone' where the bowlers could have put it anywhere and I would have hit it wherever it needed to go.

June 6, 1993: ABSOLUTELY STOKED — AS WAS
TUGGA. Worked hard on each ball and stayed positive but
composed ... Team thrilled with my hundred. Simmo and
Babs, Maysie, Warney — amazing joy.

AB declared immediately, with the partnership worth 180 runs and the lead 511. The next day, despite a brave century by Gooch, we won by 179 runs with nine overs to spare, to take a 1-0 lead in the series.

I also wrote in my diary, 'Great day in my life.' But that was after the final day. I was so proud of the way I performed throughout the Poms' second innings — 'kept brilliantly all day,' I wrote — and we won so well, with Warney and Merv each finishing with four wickets for the innings. It was very satisfying to have played a pivotal part in our victory, and I was delighted, too, that Mum was in the stands to see it (she had flown over with Helen's mum to watch the early part of the series).

This Test was one of the most important of my cricket life. From this moment until just about the day my international career finished, I always felt confident about my place in the Australian Test XI. Late in the tour, at Canterbury against Kent, I took a stumping off the bowling of ... Tim Zoehrer. 'Ziggy' would actually top the tour bowling averages, spinning leg breaks well enough to take 12 first-class wickets, and was even spoken of as an outside chance to make the Test side when Maysie was in doubt at one point. But from that first Test he was never again a chance to take the Test keeping gloves. They were mine.

— ¤ —

DURING THE CELEBRATIONS that followed our first Test victory, I was brazen enough to challenge Merv Hughes to a wrestle — a couple of drinks and a Test century can make you do silly things. A bit later, Merv attacked Boonie with a fire hydrant, the blast enough to cover our little Tasmanian champion with foam and blow him into a pot plant but not sufficient to spill a drop of his beer or douse his cigarette. Boonie was terrific, reminding me all night about how well I'd played. In return, I sledged him gently about the fact that he hadn't scored a Test century in England. 'Keep trying, mate,' I advised him, 'you'll get one eventually.' In fact, Boonie was good enough to score centuries in each of the next three Tests, one of a succession of memorable Australian achievements during this brilliant English summer.

This was the first time I'd repeated a major tour, and I found things much easier the second time around. Whereas in 1989 I'd often been wary and apprehensive, this time I coped much better. I found it amusing during the early weeks of the tour, as we attended the same functions we'd been to early in '89, the lines from the gentlemen at the British Sportsman's Club and the MCC dinner were identical. 'Is this your first tour, son?' they'd ask, as they did on my first tour and would again on my third in 1997. The convict jokes were the same, too, as were the bold predictions that we'd struggle in the Test matches. One thing I do remember is the speech given by Sir Edward Heath, the former British Prime Minister, at the Sportsman's Club luncheon, which was quite magnificent.

Cricket-wise, the big plus we had in '93 that we hadn't had four years before was Shane Warne. When we arrived, the Poms were bracing themselves for an assault from McDermott and Hughes, but dismissed Warney on the basis that he was young and blonde and leg-spinners don't succeed in England anyway. When he struggled in our opening first-class game, after Graeme Hick smashed a big hundred for Worcestershire, the wise old cricket heads around England sat back and nodded as one — Warne wouldn't be a factor. Then Shane came on in his first Ashes Test and knocked over Mike Gatting immediately, with one of the best leg-breaks ever seen in Test cricket anywhere, and everything changed.

As Gatting stumbled off, a stunned buzz enveloped Old Trafford. Into our huddle from wide mid-on came Merv Hughes, who from his angle couldn't see what the delivery might have done. He had no idea what all the fuss was about.

'What'd it do?' he asked.

'Mate, it pitched off and hit off,' I replied, poker-faced.

'Oh, is that all,' he said, but soon he was back, having been told a very different story elsewhere.

'Merv, it pitched off the wicket and hit the off stump,' I explained.

Which is about what it did, but only after starting on the off stump line and then drifting viciously so it pitched around six inches outside the leg stump. Then it buzzed back to take the off bail.

Warney hadn't played in the Texaco Trophy matches that preceded the Test series, which we won 3-0, not because there was any grand strategy to leave him out, but simply because at that stage in his career he wasn't a regular in our one-day team. We still knew he was going to be a threat in the Test matches. However, the way Gatting reacted when he was bowled, as if he'd seen some sort of ghost, built up a sudden mystique that Shane didn't let diminish for the rest of the series; he thus became a very, very lethal weapon. The Poms were spooked,

Old Trafford 1993, during my first Test hundred.

Above: I wrote in my diary of this innings, my first in a Test in Australia, against the mighty Windies pace attack at the Gabba in November 1988: 'In at 5-76, hung around a couple of hours … hooked! Idiot!!' I was finally out for 27, off a slower ball, caught by Gus Logie, the short-leg fieldsman here.

Left: This was the shot that caused me a great deal of embarrassment in our second one-dayer on the 1989 Ashes tour. At the time I had a runner, Dean Jones, because of an injured knee, but I was so excited to hit the ball in the middle that I took off and ran one of the quickest twos of my life!

Above: Jack Russell, caught behind on the last day of the first Ashes Test of 1989, off Merv Hughes.

Below: Another wicket for Big Merv. Pakistan's Wasim Akram is caught behind at the MCG in January 1990. The slip cordon is (left to right): Terry Alderman, Mark Taylor, Allan Border and Steve Waugh (obscured).

Above: A victory shout in Adelaide during the 1990–91 Ashes series. The jubilant fieldsmen are Greg Matthews (centre) and Allan Border.

Below: Down and out during the 1992 World Cup, after tearing my hamstring against South Africa. Our long-serving physiotherapist Errol Alcott is trying to get the leg right, while Steve Waugh is the other batsman. These days Tugga is in such commanding form he wouldn't have to bend down to pick up his helmet — when he asked, it would just rise up to him!

Batting in the second Test, at Georgetown, Guyana, during our tour of the Caribbean in 1991, when I managed to get myself run out in both innings. As the scoreboard shows, I made 53 in the first dig. This photograph was taken late in our second innings, and I'd finish with the second top score of 47. Highest was sundries, with 53, including 28 no-balls!

Above: Brian Lara run out for 277 in Sydney, January 1993.

Below: Two of Australian cricket's finest players, and two of my all-time favourite team-mates, Allan Border and Merv Hughes, celebrate Merv knocking over England's Mike Gatting with the last ball of the fourth day's play, first Ashes Test, 1993, at Old Trafford. Gatting turned 36 this day, and given that he'd been knocked over by Warney's wonder ball in the first innings, the Test was hardly an ideal birthday present for him.

England captain Graham Gooch, stumped off Tim May's bowling during the fourth Ashes Test of 1993, at Headingley.

In the top photo, I've only just recovered from slightly fumbling the ball.

Above: These were always good nights. The Australians in Sydney after winning the World Series in 1993–94. Standing (left to right): Paul Reiffel, Glenn McGrath, Dean Jones, Mark Waugh, Craig McDermott, Matthew Hayden, Errol Alcott, Tim May, Ian McDonald (team manager). Front: Shane Warne, Steve Waugh, David Boon, Allan Border, me, Mark Taylor, Bob Simpson (coach).

Below: With skipper Mark Taylor and the Frank Worrell Trophy, during the ticker-tape parade through the streets of Sydney that followed our famous victory in the Caribbean in 1995.

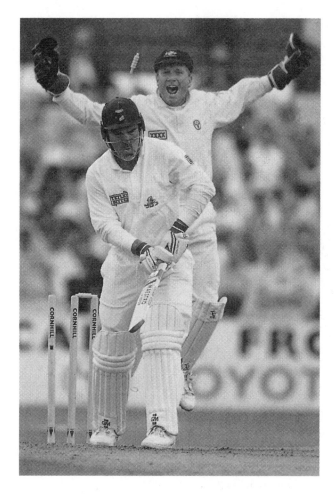

The ball of the century … Gatting, bowled by Shane Warne's first ball in Ashes cricket. Poor 'Gatt' couldn't believe it, but we already knew what Warney was capable of.

Warney's confidence skyrocketed, and he finished the series with 34 wickets, the most ever by an Australian spinner in an Ashes series in England.

For me, one of the most significant stats of that series is that while Shane captured those 34 wickets, Merv also got 31. Everyone remembers Shane's tour, but Merv's has been forgotten to some degree. The big fella got those wickets despite the fact that his pace bowling partner, Craig McDermott, fell seriously ill during the second Test and wasn't a factor during the Tests. And, most impressive of all, he got them despite the fact he had an ever-worsening bung knee that later required major surgery and five months' rehabilitation. Two pieces of Merv's bowling that series stand out. One was the way he dismissed Gatting in the second innings of the first Test, sending Gatt's stumps everywhere with the last ball of the fourth day, a fast yorker, when the batsman was clearly expecting a bouncer. The other was the way he kept charging in during the sixth Test, at The Oval, even though we were losing and his knee was killing him. There was no one else to do the job, so big Merv kept going. Off the field he was a million laughs, a walking anecdote and an intolerable pest, as he always will be. He's one of my all-time favourite people, and one of the gutsiest cricketers I had the pleasure to play with.

—¤—

MY FIRST GAME AS keeper after the first Test was at Bristol against Gloucestershire, on a wicket that was two-paced. Fourth over of the day, one stayed down and I wore it on the thumb. It was sore, but not too bad. I managed to get through the day and also survived a sponsor's promotion that night, even winning the trivia quiz. When I finally returned to my hotel room, I put the ice on it and first thing next morning Errol convinced me I needed to have the joint x-rayed. The x-ray confirmed that the joint was broken, which at least explained why it had been sore. Unfortunately, the second Test was just five days away, not that that mattered to the doctor, who flatly told me that the thumb needed to be in a splint for 28 days. 'Well, I've got three,' I responded. On the way back to the ground, Errol and I agreed it would be a good idea to not bat or keep for the remainder of the Gloucestershire game.

I was left to gently catch tennis balls, and rely on ice and heat treatment to try to get the thumb playable. I couldn't see any improvement while we were in Bristol, but by the end of our first night in London — the second Test was at Lord's — I felt things might be coming right. I had my roommate, Merv, gently throw an orange across the room, which I gloved okay. Then another one, maybe a bit harder. Tim Zoehrer was told to prepare himself for his first Test in six-and-a-half years. The next day at practice I gave the thumb a reasonable workout. Catching a tennis ball was no problem; the much harder cricket ball was not so easy, but possible. Batting was okay, but only after I modified my grip slightly. I walked away from that net sure I would play, but still obliged to face a fitness test on the morning of the game, two days away.

On the morning of the game, AB revealed at a brief team meeting that we were going in with two spinners, which for me was a bonus — not too much fast bowling to keep to. I flew through the fitness test, although in reality the responsibility for the decision was always in my hands, and I felt 100 per cent sure I wouldn't be letting anyone down by playing.

While I was telling Errol and Simmo that I was in, AB was preparing for the toss. I actually passed him in the Lord's Long Room, he on the way out to toss, me on the way up to our dressing room to get ready for the start. We didn't say a word, but a bit later, when he came back in to say we were batting, he looked at me and said, 'By the way, are you in?' I don't know what would have happened if I wasn't able to play — AB had simply assumed that I was right, and at the toss had confirmed our line-up to the game officials. I was grateful for his confidence.

And then fate bought me some extra recuperation time — we batted for two and a bit days, losing only four wickets in the process. And even luckier (for me), Billy got crook and couldn't bowl, and I was left to keep to only one fast bowler. And Merv didn't bowl very much anyway, with Warney and Maysie doing the

Above: Robin Smith, stumped off Tim May at Lord's in 1993. This was the first dismissal given by a video umpire in Ashes cricket. Below: Graham Gooch, caught behind off Warne later in the same Test.

bulk of the work, and doing it superbly. I did manage to stump Robin Smith in the first innings, which meant that he became the first man to be given out by the video-replay umpire in an Ashes Test. Merv might have been a bit tricky for me with the new ball, wobbling them about as he did, but otherwise the thumb worked okay. It was a bit sore late on days three and four, but I had no problems on the final day, when we captured the last seven English second-innings wickets to go two-up in the series.

Billy's illness was a huge shock. On the second afternoon, as our first innings score mounted towards its eventual 4-632 (Slater 152, Taylor 111, Boon 164 not out, Mark Waugh 99, Border 77), it quickly became apparent that our pace spearhead was very ill. When we first heard his groans we thought he was play-acting, and someone yelled out, 'It's all right, mate, the wicket's not that flat.' But then Tugga found Billy in agony in the toilet, fighting for air and unable to move. The preliminary diagnosis was severe appendicitis, but in fact he needed major bowel surgery, spent a week in hospital, and was out of the tour.

In contrast, my thumb was so good it never cost me a game. As usual, I had the game immediately after the Lord's Test off, and stayed in London with Helen and Emma while the team journeyed to Oxford for a three-dayer against Combined Universities. Then it was off to Southampton to play Hampshire, where I even opened the batting in the second innings.

I thought my injury worries were behind me, but after struggling to a draw in the third Test, my 50th, at Trent Bridge, I hurt an ankle in our tour game at Durham — Ian Botham's farewell first-class game — and thought I was in serious trouble once more. This time I was taking a return from Paul Reiffel and stepped back into some bowlers' footmarks. I heard a crack and thought, I'm gone here. Over the next couple of overs I became a little concerned with the noise the ankle was making, so I went off for a while and showed Hooter. We put an ankle brace on it and I returned to my keeping duties believing it would be all right. It never swelled up like a sprained ankle, hardly bruised at all, and I kept playing. But in the days that followed it became more and more apparent that the brace wasn't working, so I had Errol strap it up before play each day. And every day, that strapping got firmer and firmer. Months later, I was still having the ankle strapped — 'Any danger of getting this ankle right?' AB kept asking. 'If you're after sympathy you won't get it.' — and it wasn't until after the South African tour, in April 1994, that I had the doctors open it up, and they found that I'd wrecked the lateral ligaments.

Throughout my career I enjoyed the stress that came with fixing an injury, and the satisfaction that came from playing effectively when others reckoned I couldn't. I'm very proud of the fact that I only missed one Test through injury in my 11-year international career. I didn't like the hurt, but I was dedicated enough to do everything possible to get it right and to fight through the pain that is part of that process. Staying off the grog, plenty of sleep, late nights with the physio, ice and heat, then more ice, every hour ... I became familiar with all the steps of a quick recovery routine.

Some guys miss games, on the basis that by playing they could make things worse, more easily than others. At times, I thought these players could have tried harder. I never understood blokes pulling out because of a problem, such as the flu, that would only affect them for the first part of a game. If you're the only wicketkeeper on tour and you wake up with the flu you have to play, because there's no one else. Never once, I must stress, did I feel that I was putting myself ahead of my team by playing with an injury. But if I could possibly get through without letting the side down then I was out there.

— ¤ —

HELEN AND I LEARNED that she was pregnant again while we were on tour. I was appreciating my time with my wife and daughter more and more as we got older. Throughout our married life until this point, my entire focus had been on my sport and career — I worried most about my form, practice, preparation, injuries. When AB said no wives on tour, I agreed 100 per cent. You need the team together, thinking about cricket, I firmly believed. Even in the bar, you're thinking cricket, talking cricket, with cricketers, planning for tomorrow's cricket. However, when I wrote in my diary in June 1993 that 'total obsession with cricket not good enough this match — enjoyed family immensely (most important thing to me)', it reflected the fact that I was mellowing. During the fifth Test of this series I marked scoring 80 in the first innings by spending the night in my hotel room babysitting Emma while Helen went out with a few of the girls. I wouldn't have done that in 1989, but by this time looking after my daughter was as perfect a form of relaxation as I could think of.

Our wives, partners and family had travelled with us to New Zealand in 1993, and though I can't speak for the other guys, I know having Helen and Emma there definitely softened my approach to the cricket. Having them there was fantastic; it made me realise that there was something more important than cricket. But after such a long haul on the road, their presence did take the hard edge off the Australian team on the field.

— ¤ —

WHILE IN 1989 WE had thought we were playing top-drawer opposition in England; four years later we knew this wasn't the case. We had it all over them. New players such as Mark Lathwell, Matthew Maynard, Andrew Caddick, Mark Illot and Martin McCague were nailed as soon as they came in, to ensure that they never got up and running against us. A few, most notably Nasser Hussain and Graham Thorpe, battled hard and left us feeling they'd be good players. But really our colossal victories at Lord's and in the fourth Test, at Headingley, when AB hit an unbeaten 200, Tugga was 157 not out and Pistol Reiffel took eight wickets, reflected the vast chasm between the two teams.

The biggest change between 1989 and this trip was that this time we had respect from day one. AB had the same give-'em-nothing attitude that he had initiated in 1989, and the tour became something of a triumphal march for him.

It's party time at Leeds in '93, after our big win gave us an unassailable 3-0 lead in the series. Left to right: Bob Simpson, Merv Hughes, me, Michael Slater (obscured), Brendon Julian and Allan Border. Not a lot of things during our careers matched this winning feeling.

In contrast, their captain, Graham Gooch, walked around the field like a kid taking a bad report card home to Mum. They didn't like our on-field bravado, our aura of invincibility, but they did nothing to confront this or to discover anything about how we approached our task. Had they come into our dressing room after a Test, we would gladly have shared a beer with them. But we never saw them. They stayed on their level, we on ours.

I have always felt that if a team is beating you, the one place you must go is their dressing room, to try to discover what they're doing right. In Pakistan in 1988 we never went into their rooms, so we never learned what they did, who they were, whether they were finding things as hard as we were. Through the 1990s, England's players should have been camping themselves in our dressing room. They would have learned that we were blokes with the same form battles and self-doubts that were crippling them. They might have found out how we planned our campaigns. I think we did this to some degree with the West Indies in the 1990s, taking a few of the masks off some of their players, though in the case of their fast bowlers this can be difficult, as they stick so religiously to themselves.

July 25, 1993 (during fourth Test): Papers have placed ultra-sensitive microphones to try to detect our sledging! Can even pick up our conversations. Boys are baiting 'em now ...

At Edgbaston for the fifth Test I had another good day with the bat, smashing 80 and sharing a century stand with Merv. I was thrilled with the way the runs and keeping dismissals kept coming, and the way I was constantly focused on the job at hand. I especially enjoyed a dismissal of Graham Thorpe in this match, which came after a gentle but highly effective sledge by Steve Waugh. England were eight down in their second innings, Thorpe was unbeaten on 60 and defending well, and Tugga said to me, within earshot of the batsman, 'You watch, he'll play for the not out.' Almost immediately, Thorpe rushed out at a wide one from Warney, and swung and missed — I had a lot of work to do to get the ball back from high and far from the stumps to complete the stumping, but I did it. We eventually won by eight wickets. At The Oval, however, we crashed to a 161-run defeat; the first but not the last time we'd mar an excellent series by losing the final 'dead' Test.

There's no doubt we were ready to go home, which was only natural after such a long campaign. I remember one night late in the Test, when it was clear we were losing, and Mark Waugh disagreed that we had let ourselves down.

'We just got out,' he reckoned. 'We didn't try to get out, did we?'

'How come then,' I shot back, 'we didn't get out like this when the pressure was on?'

I was always cranky, when we lost these dead Tests, if I heard teammates saying, 'Oh well, it doesn't really matter.' It mattered to me. I was frustrated, too, that we didn't really address what was going wrong, and in the seasons following lost four Tests against England (1993, 1994–95, 1997, 1998–99) after we'd retained the Ashes.

After England had won that final Test, and we'd spent a bit of time among ourselves bemoaning the defeat, someone jumped up and said, 'Let's go in and have a beer.' So off we went to the home dressing room. But they'd gone, all but two of them, and the pair remaining were in their blazers and ties, zipping up their bags, ready to depart. Scattered around were a few champagne bottles and a few flutes, so there had been a brief party, but that was it. Apparently they all had county cricket commitments they had to dash off to. We couldn't believe it, and returned to our own room to commiserate some more over our defeat, and then to toast the tour's success.

What's the point of winning if you haven't the time to celebrate?

CHAPTER 11

THAT'S FOR YOU, GRANDPA

THE FIRST THING I NOTICED when I went out to bat in the first Test of the 1993–94 Australian summer, against New Zealand in Perth, was that the boos that had been prevalent whenever I'd played at the WACA in the past were gone. I appreciated that. The scoreboard as I walked out on that opening day showed that we were 5-164, and it struck me how often I'd come to the wicket in difficult situations against these 'weaker' Test nations. My theory is that our top order were a little more reckless against these teams than they might have been against the 'top' countries, and got themselves out trying to smash them around. Steve Waugh and I added 34 before Tugga was caught behind, after which Paul Reiffel helped me get safely through to stumps.

After play, I was pulled aside and told some dreadfully sad news, that my grandfather, George Healy, had passed away earlier in the day. While I didn't immediately swear to go on and score a hundred for him, he was in the back of my mind when I resumed batting the next morning and, once I had my eye in, his memory provided real motivation to keep going. When I did reach three figures, by slamming Danny Morrison down the ground for four, I looked straight at the Channel Nine camera beyond the mid-off boundary, pointed the bat in that direction and declared, 'That's for you, Grandpa.' It's a memory I treasure.

After that knock, I really felt that I had found *my* way of batting. This process had really begun in Sri Lanka in 1992, when I was more patient and focused, and continued in England, where I'd averaged 59 in the Test series.

Aside from that hundred, this was for me a fairly nondescript series. The Kiwis were weakened by injuries to their two most important players, Martin Crowe and Chris Cairns, and some of the side struggled against our robust approach. For example, in Hobart two weeks later, Blair Pocock and Ken Rutherford put on a 50 partnership in New Zealand's second innings and when they reached that mark the ground announcer gave the crowd details of the stand. The score was 2-84, they were trying desperately to salvage some pride after conceding a massive first-innings deficit, and Pocock had made just 15 off 97 balls. As the announcer continued, Rutherford met his partner in mid-pitch to offer some inspirational words and an encouraging pat on the shoulder, but they were interrupted by Maysie, standing nearby, who said to Pocock, 'Mate, it had absolutely nothing to do with you.' The very next ball, the Kiwi opener tried

On the way to my first Test hundred in Australia, v New Zealand at the WACA, November 1993.

to slog Shane Warne into the Derwent River and was stumped. As we celebrated the end of what proved to be the only significant stand of that innings, Maysie was quick to claim a part of the dismissal, and he was entitled to. We ended up winning by an innings and 222 runs, and then won again at the Gabba for a 2-0 series victory.

In just about every way, the New Zealand series was merely an entrée before the main event — the first Test series between Australia and South Africa since 1970, the first in Australia since 1963–64. I didn't see it as a historical moment as much as another big cricket challenge. We'd learned during the 1992 World Cup that the South Africans could play, and that in many ways they were similar to us — abrasive blokes on the field who enjoyed a battle. To many, the South Africans quickly came across as arrogant, but I bet to many observers outside Australia the Australian teams of these times and later appeared to be the same. We went hard, appealed hard, encouraged each other, had a lot of fun together and played as a team. So did South Africa, right from the word go. We discovered rapidly that while they weren't going to be super aggressive, tactics-wise, they would fight aggressively to avoid defeat.

In many ways, even for their older players, this tour was a learning experience, but we would soon see that they were learning quickly about this Test cricket business. Their senior men appeared delighted to finally have a chance in international cricket, rather than bitter about opportunities missed, and perhaps this is why they were so tough to put away from day one. In Sydney for the second Test of the series, we could have killed the match many times, but men such as their young batsman, Jonty Rhodes, the left-handed opener Gary Kirsten and the indefatigable pacemen, Fanie de Villiers and Allan Donald, persisted and persisted and finally won them a famous victory.

January 6, 1994: This was my chance to do what I had wanted to v West Indies in Adelaide ...

Lose by six runs. Billy played a sensational innings to get us close. Me — 1, bowled, chopped a half drive onto leg, then stumps when we needed 44. Wicket was difficult but we all made no special effort to go for it. Hence we dug a big hole for ourselves while wickets fell.

So I failed to pull this one off also. One close finish soon I will be the man ...

This was a very bad loss for us. From early on the first day, as Shane Warne spun them out for 169, we believed we were going to win, and it wasn't until the fifth morning that we suddenly realised we were in trouble. On the fourth day, Rhodes had played a critical knock, an unbeaten 76, and added 36 with last man Donald, whom we had thought was a real rabbit. On the fourth afternoon, needing just 117, we made it to 1-51, but then lost David Boon, nightwatchman Tim May and Mark Taylor in the last half-hour. We still thought we were okay, but had we looked closer we would have realised that the pitch was deteriorating. The next morning, de Villiers continually aimed at a dusty patch fractionally short of a good length, Donald gave away little at the other end, and we crashed 5 runs short. It would have been worse but for a barnstorming 29 not out from Craig McDermott, batting at No.10, who added 35 dramatic runs with Damien Martyn for the ninth wicket. In hindsight, we could have bowled better to Rhodes and Donald, and should definitely have shown a greater urgency when we batted on that fourth afternoon.

One South African who wasn't having a happy time in Australia was their young batsman Daryll Cullinan. From the moment the first Test, which was rained out in Melbourne, began, Cullinan kept mouthing off in the slips ... and dropping catches. It was a crazy mix. Whenever he came out to bat, he was sledging Warney, who'd respond by getting him out. Many reckoned he was a fantastic batsman, but we just thought he was a goose. You don't bag proven Test players if you are a fledgling yourself; neither do you irritate a bowler you can't play — what you need to do is meet him, learn about him, find out he's human. In the seasons that followed, while he scored plenty of runs against other outstanding bowlers, Cullinan never came to grips with Warney. And he probably never will.

Shane was the stand-out player of the summer, taking wickets wherever he went, including in the World Series. By summer's end another high-profile figure was umpire Darrell Hair, who upset the South Africans with some decisions in the Adelaide Test to such an extent that he became public enemy No. 1 on the streets of Johannesburg. By the time we arrived there in early February, someone had even written an anti-Darrell Hair song that was getting airplay! The reason was a string of lbws he gave, which we all thought were out but which our opponents didn't. Their opener, Peter Kirsten, was later fined for disputing his decision and then getting a bit excited in the Adelaide Oval viewing room after he was given out, but we thought *we* were copping a raw deal from the umpire at the other end, my old mate Terry Prue. Because we won the Test and levelled the series we didn't make a fuss about it.

By this stage of the season my ankle, sore since my stumble back at Durham six months before, was really aching. I was reduced to wearing rippled-soled

That's for you, Grandpa.

boots, because every time my sprigs caught in the turf the ankle screamed. I was also taking painkillers all the time and taping it up ever tighter. Still, to be able to get through and not have anyone know I was injured was a sure sign that my confidence was good. During the Adelaide Test I took a beauty to dismiss Cullinan — after he ducked a McDermott bouncer, the ball clipped the back of his bat that he'd left poking up behind his body like a periscope, and I dived down the leg side to snare it. Those sorts of catches, from a deflection you don't expect, are always pleasing. When I came up from that catch I was limping, not because I was in pain but because the strapping was so tight I couldn't flex my ankle. After Adelaide, I went off the painkillers but I really struggled through the first week in South Africa, so I went back to them and kept on them until I returned home.

By 1994, I felt that I understood my wicketkeeping technique and was aware of what it took for me to be consistently on top of my game. If a bad day came along I was able to rectify things immediately, rather than pray for the answer, while my diaries, which comprehensively documented my ups and downs, were invaluable. I now rarely had two bad Tests in a row. As my expectations peaked, a bad day might involve just a fumble or two. My confidence was further boosted by the way I'd risen to the challenge of keeping to Shane Warne, and to

On the balcony of the SCG home dressing room with Mark Waugh, watching us crash to a five-run defeat against South Africa.

Tim May, too. Originally I resolved not to let mistakes worry me when I kept to the spinners, but to learn from them, and this approach helped me really enjoy keeping to them. I found staying positive to be a real benefit — it's amazing how the mind can shape the way your feet and gloves move. As a person and cricketer I was really starting to understand the scale of the stage I was playing on and my part in the action taking place on it. I was aware of the influence we might have on children and adults watching us — perhaps having a child of my own had an impact. Some players and observers mightn't like me; most, I think, respected me. I saw myself as 'the drummer in the band', as Kiwi keeper Ian Smith called his autobiography, at the hub, constantly driving the team but rarely at the forefront.

— ¤ —

I'VE NEVER SEEN MYSELF as a political animal — either cricket politics or that stuff they do in Canberra. But I must confess to being a little intimidated by the potentially explosive political situation in South Africa when we arrived there in February 1994. I certainly had no idea what to expect, so you can imagine how we felt when just about the first thing that confronted us on the way from Johannesburg airport to our hotel was a terrible car accident, involving a mini-bus. Bodies were strewn everywhere, as were pieces of wreckage, and it really did look as if a bomb had gone off. My first thought was, 'Get us outta here, I want to go home.' Then, on our first day, after a sleep-in in our rooms, we decided we wanted to go out for a drink and the guy on the concierge's desk at our hotel recommended a pub called 'Foxy's'. As soon as we walked in, not long after we'd been frisked at the door, they started playing the Darrell Hair song and from that moment we had a fantastic time. However, when we returned to our hotel, we were greeted like prodigal sons. The hotel manager couldn't believe we'd gone there; most locals were steering well clear after a man had been shot in that same beer garden earlier in the week. Occasionally at matches I'd ask why helicopters were hovering overhead and the answer would be that there was an African National Congress rally taking place nearby, while the security guys shadowing us sometimes had frightening stories of skirmishes at political demonstrations. And everywhere there were guns. It didn't feel a safe place, even though we were more sheltered from the divisions between colours and classes than exposed to them. Meeting both Nelson Mandela and FW de Klerk was quite inspirational, but as was always the case when being introduced to famous people on tour, there wasn't enough time to enjoy a long, meaningful conversation.

> *March 5, 1994 (after second day, first Test): 10-248 and could've been worse. Billy made 31 at the end, and Tugga 44 not out. Two silly run outs in middle. I made 11 and chopped one on. South Africa fielded very well. Many undisciplined shots. Once again, we've gone off the boil. AB spits it — team mood has turned desperate ...*

This was the first tour where we played a lot of one-day internationals. There were eight in all, four each side of a three-Test series. Coming as it did at the end of the best part of 20 months of cricket, it might not have been surprising — though no excuse — that at various stages our tempers were frayed, not least in the first Test at the Wanderers Ground in Jo'burg, when Warney had his infamous run-in with South African opener Andrew Hudson and Merv had his equally infamous clash with a spectator. I had no idea Shane's blow-up was coming, I don't think any of us did. He might have been niggled by the crowd down at fine leg, but basically he bowled Hudson after the opener had held us up for three hours and then charged at him, abusing him as he did so. I got the shock of my life and even had to physically restrain Warney from getting too close to the batsman, though I know he had no plans to manhandle him. It looked ugly and was ugly. Merv simply lost patience with a bloke in the crowd who spat at him and then abused him. We'd all copped plenty from the mob surrounding the race up from the ground to the dressing rooms and could understand Merv banging the fence to get the so-called fan's attention. But we also knew it was wrong.

Shane and Merv both fronted the ICC referee, Donald Carr, and were each fined $400. Significantly, Merv was not reported for the clash with the unruly spectator but for an earlier incident where he'd given Gary Kirsten a spray. Our manager, Cam Battersby, thought the provocation was so great that he decided to forget about the confrontation with the spectator in the race. Another fellow who'd been close by when it happened offered to pay Merv's fine, unaware that he had actually been penalised for another offence.

We didn't learn that the ACB were dissatisfied with the size of the fines imposed on the two guys until we arrived at the Sun City resort for a couple of days off. At a meeting in the manager's room, rumours were confirmed that the

With Steve Waugh (left) and Matthew Hayden, atop Table Mountain overlooking Cape Town and with a glorious sunset in the background, during our tour of South Africa in 1994.

two incidents had been replayed ad nauseam on TV back home and as a consequence the Board had reviewed the matter and fined the pair $4000 each. I thought that was an appalling overreaction, we all did, and wondered exactly who these Board members were who had come up with the decision. There had been no attempt to get the guys' version of events and no avenue of appeal. Four days later, when we were at Stellenbosch for a game against Boland, we specifically requested that the ACB officials who had flown over to South Africa stay out of our dressing room.

At this point, the tour wasn't going well. We had lost the first Test and were down 3-1 in the one-dayers. On the bus to Sun City, AB was into us for our attitude, suggesting it was as if we were in South Africa on holidays. But in the week after the first Test we turned it around, using the feeling that everyone was against us to our advantage, and in the second half of the tour we fought back to square the Test and one-day series.

However, while our morale picked up before the second Test, in Cape Town, it wasn't until the last 30 minutes on day four that things began to come good, as the home team crashed from 2-94 in their second innings to 6-100 by stumps. As we'd gleaned a first-innings lead of 74 over the first three and a half days, it meant the game had stunningly turned from a boring draw into a probable Australian victory. The heroes were Steve Waugh, who finished the innings with five wickets and Shane Warne, who took three.

My favourite wicket, though, was not one from that late-afternoon collapse, but the first one to fall the next morning. When we arrived at the ground we looked over the nets and saw big Brian McMillan flaying away at his net bowlers, most of them spinners. He was hitting them a million miles, and looked in imposing touch. Was this the way he was going to attack the bowling when play resumed? We hoped not. We much preferred that they, and especially him, did no more than try to defend the day out.

During the first over, as soon as McMillan came on strike, I turned to a fieldsman near me and said, 'We're going to have to bowl really well here, because I saw McMillan in the nets this morning and he was smashing 'em everywhere.' Soon after I added, 'Brian's fast becoming one of my favourite players. We're gonna have to bowl really tight here, Tugga.'

For half an hour McMillan did no more than stonewall, a shadow of the Colossus from the nets. He fell, lbw to Steve Waugh, for 3. A few days later, in the final Test, in Durban, he stopped at one point when he was batting and quipped, 'You know, Heals, you're one of my very favourite players.' That was when I realised just how well some of the one-liners had worked back in Cape Town. Like Maysie back in Hobart, I thought I'd done my bit.

There was a huge build-up to the third Test, in Durban, but the game fell flat — largely, in my view, because the home team weren't adventurous enough to win. After we were sent in on a lively track and managed to make 269, South Africa batted for more than 200 overs, nearly 14 hours, for 422. It was a pity that what should have been a thrilling finale turned into a dull draw. No wonder Warney said to me, when we went for a jog before play that day, 'Heals, there's no way I'll be playing cricket when I'm 30!'

Even today, the South Africans play too conservatively in my opinion. Their emphasis is too much on not losing, when it should be on entertaining and making players face the pressure of having only two choices, winning or losing, rather than the soft, opt-out option of the draw. I believe one of the greatest strengths of the Australian teams of the 1990s was that we played aggressive cricket naturally, a style that evolved when Allan Border was captain, even though he was by nature a conservative leader. The team had a naturally aggressive bent and AB went with it. Mark Taylor was the captain who made this style of cricket our mantra, arguing that we were good enough to win in most situations so long as we backed our natural ability. Steve Waugh's team in 1999–2000 took this approach to an even higher level and won a string of Test matches and one-day internationals, sometimes from well behind, largely on the back of it. The NSW teams that Tubsy and Tugga were a part of in the late '80s and early '90s played this way at Shield level and it was a style we successfully brought to the Queensland team in the '90s.

> *April 5, 1994: Good tour; can improve my overall keeping intensity and desire to repeat my Ashes tour. Great effort with ankle injury. With this rest, I will be ready to produce some of the most authoritative performances yet. Really looking forward to next summer.*

THAT BORING DRAW IN Durban turned out to be Allan Border's last Test. In retrospect, and having been through the same scenario in 1999, I have no doubt that the pressure of trying to work out how to end his career preyed on his mind throughout that tour. The team itself was a bit tired and grumbly and AB was the worst, too often pushing a negative vibe and by doing so making it harder for anyone else to pick the team's spirit up. It's so hard, though, I know now, when you've got more on your mind than others realise. His team wasn't winning, and he was only trying to decide what to do with the rest of his life. Career-wise, AB's problem was that he didn't want to go to Pakistan, which was where we were scheduled to tour from August to October. Maybe he would have liked to play another summer with the Test team, but his attitude was you either play all the games or you play none. Maybe AB was ready to retire after South Africa, but it's such a hard decision. You're a long time off the field once you're gone.

After the tour, I reckon the ACB should have offered AB the chance to skip Pakistan and have another season at home. Such was his skill and toughness, he wouldn't have let anyone down under those circumstances. That's how the team felt, but instead, for some daft reason, the Board ignored him while calling Tubsy, Stephen, Boonie and me to Melbourne for what amounted to individual job interviews. At least it felt like a job interview, and I'm sure AB back in Brisbane would have perceived it as such. Soon after, he called reporter Pat Welsh, whom he was good mates with, at Channel Seven in Brisbane, teed up an interview, and told the world he was retiring. Just like that.

I'm sure AB and Simmo had been copping flak from the Board over a number of issues relating to the Australian team. I don't think the ACB liked the way that we were prepared to throw a positive image out the window for the sake of winning. The Board members were big on the term 'siege mentality' which I think meant that, as far as the Board members were concerned, we saw our relationship with them as us against them. Which, unfortunately, was often about right. However, it was near impossible to build a bond with men we never saw and didn't know, who had great power in Australian cricket, made important decisions about Australian cricket, but rarely seemed accountable for those decisions. If these officials were better known to the players, then the players would have known what these official's roles were and how best to put their complaints about and suggestions for the way the game was heading. In return, the Board would have been better able to put their arguments to the players.

I was always confused about a philosophy that certainly was within the ACB, and still is to a degree, that being proactive can cause trouble rather than improve things. One thing I've learned in business is that making decisions can be difficult, but it has to be done. In the corporate world, every board member needs to be fully informed, and procrastination can be a killer. But as far as the players of the early and mid '90s were concerned, the Board was neither enlightened nor dynamic.

Those interviews that might have precipitated AB's retirement were a real case in point. Four of the country's leading players were invited to a 'get to know you'

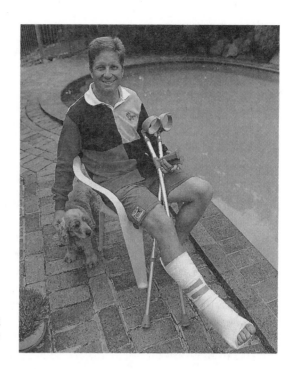

Back home in Brisbane, soon after having surgery on the crook ankle that I'd carried through the 1993–94 season.

interview, one player grilled by 17 Board members. Perhaps they were attempting to right past wrongs, but it seemed very peculiar. Together, the four of us had been playing international cricket for a combined 29 years, yet the Board members felt they knew so little of us they needed to haul us in to learn more about how we thought and who we were. I quickly realised that they seemed to know much more about my 'image' than they knew of me. They sought my opinion on a number of subjects, including prize money levels, player-of-the-year awards, contracts, the role of the captain, senior players and the coach, on and off-field player behaviour, the players' 'siege mentality', how the administrators were perceived by the players. I couldn't stop thinking it was a test. I was upfront and honest, which I hope helped.

In the lead-up to those interviews, we four players never discussed who would be AB's successor. I think we just accepted that unless something strange happened Tubby would get the job. As for the vice-captaincy, I was pretty sure I'd get it, if only because cricket politics demanded that if the captain was from NSW, as Tubby was, and the coach was from NSW, as Simmo was, they weren't going to make a Bluebag vice-captain as well. I even made a few dollars out of that — $800 to be exact. On the way home, I learned that Centrebet, the sports betting agency, was offering 4-1 about the Taylor-Healy exacta, so I rang them up, told them who I was, assured them I had no inside information but informed them of the interviews we'd just completed, and put $200 down. My brothers and sister got a bit of the 4s too, but when my uncle phoned, the odds had been tightened in. That's the only bet on cricket I've ever had in my life.

CHAPTER 12

BAD BREAKS
IN PAKISTAN

THE FIFTH TEST OF THE 1993 Ashes tour was a good one for me, and the team. Our eight-wicket victory gave us a 4-0 series lead, and I was delighted with my performance, which featured an 80 and five dismissals. However, we were intrigued and mystified by an incident that occurred before play on the final day. At the time we were 0-9, needing 120 to win. On the televisions in the members' bar, replays of England's victory at Edgbaston in 1981, when Ian Botham took 5-1 and Kim Hughes' Australians were bowled out for 121, chasing 150, were being shown.

A call came out for Allan Border. A former Pakistan Test player had sent a message to the Australian captain, asking if he could talk to him for a minute. When AB returned after that brief chat he had a curious look on his face. He had, he told us, just been offered a considerable amount of money if he could arrange for us to fail in our run chase! When confronted later, the man who made the offer dismissed it as a joke, but AB was adamant this was not the case. We couldn't believe that such a proposal had been made, and laughed at it, treating it as unique. As we know now, we should have been much more suspicious …

—✠—

IN SOUTH AFRICA, I'D APPROACHED Bob Simpson to ask him if it would be okay for me to skip the trip to Sharjah that had been tacked on to the end of that tour. I'd already spoken to Laurie Sawle, back after the Adelaide Test, and he had told me I could miss Sharjah if I wanted to. I was sick of the ankle and wanted to get home to my heavily pregnant wife. Laura, our second daughter, arrived on April 19, and a week later I was in hospital myself, for an ankle reconstruction. The plaster cast and surgical boot stayed on for six weeks, and for much of June the lower leg was as stiff as a board. By the time I regained my mobility, not long before the pre-tour camp, I was fatter than I'd ever been in my life, but also far removed from the fatigue I'd felt after the 20 months of cricket we'd completed in April. Losing that extra weight was bloody hard work, but enjoyable, too, once I got started.

The vice-captaincy was an added spur. At that point I saw myself as something of a successor to Geoff Marsh, and knew that Swampy, always conscious of his responsibilities and a firm believer in the adage 'do as I do', would never have turned up to a pre-tour camp way out of nick. When the appointments were announced, I'd been asked, naturally, if I saw the vice-captaincy as a stepping stone to the top position when Tubby's reign was over. No, I said, and I meant it. I was more concerned with being a good deputy, which to me meant making sure all the blokes are happy, that the atmosphere within the team is fine, and that any complaints are dealt with through the right channels. On the field, I've always thought the wicketkeeper was in the perfect position to be vice-captain, as he is in the thick of it, can see how the batsmen are going about their tasks and how the wicket is playing. And he can tell better than even the bowlers how the bowlers are going.

The fact that I was vice-captain made little difference to the way I approached the tour of Sri Lanka and Pakistan. The biggest change Tubby brought was to make each of us more accountable for our roles within the team. Nothing was left to chance. I probably felt a tinge of extra responsibility, especially with AB absent, but I doubt that was reflected in any major change in the way I prepared or interacted with my teammates. Without doubt, I reacted positively to the way Tubby wanted everyone and everything to be organised. My personal ambition was to regain what I called my 'Ashes '93 intensity'.

By the time we arrived in Karachi for the first Test of the tour, we'd already failed to make the final of a limited-overs tournament in Sri Lanka after beating Pakistan but losing to India and our hosts. I felt that I was heading into the Test matches in pretty good form, especially considering my 'lazy' off-season.

That game we won in Sri Lanka is a match that has aroused much suspicion in the light of the ongoing cricket bribery scandal. In late 1998 Pakistan's left-hander, Saeed Anwar, told a Lahore court that in his opinion the game was rigged. At the same inquiry, a bookmaker admitted he'd offered two of the Pakistanis big money to throw a match against Australia (he didn't specify which one). I think this is the game their captain at the time, Salim Malik, allegedly alluded to years later when he said there was an Australia-Pakistan one-dayer in the '90s where both teams were trying to lose. However, though we were a bit rusty, first up from a spell, I can assure him we were doing our best. We made 179 from our 50 overs, on a pitch I described in my diary as a 'slow turner making it difficult to play big shots'. It was very, very hot and sticky, and Warney and I were exhausted after we added 46 for the seventh wicket without hitting a boundary. In reply, Pakistan was looking good at 1-77, but from that point their run chase slowed to a crawl and they finished at 9-151. It never occurred to me at the time that anything was wrong. In my diary I wrote of our performance, 'Fielding great, bowling excellent. Anwar went after Maysie. Me: catch and stumping. Great win.' I've thought since that maybe some of the Pakistanis weren't as decisive as they could have been, but that's the trouble with all this bribery business — you can take any number of performances in any number of games and put your own bent on them. I prefer to think that we bowled well and under the pressure we built up they struggled.

Before the Karachi Test I wrote, 'Going to have a dirty big go here — won't be easy.' This, of course, was a return to the scene of my Test debut, and I was determined to make up for that defeat. Since the early '90s the team had adopted the motto 'to lose patience is to lose the battle' and this was the tour when we really set out to apply that mantra — umpires and inadequate facilities were not to be whinged about, practice was to be as effective as possible. And for the best part of three days, the match was a beauty for Australia, but only after Tubby marked the start of his Test captaincy career by winning the toss, and then getting himself out for nought. But though we struggled to 4-95, Michael Bevan, on debut, played beautifully for 82, Tugga made 73 and I scored 57 as we totalled 337, which proved sufficient for an 81-run first-innings lead. After Tubby completed an unfortunate pair, Michael Slater, David Boon and Mark Waugh set about giving us a huge advantage, and by late on the third afternoon we were 2-171, a lead of 252. There was hardly any time left, and I started to pack up my gear, but Warney saw me and quipped, 'Geez Heals, you wouldn't want a couple of wickets to fall.'

I just laughed. Seven balls later, I was out there, after Pakistan's awesome pace duo, Waqar Younis and Wasim Akram, blasted out Junior, then Bevo, then Tugga. I was in such a rush I forgot the inside thigh pad for my back leg, and we all know where the first ball I faced was going to hit me. It was typical Pakistan cricket. They could go along at their own pace and then, boom, boom, they changed gear. Wasim and Waqar were quick and they were swinging the old ball. All of a sudden we had a game on. Bar Boonie, who batted through the next day for 114 not out, no one after Junior reached 10, and we ended up setting them 314 to win. At stumps on day four Pakistan were 3-155.

Loosening up in Rawalpindi, in the early days of our 1994 tour of Pakistan.

October 1, 1994: Keeping well again — drifting a little with the tension. NOT THE OUTCOME.

We'd gone into the Test with a very inexperienced pace attack, after Craig McDermott pulled out because of an infected ingrown toenail. Glenn McGrath had made his Test debut the previous Australian summer, while Jo Angel was playing in his second Test, after first appearing against the West Indies in Perth in early 1993. On this last day, while 'Pigeon' McGrath was off the field because of a strained quadricep, Joey was fired-up and excellent, despite getting himself reported for dissent after an lbw appeal was turned down. Most of our hopes, however, depended on our two class spinners — Warne and May — with Steve Waugh offering medium-pace support.

Next morning, I learned that the previous night, Salim Malik had contacted Warney around 10.30pm with an offer we couldn't believe. If he and May bowled badly, and Pakistan won, there would be US$200,000 for each of them, Shane was told. Warney came back to Maysie, his roommate, and told him what had just happened, and Maysie replied, 'I hope you told him where to go.' But Warney was so stunned he hadn't said anything.

The last day was one of the most dramatic I have ever been involved in. Maysie had woken with a crook neck, and with McGrath also out a huge load fell on our champion leg-spinner, but we started brilliantly, with Warney causing problems with his flipper. He quickly took three wickets, Angel chipped in with the key scalp of the Pakistan captain, and at 7-184 it looked as if a rare Australian victory in Pakistan was about to occur.

Inzamam had been held back to No. 8 and he and their keeper, Rashid Latif, added 52 for the eighth wicket before Tugga got the breakthrough. Then Inzamam and Waqar Younis added a further 22 before I took a good catch to dismiss Waqar off Warne. Inzamam had been scratching around and they needed 56 to win, an ask no last pair had ever made to win a Test match.

Until now. I remember the tension, and how excited the spectators were. With the little leggie Mushtaq Ahmed, Inzamam suddenly found his hitting form and rapidly pushed Pakistan towards a dramatic victory. They hit superbly and very sensibly while we refused to yield. It was bloody good, tense cricket. I thought Warney was outstanding throughout those final overs and Tubby's captaincy was excellent.

With three runs needed, the great spinner and new captain had a conference, and then created a gap at midwicket. The hope was that Inzamam would go for the empty space and maybe get a leading edge.

In fact it worked even better. From around the wicket, Warney bowled a beauty and Inzamam, I'll never forget it, went to work it through the legside, his feet came together, and the ball spun through him, between bat and pad. I thought it was going to bowl him and got a bit stiff with my gloves and body — if your eyes don't stay with the ball as it spins past the bat you're in trouble. The height wasn't a problem, but my gloves didn't move to the ball, so when it missed

Worse miss of my life. Inzamam-ul-Haq has swung and missed, but with the stumping on the ball has shot through me and down to the boundary. Bowler Shane Warne, silly point Steve Waugh (obscured) and slip Mark Taylor can only choke on their appeals. I still find it very hard to look at these photographs.

the off stump it buzzed low between my legs and down to the boundary. Four byes! It wasn't an easy stumping but I should have made it, especially in that pressure situation. I couldn't believe it. While my teammates choked on appeals and held their heads, in total despair I kicked over the stumps.

That last ball ruined a fantastic Test for me. To that point I'd been rapt in the way I was keeping, and I'd also made a key half-century in our first innings. What went wrong?

> *October 2, 1994: My first real blemish for the game. UNBELIEVABLE feeling (numb, can't talk). The game we shouldn't have lost.*

> *October 3, 1994: Started to speak an hour or so later (swear words). Can't believe we lost. Few beers at British Embassy — good chat with Simmo, Tug, Tubs, Hoot, Slats, Warney, Maysie. Must now get on with it. 'Use it as an experience — life's realities experienced from the canvas.'*

That night, Warney and Maysie told Tubby, and later, Simmo and manager Col Egar about Salim Malik's approach, and a report was passed on to the ACB and International Cricket Conference (ICC). Thus began a process that by 2000 had exposed a web of corruption and deceit that involved many of cricket's biggest names. And in a sense, I was involved too, because every time this match is referred to in media stories about possible match-fixing, the reports always add, sometimes in an almost sinister way, that the match ended when Australian wicketkeeper Ian Healy missed a stumping. One Australian journalist who certainly wasn't there in 1994 and has rarely written about cricket in the past described my mistake in May 2000 as a 'regulation' stumping, which it certainly wasn't, in a story that told again how the Pakistan captain had tried to bribe Australian players to throw the Test. Maybe I'm paranoid, but it's as if I'm guilty by association — the bribe was offered, the stumping missed, game lost, I'm a part of it.

In the years since, as the cricket match-fixing scandal has earned more and more headlines, any number of unsubstantiated allegations have been made. People recall South Africa's Herschelle Gibbs dropping a sitter at the World Cup and assume he's throwing the game, without mentioning that he'd earlier scored a century in the same game. All I know is that that stumping error of mine in Karachi in 1994 was the cruellest miss of my cricket life. If I'd made it, it might have been the greatest dismissal of my entire career — the tricky stumping that won us a Test in Pakistan by two runs. Instead, I hated the fact that I'd cost the team the game.

— ¤ —

UNFORTUNATELY, WE HAD TO back up for another Test just two days later in Rawalpindi. All I could think of was where my hands and feet were — not surprising, really, because for two days I'd been reliving the fact that on the

Bags packed, broken thumb in a cast, I'm preparing to leave a tour early for the first time in my life.

fateful ball my hands and feet were in the wrong place — which meant I wasn't moving naturally. I put myself under so much pressure to perform perfectly that, of course, I had a shocker. In the two weeks after the second Test, we played limited-overs internationals in Lahore, Multan, Faisalabad and then back to Rawalpindi, and I felt my timing was coming back, but then in that fourth game I misjudged a delivery from Craig McDermott which ran along the ground, and smashed my left thumb. This was the same game in which Mark Waugh was offered a lot of money to bat badly and went out and made 121 not out. He immediately reported the approach to management.

When the ball struck the thumb, I whipped my glove straight off and shook my hand, which I couldn't remember doing before and have certainly never done since. It was purely instinctive. And then it was desperately painful to get the glove back on. I kept for a couple more overs, two by Billy, two by Maysie, but then decided to go off and have it checked out. It just didn't feel right, but Errol couldn't find anything wrong. He pushed at the tip of the thumb, where the ball had hit, but that didn't hurt. Then the first joint. Still nothing. 'Hooter,' I said, 'let's just strap it up and I'll go back out there.' And then he asked, 'What about this,' as he pushed at the base of the thumb, near the wrist, and I said 'Ouch!' or words to that effect. Boonie, who was having the game off, said he'd accompany me to hospital, so off we went in what would have had to be the world's dirtiest ambulance. I sat on the spare tyre, Boonie on the floor. There were no beds, no seats, I was having all sorts of scary visions of where they were taking me but from the moment we arrived at the hospital they looked after me magnificently. It took about 20 overs, that's all, to get through the traffic, into the hospital, x-rays, treatment, plaster and back to the ground. I had the way they set the broken bones checked when I arrived back in Brisbane and was told everything had been done excellently.

I knew even before a doctor looked at it that my unbroken run of 64 Tests was over. The thumb wouldn't function, and Errol had confirmed that there was something wrong, so I would have made a fool of myself if I'd tried to keep with it. I'd managed with broken bones lower in the fingers, but this fracture was at the base of the thumb joint, and the tour management was straight on the phone to call Phil Emery over to replace me. Justin Langer filled in for one one-dayer, then 'Emers' played in the one-day tournament final, which we won, and then in the drawn third Test.

So now it was back to Dr Peter Myers, who set me a program that involved two weeks of doing absolutely nothing, keeping the thumb as immobile as possible, then off with the plaster and start squeezing tennis balls, squash balls and putty. The last week, he programmed a series of exercises which had the joint pretty much fully operational by the time the opening tests of the '94–95 Ashes series began, though Peter was still fearful that the bone would be more like hard toothpaste than strong enough to catch a cricket ball for five days. Luckily, the bone stood up to that test. I was fortunate, too, that the selectors took a benevolent view — despite the fact I was going into the match without a Shield game under my belt they took the attitude that a thumb was something that was either right or not right, and if Errol and I felt it was okay then I could play. Errol did give the damaged digit a routine fitness test, which I sailed though.

One thing I look back on in regard to my cricket injuries is that I was very lucky in terms of timing. People look at my record, missing only one Test in 120, and reckon I was injury-free, which of course I was to some degree. I did get hurt, but luckily managed to time the injuries so I hardly missed a game. That thumb cost me six weeks, but only one Test; at another time it might have kept me out of an entire series. Similarly with the busted finger in 1991, which occurred on the last day of the fifth Test. Had that happened in the second Test, I might have missed a couple of Tests and a string of one-dayers. The knee in the one-dayer in England in '89 … had that occurred in the third one-dayer I might have had to miss the first Test, and at that point in my career missing one Test might have changed my career path dramatically.

— ⌧ —

THE MATCH-FIXING STORY took another turn during the following Australian season, just before we were to leave for the Caribbean, when we became aware that Shane Warne and Mark Waugh had accepted money from a gentleman while we were in Sri Lanka for the one-dayers that preceded the Pakistan Tests. This had come out after ACB team manager Ian McDonald had asked some questions in response to persistent rumours about a connection between the Australian team and Indian bookies, and when the two blokes admitted what they'd done, the Board fined them. A number of us didn't agree with them being penalised, because we saw them as having being paid for supplying nothing more than details they were also giving out in media interviews. Of course we were naive to think that, but we had no idea how widespread cricket betting was. Certainly, as far as the Board and the players were concerned, once the matter with Shane and Mark was dealt with that was it — the Board wanted to keep the matter in-house, as did we, and we'd all been left in no doubt as to what to do next time a benevolent bookie turned up seeking seemingly innocent information.

I thought the Board's thinking was right — they wanted to protect the players — but, of course, I would think that. I didn't see keeping the information from the public as being morally wrong, and like everyone aware of the fines imposed on my two teammates I badly underestimated the extent of the media scrutiny. Maybe it was inevitable that the story would come out. But again I stress that at the time we had no idea how big this scandal was. When the full story emerged in late 1998, the fact that it had been kept secret for nearly four years didn't help Shane and Mark's reputations at all, but I still believe that the decision made back in 1995 to try to keep it private was right, even if hindsight says it was misguided.

CHAPTER 13

ASHES PAIN, SHIELD GLORY

WHEN I WAS A BOY, no more than 11 or 12, my mother sat me down to give me a quick cricket lesson. 'Ian,' she'd gently begin, 'you'll never make big scores if you keep getting out to that hook shot. Why don't you give the hook up until you're past 50 runs.'

I'm not sure I ever listened; if I did I didn't do it very quickly. Even when I made my first Test hundred, at Old Trafford in 1993, for most of it the Englishmen had two men back for the lofted shot and I kept trying to hook the bouncers either side of them. Mum was there that day; I knew exactly what was going through her mind as I flailed away. At another time, after I was caught on the fence at the Adelaide Oval after playing a feeble 'flip' shot, I took a call from Mum, who began with, 'Ian, what have I told you about the hook shot?' Just like my hook shot, I acted instinctively … and hung up on her! Which, of course, only made me feel worse, so I called her straight back, to let her finish. I had to … I knew she was right.

During the 1994–95 summer, after I'd captained Queensland to a critical loss against Western Australia at the Gabba, I had a similar 'non-conversation' with my father, who'd seen me bat during the match.

> *January 24, 1995: Dad rings up to tell me, 'You're low at the crease, arms are in a diamond shape, not allowing you to hit through the ball.' I hang up!!*

Now before you start thinking I am, or was, an impulsive hanger-upper, these are isolated incidents. As had happened with Mum, I was soon back on the phone, constructively discussing my cricket with Dad. Later, I added in my diary entry for that day, 'Must compose my thoughts and improve my energy for this Test.' I hadn't been in good batting form in the first three Tests of the summer, and was in my room developing a firm strategy for the upcoming Adelaide Test.

> *January 25, 1995: BATTING: 1. Low and strong; 2. Ball — maximum energy on each one; 3. NEVER WORRY ABOUT GETTING OUT.*
>
> *With No. 3 have definite plan as to what I can do to each bowler. Achieve low, strong, invincible position. Make them bowl to me — play straight or leave on offside.*
> *WORK STARTS TODAY.*

My diaries became something of a bible for me, a resource I could consult when things were going well or badly. It was where I recorded my desires and ambitions, such as when I wrote in October 1990, 'I want to be the best keeper in the world. Tomorrow is a good place to start.' And two weeks earlier: 'Think about it. Love your job. Bat like a batsman and not like a tailender. Too many things flood the mind. Have fun.' A constant theme was 'Not the Outcome', meaning I should be concerned about exactly what was in front of me, not what might or could happen. For example, in March 1995, in Barbados, I wrote, 'A little hesitant, be positive. Worrying about outcomes — will this one spin a lot? — just stay down, move and watch it so that I'll react appropriately.'

My diaries were also where I reminded myself about my role in the team, such as in November 1988, when I wrote, 'When we are down, myself included, I must be the determined, positive and encouraging person. My performance will rub off on the team.' And I was also prepared to be critical, such as this bagging in January 1992: 'The most gutless shot I have played in my career. I deserved to be dropped for lack of pride. Attempted swish across the line against the spin. Straight up in the air, caught by Prabhakar off Shastri. One session to bat, five down ... nice time to have brain fade ...'

The diaries were also where I'd record the occasional amusing line from my teammates, such as when Allan Border said to Merv Hughes, 'If you want to sort your control out why don't you look at a place on the pitch, just short of a length outside off-stump.'

'What for?' my 1989-90 diary reckons Merv replied, 'I never bowl there.'

There was the time in Sri Lanka in 1992 when AB recalled an incident from the tied Test in Madras in 1986. Allan had got himself involved in a blue with the umpire that ended with AB aggressively pointing his finger at the ump. Apparently it all looked very menacing, and the crowd would have thought that AB was very sure of himself. In fact, when AB stormed away from the umpire and walked over to his vice-captain David Boon, the first thing he said was, 'The ump can't send me off, can he?'

What about Mark Waugh after he'd made a hundred in his debut Test in early 1991? 'They should have given me a game two years ago,' he quipped.

And then there was the one-day international against Zimbabwe at the Bellerive Oval in Hobart in December 1994. Tim May was bowling to the Zimbabwean captain, Andy Flower. He flighted one down the leg side and I managed to complete the double — Flower, caught behind *and* stumped Healy, bowled May, 39. Of course it went in the book as merely caught. Afterwards, the journos in the press box raced to talk to me to discuss my cunning gesture to the bowler immediately before that delivery, how I'd advised Maysie from behind the batsman's back that he should spear the ball outside the leg stump. Sorry to disappoint you, guys. The truth was I was simply throwing a piece of dirt away — I wasn't signalling to Maysie at all! And he wasn't even looking at me at the time.

—¤—

THAT ZIMBABWE GAME WAS one of the seven one-day internationals we won during the '94–95 Australian summer, our only loss being to England in Melbourne in mid-January, despite an innings of 56 in 63 balls by I. Healy, which ended up being the highest score of my one-day international career. I was in at 5-76 that day, a situation that didn't happen too often but when it did I always tried to take advantage. Being in that early also meant that we were struggling, and it wasn't easy, but I did relish the challenge of chipping away, keeping the run-rate going while trying to restore the innings. That World Series demonstrated how rare my opportunities were with the bat. In seven one-dayers that season — I missed one game because of a slight injury — I only batted four times, and one of those innings was a 9 not out that involved just 11 deliveries. My other two innings were a 40 off 43 balls and 15 off 20.

The game I missed was against Australia A, who were involved in the World Series apparently because the ACB didn't think that Zimbabwe were a big enough attraction to be the 'third' team after Australia and England. As in Pakistan, my replacement was NSW's Phil Emery, but until then he'd been playing in the Australia A team. This swapping between the two Australian teams blurred the competitiveness of the tournament, and the issue came to a head during the finals after Australia A qualified ahead of England: Paul Reiffel, who'd played six matches for Australia A in the preliminary rounds, was co-opted into our squad for the finals and was promptly made 12th man. The members of the 'real' Australian team struggled with the concept because it seemed to give local fans a chance to cheer the team we were playing rather than us. In Adelaide in December, when we narrowly defeated our fellow countrymen in an excellent match, it seemed the home crowd was genuinely disappointed when we prevailed. This wasn't quite so apparent in the finals, which we won fairly comfortably in two matches, but by then our captain, Mark Taylor, had complained publicly about the situation, which may have made those fans who'd automatically supported the underdog think again. I guess it was an idea worth trying, and I'm all for an Australia A team being brought together for matches against touring teams, but, for the players' sake, I hope we never see such a side in the World Series again.

— ✠ —

THE ASHES SERIES BEGAN at the Gabba with Michael Slater hitting the first delivery, from Phil DeFreitas, for four, a stroke that set the tempo for the first two Tests. In Brisbane, Slats and Junior both hit big hundreds, Shane Warne took eight wickets in England's second innings and I finished the match with nine catches — five of them off Billy McDermott — which equalled the Australian Test record. Then, in the second Test, in Melbourne, I made another eight dismissals and was on track for a record-breaking season.

Not that I thought such landmarks were any big deal. If a team's consistently knocking over the opposition twice, and includes bowlers of the calibre of Warne and McDermott, who both know where the outside edge of the bat is, that team's wicketkeeper is going to be taking some catches and making the odd stumping. I never measured the quality of my performance by the number of dismissals, rather by the way I gloved them throughout the innings, match or series. Some of what I considered to be my best performances were on days when I hardly made a dismissal but I didn't misglove a thing. In contrast, I had awful Tests where I managed to take a couple of screamers, which meant the highlights package might have looked brilliant, but I knew better. This said, for the most part I was in excellent form this summer.

The most memorable of my dismissals at the MCG in '94–95 was the snare from Warney's bowling, a thick edge that needed some catching, that dismissed the Poms' fast bowler Darren Gough. This was the middle leg of a thrilling hat-trick that had started when DeFreitas was lbw and ended when Boonie took a stunning catch at short leg. The final day had begun with England 4-79 chasing 388, but the match was over before noon, as the last six wickets crumbled in 12.5 overs. After two Tests, Shane had taken 20 wickets and Billy 16, while Slats, Junior and Boonie had all made hundreds and Steve Waugh an unbeaten 94. We were on top of our games, while our opponents seemed shellshocked.

Their struggles were personified by Graeme Hick, who had been lauded as their white knight before he first appeared in Test cricket but had been given a torrid time by Merv Hughes in England in 1993 and again by Craig McDermott here. Although he played one or two significant innings on this tour — most notably an unbeaten 98 in Sydney when England captain Mike Atherton declared on him, something I couldn't fathom no matter how hard I tried — Graeme was not the major force his side needed. Having played with him when he had a season of Shield cricket with Queensland, I know he's good enough to play at the highest level, but perhaps he's just too nice a bloke to dominate Test-match bowling attacks. He's the sort of batsman who can score runs in beautiful, delightful style but seems to lack that necessary tough edge to dig himself out of the difficult situations and give it back to aggressive opponents. Our batsmen could do that, and we all revelled in the fact that, while man on man there wasn't too much between the teams, we appeared to be so much mentally tougher than England.

On that final day in Melbourne, we hadn't expected our post-second Test celebrations to begin so quickly, but we still managed to party hard in the dressing room until around 4.30pm, toasting a 2-0 lead, Warney's hat-trick and Boonie's 34th birthday. From there we headed back to our hotel, where I soon found myself involved in an argument with an Englishman who annoyed me when he muttered, 'You blokes think you're pretty good but you've only beaten England.'

'You're right,' I responded. 'They are soft and don't care enough for their country. You're probably the same.'

I learned soon after that this bloke's wife had immediately rushed off and complained to the concierge desk, who contacted team manager Ian McDonald and, we were soon to discover, the police. 'Macca' insisted I go back and

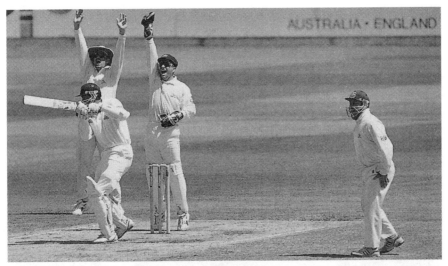

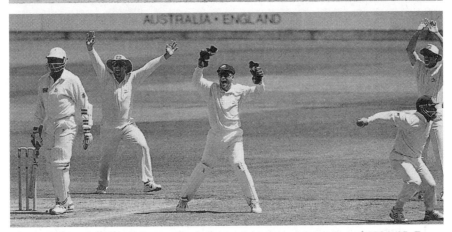

Shane Warne's famous hat-trick on the last day of the second Ashes Test of 1994–95. Top: Phil DeFreitas, lbw; Middle: Darren Gough, caught behind; Bottom: Devon Malcolm, caught by David Boon (in helmet) at short leg.

Craig McDermott, Australia's most lethal fast bowler for the first half of the 1990s, has England captain Mike Atherton caught behind in Melbourne in December 1994.

apologise, which I did. Then we headed up to our rooms to prepare for dinner at an Indian restaurant and then on to the Crown Casino for a few more drinks.

Back downstairs, we saw a policeman in the foyer, and Helen jokingly said to him, 'Here he is, officer, take him away.' Which was very funny, except he *was* there to see me. Everything was sweet, but afterwards in my diary I wrote succinctly, 'Must curb this.' I was aware that this was not a good example being set by an Australian cricketer, let alone the vice-captain.

The following day we flew to Sydney, where on New Year's Eve we enjoyed a 5.30pm premiere of the musical *Cats*, followed by a party in the Botanical Gardens. It was a wonderful set-up, enjoyed by all the players and their wives and partners. When it was over we strolled back under clear skies to our hotel, accompanied by bodyguards! I'm sure this didn't have anything to do with my verbal altercation with the Englishman in Melbourne; whatever the cause it was in a way a little unsettling. Like it or not, we were now fair dinkum celebrities.

The Sydney Test was a disappointment. I had my worst game of the summer and the team was pretty ordinary as well. We started with a rush, reducing the Poms to 3-20, but after they made 309 we needed a substantial ninth-wicket partnership between Taylor and McDermott to avoid the follow on. From 8-65 our skipper and leading fast bowler pushed our total to 116. Though we had a bit of a gallop at a fourth-innings target of 449, with Slats and Tubby both making hundreds in an opening stand of 208, we ended up needing the eighth-wicket pair, Warney and Maysie, to bat out the final 77 minutes to force the draw. This they did, in fading light and with eight fieldsmen around the bat, which was enough for us to retain the Ashes.

After the Sydney Test our focus shifted a fraction, to our impending tour of the Caribbean. We knew we still had the World Series to win, and two Tests, and a brief triangular one-day tournament in New Zealand (also involving South Africa) but the guys who'd played the West Indies before knew this tour was our big chance and we were keen to see how we'd go. In my view, that was why we were below our best in Adelaide, when England won the fourth Test, but that defeat was like a wake-up call for us. In the lead-up to the fifth Test, in Perth, everyone was talking about the fact that the series could be squared, but we kicked back into action whereas the Poms folded badly. Slats hit his third hundred of the series, Stephen made 99 not out (when his twin, running for last man in, Craig McDermott, managed to get himself run out at the bowler's end), Greg Blewett scored his second Test century in his second Test, and Billy took 6-38 in England's second innings. We won by 329 runs.

Billy finished that series with 32 wickets, having moved passed Richie Benaud into second place on the all-time Australian Test wicket-taking list. By the time his career ended prematurely because of injury in 1996, he had 291 Test scalps, an impressive performance by any standards, yet because the end of his career fitted in nicely with the emergence of Glenn McGrath, Australia never desperately missed him. I guess we never stopped to consider how good he was.

Craig is a very good mate of mine, whom I've known since I was 11 years old and he was 10. Off the field, he's one of the neatest, most meticulous men I know. On it, he's always had natural athleticism, and I reckon he was earmarked to be a Test bowler from about the age of 16, when he made the Australian Under 19 side for the first time. He was taking West Indian Test wickets before his 20th birthday, and leading his country's bowling attack in England not long after, but in the seasons that followed his body took a pounding from all the training he did and all the overs he bowled. He sometimes became a very serious and sensitive man — which he normally wasn't — when he worried about the possible consequences of failing. These are some of the typical pressures that cricketers must cope with when they are not physically 100 per cent right. However, there were many points in his career — and this 1994–95 series is an excellent example — when he was as good and relentless as any fast bowler I ever kept to.

— ✠ —

THE ASHES SERIES HAD a painful end for me, and not just because I strained a calf muscle late in the Perth Test and needed some heavy strapping to get me through. In fact the strapping was my undoing in the second innings, when it was wrapped a little tight but rather than go off to get it fixed I soldiered on, distracted, and was out soon after.

This was Graham Gooch's last Test, and Mike Gatting's, too, and after the match we decided we had to see Gatt and Goochie off properly. We were in our dressing room, as was Gatt, but Graham had returned to their hotel, so someone got on the phone to tell him to get back here as soon as possible. This he did, with a carton of Tetley's beer under his arm. From the ground, we were required to attend a sponsor's dinner, which we did, so by the end of the night I'd drunk more than I needed to. I had arranged to meet a group from one of my sponsors after the function, but missed them, so I arrived back at our hotel on my own, to be greeted by a couple of England supporters who proceeded to give me a gobful. Apparently Mark Waugh had arrived at the hotel not long before me, but he was smart enough to ignore them ...

At first I just asked them what their problem was, and told them to calm down. One of the two was fine. But his mate kept coming with the abuse, so I asked him, standing a step above him on the stairs into the hotel, 'What kind of loser are you, following this bunch of no-hopers around the country?'

I'd hardly got the sentence out before he jumped up and head-butted me. I went to grab his T-shirt, but they bolted. Hotel security, who later told me they'd just kicked the pair out of the hotel because they were causing trouble, came out and raced after them but they'd scampered away. I told the security guys not to worry about calling the police, let's forget about it. After they helped clean me up a bit, I went up to my room and had only just got in, when the phone rang. It's the police. I invited them up, and when they arrived the first thing the officer said was, 'Is your nose always bent?', I looked in the mirror, it didn't look too much worse than usual.

'We'd better,' he continued, 'get you up to the hospital.'

That, in hindsight, was silly. I didn't think I'd done anything wrong on this occasion, but I knew there'd been other times when I probably should have been belted but got away with being a goose. Now I was in Royal Perth Hospital filling out forms, so I could get my nose checked out, and when the doctor came to look at me he quickly explained that there was nothing he could do until the swelling went down. But my visit to the hospital had alerted the media and by early the next morning there was a story about that an Australian cricketer had been bashed.

At the breakfast table the next morning, I sat very quietly reading the morning paper through my sunnies. The only marks I wore from the skirmish the night before were a little graze on my eyebrow, a nicked lip that you couldn't really see and a still-swollen nose. An ABC reporter came up to me and said, 'Ian, I believe one of your team was bashed last night. Do you know anything about it?'

'No, mate,' I replied, 'that's the first I've heard of it.'

There were only three or four of us down at breakfast at this point, as many of the guys had caught the midnight horror home straight after the dinner. Slats was one, and after he was asked the same question, he looked over at me, lifted up my sunnies slightly, and said, quietly but wide-eyed, 'It was you, wasn't it?'

I told him the story, and asked him to keep quiet. Which he did. Slats was more concerned about his thumb, which England's fast bowler Devon Malcolm had broken at the WACA and would cost our little opener the New Zealand trip. I flew home to Brisbane later that morning and when Helen picked me up at the airport she'd heard nothing about the fracas but immediately spotted the damage. To say she was disappointed would be an understatement. By two days after the Test, the media were right onto the story, having received confirmation from the hotel manager, but I wasn't commenting and neither the ACB's Ian McDonald nor my manager, Paul Smith, knew anything about it because I hadn't told them. I wanted the story to die, which it gradually did after I relented to media requests for interviews while I was at the Gabba for an advertising shoot. 'You don't have to be a great shot to hit my hooter,' I laughed during the interviews.

But really, it was no laughing matter. More a very serious lesson learned.

> *February 8, 1995: Not going further with incident. Very lucky. Cheek, teeth, etc, all okay.*
>
> *My behaviour when drinking has been too confrontational when people are abusing/sledging me and the team. I will either get myself into trouble properly, upset people or get badly hurt even if I am bullet proof. Must make an effort here to curb this behaviour because it is no longer appropriate to my team role and profile.*
>
> *IMPROVE THIS AS OF NOW!*
> *(I am no longer a normal person.)*

— ✠ —

I WAS CAPTAIN OF Queensland for seven years, from 1992–93 until my retirement, so technically I was captain when Queensland first won the Sheffield Shield. Because of international commitments, I only led the team in 26 first-class matches in those seven seasons, though I still gained enormous pride from being the leader and tried to do as much as I could to help give the team the courage and confidence it needed to be successful.

From the 1987–88 season, when I had played in the state's final four Shield matches and the team had squandered a big lead at Christmas, I sensed that there were two major factors holding the team back. One was the simple stress of having not won the trophy before, which had players, officials and supporters constantly looking over their shoulders during the second half of the season, waiting for something to go wrong — a classic case of worrying about the outcome rather than the task at hand. The other stumbling block was the lack of cohesion within the squad. The players just weren't tight enough as a group, which led to experienced players ribbing up-and-comers rather than nurturing them, and the youngsters waiting for the stars to perform rather than inspiring them. The team relied on individual performances rather than team strategies. Some saw themselves as better or worse than others, because of what they'd done rather than what they were doing. For a while Queensland could get by on natural talent, but in the pressure situations that came up late in the season the team's focus inevitably fractured and crucial matches were lost, sometimes embarrassingly.

When I was given the Queensland captaincy, I wanted to facilitate some improvements. Then, in 1994–95, John Buchanan, a man I'd known for many years and a man who was even more adamant about this need for a change of philosophy and focus within the squad than I was, was appointed coach of the Queensland Shield team. 'Buck' had been a modest Shield player himself in the late 1970s (and a prolific runscorer and more-than-handy wicket-taker in club and English league cricket), and as he worked through the coaching levels within Queensland cricket he quickly recognised the hurdles that were holding the state's Shield fortunes back. From 1994-95 on, whenever I returned to the Queensland XI I knew that I was slotting into a tight team unit and that there would be pressure on me to contribute.

My first contact with Buck, or 'Pluto' as I know him, was in the early 1980s when he coached and captained Colts in the Brisbane grade competition. His attention to detail was eye-opening. Buck is very organised, as am I, and big on goal-setting, the effectiveness of which is something I've always reckoned is very underrated in the cricket community. Before each club round, we'd scrutinise every scorecard and article about our upcoming opponents, to ensure that we knew exactly what were up against. I thrived on such detail — some didn't — but as a team we went all right. I'm sure even today there are some who wouldn't enjoy his precision. Mark Waugh, a batsman who likes to rely on his instincts and think on his feet in the middle, is the type of player who would love to play without too much detail. Greg Blewett, Damien Fleming and Andrew Symonds are probably in the same boat, but Buck is smart enough to recognise that not everyone is alike, that too much analysis can bog some people down, and is happy to meet such cricketers halfway.

I know Buck was slightly intimidated by the us-and-them atmosphere that had pervaded Queensland Shield teams in the past, because just before applications closed for the Queensland coaching job he asked me whether I thought he should apply. The last thing he wanted, he told me, was to have to confront disaffected senior players. Things were changing, I told him, and the Borders, Rackemanns, McDermotts and Healys of this state weren't going to cause him grief. AB might not have agreed with Buck's meticulous, goal-oriented approach, but he was such a team man that I knew he'd support the new coach

As acting captain, I'm leading the Australians out for our opening match of the 1995 West Indies tour, a one-dayer against a Barbados second XI at Kensington Oval in Bridgetown. The banner in the grandstand was a little bit premature, because the Shield final was still three weeks away, but the bloke who made it clearly knew his cricket! This was the first time I'd captained Australia in any match.

enthusiastically. And Mocca, though a close ally of the former coach, Jeff Thomson, is such a loyal Queenslander, good bloke and positive person there was no way he'd be a problem. Billy and I, both of us very organised people by nature and aware of Buck's coaching philosophy from our days at Colts, were keen from the start.

Since October 1999 John Buchanan has been the Australian team's coach (in fact, his appointment was announced the same day I retired) and he has played a significant role in the great success enjoyed by Steve Waugh's Test and one-day sides. However, while some may rate his performance with the national team as his career highlight, in my view his efforts with Queensland, where he improved the confidence and consistency of the entire Shield squad, has been his greatest triumph to date. He was so successful in revving up the 'fringe' players in that squad that it reached the stage where the international players were left behind if they didn't slot straight back into the team's methods. I loved that; it was extremely refreshing.

Buck is a bloke who continually writes notes — I have no idea where he stores them all — and can see value in every statistic and computer program ever invented. And he's often been ahead of his time. Way back in the mid 1980s he proposed a 'Second XI' state competition, his logic being that another rung was needed to reduce the extent of the jump from club to first-class cricket. Then the idea was dismissed almost immediately; today such a scheme is a part of the Australian cricket landscape. Certainly, the path from Brisbane grade cricket to Queensland Shield cricket is much less intimidating for rookies these days. As coach of Queensland, Buck proposed a schedule that would allow the international stars to play more Shield cricket and Shield players to play more club cricket. Again that was ignored, and still is, though I for one would like to see such an idea encouraged. I wonder what Buck thinks of that proposal himself today, now that he's part of the 'show'.

Buck was a Shield coach who asked a lot of his players, starting a trend that quickly spread across the land and became one of the contributing factors in the formation of the Australian Cricketers' Association. He was a coach who asked a lot from his part-time Shield cricketers: pre-season camps, early training start times, morning sessions, innovative three-day games as lead-ups to vital fixtures and winter sprint and speed sessions. Players who had full-time jobs struggled to find the time, and Buck's demands of his squad also impinged on the grade clubs, who were losing their best players to more than just Shield games. However, because of the results Buck's methods delivered, there were rarely any complaints from the clubs or the players. Everyone just jumped on board and enjoyed the ride.

That game against Western Australia we lost at the Gabba in January 1995 — the one that led to me hanging up on my dad — was my only Shield game of the 1994–95 season. So from a playing angle, even if I was the captain I couldn't lay any great claim to our historic triumph that summer. However, my view was that the guys on the field for that final were playing not just for themselves, but for everyone who had ever played for Queensland, myself included. And they were representatives of everyone who'd ever shed a tear when we'd thrown away possible Shield victories in the past.

The final was played at the Gabba from March 24 to 28, 1995, against South Australia, while I was on the tiny Caribbean island of St Lucia. Throughout the match, I received regular phone updates from Helen, who, like all Queenslanders

Friends and family with the most important prize in Australian domestic cricket.

at the time, seemed more interested in the Shield team's fate than she'd ever been in a Test match, and also reports from the two Queensland cricket writers on the West Indies tour, Robert Craddock and Jim Tucker. By this stage of the tour, Billy had returned home after badly hurting his ankle, and I was the only Queensland player in the Australian team.

> *March 24, 1995: Queensland play sensationally. South Australia 214, Qld 0-36. Helen is as excited as anyone. Great first day. Go the lads!*

> *March 25, 1995: Qld 0-110 at lunch. 3-409. Tank [Trevor Barsby] 150, Lovey [Martin Love] 114 not out. HOME!!*

In St Lucia we were playing a four-day game against a West Indies President's XI, but I must confess I was more concerned with the cricket being fought out at the Gabba than the match I was playing in. Fortunately, with the time difference, the Shield was being played in the middle of my night, and I was awake for most of it, waiting for the next call. I was also helped by cricket's weather gods, who washed out the first day of the game on St Lucia and the last day, too. During the final, I received pre-arranged calls, at around 2.30am St Lucia time, from the Channel Nine commentators at the Gabba, which made me feel as if a little bit of Ian Healy was there. This was especially true when the call came immediately after the final wicket fell and I could hear all that Queensland joy in the background.

March 28, 1995: Good chat to Pluto — so happy for him.
SA 10-340 odd. Qld goes berserk!!

Helen rang me at 4am, God love her. I don't want to be in St
Lucia at this stage …

Queensland's winning margin was an innings and 101 runs. Inevitably, I was in glorious form on the washed-out final day of our match in St Lucia and made sure the boys from NSW — the Waughs, Taylor, Slater and McGrath — copped it most of all. They, after all, had been the ones keenest to remind me in the days long gone that Queensland had never won the Shield. For his part, Tugga was more concerned with bagging the two South Australians in our squad, Blewey and Maysie, whose state had let this disaster (in his eyes) happen.

Although I was due to be at the airport the following morning at 6am, for a flight to Barbados, I was up for a fair piece of the night with my two Maroon comrades, Messrs Craddock and Tucker, celebrating the Shield triumph. Jim was even clever enough to bring a bottle of Bundy rum over with him, especially for the occasion. We weren't sure what the locals thought of us, three proud, happy Queenslanders constantly toasting an event they knew nothing of, but we didn't care.

A few days later, that great Queensland warrior, Carl Rackemann, joined the Australian team's tour, having been called into the squad after Damien Fleming and Craig McDermott were injured. Mocca came suitably armed with a range of 'Sheffield Shield champions' T-shirts, which he and I proudly wore to breakfast in Barbados the morning after his arrival and then kept wearing, morning after morning after morning. One morning Mark Taylor even had a go at us, as if wearing Queensland shirts was bad for team morale. I didn't agree, and whispered quickly to myself, 'You beauty, there's cracks in the NSW ship showing.' That Tubby lecture apart, for some reason we struggled to find teammates to share conversations with over breakfast, but I didn't care, so long as I kept hearing stories from my Queensland comrade about the final, the team, the crowd, the atmosphere. A little later, Allan Border came over to do some media work and I was able to hear about the big game all over again. Today, even though I wasn't at the Gabba, I know a little bit of me was. I'm so proud to have been a part of it.

CHAPTER 14

WAUGHSOME!

OUR WEST INDIES TOUR from March to May 1995, was the cricket highlight of my life. To succeed in this toughest of all cricket environments was as satisfying and glorious as it gets at the top level of our sport, and I especially enjoyed the triumph for a number of reasons. Foremost was the fact that we'd been physically smashed by the Windies in my first three series against them (and many more before that!) and emotionally devastated by that one-run loss in Adelaide in early 1993. As vice captain, I was privy to and played a part in the development of our strategies, and the team spirit on the tour was magnificent, so it was a joy to be part of the team. And there was the way we won, coming back from a potentially morale-sapping loss in the third Test in Trinidad to win decisively in the fourth and final Test in Jamaica.

It is somewhat ironic, then, that this pinnacle of achievement for the Australian team should happen at a time when the relationship between the players and the Australian Cricket Board was reaching its lowest ebb. Not even two and a half years later, when we threatened to go on strike over a pay and conditions dispute, did I personally feel as dirty on the ACB's officials as I felt in the lead-up to the '95 West Indies tour.

I should stress straight up that most Board officials are good people who genuinely have the best interests of the game at heart. It was the way they often went about things during my career that perturbed me. And the lack of trust; too often, their words did not appear to match their actions.

It always annoyed me that when the Board's senior officials addressed the players it was usually in a hotel room, with the players strewn like disobedient schoolboys around the room, lying on the floor, perched in a corner, hidden behind a bed or a lounge, while the chairman or the chief executive stood among us or sat on a chair and began his spiel. No wonder they felt superior to us. Why weren't we seated around a table, business-like, maybe even with an agenda when there were a number of issues to be discussed? By 1995, international cricket was a big business and the elite players were key employees.

A meeting in late February 1995 was typical of the way the ACB did things in the mid '90s. Six or seven of us were on the bed of the hotel room, the rest on the floor. The Board's representative went through a number of incidents that had disappointed them, including the head butt I wore in Perth. We heard the Board's views on the question of workers' compensation for their players, and problems that had arisen when personal sponsorships had conflicted with the ACB's sponsors. We were told the Board was doing everything it could to communicate with the players but had been disappointed that an unnamed senior player had allegedly described a series of one-on-one meetings in Adelaide as a 'waste of time'. The only problem with that rebuke was that none of we senior players could recall having made that comment. We believed that it might have been better for the Board to confirm that the comment had been made before tarnishing us as cynics. Finally, the subject of the bribery allegations from Pakistan and the fining of Junior and Warney for being paid to provide information was raised, with a firm reminder given that the matter of the fines was being kept in-house. The insinuation was that one of the players had leaked scraps of the story to the journalists who seemed to be onto the story, but our understanding was that if anyone had let his guard down it might actually have been an ACB official.

> *February 22, 1995: Board/player communication still two-faced ... my game must continue above all else and petty problems perceived to be big by a few can't interfere. Toughen up and play well.*

Throughout the West Indies tour, I would have a number of meetings with Tubby and some former and current senior Australian players on the subject of player contracts. I was fearful that we were being treated unfairly and also worried about the extent to which we were signing our lives away when we autographed the ACB contracts. Perhaps I was being a little paranoid, but two conversations I had with former players during the tour reinforced my view. One of these chats was with an ex-West Indian fast bowler who said to me, 'Amateur administrators are trying to keep cricket as a sport. But it's now a job.' The second conversation came later in the tour, when a former leading Australian player, who'd lived through the World Series Cricket dispute of 1977 to 1979, told me in a bar in Trinidad, that while our salaries might have increased, 'in many ways cricketers today are no better off than we were 18 years ago'. But even from a money point of view, I looked at our football cousins and saw them making considerably more than we were, even though we were now playing nine months of every year. I was fully aware that the Board had a huge sport to run at every level from Tests to grassroots, but I wondered whether the elite players were seeing a fair proportion of the Board's total revenue.

—◻—

IN MANY WAYS OUR tour of the West Indies in 1995 was *the* benchmark tour for the Australian team in the '90s. Before this Caribbean challenge, we were a good side, maybe a very good side — better than England and New Zealand, better than Pakistan in Australia, probably better than South Africa, not very good away from home. This tour proved our quality, demonstrated that we could perform outside Australia and validated Mark Taylor as an effective leader. The ghosts of past losses to the Windies were put to rest. Glenn McGrath emerged as a worthy and belligerent successor to Merv Hughes and Craig McDermott.

Practising my hook on the beach in the West Indies with (left to right) David Boon, Errol Alcott and Paul Reiffel in the slip cordon. It looks like, for the 1000th time in my life, I'm going to hit it up in the air, to be caught again in the deep.

Steve Waugh's famous confrontation with Curtly Ambrose in the third Test, in Trinidad, established his and the team's courage and liking for a stoush. And then Stephen's remarkable double century in Jamaica confirmed his class, giving us a batsman whose aura and reputation were as critical to our team as Tendulkar and Lara were to India and the West Indies respectively.

> *March 4, 1995: Tubs not overly concerned with ODIs here. Wants to play well but not be all and end all. This, I feel, is not aggressive enough but it's not for me to say — could turn out to be a masterstroke in build-up to Tests.*

The climax to this famous tour is well remembered in Australia. The first fortnight, however, is not, which is lucky because those early days weren't too terrific. In our early team meetings, Tubby pushed the line that we were gearing up for the Tests. In 1991, we'd won the one-day series but when we quietly returned to Australia after losing the Test series no one rushed up and congratulated us on our limited-overs achievement (and it was an achievement, beating that Windies side 4-1 on their turf). My feeling was that in 1995 we were capable of winning both ... and why not try. However, we were short a fifth bowler in the one-dayers, because the Waughs were carrying minor injuries and Greg Blewett was bowling badly. All three were going to be in our Test batting line-up and Tubby wanted them to get the batting practice, so rather than include a better bowling option we continued to hope that our existing fifth bowler's overs would not be too expensive. However, in game three Blewey went for 32 off three overs, then 26 off three in game four. By that fourth game, we even had Boonie bowling, which suggested our attack wasn't as potent as it could have been. I must point out that our batting wasn't too flash at times either — our blokes got into the habit of making starts and then getting out — and we lost the one-day series 4-1 as conclusively as we'd won it four years before.

We were very concerned in the lead-up to the first Test. The injuries to McDermott and Fleming left our pace attack, on paper at least, looking decidedly thin. At separate meetings for the batsmen and bowlers (I attended both, which were held in St Vincent) Tubby was justly critical of the guys' performances, but he ended each get-together with the comment, 'I'm not concerned yet, but we *must* start switching on now.' Tubby bluntly told the bowlers what we expected of them. The loss of McDermott and Fleming was not a catastrophe but a challenge; our quick bowlers were still going to show their late-order batsmen no respect at all. Retaliate first! Tubs asked Glenn McGrath to step forward, which 'Pigeon' did in magnificent style. This was a task he was ideal for, because while he might not be the most talented batsman in the world, he's a fearless character not about to get concerned about likely reprisals from fast bowlers such as Curtly Ambrose and Courtney Walsh. Glenn's bowling in this series was comparable to the fastest I have kept to; and, most importantly, it was as fast and intimidating as anything the West Indies threw back at us.

We knew that if we targeted their tailenders, they'd respond in kind. And that our top order was going to get plenty, whatever our bowlers did. As a consequence, our pre-Test preparation was as intense as I've experienced, with pacemen practising their bouncers in the nets, often with new balls, and the batsmen gladly facing them, hooking them, dodging them, fending them away, whatever was their method. In this regard, we were lucky that the Test series began in Barbados, because the practice facilities there were infinitely superior to those anywhere else in the islands. Had we undertaken this sort of rehearsal anywhere else someone might have got killed. In the week leading up to the Test the team knitted together really nicely, which showed up in little ways such as the whole team dining as a unit most nights, rather than dividing into four or five groups every night except for the official pre-game team dinner. There was one moment of levity I recall, which came when Simmo, after pointing out that the wicket might be a little two-paced, asked where we thought the slip fieldsmen should position themselves. 'In the slips,' Maysie responded. Simmo wasn't amused.

March 31, 1995: Test 1. Barbados. Lost toss, bowling.
WI 3-6!! WOW! — everyone was stunned.

This first Test developed into one of the most impressive and systematic victories by an Australian team in my experience. It began in dramatic, pulsating fashion, as Tubby opened the bowling with Paul Reiffel and Brendon Julian, rather than McGrath, and within minutes Stuart Williams, Sherwin Campbell and Richie Richardson were all dismissed. Then Carl Hooper launched a daring counter-attack on Shane Warne and by lunch the Windies were 3-116.

At this point, Hooper and Brian Lara could have established a theme for the series similar to what had occurred in the past — Australia gain an advantage, but the West Indies come fighting back. Remember, this is what happened in Barbados in 1991, after we bowled them out on the first day for 149 and they came right back to bowl us out for 15 less and ultimately win the Test by 343 runs. And so cruelly in the 1992–93 series, too. However in 1995 things were different. Soon after lunch 'BJ' had Hooper caught at slip, Pigeon dismissed Jimmy Adams, and then Lara, on 65, slashed at BJ and Steve Waugh took a juggling grab in the gully. This was a controversial moment, but not so much on the field, where everyone with a clear view — including Lara — thought Tugga successfully made the catch. But in the press box, video replays suggested the ball *might* have hit the ground. After stumps, Simmo asked Tugga, 'What are you going to say to the media?' and Tugga just looked at him and said, 'What about?' My opinion was that the replays were inconclusive, while the fieldsmen (and umpires!) were adamant the catch had been made. So it was out, end of story.

The Lara dismissal made it 6-156. Junior Murray and Winston Benjamin took the score to 184 before Benjamin was caught at slip, and immediately Tubby brought McGrath back to bowl at Ambrose. The impact was immediate: the last three wickets fell for just 11 runs, and both Ambrose and Walsh seemed to take the barrage personally. We saw their reaction as a big win for us, almost as important as the fact that we'd knocked them over for less than 200.

When we replied, all our batsmen made starts but no one made that big score we needed. So when I came to the crease at 5-194, two balls before lunch and still one run behind, I knew the match was precariously poised. Again, here was a chance for the game to tumble the same way as in the past, where 5-out had meant all out; but I noticed from soon after the interval that the Windies' presence and intensity weren't quite as ruthless and intimidating as they had been in the past. I made 34 in the session between lunch and tea, when we lost just one wicket and survived the second new ball, and was rapt with my patience and composure. I noted, too, with some satisfaction, the absence of chat from the fieldsmen. In the bad old days, the support the fieldsmen gave their bowlers — some of it disturbingly 'anti-white' — was incessant. Here, the larger our lead the quieter they became, our last four wickets added 116 runs, and I finished unbeaten on 74 including two sweet sixes. In the process, we severely dampened the notion that our lower order couldn't score runs against the Windies quicks.

It was a beautiful day and we topped it off with a relentless, excellent spell of bowling before stumps. For 15 overs Williams and Campbell defended grimly for just 13 runs. In previous series, we might have knocked the West Indies out once for less than 300, but never twice. It was an almost surreal feeling, being in the Caribbean and having the home team on the rack, their body language negative, the crowd quiet … our personal satisfaction enormous.

We didn't let up on day three, instead powering to an emphatic 10-wicket victory. McGrath took five wickets, no batsman reached 40, the last four wickets fell for just 19 runs and we were given the sight of Courtney Walsh losing it in bizarre fashion during his brief time at the batting crease. This was the same bloke who had clobbered Craig McDermott at the start of the 1991 tour, and then dismissed Billy two runs short of a series win in Adelaide in early 1993. Here, after Pigeon greeted him with a bouncer, Walsh ran down the pitch at him and then took off towards square leg. It looked to me that Walsh was out of control. His helmet was askew, ineffectively fastened, hardly the look of a senior player. Then, when Tubby and Slats walked out to get the 39 needed to win, Ambrose stood alone in the field while Walsh and Kenny Benjamin deliberately charged through the crease when they bowled, apparently so they'd be that much closer to the batsmen when they let go their bouncers.

From the dressing room, it appeared that their back feet were landing where their front feet should have been. More significantly, it confirmed that our pugnacious outlook had left a mark. *Under the Southern Cross* has rarely been sung with greater verve than it was in Barbados after that win, both in the dressing room (with many fans outside the room joining in) and on a cruise we thoroughly enjoyed that night.

There were more signs of the West Indies' declining confidence in the second Test, in Antigua, a potentially great match that was ultimately wrecked by rain. For example, on the first morning we heard there was conflict in the West Indies camp as to what to do if they won the toss, which struck us as strange because in previous series if there had ever been anything in the wicket they'd be bowling first. Tubby told us that Richardson hesitated for a moment before saying, 'We'll bowl.' It struck me that unlike his predecessors, Richardson needed to really think about his strategies. There was no certainty that his bowlers would steamroll the opposition if he bowled first, or that his batsmen would pile on the runs. However, there were also moments when we were reminded that their pride was still simmering. When Tubby and Slats went on the second evening to face nine overs, after the West Indies batsmen had failed to establish a substantial first-innings lead, they were peppered by Walsh and Ambrose, and needed a stockpile of icepacks for their bruised bodies when they returned, still not out, at the close of play.

At our team meeting before the third Test, I pointed out that the match offered us a chance to 'take another step forward in our cricketing lives'. I felt in top form with the bat and gloves, and the team's preparation was excellent. Unfortunately, the pitch in Trinidad wasn't. When I walked out to the centre to look at the track, I crouched down, ran my hand through the two-centimetre long, wet grass, and then looked up at Tubby and asked, 'Are we going to start on time?' My guess was that it needed another 24 hours, at least, before it would be close to ready for Test cricket, but the officials wanted none of that. At least rain was about, so there was no chance of a full day's play.

David Boon has just taken a screamer at short mid-on; to dismiss Brian Lara off Steve Waugh's bowling during the second Test, in Antigua.

Of course we lost the toss, and this time Richardson had no second thoughts about sending us in. The pitch was a seaming minefield, and we did well to only lose seven wickets in the 39 overs possible on the day. Steve Waugh was magnificent, improvising courageously to 54 not out, and having a very public spat with Curtly Ambrose along the way. That blow-up occurred after Ambrose bowled a particularly nasty ball that flew up and nearly took off Stephen's chin. Ambrose followed through up close to Tugga, who nonchalantly asked the big fast bowler what he was looking at. Ambrose, sucked in, stepped a bit closer, Tugga suggested he go back to his bowling mark, Ambrose asked Tugga not to speak to him like that and then Richie Richardson jumped in and pulled his fast bowler away. That incident added considerably to the Steve Waugh legend.

There were a lot of Aussie supporters in town for this Test and, not surprisingly, they were a little disheartened after the opening day. I remember seeing a group of them after stumps and telling them to hang in there because the wicket was doing so much. The following day justified my optimism, as Glenn McGrath took six wickets and kept the Windies first-innings lead down to 8. By stumps we were 12 runs in front, still with 10 wickets in hand and our fate very much in our own hands.

The atmosphere in the rooms after the second day was fabulous. The following afternoon the room was like a morgue, after we managed to lose 10 wickets for 85 runs, our last seven for 20, and then watch our cock-a-hoop opponents play very well to storm to a nine-wicket victory in 20.5 overs. The wicket, by this point, was much improved but still not easy. Still, we batted very poorly indeed, at least in part, I believe, because we got our goal-setting wrong. Before play, I was as bad as anyone, emphasising that our objective was to bat right through the day. In these conditions that was unrealistic; we should have been looking at getting a lead of 220 or 250, which would have been very hard to get. Not too many Test teams make 250 in the fourth innings to win on the best of decks, and this grassy Trinidad wicket was never going to be benign.

I was worried after that loss. On what had been the scheduled rest day for the third Test, most of the boys set off on a pre-arranged cruise to a privately owned island off the Trinidad coast, but I preferred to stay in. I needed to contemplate the loss and preferred to do some fitness work. You can't move on until you've put the past behind you, and this defeat rankled with me. The 'past', I knew, was not only the Test just lost, but the three previous West Indies series I had been involved in and the many before that that my old teammates had played in. I resolved to do all I could to make the fourth and final Test turn out the way I wanted and needed it to.

At a meeting of the batsmen two days before the decider we had a very frank and open discussion about our performances in the three Tests to date. To that point no one had made a hundred in the series, which was disappointing, especially seeing that the Windies pace attack contained only two real threats instead of the four we'd been obliged to face in the past. Three criticisms were put forward: that we were relaxing after seeing off Walsh and Ambrose; that we weren't concentrating as well late in overs as we were at the beginning; that we might be simply putting too much pressure on ourselves.

> *April 27, 1995: Must employ the purest of concentration.*
> *BALL ONLY. Total trust in instincts acting for you, bringing*
> *you runs. Can't pre-empt at any time — that creates even*
> *slight indecision which makes you late on the ball. Have been*
> *getting out all tour at lazy times.*
> *'Nike' Test … Just Do It.*

This fourth Test wasn't like Perth in 1992–93. The WACA wicket that summer was tailor-made for Curtly and Co., whereas this time we were on a level playing field. We were pleasantly surprised when we set eyes on the new Sabina Park in Kingston, Jamaica. The wicket was still the same as 1991 — totally bare, built on red clay and polished so you could almost see your reflection in it — but the outfield was now good, the stands were good, everything was good. We truly thought we were a better side than our opponents; all we had to do was prove it.

Richie Richardson won the toss, four straight, and batted for the first time in the series. That showed what the Windies thought of the wicket, but we still bowled them out for 265, one run more than they'd made in Jamaica in 1991. Richardson batted bravely for an even 100, but the key wicket was Lara, caught behind off Warney for 65 just before lunch. They were 1-103 at the time, after

With the ball spinning, kicking and occasionally scuttling, Tubs suggested I don a helmet while keeping on the last day of the series, in Jamaica.

Williams was out in the first over, and looking as if they were on their way to a big total.

Day two, my 31st birthday, was dominated by the Waugh twins, who put together the finest partnership I've ever seen in cricket, a stirring stand of 231 built on great skill and impeccable concentration. Everything we talked about in the batting meeting before the Test was played out perfectly in this partnership. Mark was at his commanding best, while the West Indies made the mistake of overdoing the short stuff to Tugga, who often doesn't look too pretty handling it, but rarely gets out to it.

On the third day, the Windies bowlers dished out more of the same, as Steve moved relentlessly on to his double century in a display of commitment and concentration as good as you could ever see. Blewey and Pistol offered considerable support, and our lead amounted to 266, when the last wicket — Steve Waugh for exactly 200 — fell. Our mood through that day was buoyant, but it was very different from how we'd felt in, say, the first Ashes Test of 1989, when we were excited because we couldn't lose. This time, nothing short of a victory was good enough, so we knew there was plenty of work still to do.

A critical period in the Test was the 90 minutes between the end of the Australian innings and stumps on day three. Had the West Indies gone into the rest day with 10 or nine wickets in hand on that flat track then I reckon we might have had a real battle digging them out when they came back refreshed after the rest day. But Pistol Reiffel stood up and took three crucial wickets, including Richardson and Lara, before stumps, to leave us in a magnificent position with two days to go.

> *May 2, 1995: Crunch day tomorrow. Work hard and enjoy the challenge that this wicket presents. It's what we've dreamt of for my whole career ... can come true!!*

I could hardly believe it when I took a look at the pitch before start of the fourth day. It looked as if a Test match had been played on it during the rest day — cracks had opened up, and on the edge of many of those cracks the red clay had gone white and fragile. First ball of the day, I managed a good one-handed take; second ball, I spilt a regulation nick off Jimmy Adams. 'There's nothing more embarrassing,' I diarised later, 'than picking the ball up from behind the slip fieldsmen who are advancing with their appeals.' From there it was a battle for me; I went for the sunglasses, to fight the glare, and then a helmet, of all things, on Tubby's suggestion to guard against the inconsistent bounce. Just before I made this move a ball from Warney had kicked up over my head ... immediately after a delivery had scuttled between my legs.

Wickets fell at regular intervals during the day and from around lunchtime we were confident of ending the series before stumps. I dropped another one, their keeper Courtney Browne, when they were eight down, but soon after Warney spun one across Kenny Benjamin who snicked it to Tubby at first slip and the battle was over.

> *May 3, 1995: WE WIN!! HOW GREAT IS THIS? The plans, the execution, the result ... huge sense of satisfaction. Most complete feeling of my career, probably because I've been privy to the plans.*
> *THERE'S A LOT OF LOVE IN THE ROOMS!*

Afterwards, Richie Richardson made a comment that this was on paper the worst Australian team he'd played. In effect, he was signalling the demise of his own side. If only he'd added, 'but full credit to the Australians, they outplayed us'. I'm sure that's what he wanted to say, perhaps his pride and the pressure he'd been under stopped him. Richie was a great cricketer, and is a good bloke, but he was tired throughout that series, fighting the chronic fatigue syndrome that sapped his energy in the mid '90s. That hundred he scored in the first innings of the final Test was probably the bravest of his life.

Whatever Richie said or thought, we didn't really care. We had a big party planned, which started chaotically in our champagne-drenched dressing room, extended long into the night and involved not just the players in the 1995 team

With captain Tubs and the Frank Worrell Trophy ... probably the most satisfying triumph of my career.

but also a number of past members of the side who were in the Caribbean. AB, Deano, David Hookes and Geoff Lawson were among the heroes who joined us in the room and then on the 17th floor of the Pegasus Hotel in Kingston. Most of the present players stayed in their whites, many in baggy greens, Justin Langer draped in an Australian flag, Steve Waugh still in his spikes. The night ended with us all in one big circle, sitting on chairs, drinks in hands, sharing the moment. Who knows what we were talking about, but it was good. Gradually, one or two at a time, tired and emotional cricketers broke off to go to bed, and I was one of the last to leave, not long after Tugga. To see our exhausted champion trudging off to his room, still in spikes, whites and baggy, is a memory I cherish. The '10-to-2' feet, the one bowed leg and the casual swagger reminded me of the conclusion to the movie, *Chaplin*. I followed him down the corridor, watching as he tried his key in every door, until he finally found his room ... room 200.

From Kingston we set sail for Bermuda, for a golfathon and one more record, an astonishing effort where we ran up a bill of nearly US$7000 for a dinner shouted by the ACB. We toasted our success, relishing the fact that our performance was as well planned as it was executed. The credit for that, we acknowledged, went first to our coach and captain.

Tubby's approach had been thoroughly vindicated. Just as he'd predicted back at the start of the tour, now that we'd won the Test series the losses in the limited-overs matches were long forgotten. I certainly can't remember anyone bringing the one-day series up when we were showered in ticker-tape on our return.

CHAPTER 15

UNDER THE
SOUTHERN CROSS

I CAN'T IMAGINE the Australian Cricket Board's accountants being overly excited about the itinerary for the 1995–96 season when it was first programmed a few years before. In the previous four years' seasons these money managers had received funds generated by a World Cup, then Test tours by the West Indies, South Africa and England. For '95–96, however, the schedule was built around three-Test series involving Pakistan and then Sri Lanka, the former without much winning form in Australia and the latter with none at all. Yet the season evolved into one of the most controversial and headline grabbing for many years. The story involving Salim Malik's offer to Shane Warne and Tim May in 1994 had well and truly broken and inevitably the papers were full of speculation surrounding the impending meeting between the accused and his accusers. Then, after the Pakistanis departed, the Sri Lankans became embroiled in ball-tampering allegations and a momentous throwing controversy, which led to death threats being sent to the Australian players and Australia's preparations for the 1996 World Cup being severely disrupted. Cricket spent as much time on the front page of the papers as where it belongs at the back.

Before any of this happened, my early season was disrupted by a hamstring injury that dragged on for six or seven weeks and cost me two domestic one-dayers and two Sheffield Shield games. At first it was a minor strain that happened while I was sprinting during a fitness test at Queensland's pre-season camp and wouldn't go away. Right away, I was silly, continuing through the rest of the session because I was worried I'd be seen by some as a piker if I stopped. That's not the thing for a captain to do. The niggle persisted through a three-day trial game in Cairns against a Queensland Country XI and was still there throughout a game for Queensland against the touring South African provincial team, Western Province. As the days flew by I began to worry that I might miss the first Test of the summer, but I managed to get through a one-dayer and the Shield game against Tasmania and felt ready for the Pakistan series.

Salim Malik came to Australia as a man under extreme pressure, and not surprisingly he did all he could to dodge the limelight by arriving after the rest of his teammates and then spending most of his non-playing hours locked in his hotel room. In the Australian camp, we looked at Salim as just another opponent, though we knew Shane was keen to get his wicket. In the lead-up to the series Warney had been a little on edge, not quite knowing what to expect and

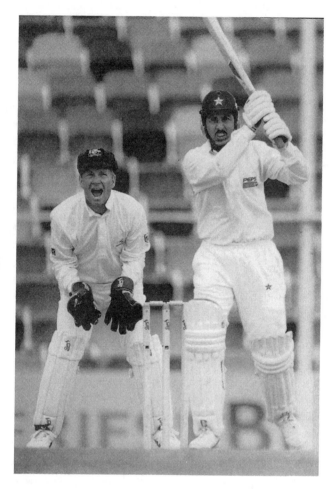

Salim Malik, the central figure in the match-fixing controversy that had its origins in 1994, came face to face with one of his accusers, Shane Warne, at the Gabba, in late 1995. Here Malik has miscued Warney to mid-off. Malik didn't bat in the first innings of this Test because of a hand injury, and struggled here in the second.

wondering why he was being pushed under the harsh match-fixing spotlight. In his mind, and ours too, he'd done precisely the right thing by promptly telling the authorities about Salim's original approach.

As things turned out, Shane bowled beautifully in the opening Test of the summer, in Brisbane, taking 11 wickets for the match, and the hyped up on-field confrontation with Salim was ridiculously brief. The former Pakistani captain couldn't bat because of a hand injury in their first innings and then made a fourth ball duck, caught McDermott at mid-off bowled Warne, batting under difficulties in the second. Earlier, Steve Waugh had made another hundred, and our final victory margin was an innings and 126 runs. Pakistan improved somewhat in the second Test, in Hobart, but we still handled them fairly comfortably, even though Warney had a big toe broken by a Waqar Younis yorker. However, in Sydney they were excellent, defeating us by 74 runs after Mushtaq Ahmed spun through us on a typical SCG turner.

I don't think the Pakistan team was helped by the scheduling of this tour, which from a Test-match perspective was over for them before it began. Throughout most of the 1990s they were a very talented and competitive side, who rarely did themselves justice in Australia. In Wasim Akram and Waqar Younis they had two magnificent fast bowlers; in fact, I always rated Wasim as the fastest bowler I faced in my career, based on a spell he fired at me during the 1989–90 season. Their spinners, Mushtaq Ahmed and Saqlain Mushtaq, were also outstanding, while a number of their batsmen were definitely Test-class. I reckon their problems in Australia are probably not too dissimilar to the difficulties that used to hinder Australia in Pakistan. The Australian conditions and Aussie culture, so different from what they're used to at home, intimidate them. Rather than trying to transform their techniques and strategies to suit the wickets, and backing their ability to do that well, they play the way they've always played and struggle as a consequence. One example is the way their batsmen have never come to terms with the extra bounce in Australian wickets, just as we refused for a long time to come to grips with the turning tracks you sometimes see on the Indian Subcontinent. Until Pakistan, and India and Sri Lanka, too, face up to this fact and come to Australia with a clear and appropriate plan as to how they're going to play, they won't do any good.

The Sri Lankans' problems in regard to ball tampering occurred during their first Test of the Australian summer, in Perth, when the neutral umpire, Pakistan's Khizar Hayat, questioned the way the visitors were picking at the ball during our only innings. As the matter was raised very early in our innings, I wasn't privy to the on-field debate, but it soon became clear to us that the umpires handled things badly. If they had a concern with the ball, they should have taken it out of the game, but instead, having decided in their own minds that the ball had been illegally damaged, they handed it back to the Sri Lankans and told them not to do it again. When the ball was examined later, no one could tell whether the ball had been doctored or not, so, quite rightly, the Sri Lankans were cleared, though a cloud hung over them.

All I can say is that while there were a number of occasions during my career when an old ball suddenly started swinging strangely, this wasn't one of them. I am convinced, though, that it is possible to accentuate this 'reverse' swing by scratching and scraping at one side of the ball while polishing the other side. In such circumstances, while a new ball will swing 'away' from the shiny side, an old, scuffed-on-one-side ball can swing even further 'towards' the shiny side. We tried it ourselves in net sessions and were astonished by the way the scratched ball swung, even into a cross breeze.

This ball-tampering episode was small fry compared to the chucking controversy that engulfed the rest of the Sri Lankans' tour. The trigger came midway through the first day of the Boxing Day Test at the MCG when umpire Darrell Hair called their outstanding offie, Muttiah Muralitharan, for throwing. 'What was that for?' someone shouted in our room. First there was disbelief, although some who'd been quietly and privately critical of Murali's action muttered that the umpire's action was overdue. In the middle, the Sri Lankans were fuming, as umpire Hair continued to no-ball poor Murali. Arjuna Ranatunga, the tourists' captain, switched his ace bowler to the other end and this is where I believe the affair descended into farce. For the rest of the innings — our only one of the Test — Murali bowled 32 overs without censure from New Zealand umpire Steve Dunne's end, having been called seven times in three overs by umpire Hair. No wonder the Sri Lankans were confused and hostile.

I am not suggesting that umpire Dunne should have automatically called Murali because his fellow umpire did. What I couldn't understand was that he didn't want to have a look at his action. Umpire Hair had stood back from the stumps for two overs before making his first call; umpire Dunne stayed rigid, right over the stumps. There was a lack of teamwork between the umps that I thought was very disappointing. We knew that a few umpires had questioned Murali's action in recent times — including, we learned later, both Hair and Dunne — but that nothing had been done by the ICC to confirm whether he had a problem. It was that confirmation that was desperately needed — when I first saw Murali bowl in Sri Lanka in 1992 I thought he had a suspect action, but when I talked to a few people who'd seen more of him they said he was okay. It should have been obvious to the authorities that Murali was a gifted bowler who could be wonderful for the game, so they should've had the matter cleared up as quickly as possible. Instead, they dallied. Consequently, I reckon Darrell Hair was right to call him, given the ICC's inaction, because he personally and firmly believed that there was a doubt over the bowler's action. And remember, the laws of cricket clearly say that if the umpire is not entirely satisfied with the absolute fairness of the bowler's action, then he or she should call 'no ball'. I respected him for backing his convictions, and told him so when I saw him after play. Perhaps he didn't need to keep calling Murali, but that's what the laws of cricket asked him to do.

Throwing is such a contentious area, because different people see different things in a bowler's action, most chuckers don't throw every delivery, and very few do it deliberately or know they've thrown one when they have. Murali claims he's unable to fully straighten his arm because of a birth defect, and there's plenty of good judges who, having watched the videos of his action much more closely than I have, reckon he's sweet ... throughout his delivery the bowling arm stays bent. I found him awkward to bat against, and very hard to read, a bowler with freakish talent. Certainly, there have been some much worse actions in world cricket in the past decade, and maybe a West Indian fast bowler or two who didn't mind chucking the odd delivery. One bloke in particular had this nasty habit of bowling three different bouncers. One you could hook, one you could duck out of the way of, the third hit you in the head.

Some animosity built up between the two sides after these incidents, but for a long while the rancour was beaten up by the media and the Sri Lankan community in Australia far beyond what was actually happening. The second one-day final, in Sydney, was the one game that did turn nasty, and I wondered whether we had finally fallen into the roles sections of the public and media had

Angry nights against Sri Lanka ... in consecutive one-dayers I had very public arguments with Roshan Mahanama in Melbourne (above) and Arjuna Ranatunga in Sydney.

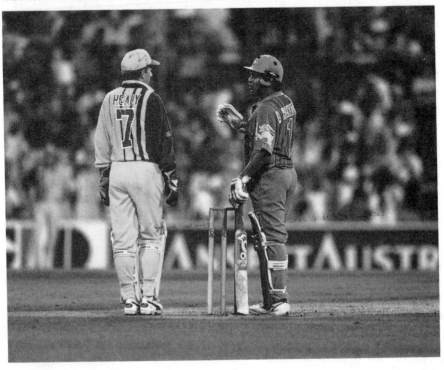

wanted us to play. I was at the centre of it, in a brief but very public disagreement with Ranatunga during their run chase. I'd already had a barney with Roshan Mahanama in Melbourne in the first final, after he got in my way when I was keeping and he was batting with a runner. But we were both fine afterwards — he's a good bloke who played it as tough as I did on the field. At the SCG, it was different. We had made 273 batting first, more than enough we thought, but then a thunderstorm moved in and reduced the tourists' target to a very gettable 168 from 25 overs, with all but two of the fieldsmen being required to stay up in the circle for the first 15 overs. Ranatunga came out with the score 4-66, with a maximum 15.5 overs remaining, but almost immediately went down with an apparent cramp and requested a runner. I thought his behaviour was ridiculous, we all did, and told the portly Sri Lankan captain so.

'Mate, you can't have a runner just because you're unfit,' I snarled.

'It's nothing to do with you,' he replied. 'I have cramp.'

'Have a look at yourself, Porky. That's why you've got cramp,' I added mischievously. Ranatunga spun around and gave it to me, pointing a menacing finger as he did so. I didn't say another word. I'd made my point, and Mark Taylor was in my ear, telling me to shut up.

Eventually, but not straight away, the umpires gave Ranatunga his runner, and the much quicker Sanath Jayasuriya dashed out to do the job. Both sides were filthy. Soon after, another quarrel erupted, as Jayasuriya and Glenn McGrath collided while the Sri Lankans were completing a desperate run, and this time the angry words were accompanied by the odd push and shove. I think fault was pretty evenly shared in that one. Then, after we won the game to take the trophy two games to nil, many of the Sri Lankans refused to shake Tubby's hand. Dav Whatmore, their coach, who had played Shield cricket for Victoria and a little Test cricket for Australia in the late '70s, did come over to congratulate us, but then took a comment I made the wrong way, which didn't help matters. I told him I didn't like the way his team had played that night, but he thought I was suggesting he was responsible for their behaviour. I didn't mean that at all, and rang him when we got to Adelaide for the third Test to clarify the remark. I don't think what I said was inaccurate, but maybe I said it at the wrong time.

What really annoyed us was that through all this we were being painted as villains, while the poor Sri Lankans were angels. This was typical of my time in the Australian team. It was assumed by many, including ACB officials sometimes, that we were always in the wrong. Few seemed to want to listen to our version of events; fewer still wanted to believe us. During the 1995–96 summer, and before and since, the Sri Lankans gave as good as they got on the field, but when the inevitable on-field clashes were publicised, they suddenly ran behind their 'we're just rookies' skirts and let their countrymen and sections of the media come down hard on us. Sure, they were totally frustrated with the umpires and administrators, who in their opinion had stitched them up with the ball-tampering accusations, the throwing calls, and every 50/50 umpiring decision that didn't go their way. But we were just as heartily sick of their whingeing and, when things got competitive out in the middle, we told them so. In my opinion, the biggest problem was Ranatunga, a provocative opportunist on the field and a genuine political animal off it. After that acrimonious second final, Tubby told reporters, 'I think it is time that we mend any bridges that were burned the other day in Sydney. Tempers might have got a little bit out of control.' He then added, 'We would like to hear some positive vibes from the number one Sri Lankan player ... and that is Arjuna.' Throughout, Graham Halbish, the ACB Chief Executive, was desperately trying to bring the teams together.

But Ranatunga would have none of it. 'I'm not answering for Mr Halbish or Mr Taylor,' he responded. 'I'm not going to dance to what they want. I do the right thing for my country.'

By the time of the Adelaide Test in late January 1996, many of the Australian players, including me, had received death threats and the whole saga was spinning out of control. We were scheduled to play our opening group match of the cricket's sixth World Cup in Colombo on February 17, but were now being told that to do so would be to put our lives on the line. At the time, the Sri Lankan nation was wrought with internal divisions that went a million miles beyond cricket, and we were now caught up in it. Sadly, bombs and guerilla warfare had become a fact of life in some areas of Sri Lanka, and when we heard reports of bloodshed it exacerbated the impact of the sick letters we had received. One day, Craig McDermott opened a particularly descriptive and specific bomb threat, posted to his home, which he promptly handed on to the federal police. Soon after, Glenn McGrath received an envelope in the Adelaide Oval dressing room, which had been forwarded from our hotel, which was just as sick and frightening. A fax had come through the ACB offices in Melbourne, which contained a threat that when the Australian team arrived in Colombo they'd be greeted by a suicide bomber. What should we do, just put smiles on our faces and go? Right at the moment, few of us wanted to. On the field, a couple of the Australian players had been told by one of the Sri Lankans, 'Wait till you get to Sri Lanka ...'

A meeting had been called before the Adelaide Test. It was attended by all the players plus Denis Rogers, the new ACB Chairman, Graham Halbish and Des Rundle, the ACB Treasurer, and we went through the three alternatives: we go to the World Cup as planned; we don't go; or we stay out of Sri Lanka but play our other World Cup matches in India and Pakistan. The ACB was aware of our concerns, but worried too about the long-term ramifications for cricket and Australia–Sri Lanka relations of a 'boycott' of Colombo. We were told of the elaborate security arrangements that would be in place, akin to that given to touring Heads of State, and welcomed Mr Rogers' statement that the players' safety was the ACB's highest priority.

While we'd been very disappointed with the way the officials had handled the ball-tampering issue and especially the throwing affair, in this instance the Board's response appeared shrewd and sensible. We came away from that meeting reasonably certain we'd be playing all our matches in the World Cup and decided at a later meeting during the Test that we would go to Colombo, though we'd minimise our time in Sri Lanka outside the game itself. We also resolved to immediately improve our relationship with the Sri Lankan team.

The Adelaide Test was played in a much better spirit, thanks in part to the efforts of the two captains — Tubby, who instigated a beer between the two sides after the match, and Aravinda de Silva, who was filling in for the injured Ranatunga. We came away from that game with a 3-0 series cleansweep and wishing we'd got together earlier than when we finally did; had we done so I'm sure we could have avoided the pressures and consequent bitterness of that Sydney final. Two days after the Test finished, however, a suicide bomber launched a ghastly attack in the centre of Colombo, not far from the hotel where we would be staying. Early media reports had the death toll at more than 100. The Australian players were quickly on the phone to each other, and all the conversations had the same theme: now we definitely don't want to go to Sri Lanka.

In my view it was too much to stage a cricket match in potentially the wrong place at the wrong time, and the ACB agreed. Once the Board was armed with advice from the Department of Foreign Affairs that all Australians should avoid Sri Lanka unless there they had a desperately good reason to be there, they moved swiftly to call off Australia's match in Colombo, even though the ICC threatened (and eventually ruled) that the decision meant we were forfeiting the match. Around the same time, the West Indies Board did exactly the same thing on behalf of their players.

When we gathered in Brisbane for our pre-Cup training camp a few days later, I was still very apprehensive about the trip. I'd just spent some time in my own home, with my pregnant wife (we'd just found out that Helen was due in late September) and two beautiful daughters, and was thinking, 'I'm only a cricketer, is it really worth it?' Simmo came over on the first morning of the camp and asked me what was wrong.

'Simmo, I don't really want to go,' I said quietly. 'The flak we're going to cop once we get over there won't be worth it.'

The truth was that in all the discussions we'd had about the Cup we always talked in terms of 'one out all out', and I am such a strong believer in the team and loyalty that there was never any real chance of me pulling out. But that didn't mean that I had to want to go.

— ¤ —

AFTER ANOTHER BIG hundred from Steve Waugh and some excellent bowling from Paul Reiffel and Glenn McGrath had beaten the Sri Lankans in the third Test, David Boon, who'd announced before the match that this would be his last game in international cricket, led the team in a final, heartfelt rendition of *Under the Southern Cross*. Then he quietened the room to announce that I would be the one to lead the team in their victory song in future. When I joined him on the dressing room table it was one of the highlights of my cricket life, and one of the most nerve-racking — I reckon I was as anxious as I'd been before my Test debut.

Rod Marsh — who'd passed the honour to Allan Border, who in turn had passed it on to Boonie — was in the Adelaide Oval dressing room that day, but refused to jump on the table with us. His time, he said, was gone, but he was happy to be in the team circle. The singing of that song that day was one of those emotional moments in the life of an Australian cricketer, one that reminds you of the true and unique value of the baggy green. Today, I remember Boonie's farewell with great affection, not just the song but everything — when he choked up telling the team he was retiring, his final innings, walking off the field one last time, his wife and family shedding a quiet tear in the grandstand …

Still, I will always believe Boonie retired too early. He first started talking about giving it away in 1995, on the West Indies tour, and I thought he was kidding, just looking for a little reassurance from his peers that he was still wanted. Which, of course, he was. Boonie was the rock on which many an Australian victory was based, a guy whose body language never changed, never gave much away. He was a wonderful concentrator, and a tough man, very difficult to get on top of, which is why I rated him so highly: I always wanted to be that style of combatant myself. Boonie was very similar to Mark Taylor in the way he approached the game and put a very high price on his wicket. He rarely strayed from his own style, sacrificing the shots that he considered too risky, and in doing so forced disheartened bowlers into trying to be different or special to get him out. Then, when the bad ball came along, he hit it for four.

Boonie is a proud Tasmanian, a man who loves a red wine and loved a wrestle on the team bus. I only saw him lose his composure once during his long career, and that was when, on the 1993 tour of England, he was joined in a Manchester men's room toilet by Tim May. As they stood at the urinal together, eyes straight ahead, Boonie decided to give Maysie a gentle touch-up. Only trouble was, it wasn't Tim May at all. The poor bloke bolted, and our man of stone went to water. That miscalculation aside, Boonie was at his most prolific that year in the UK, when he started the series with a 93 in the second innings of the first Test and then made three hundreds in three consecutive matches.

During his 'retirement' season, and maybe the summer before, I thought that if he could just lift his enjoyment level and training level by one percentage point he could have bounced his Test career back to its best. But it seemed he'd lost his enthusiasm by that critical fraction and didn't really train as intensely as he had in the past. Finally, he retired, after he learned that he wasn't going to be a member of the Australian World Cup side. I wonder now if he regrets that decision just a little. He could have taken it on the chin, and worked hard to get himself right for the Test series against the Windies in 1996–97 and then another Ashes tour. As it was, he played three more years of Shield cricket, and county cricket for Durham, when he could have still been playing for Australia. Until Justin Langer started scoring heaps of runs for Australia in 1999–2000, I don't think we ever genuinely replaced Boonie at No. 3. It wasn't easy to do.

WE FINALLY LEFT FOR India on February 9, 1996, two days before the World Cup opening ceremony, still unsure of what we'd be doing in the two weeks between our departure and what was now our opening game, against Kenya in Visakhapatnam. As it turned out, we spent a very long 12 days in Calcutta and Bombay, before finally travelling to 'Vizag' via Madras to begin our campaign. Fortunately, we weren't outcasts in India; in fact in the main we were made to feel welcome by the public, though the organisers and sections of the media obviously didn't like us. We sensed, too, that a few people weren't going out of their way to help us through that first difficult fortnight. Good and available practice facilities were hard to find. But on the bus trip from the airport in Calcutta to our hotel in the city centre the streets were lined with thousands of cricket fans, all of whom seemed happy and passionate and delighted to see us.

At times the lead-up to our first game descended to farce. It took the uniform-makers three goes to spell 'Healy' without a second 'e' after the 'l' on the back of my shirt. In Calcutta, my sleep was disturbed by room service: 'Mr Healy, would you like to order anything?' And everywhere we went there were security guards, armed with the very latest in high-tech submachine guns.

Despite the fact that we were starting two points behind everybody bar the West Indies, we went into the Cup as one of the favourites. A highlight of our early rounds was the clash with India in Bombay, a wonderful carnival of a day/night that we won by 16 runs despite an astonishing 90 by Sachin Tendulkar. Earlier Mark Waugh had made a brilliant century, and then Damien Fleming took 5-36.

Our bowling plan to Tendulkar was to aim just short of a length, hoping he'd still try to hit fours on the rise or across the line. Glenn McGrath did this superbly, three maiden overs straight, but then Sachin said 'enough of this', and smashed two beautiful pull shots to the leg-side boundary. Pigeon pitched further up, yorker length, and the ball rocketed to the extra-cover fence. The cacophony from the full house delivered at this point was remarkable. Tubs turned to Warney, and the crowd held its breath, but after a tough catch was dropped at deep mid-off, Sachin was off again. While he was there India were cruising, but when Mark Waugh speared a ball quicker and wider, well outside the little champ's off-stump, I completed a stumping and the game was ours. Just like that. Sachin means so much to that Indian team, and the entire nation.

We finished the group matches with three wins (Kenya, India and Zimbabwe), one loss (West Indies) and a forfeit, which set up a quarter-final against New Zealand in Madras. Gee, it was hot that day. It's the only game I've ever played where I had to dash off during a drinks break to use the toilet. It might also have been the game when Junior played his best one-day innings, a brave and brilliant 110 that spearheaded our successful pursuit of the Kiwis' big total of 286. Amazingly, when Junior went out to open our innings he was already cramping up a little in the calves, but he overcame that to play superbly. Afterwards I did my first solo victory song, which we'd decided we'd do through the knockout stages of the tournament. I loved it!

Security was ultra-tight during the 1996 World Cup — to the point that if we went for a run our guards would jog along with us — but I still had opportunities to get a kick and a mark in. Unfortunately, while this might look like an impressive grab (left), I never really got the hang of Australian football.

This was a run chase in which we used Shane Warne as a pinch hitter. In at 2-84, Warney belted 24 off 14 balls, to get our run-rate back on track. It was an idea that we'd toyed with in the past, and on this occasion I mentioned the idea to Michael Slater, who was sitting next to me, a couple of minutes before Steve Waugh came over and suggested the same thing. So I went over to Tubby and soon after Warney was putting the pads on. Warney's cameo made our batsmen's job that crucial little bit easier, and even if it hadn't worked, we wouldn't have lost anything like what we stood to gain.

Although we were into the semi-finals, I wasn't enjoying the tour very much. 'Irritable tourist,' I wrote in my diary on March 11, the day of the New Zealand game, 'spare time, injury, form ... get happy.' I was struggling a little with back, finger and thumb injuries — none serious, all frustrating — and was finding the unending plane and bus trips, complete with inordinate delays and ridiculous scheduling, overwhelmingly tedious. By the time of the quarter-final I was jack of it all. And the thought of venturing out onto the streets to take in the sights was impeded by the ever-present armed personnel who shadowed us wherever we went.

From Madras, in the south of India, we had to get to Chandigarh in the north. This involved a trip to New Delhi, stay overnight, and then on to Chandigarh on a flight we shared with our semi-final opponents, the West Indies. During that flight, Brian Lara passed a letter to Warney, which he said he'd been given by a woman sitting further up the plane. Warney opened the document, which was written by someone sitting in seat 22F and claiming to be a former Miss India. Would Shane like to come up and say hello? Warney looked up to row 22, moved his eyes across to seat F, and there was ... Curtly Ambrose, eyes shut, listening to his walkman! Any laugh on those bloody plane trips was a good one.

> *March 14, 1996: Win toss: batting. 4-15, then Law and Bevan add 138. 5-153 — 41 overs. Me: 31 run out, last ball. Total: 207. WI 2-165 in 42nd over — 10-202.*
>
> *Unbelievable huddle on ground, rooms afterwards same as Ashes '89, WI '95!! Hotel crazy when we return! Drinks in team room, singing, GREAT SCENES ...*
>
> *Ring Helen at 4am!*

This game made it all worthwhile! With nine overs to go, there's no doubt the Windies had us, but they panicked just as we began to bowl and field very, very well. Warney was superb, as was Glenn McGrath, while Damien Fleming held his nerve magnificently in the final over. There was no one key dismissal, or one specific moment that won it for us, just a case of our main bowlers picking a very major stage to show their stuff, and the whole team backing them. The pressure was intense, and on this important occasion we thrived on it. It was unbelievable. My major contribution was to run out Ambrose in the last over when he and

My dismissal in the World Cup final in Lahore, bowled by Aravinda de Silva for 2.

Richardson attempted a cheeky bye. Someone later said I was lucky to hit the stumps like that, but they didn't know about the 1000-odd times I'd rehearsed that very underarm throw at practice every summer.

The final, in contrast, was a major disappointment for us, and by this I'm not just referring to the result. We'd been playing in India for so long that to go to Pakistan, where we weren't nearly as popular, for one game was unsettling. Getting through customs was an adventure, then we got to Lahore where the hotel was excellent but the practice nets provided were not — just one net for each team. Every day in the lead-up to the final there were so many people in the hotel foyer that I could never escape to find some private time or to do my golf ball. It was all so rushed, there was no sense of normality at all. There were ticket hassles, the organisation at the official pre-final World Cup dinner was disgraceful and then when the morning of the final dawned wet, we were told the match wouldn't start on time, and might even be postponed until tomorrow. When we arrived at the ground, late, we learnt that the pitch was dry and the final would begin as scheduled. Thus, we had to snap from easygoing to ready-to-play in very quick time. I'm not making excuses — the Sri Lankans faced many of these hurdles as well. This was supposed to be one of the biggest experiences of my cricketing life but things became so hectic and disorganised in the lead-up that I never had an opportunity to savour it.

Our opponents were … Sri Lanka! Ranatunga's men had beaten England in a mild surprise in the quarter-finals and then shocked all of India in the semis, prompting riots and recriminations across the land. The Pakistanis, meanwhile, were still mourning their loss to India in the quarter-finals. Tubby won the toss and batted, and for a while it appeared we'd amass a huge total, but we became bogged down in the middle overs. We actually managed to score 1-134 from the first 25 overs and 6-107 from the second 25, and didn't hit a single boundary between the 19th and the 43rd over. The key point here is that the Sri Lankan spinners bowled magnificently, and Ranatunga's captaincy was very clever.

During the break between innings, the floodlights went out, so we were left, ready and rarin' to go, but stuck in the barrier stalls. When play finally recommenced we managed to dismiss the pair we'd identified as the biggest dangermen, the openers Jayasuriya and Kaluwitharana, for just 23, but from there it was all downhill, as Gurusinha, Ranatunga and especially Aravinda de Silva batted excellently, while we found it hard to handle a ball made slippery by a heavy evening dew.

Perhaps we were tired after all the distractions we'd faced over the previous two months. I do remember being very nervous before the final, which was unusual for me. I usually coped with the pressure of big games pretty well, and the nature of international cricket is that most games are big games anyway, so you get used to that pressure. But I was a little anxious, which suggests to me that I was a little tired. If you're fresh and ready to go, nerves disappear very quickly. I wonder whether we'd used up our intensity in the quarter-final and semi-final. One thing we didn't do in Lahore was underrate our opponents, who we knew were suited to the conditions and would keep wearing away at us all day and night. Later, we suspected we revelled too passionately in the joy of our semi-final victory, not in terms of the amount of grog we put away (in fact, we hardly drank at all) but just in the way that, perhaps subconsciously, we thought we'd become bullet-proof. Certainly, in 1999, when Steve Waugh's Australians won through to the seventh World Cup final after a once-in-a-lifetime escape against South Africa, the celebrations were well and truly tempered. There was no rendition of *Under the Southern Cross* as there had been in Chandigarh. Stephen wanted the '99 team totally focused on the final.

We made a low-key return to Australia after the '96 World Cup. Every one of us — players, fans, officials and politicians — were relieved the campaign was over, disappointed that we hadn't played as well as we would have liked in the final, and more than happy to have a break. I came back to try my best to help Helen and reintroduce myself again to my daughters. We were scheduled to play an eight-a-side competition in July in Kuala Lumpur, a domestic eights comp in early August, and then depart for Sri Lanka in mid-August for a one-day tournament featuring the hosts, India and Zimbabwe. Inevitably, this would be a tour requiring exemplary diplomatic skills from our captain, who would be accompanied by a new Australian coach, Geoff Marsh, after Bob Simpson's 10-year reign had been brought to a close. In early August I had dinner in Sydney at Mark Taylor's place, where he told me that he was struggling with his back and was no good thing to make the trip to Colombo. A few days later I was back in Brisbane and the phone rang. Tubby was out …

'Congratulations, Heals, you're in charge.'

CAPTAIN DIPLOMACY

IT COULD BE THAT I nearly lost the Australian captaincy before I had it. Early in August 1996, I launched my first book, *Playing for Keeps*, and the media immediately honed in on the sections of the book where I criticised Arjuna Ranatunga's behaviour during the previous season and told the story of the threats that had been made against the team. 'DEATH THREATS — Healy accuses Lankan skipper' roared the *Sunday Telegraph* of August 11. The following day, I received a message to ring a senior ACB official. At this point Tubby had not withdrawn from the tour, but everybody was aware that he was 1000-1 to be available.

That official told me that the Board was concerned about the previous day's story and the ramifications in Sri Lanka, given that the Australian team was about to land there. He told me that he had received some calls from 'friends in Sri Lanka who aren't happy', but he couldn't tell me why they were unhappy. I asked the official if he'd read the extract from my book and he admitted that he hadn't. Then came the bombshell.

'Ian, I must tell you,' he said gravely, 'that we'll be reviewing your position as Mark Taylor's replacement as captain for the tour.'

Taken aback, I asked the official if he had heard any of the 20 or more media interviews I'd done in the past week in which I had consistently pushed a very positive line about the tour. No he hadn't. He then muttered something about 'damage control', and I replied that once he read the article he'd realise that this wasn't necessary. I reiterated that I'd been proactive anyway by being ultra-positive in my press comments in the previous week, even when I was told by a journalist that more than 30 people had been killed in yet another bomb attack. The conversation ended abruptly with a reminder that the Board was meeting later in the week, and that I'd be told immediately of their decision. Nice to talk to you …

I never heard another word from the ACB about the book, and by the end of the week I had been confirmed as Mark Taylor's stand-in.

—◻—

FOR MY FIRST PRESS conference as the Australian captain I was flanked not by Bob Simpson, but by his successor as Australian coach Geoff Marsh. Swamp had the job after the ACB decided in their wisdom that after 10 years it was time for a coaching change. I, for one, was sorry to see Simmo go, though my disappointment was tempered when I learned that Geoff was his replacement. I knew Swamp would do a decent job, but I still wondered why Simmo had been dumped and especially why he had gone with such little ceremony. If anyone deserved a huge testimonial dinner with all the trimmings it was Simmo, who had given so much to the game and the Australian team over the previous 40 years. Instead, he went quietly, I'm sure very satisfied with what he'd achieved with the Australian team between 1986 and 1996. Perhaps he wanted to depart without fanfare? Maybe he'd upset someone at the ACB? I don't know.

My favourite Bob Simpson story concerns an episode that occurred during our match against Surrey on the 1993 Ashes tour, after Paul Reiffel came back into our dressing room after being dismissed for a duck and threw his bat across the room. Immediately, Simmo was into him — it was a pet hate of Simmo's to have guys damaging their equipment because they made a mistake. Cricketers should learn from their errors, he argued. And Simmo hated dummy spits and sudden displays of rage, which he thought upset the ambience of the dressing room and potentially the morale of the team. 'You don't need to show other people you're upset, Paul,' our coach said firmly on this occasion.

After Pistol was dismissed, Allan Border declared to give us a few overs at the Surrey openers before stumps. Shane Warne, who'd been batting with Pistol when our now contrite pace bowler lost his wicket, was many metres behind when the bat throwing and Simmo's brief lecture took place. When Shane entered the room, he was a little agitated himself, because he didn't get a decent hit, and gave no one in particular a quick spray and then threw his bat at his coffin. As soon as we saw the bat spin through the air — for me, it was as if it was in slow motion — we knew Shane was in for the same sermon Pistol had just copped, but then the bat hit the coffin and rebounded, bang!, straight into Simmo's bung knee.

'For Christ's sake, Shane, that's bloody stupid!' Simmo exploded.

So much for not showing people you're upset. We broke up, all of us, and even Simmo eventually saw the funny side of it. Maybe you had to be there ... or you had to know Simmo.

Ninety-nine times out of a hundred he was a very sensible, sober man, a bloke with a tough exterior who is absolutely devoted to cricket. Simmo's enthusiasm for the game is undeniable; he never tires of watching it, talking about it, mixing with other cricket people, loving it. He has an enormous respect for the traditions of the game, but is the first to welcome innovations when he sees they will benefit it. He understands the intricacies of technique better than just about anyone, but encourages unorthodoxy and improvisation, again, so long as he sees a profit in it. I think he understands the game better than anyone else I've met.

Soon after he was appointed coach, Simmo cut a swathe through the Australian team, bolstering Allan Border as captain, identifying and nurturing players whose attitude to cricket matched his and ruthlessly casting aside those he saw as flippant, lacking a work ethic or disrespectful to the sport. Some of those who were cast aside reckoned Simmo destroyed their careers unjustly, but as he

Bob Simpson with Damien Fleming, after 'Flem' had bowled a fantastic final over in our World Cup semi-final against the West Indies in Chandigarh.

always said, he helped a hell of a lot more cricketers than he burnt. I know some people felt threatened by Simmo the coach also being Simmo the selector, but I always felt that was unfair, too. It always appeared to me that he was much keener to help a bloke get over a form slump than to flick him at a selection meeting. After all, if the team was playing good cricket it reflected well on his coaching ability.

While some felt threatened by Simmo, I never did. Maybe that was because I came into the team with such a rush and recognised immediately that he was out to help me. I always found him very loyal to people who were honest with him. I recall back in 1991–92, against India at the SCG, I played an awful, ill-disciplined shot and was caught near the boundary when I should have been playing for time. I came off and declared to no one in particular but everyone around me, 'You shouldn't be doing that sort of thing in a baggy green cap. If I was a selector I'd drop me straight away.' The bloke standing closest to me *was* a selector, and he could have taken that remark back to the next selection meeting. Instead, Simmo sat down and said quietly, 'You made a bad mistake. It wasn't bad luck. Make sure you learn from it and don't let it happen again.'

To Simmo, a mistake is never a mistake unless you do it twice. I believe in that adage, too.

Simmo and I had plenty of arguments about whether as a team we drank too much. He used to really keep an eye on us to make sure we didn't fall into what he called 'the disco syndrome', but I countered his displeasure by explaining that in my eyes we were only drinking at the appropriate times. I don't think we ever agreed with each other on this one, but he always found time to listen to my case, as I did to his. I always felt we needed an outlet to escape the pressure of the game, especially when we were playing a lot of cricket in a short space of time, and that it was essential we celebrate our successes. Simmo, in contrast, didn't want *anything* to impinge on our performance. I didn't think our partying did that, sometimes he wasn't so sure.

One of his greatest skills was his ability to recognise a player's fault, technical or mental, and then fix it. He worked hard with Steve Waugh when Tugga was having problems with the short ball in the early 1990s, getting him less side on and convincing him that it didn't matter what he looked like as long as the short ones didn't get him out. He also gave Boonie a very effective rev-up when he felt our No. 3 had become a little comfortable with life and wasn't operating on all cylinders. 'In the comfort zone' Simmo called it, and I never forgot the lesson, especially later in my career, when occasionally I thought my standards and enthusiasm were slipping. When he was coach, Simmo was forever on my back, reminding me that I didn't need to hit fours and sixes to be an effective late-order batsman in one-day cricket. 'Keep hustling,' he'd say, 'take the one and twos and threes off every ball.'

In 1991 Simmo wrote down a piece of advice for me that I valued so highly that I put it in the front of my yearly diary. I can remember reading it fondly not long after I made my first Test hundred. He wrote of my batting:

> … *So far only a small part of your talents have been exposed. I still feel your self-destruct button gets pushed too frequently. It is almost as if you accelerate into disaster and if you get 4, 5 or 6 an over you can't get off the roller coaster. This continued acceleration ends in dismissal. Once you learn to control that aspect of your batting you will score Test 100s.*
>
> *You must never repress completely your natural aggression, just temper it with a higher level of commonsense and calm.*
>
> *No use getting the shits after the dismissal; more control and composure before the act is the way to greater success.*

Simmo has not received the credit he deserves for his major role in getting the modern Australian team back on track. He wanted us to be as professional as possible in regard to our preparation, ensuring we got the fundamentals right. He wanted us to be sensible cricketers, and do the little things, such as hitting the ball into the gaps, bowling to a plan, getting the slips in the right position, taking every run. He never gave blokes the easy option, but was always prepared to work with his cricketers to get things right. And like the best players in his teams, he was prepared to back his beliefs and judgement, until someone was able to show him there was a better way. There very rarely was.

—◻—

SO NOW, WITH GEOFF Marsh at my side, I was captain of my country, though everyone knew this was a fill-in role, as Tubby was sure he'd be right for the tour of India in late September and October. We were also without Shane Warne, who had decided to have surgery on his spinning finger after the World Cup and

With injured captain Mark Taylor at the press conference in August 1996 when it was announced that I'd be taking the Australian team to Sri Lanka later in the month.

wouldn't return to the Australian side until November. With or without them, all involved with the Australian team recognised that this Sri Lankan visit was going to be awkward, and I knew that my diplomatic skills were going to be tested. 'I would be lying if I said there were no fears whatsoever,' I told reporters at the press conference after we arrived, when asked if we still had concerns for our safety. 'But the reception we have received so far has gone a long way to dispel our fears.' I had been told by our manager, Dr Cam Battersby, not to talk about the previous Australian summer or our decision not to play in Sri Lanka, and Cam was later slammed in one Colombo daily for refusing to respond to questions about these issues. However, I was still learning, and rather than say nothing, I remarked when asked, 'We just got a bit cranky last summer with Pakistan and Sri Lanka because they weren't communicating that well. Our intention here is to play as fair and hard as we can without making a scene for anyone.'

From that point on I tried to make myself available for media interviews as often as I could, always trying to steer the conversations towards the future. The locals were grateful for such access, which they weren't used to, and surprised we weren't bitter and twisted, as we'd been painted by the Sri Lankan papers before and during the World Cup.

Overall, the tour went off without any major dramas. Off the field, our movements were restricted by the ever-present security. On it, we won two of our four matches, defeating India and Zimbabwe but losing twice, including in the final, to the home team. In our first game against the Sri Lankans, I was roundly hooted when I came out to bat, at least in part because extracts from my book were published in the local papers that very morning, and my dismissal soon after — caught Ranatunga bowled Muralitharan —inspired unrestrained glee throughout the stadium. However, in the main the locals were good-natured, applauding warmly when Mark Waugh and Michael Bevan reached 50. A week later, rain threatened to ruin the final, and the match was eventually reduced to 35 overs a side. I won the toss, sent them in, and watched their ultra-confident batsmen smash 3-234, with Aravinda de Silva smashing 75 not out from 64 balls, giving him a tournament aggregate of 334 runs from four unbeaten knocks. This was on top of his effort in the World Cup, when he belted us for an unbeaten 107! In reply, we were never likely, and finished 50 runs short. Perhaps the conditions suited them, but such was the Sri Lankans' confidence at this time, it was very hard to argue that they weren't the best limited-overs team in the world.

I enjoyed the captaincy. The only time I found myself in any trouble was against India, when I was given not out in a close run out call, but then the fieldsmen convinced the umpire, Mr KT Francis, to consult the video umpire, who gave me out. I was very disappointed, not because of the decision — if the TV said I was out, I was out — but because the ump allowed himself to be influenced by the Indians. The tour conditions clearly stated that players weren't allowed to ask for the video replay, and I reminded the umpire of that fact before I left. I enjoyed devising and implementing tactics and occasionally experimenting, such as when we held back Glenn McGrath and Damien Fleming and opened the bowling instead with Stuart Law and Steve Waugh in our first match against Sri Lanka. Our logic was that the slower pace of Tugga and Lawey might hinder their swashbuckling openers Jayasuriya and Kaluwitharana. Tugga did get 'Kalu', but Jayasuriya took to the slower balls as savagely as he'd belted the quicks during the World Cup, finishing with 44 from 28 balls. Still, it was worth a try. We also ensured that everyone got an opportunity, and two new players — the wrist-spinning all-rounder, Brad Hogg, and a young Adelaide quick named Gillespie — made their one-day international debuts during the tour.

'Dizzy' Gillespie, as he quickly became known, had first been introduced to us during the 1996 World Cup, when he was flown over as a replacement for the again-injured Craig McDermott. Before Dizzy's selection, there were no South Australians in our squad. He'd come from nowhere — so much so that most of us hardly knew him — and I'll never forget Simmo, who was no longer a selector by this stage, coming into our room and saying, after the selection was announced, 'Yep, his name's Jason ... I've checked.' But we quickly learned exactly who Jason Gillespie was and how good a fast bowler he was going to be.

I always knew, in one-day cricket at least, that the captaincy wouldn't impinge on my wicketkeeping. At the time, I wasn't so sure that this would be the case in Test cricket, especially given that much of my time would involve keeping to Warney. But to be honest, it wasn't something I gave much thought to — my job at this time was vice-captain, a position I was proud of, and my ambition was to be as good a deputy to Tubby and for the team as I could be. Worry about the moment, let the future look after itself, was my philosophy.

OUR SHORT SOJOURN TO Sri Lanka was the beginning of a cricket travelogue that would continue, with only short breaks in between series and tournaments, until April 1998. By September '96, I had played in 79 Tests and calculated that there were 21 Tests scheduled up until the end of the 1997–98 Australian summer. It had become something of a goal of mine to play 100 Tests — no keeper had ever reached that landmark — and I decided to use that figure as a bit of a carrot. It was funny, because when I had returned from Pakistan in 1988, the then Queensland coach, John Bell, had said to me, 'I want to work with you so that I can get you to 100 Test matches for Australia.'

'Whoa, mate,' I replied, 'I might not get to four!'

Mark Taylor was fit enough to take back the captaincy for a tour that featured just one Test and a one-day tournament involving our hosts, India, and South Africa. Unfortunately, while Tubby had an excellent one-day series with the bat, as a team we had a shocker, losing not just the Test but all our one-day matches as well. The South Africans were much too good for us, but our two losses to India were much closer.

At this point, while the amount of cricket we were playing wasn't bothering me, what was wearing me down was the amount of *one-day* cricket we were involved in. That one Test, which we lost by seven wickets in Delhi despite a superb display of patient, defensive batting by Steve Waugh, was only the second Test we'd played so far in 1996. But in the same timeframe we'd played World Series matches, World Cup matches, Singer Trophy matches in Sri Lanka, now these Titan Cup games in India. For a keeper, limited-overs games are not particularly challenging — you're there to catch and you don't get too many dismissals. As a No. 7 batsman I was rarely required to do more than get going straightaway. But the strain on my body from these contests and all the travelling in between was ongoing. Perhaps more than at any other time in my career, my diary was full of reminders to stay positive, and also complaints about my lack of good fortune. I had become a little disillusioned with life on the merry-go-round. Despite all this, I still loved playing for Australia in every form of cricket and never wanted to miss a game, and still enjoyed treating my injuries and getting myself up for future challenges, whatever they might be.

In the second innings of the Test I was the victim of one of the best stumpings I've ever sensed. I say 'sensed' because, of course, I didn't see it live because it all occurred so quickly behind my back, but I knew immediately that I'd been the victim of something special. What had happened was that Anil Kumble, India's outstanding almost-medium-pace leggie, had got one to drift in to me, and I went to work him on the legside but missed. I overbalanced, no more than a fraction, as the ball speared between my legs. No way could Nayan Mongia, their keeper, have seen it until very late, and the delivery was one of Kumble's quicker ones, but he grabbed it, low down, and had the bails off so rapidly that I couldn't get back, even though I only needed to recover a few centimetres. As I said, I sensed I'd been beaten by something special, and when I saw the replays I marvelled at just how brilliant the Indian keeper had been.

Trying to stave off a big defeat against India in Delhi in October 1996. Unfortunately, my ambitions were destroyed by a brilliant stumping by the Indian keeper, Nayan Mongia.

In our one-dayer against India in Bangalore after the Test (a match we eventually lost by two wickets), I felt my hamstring tighten as I skied and madly ran the last ball of our allotted 50 overs. The niggle didn't stop me keeping throughout the Indians' innings, but I did have to ice it that night and knew I'd have to miss the following game, which was scheduled for four days later against South Africa. But that was all. Imagine my surprise then, when I received a phone call from an ABC Radio reporter early the next morning seeking confirmation that I'd be going home early. This was the first I'd heard of it, but I soon learned that Western Australia's impressive young keeper-batsman, Adam Gilchrist, was on his way, and that Graham Halbish had released a press statement saying that 'it was in my best interests' to return to Australia as soon as possible. Instead, I decided to stay on the tour, and work with Errol to get the leg right. In the old days I would have been consulted before any decision was made as to the need to call in reinforcements. I now had time to contemplate the reality that for the first time in three-and-a-half years I had a real challenger to my place in the Australian set-up. My gentle concern about my form was turning into real paranoia about my future and what my colleagues thought about me. I resolved to get myself in a better, more positive frame of mind before the Test matches began back home.

'Gilly' made his one-day international debut against the South Africans and played again in our next match, and then I came back for our last encounter, a do-or-die affair against India. Because India, like us, had lost their three matches to South Africa, and we had lost once and had one game washed out against the home side, we could still have reached the final with a high-scoring win. In the end, we hit enough runs, 284 in all, but sadly we finished six runs short of our victory target, when Glenn McGrath was run out by the first ball of the 50th and final over. And so ended the least productive (in terms of victories) Australian tour I was ever involved in.

Looking back, I reckon one of the problems with that Indian tour was that we were too focused on the upcoming West Indies, South African and England Test series and let the matches we should have been concentrating on pass us by. I remember after Gilly arrived, he came up to me at one point and asked why we didn't have a specific plan going into our second one-dayer against South Africa. What were the jobs that everyone in this team was supposed to do, he wondered. It was a fair criticism, and I, as vice-captain, had to accept some of the blame. We'd subconsciously prioritised our games and series and put this Indian tour well down our list.

This attitude is rare in Australian teams, because they are usually excellent at treating every game specially, but the fact that there was a degree of prioritising reflects just how much importance we placed on winning the home series against the Windies. We all knew that if we didn't win that one, the critics would be quick to label the 1995 triumph a one-off, but if we won ... then it would be like a repeat of that glorious triumph in the Caribbean, only in front of our own supporters. That would be something to savour.

CHAPTER 17

KEEPING
THE FAITH

IN THE LEAD-UP TO the 1996–97 Australia–West Indies Test series in Australia, the *Australian's* senior cricket writer, Mike Coward, wrote a lengthy article that bluntly questioned whether I should retain the vice-captaincy of the Australian Test team. From there, speculation snowballed, as the entire media began questioning not just my claims to the vice-captaincy but also my spot in the side. While I recognised Coward's right to form opinions and to put his views in print, I was disappointed that sections of the media interpreted the article as a statement of fact, which meant that I was then obliged to participate in an extended series of interviews on my playing future.

Strangely, though, while the media scrutiny angered me, it also galvanised me, and having fought through the final stages of the Indian tour riddled by mixed thoughts, I enjoyed the fact that I found myself eagerly looking forward to the first West Indies Test.

> *November 14, 1996: I think I will now find out just how*
> *good I am — funny feeling of inner strength and calm.*

From the moment Coward's article hit the newsstands the questions in the lead-up to the first Test were all about my future, my form, my confidence. I had never expected an armchair ride from the media, especially given Adam Gilchrist's success at Shield level, but I was astonished at how quickly they were writing me off. I'd reached the point where I thought I deserved a little more respect for what I'd achieved during my career, but instead it seemed as if the previous eight years amounted to nothing. Still, I answered all their enquiries as patiently and candidly as I could, all the while fervently hoping that my on-field performance in the upcoming Test would prove them wrong.

The night before the toss, during our team meeting, Tubs had gone right around the room, asking each member of the side why they saw this series as something special. The general theme was that we needed to reinforce our '95 victory; I commented, too, that I wanted to prove my inquisitors wrong and was encouraged by the way my teammates rallied around me.

That meeting gave me a really positive feeling about the entire series, reminding me of how much I wanted to be part of the team, and why I'd worked so hard to be the cricketer I was. In all the commotion of the previous 12 months — the throwing controversy, the Sri Lankan antagonism, the death threats, Ranatunga, the World Cup loss, Tubby's injury, the Sri Lankan tour, the endless one-dayers, my injury, the media conjecture about me — I'd almost forgotten about all the plusses.

When I strode out to bat on the Test's opening day, I was bolstered further by the enthusiastic cheers of the Gabba crowd. The best cricket fans in the world are the ones who back you when you're down, when you most need support. Two wickets had just fallen in successive balls, leaving the scoreboard tottering slightly at 5-196 and the bowler, new Windies captain Courtney Walsh, in a menacing mood. Up the other end was a friendly face, Steve Waugh, my partner in many a fighting partnership.

Fortunately, the Gabba wicket was as magnificent this day as it always was during my career (even in 1988–89, when we were flogged in two and a half days, it was an excellent batting track) and I came in at a time when the Windies bowlers were overdoing the short stuff. The sight of Stephen had made them go bumper crazy, which was silly, because he'd handled that sort of bowling so well in the Caribbean and wasn't suddenly going to falter now, no matter how awkward he might occasionally look. When I was on strike, Curtly Ambrose gave nothing away, but I was as patient as I have ever been, letting balls go and waiting for the off-line deliveries from the other bowlers. The ball was coming beautifully onto the bat. By stumps we were 5-282, Tugga was 48 not out and I was 47 not out. I went to bed that night feeling a lot better about the world than I had two nights before.

The following day was like a dream. Had I sat down in the morning and mapped it out I couldn't have done any better. Before I left home for the Gabba on that second day I told Helen my plan was just to stay with Stephen for as long as I could, but while he had a tough time first up against Ambrose, I started really well. Of the 56 runs we added that morning before the stand was broken, he scored only 18. By this time I'd survived the second new ball and I felt so much in control it was as if I was batting in slow motion. I finished with 161 not out, the best innings of my life. And bloody good fun, too! Tugga had been caught at first slip for 66, but I added 69 with Pistol and then 61 with Warney, as we reached 479 all out.

A nice little touch came shortly after tea, when Michael Kasprowicz came out to play his first Test innings. The ground announcer had already revealed that I'd become the first Queensland-born batsman to make a Test hundred at the Gabba. Now fellow Queenslander 'Kasper' scored his first Test run. All this Maroon glory was too much for the faithful in the outer, who started joyfully singing *Waltzing Matilda*. Gee, it's good to be a Queenslander!

> *November 24, 1996: Energy on every ball, one session at a time. No outcomes or worries, positive outlook. We will win.*
>
> *Keep bowlers thinking and fielders going with quality.*
>
> *HOLD THE TENSION. WATCH THE BALL, MOVE, STAY DOWN …*

On the way to my third and probably most satisfying Test hundred, against the West Indies at the Gabba, November 1996. For a period, everything seemed to be in slow motion, which can be handy against the West Indies.

When the Windies batted, we all fielded in our baggy greens — something we'd decided to do at our pre-Test team meeting — and I took the first catch of the innings, Robert Samuels, caught Healy bowled McGrath, 10. It was turning into a really good week. We bowled them out for 277, but Tubby didn't enforce the follow on, which gave me the chance to make 45 not out in our second dig. When Tubby called a halt, the Windies needed 420 and they finished 124 short, despite a Sherwin Campbell century. The wickets had been evenly shared, which meant, for just about the first time in my Test career, I was an absolute certainty for the man-of-the-match award, which I really enjoyed.

One thing that didn't thrill me was the media conference I was obliged to attend after the second day's play. Of course, having made a big hundred, I was a story, but I knew most of the questions would be about the pressure I'd been under before the game rather than the innings I had just played. I was happy to talk about the present and the future, but not the past, and decided to play hard ball when the negative questions started coming.

First question: 'Did you feel pressure coming into this series?'

'In recent times, definitely,' I replied, 'but I have been there before. I'm very proud of what I did today, especially in front of my family and the Queensland crowd.'

The local supporters were magnificent. I was thrilled to put on a show for them.

A senior cricket journalist then asked, 'How did the speculation about your position affect you in the lead-up to the game?'

'Look, I'm sorry,' I responded, 'I explained all that in my pre-match interviews around 10 or 15 times. I didn't knock back one interview …'

And I stuck to that line, which especially infuriated Mike Coward, of all people, and there was a fair amount of tension in the air for the remainder of the media conference. Having created and developed a story that had fizzled to nothing, they sought, one last time, to revive it. Why should I be happy with that?

— ✠ —

A THING I LEARNED in regard to batting against the West Indies was that first impressions were usually intimidating. It definitely got easier the longer I stayed in against them but often, early on, I found it hard to convince myself of that fact. More than once during my career against bowlers such as Ambrose, Walsh, Patrick Patterson and Malcolm Marshall I found myself thinking, 'I can't score here.' Sometimes I'd panic and get out shortly after. But by the late 1990s, their attack lacked variety on good wickets, so if you could see past the initial onslaught, it was possible to do more than survive.

While our Test performances were excellent, the same could not be said for our results in the one-day internationals. Nine months earlier, we'd made the

World Cup final, now we couldn't even qualify for the World Series play-offs, losing out to the Windies and Pakistan. It was the first time Australia had missed the finals since the inaugural series, back in 1979–80. One unnerving statistic was that from the 1996 World Cup final to the end of the '96–97 World Series we'd lost 13 of 18 one-day matches, including a run of 11 defeats in 13 games. I was very disappointed that we performed so poorly in these matches, but I wasn't sure Tubby saw our losses in quite the same light. Our captain always put the Test matches above the limited-overs games. Tubby complained bitterly when he was dropped as one-day captain after the 1997 Ashes tour, pushing for all it was worth the line that the Test captain should also be in charge of the one-day team, but for most of his time as skipper he didn't assign as much importance to the one-dayers as he did to the Tests. Maybe he dug his own one-day grave. Of course his record in Test series was exceptional, and he was also a superb captain in one-day cricket. However, on some tours where Tubs was captain, such as the 1995 West Indies tour and the 1997 Ashes tour, and this home summer, too, the one-dayers were very much in the back seat.

Whatever Tubs' priorities in 1996–97, the poor bloke couldn't score a run anywhere. By the fourth Test, in Adelaide, the press had picked up on it, and with my hundred in Brisbane having confirmed my place, sections of the media now turned on him. This campaign was to reach a climax in South Africa, by which time his batting form, or lack of it, had become an ongoing saga. I thought he handled the stress admirably. The only time I saw him drop his guard in my presence was when he had a go at me for a comment I'd made to the *Sydney Morning Herald's* Malcolm Knox during that fourth Test. Knox had asked me if I thought Tubby was entitled to keep his place purely for his captaincy and I replied that while normally you'd say a player was 90 per cent batsman and 10 per cent captain, in Tubby's case, because he was such a good leader, I'd move the goalposts slightly to 80/20. Tubby interpreted my remark as saying that I obviously didn't have enough faith in him and wasn't giving him enough support. I told him not to worry, that I was actually giving him a wrap and he was seeing demons that didn't exist. The team was 100 per cent behind him and hoping he'd come good. We all knew that one of the reasons behind our success was Tubby's consummate leadership skills, and it would have been a major setback to lose them.

Tubby has a good sense of humour, which his form slump was testing to the max. Normally, he's a bloke who can wear a sledge, and return serve with interest as well as anyone I know. At the same time, he's as strong-willed an individual as I have ever met. If Tubby thought that something was right, then it was right, and as captain he expected everyone else to follow close behind, whether they agreed with him or not. If he hadn't been right at least most of the time, such a hard-edged philosophy would have brought him undone. Instead, it made him one of the best captains of his or any generation.

Once he was in charge, Tubby was never slow to bring a player into line. He took nothing personally, expected the cricketers he was leading to be the same,

In the dressing room after our first Test victory. The other lads are (left to right): Michael Kasprowicz, Ricky Ponting, Paul Reiffel (in front), Shane Warne, Jason Gillespie, Steve Waugh and Errol Alcott.

and placed great credence in regular one-on-one meetings at which he made players aware of their responsibilities and how their role fitted into the team's game plan. In this regard he was different from AB, who hated having to confront people. If something Tubby perceived as bad was creeping into a player's technique or persona, Tubby wanted to talk about it immediately. What made this approach so successful was that he knew his players extremely well: how to treat them when the pressure was on, how to get even more from them when the cricket was going well. Tubby used to clash with Warney over field placements, and sometimes their discussions on the field could get quite vigorous until Tubby would snap, 'Shane, just bowl!' Tubby wasn't being the boss just for the sake of it; he felt that Warney needed strong leadership, and Shane grew to learn that his captain was usually on the money.

When Tubby retired after the 1998–99 Australian season, his status as a captain far outweighed his reputation as an opening batsman, which I think is a shame. Take out the troubles that beset him in 1996–97 and he has a tremendous batting record. His ability to concentrate during long, disciplined hours at the crease, always with impeccable shot selection, was his real strength. He was never shy, on the field or off, and had an ability to separate personal performance from team. If he failed at the top of the order, it was never long before he was back in the viewing room, chewing as enthusiastically as ever at his gum, supporting the team with the lads. He needed this last attribute more and more as the slump set in.

Tubby was much luckier than AB in that he inherited a team with plenty of

In England in 1997 … just trying to be good. Gone are the worries of the rookie of 1988.

Above: Victory in the World Series in 1995–96, and with Boonie no longer in the team I have the honour of leading the team in *Under the Southern Cross*. As you can see, I relished the opportunity.

Left: To the dismay of all India, Sachin Tendulkar is stumped off a wide arm-ball from Mark Waugh during our group game in Bombay, World Cup, 1996.

Below right: Being met at the boundary's edge by Mark Waugh after hitting that six. Mark's brilliant hundred was the main reason we won the game.

Above left: I've just hit the best shot of my life — the six that won the second Test against South Africa, in Port Elizabeth, 1997.

Right: Mid-pitch celebrations with Adam Gilchrist after Australia won the sixth one-dayer, at Centurion Park, later on that same tour, to clinch the limited-overs series. Set an imposing 285 to win, we reached the target for the loss of five wickets and with an over to spare. Michael Bevan, who scored 103, and Steve Waugh, with 89, were the batsmen who made the victory possible.

Above: Umpire David Shepherd (left) offers his thanks after I had told him I wasn't sure if a chance from Graham Thorpe had carried during the second Ashes Test, at Lord's, in 1997.

Below: This one was out! Alec Stewart, caught at Trent Bridge during the fifth Test of the same tour. It was my 300th catch in Test matches and 100th in Ashes cricket, and came about after Stewart snicked a well-pitched-up delivery from Warney. The ball flipped out of my gloves and over my shoulder, but I dived back around and grabbed it.

Right: The Healy family at the Gabba in early 1998 — Emma, me, Tom, Helen and Laura.

Below: A diving catch in my 100th Test, in Adelaide, 1997–98. South Africa's Herschelle Gibbs is the victim, off the bowling of Greg Blewett. Mark Taylor is the first slip. We were wearing black armbands in honour of my father, who passed away three days before the game.

Above: The wicket in Chennai for the first Test of our 1998 India tour was playing enough tricks for me to call for the helmet, but Sachin Tendulkar still smashed us for a glorious unbeaten century. This was one of the toughest days of my career — the heat was intense and for most of the day my head and stomach were as dodgy as the pitch.

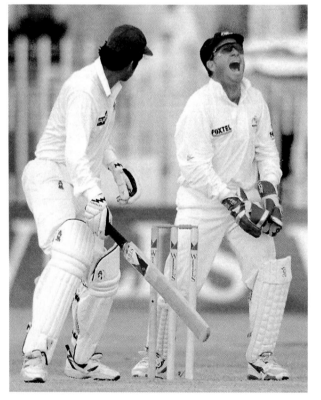

Left: The world record catch — Wasim Akram caught in Rawalpindi, October 4, 1998. We completed a historic victory the following morning, the first by an Australian team in Pakistan for nearly 30 years, making it a very memorable game for the team as well.

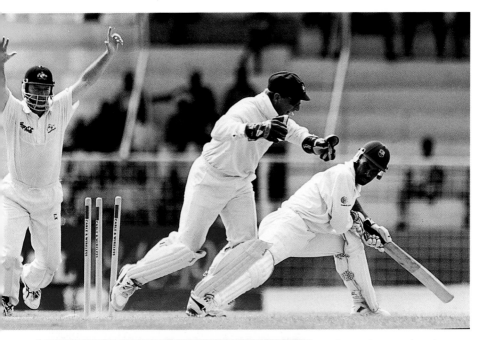

Above: Jimmy Adams is stumped off Colin Miller in Antigua, early on the last day of the fourth Test of our 1999 Windies tour. Steve Waugh is the fieldsman in the helmet. 'Funky' was bowling around the wicket, and had angled a full-length delivery just outside the line of the left-hander's leg stump. Adams missed as he tried to turn the ball behind square, and when he over-balanced a fraction I got him.

Left: Maybe I should have been doing this all along. This photo was taken during my longest bowling spell in first-class cricket — three overs, ONE maiden!, 0-14 — against a President's XI in Zimbabwe in October 1999.

Above: This is what 11 years and 119 Tests can do to a wicket-keeper's hands. This photograph was taken at the press conference on October 28, 1999, where I announced my retirement from cricket.

Left: I was very grateful to be given a lap of honour around the MCG during the Boxing Day Test in the 1999–2000 Australian season. There was absolutely no need for anyone at the ground — or anywhere else in the cricket world — to thank me for any pleasure I had given them over the years … it had all been my pleasure.

skill, confidence and experience. When AB had first taken over he was well ahead of his teammates in all three departments, whereas Tubs had people such as Steve Waugh, David Boon, Mark Waugh, Craig McDermott and me, people he'd grown up with in Test cricket. As well, in Shane Warne, Glenn McGrath and Michael Slater, he had three young and irresistibly talented cricketers, which gave him a very good side that was going to get significantly better.

This was important because it allowed Tubby to introduce a mandate into the team that we'd never let a game just drift along. We were *always* proactive, *always* had a purpose. It might not be in the last over that you don't win the game, it might be a slack hour on the first day, or an hour in the middle of a match when you were too conservative. It was a lot easier to make a game of it on the last day if you weren't dull and boring on day three. Trying to always keep the game moving became our trademark. Between the start of the 1995 West Indies tour and the end of the 1997 Ashes tour, only two Tests, both badly rain-affected, were drawn, out of 25. During this period we were trying things all the time. Something was always happening with Warney. He was either getting wickets, getting belted or out of the attack. Tubby was also a big believer in giving 'part-time' bowlers such as Ricky Ponting or Greg Blewett a bowl if the front-liners hadn't succeeded, working on the theory that batsmen often relax after they've seen off the big guns. His timing with such bowling changes was usually spot on.

It wasn't a case of us being entertaining for entertainment's sake. We played that way because we wanted to and because we believed that it gave us the best chance to win the most Tests and series. And most of the time it worked. If there was one question mark over the greatness of this team, it would have been that we occasionally lost easily and sometimes didn't fight long and hard enough to achieve a draw, when that was our best possible option. This said, my belief is that if a team, as a matter of course, prefers the soft option of playing safe for a draw, they may well reach their short-term objective and draw the game. But that team won't improve. It's not until you put yourself under pressure with both bat and ball and in the field that you're going to get better. However, there are times, when you find yourself way behind early in proceedings, that achieving a draw can become a positive.

—✠—

WE'D COME TO THE Adelaide Oval in 1996-97 leading the series two Tests to one, having won in Sydney and then been heavily defeated at the MCG, where big Curtly was back to his best. Having taken just three wickets in the first two matches, Ambrose exploded on a seaming deck, taking nine wickets and ensuring that the game was over in three days.

I missed out with the bat in Adelaide, making 12 in our only innings, but was very pleased with the way I kept throughout, especially to our newly discovered spin duo of Warne and … Bevan! Tubby had been using Bevo's left-arm high-bouncing wrist-spinners more and more, to the point that we went into this match with just two quicks and Bevo as our fourth front-line bowler. It worked

The contentious Brian Lara dismissal in Sydney. While Glenn McGrath celebrates what we all believed to be a clear-cut catch by me, Lara stands his ground.

much better than we could possibly have expected, as Bevo enjoyed an amazing game, scoring 85 and taking 10 wickets. We won by an innings and 183 runs. For me this was as satisfying a series win as we'd ever had — there's something very gratifying about proving the critics wrong. Our party, from the moment I jumped up on the table, the Frank Worrell Trophy in hand, to sing *Under the Southern Cross* was big and special. We even had Boonie on board for the celebrations, the ACB having flown him up from Launceston, a stirring gesture to mark his contribution towards getting the team to where it now was.

—✠—

BRIAN LARA'S SERIES TO this point had been gravely unproductive. The only time he made the headlines was in Melbourne, when Glenn McGrath stopped to explain to the media how he was always getting Lara out, and in Sydney when he launched an astonishing attack on me after he thought — incorrectly — that I hadn't taken the catch that dismissed him in the second innings cleanly.

For the first three Tests of this series Pigeon had it all over Lara, dismissing him five times out of six, including scores of 2 and 1 in Sydney and 2 and 2 in Melbourne. In the second dig at the SCG Lara aimed a pull at a bouncer, but bottom-edged it through to me and I grabbed it low down. It was a weird catch in that it hit one glove, bobbled out for a moment but ended up safely in the other. My gloves were tight together and in my mind there was no doubt about the catch at all, but during the break for an advertisement someone in the Channel Nine van noticed the bobble and replayed the catch over and over, trying to find something illegitimate that wasn't there. Lara, back in the Windies' room by this stage, saw the replays and angrily assumed the worst. Seconds later, there was a furious knocking on the Australian dressing room door and Geoff Marsh opened it to find one very enraged Trinidadian steaming outside.

'Tell Healy he is not welcome in our dressing room,' Lara seethed.

He had stormed through the hallowed downstairs bar of the SCG Members Stand to pass on this message. The rest of the Australian team, of course, was out on the field, so it wasn't until the lunch break when Swampy told me about it and I just shook my head. For a moment, I wanted to go straight over to sort it out, but then I thought, 'No, bugger it, it's not worth it. Let it go.' At the end of the game we went as a team into the Windies dressing room, myself somewhat reluctantly, and many of their players shook our hands. A couple did not. Lara, as far as I could tell, was nowhere to be seen. Later, the West Indies manager issued an official apology, though I never heard a word personally from Lara.

He was at it again in Perth for the final Test, though not specifically at me this time — which made for a nice change! The Windies have won every Test they've ever played at the WACA and this one was no different, with Ambrose taking five wickets in the first innings, Walsh five in the second and Lara making his only hundred of the series as we crashed to a 10-wicket defeat. Lara batted beautifully, as only he can, but lost us completely with his antics, which included crying to the media about the way we chipped away on the field at their young opening bat, Samuels, and trying to manufacture an incident when he came out to act as a runner for the injured Walsh. A few of our guys did get into Samuels, but the Windies opener gave as good as he got and didn't seem to need protection from Lara or anyone. He made 76 and was part of a third-wicket partnership of 208 in the first innings, then was 35 not out in the second, and at the time we thought he'd be a bloke we'd see more of in the future. What Lara was trying to achieve by running to the papers we weren't quite sure, but the story died a reasonably quick death, with him, I think, the only loser.

I had toned down my chatter on the field during this season, maybe from when I was captain on the tour to Sri Lanka in the previous August–September. The reason why was not one thing, more a range of things. I still believed in the value of gamesmanship and that without it Test cricket would be too close to a stroll in the park, but I was conscious of the fact that while there were many in the Aussie team who didn't mind throwing in the odd comment, I had very much become the public face of our on-field chat. Part of this was because of a few very public angry confrontations, most notably with Haynes and Ranatunga, and part was because as wicketkeeper I was always closest to the on-field microphone. But the way the Sri Lankan crisis of the previous summer had spun out of control, eventually leading to death threats, made me rethink my approach.

This was the second of two 'backhanded' run outs I managed in international cricket. The first was at Bloemfontein in 1994 — Allan Border's last match for Australia — when I caught Brian McMillan napping. This one came at the WACA in 1996–97, in the fifth Test, when I sensed Curtly Ambrose was loitering out of his ground and, without looking, flicked the ball back and hit the stumps. Curtly probably would have got back except for the fact he got his bat caught in a crack in the wicket as he tried to slide it back behind the crease.

Being vice-captain for three seasons and captain for a short while made me constantly more aware of the off-field ramifications of an on-field barney. I certainly wasn't quiet on the field, just quieter.

My third child, a son, Tom, had been born the previous September and for the first time I gave thought to when I might retire. Cricket was important to me, but nowhere near as precious as my family. No way had the cricket world seen the last of me yet, but I began to look to the future, to life beyond cricket. On the eve of the fifth Test, I'd recalled a conversation I had with David Boon in Adelaide, during which I asked him what it was like being retired. 'When you're playing you don't ever think about it,' he told me, 'and then when it comes you can't believe it's over. And then you don't realise you miss it until you return.'

'Heals,' he continued, softly and slowly, 'make the most of it.'

A week later, straight after we arrived in South Africa for a tour involving three Tests and seven one-dayers, I wrote in my diary, 'This is the most important tour of my career.'

CHAPTER 18

KARACHI'S GONE, MATE!

MY TIME IN SOUTH AFRICA in 1997 was an extraordinary mixture of joy and bitterness, with a nasty sting in the tail waiting for me when I arrived home. On the field, we won both the Test and one-day series, and I had the extraordinary experience of hitting a six to win a Test match. My keeping throughout was top-drawer. Despite our success on the field, however, the continuing melodrama of Tubs' poor form began to niggle at team morale and I, as vice-captain, found myself caught up in the debate. I also became the first Australian Test cricketer to be suspended, after a bat-throwing incident that in my view was blown up out of all proportion. It was a turbulent, thrilling and awful two months.

As we had done at the Adelaide Oval against the West Indies, we adopted a policy of playing Michael Bevan as our fourth bowler throughout the Test series, only here we were doing so on wickets much more suited to the South Africans' excellent pace attack of Allan Donald, Shaun Pollock and Lance Klusener. The impact of this strategy was far-reaching, impacting on many Australian cricketers in many different ways. Still, we dominated the first Test and won narrowly in the second, and Bevo had a reasonable series as a bowler, taking nine wickets in the first two Tests.

February 10, 1997: Attitude: enjoy it as much as any rookie
— be happy, chirpy, helpful.

The first Test was dominated by an extraordinary stand between Greg Blewett and Steve Waugh, who batted right through the third day to put us in an invincible position. When Steve was finally out they'd added 385 in a tick more than eight hours, and we were well on the way to a first-innings advantage of 326. South Africa hadn't lost by an innings since their return to Test-match cricket, but eventually they did here, by an innings and 196 runs, after Warney spun out the top order and Bevo the tail on a wearing fifth-day track. Our fielding and catching were superb, and by the end we really felt like world heavyweight champions. The people who'd suggested we'd be needing a third paceman, such as Paul Reiffel or my Queensland and now Australian teammate, Andy Bichel, to be successful on these wickets had been silenced, at least temporarily. Straight afterwards, we hopped on a bus to Sun City, and the trip there was quick and sensationally happy, so different from the long, sad journey we'd endured after our first Test loss in 1994. Once we arrived, I was straight on the phone to Helen, then Simmo, Slats and Helen again, to tell them all how wonderful it felt. Back in '94, we'd found Sun City to be a terrific place to unwind and get our tour back on track. This time, it was just terrific.

Poor Tubs' luck went from bad to worse when he hurt his back at practice before the tour game against Border at East London, and I filled in as captain. He had made an 85 in the opening tour game, against Western Province, then 50 in a one-dayer, before being a little unlucky, bowled by Pollock off the inside edge for 16 in his only innings of the first Test. But any positive momentum was lost when his back went. Instead, I had the chance to lead the Australians in a first-class match for the first (and, as it proved, only) time, and we won by an innings and 105 runs, with Blewey getting another hundred and Dizzy Gillespie taking 7-34 in the first innings.

After the game, I was asked whether I saw this captaincy experience as a prelude to greater things. To say yes, I thought, would be dancing on my captain's grave well head of his demise, so I said, 'No.'

'Why not?' the press boys asked in unison.

'If it's a fill-in thing I've got no reservations,' I replied. Then, stressing that I was looking long-term, I added, 'My view is why should I do it if there's someone in the field who's got less on his plate and is just as good at it? Either the team's going to suffer or my keeping will suffer and it's just not worth it if you've got a candidate just as good standing at gully.'

With these quotes safely recorded, the press scribes were on their way, while I gave myself a pat on the back for saying exactly the right thing. Swampy Marsh would have been proud of me. Nothing I had said would have added to Mark Taylor's stress levels. But then, as the captaincy debate intensified over the following fortnight, I started thinking, maybe it wasn't such a clever comment. All the reports were being written as if Tubs was gone, and as if Steve Waugh (who always fielded in the gully) would automatically be the man to take over. And who could blame the journos for writing that — the only other possible candidate had publicly ruled himself out of the job. In the lead-up to the second Test, in Port Elizabeth, for the first time I gave the whole issue a lot of thought, especially the question of whether a wicketkeeper working with the best spin bowler in history could also be an effective leader. Maybe he could.

After the second day's play of the second Test, I wrote in my diary, 'Tonight: Changed my mind re the captaincy. I now think it will advance my cricket.'

Why the change of mind at that moment? Well, we had fallen into a dreadful position in the Test, after going in with an unchanged side on a pitch that was covered by a thick mat of grass. Despite our combination, Tubs had no hesitation sending the South Africans in when we won the toss and McGrath and Gillespie reduced them to 7-95. But we didn't have the firepower to finish the job, and Richardson and Brian McMillan fought back well enough for them to reach 209. On day two the pitch was still lethal and we crashed to 108 all out, and then had to watch as our two quick bowlers, still weary from their efforts 24 hours earlier, were smashed around the park by Gary Kirsten and Adam Bacher.

Daryll Cullinan is caught Healy bowled Warne for a duck in South Africa's second innings of the first Test, in Johannesburg. At 3-46, having conceded a first-innings deficit of 326, the home team was crashing to a heavy defeat.

At stumps they were 0-83, effectively 0-184. 'WORST DAY EVER,' I diarised. The match, it seemed, was lost. As I sat in my hotel room that night, contemplating what had happened and what we needed to do to get it right, I couldn't help coming back to the fact that we'd gone into the Test with the wrong team because we were protecting the team from our captain's poor form. In the back of my mind I think I'd known that such a policy was eventually going to hurt us, but had put off facing that fact until it actually happened. Now it had, things needed to change. Tubby relinquishing the captaincy was one option we had to consider. And if there was going to be a new captain, then, yes, I wanted to be considered. I knew the vice-captaincy was not an automatic stepping stone to the top job; I'd said that myself many times. But if Tubby departed and I was considered the best man for the job, then I wanted to take up the challenge.

A fortnight later, after the Test series had finished, when I revealed my change of heart to reporters, they were understandably a little confused, and tried to read all sorts of things into it. But there was no hidden agenda; it was simply a case of me really analysing the Australian captaincy role for the first time and reaching the conclusion that it wouldn't hurt my cricket.

If that second day of the second Test was our worst ever, the next was possibly our best. The turnaround came, ironically, from inspired leadership. At a time when it seemed his world was about to cave in, Tubs brought us all together on that second night and said, 'Right, we're hurting, but we can still get out of this.' Before that meeting was concluded we had a very clear strategy as to how we were going to fight back. We reaffirmed that our tactics for the South African batsmen were right, so let's back ourselves and our game plans against every one of them, be aggressive, never give up, and then bat for all we are worth to try to save the game.

Save the game? The next morning, Dizzy knocked over Kirsten immediately and we were away. Jacques Kallis, Bacher and Daryll Cullinan were all dismissed before the total passed 100 and their innings never recovered. Only Cronje apart from the openers made it past 20, Bevo took three wickets, Warney two, on this supposed paceman's paradise, and we were left with a target of 270 to win. By stumps we were 3-145, with Mark Waugh undefeated on 54.

> *March 16, 1997: Who'd have thought it? Best day of our*
> *careers … positive, sensible batting needed. Partnerships vital.*
> *Nearly all walked home from the ground to the hotel.*
> *Pumped!!*

By day four, the wicket had flattened out a bit, but it was still tricky. Fortunately for us, Mark Waugh, in at 2-30, picked this moment to play his greatest innings in Test cricket, and he took us to the brink of a famous victory. As I'd predicted, the partnerships were the key — 83 for the third wicket with Matty Elliott on day three, then 54 with his brother, 25 with Blewey, and 66 with Bevo. However, just 12 runs from our target, Junior was bowled by Kallis. I was in. Straightaway, without another run being added, Bevo fell to Cronje. Still 12 to get, with only three wickets in hand.

I don't mind admitting I was very, very nervous. Second ball, Warney slogged Cronje over mid-off's head and when we took off for the first run, my legs felt like jelly. Still, we managed three. My mind was racing, and I found myself preoccupied with the noise of a large contingent of schoolchildren, and a motley brass band whose members had brought their instruments to the game. I started singing a song to myself between balls, to prevent my mind being distracted, and the song — *Have You Ever Really Loved a Woman?*, by Bryan Adams, which proved I was mellowing — lodged there. It worked, too, as I swung Cronje away over square leg to the boundary. Five to win. At the end of the over Warney and I had a conference, mid pitch, where we decided to keep it simple, win each moment, and let the result look after itself. We also chipped the umpires about the South Africans' tactic of dropping the backward square leg fieldsman back as Cronje was running into bowl. Later South African coach Bob Woolmer claimed it was legal, but we weren't so sure.

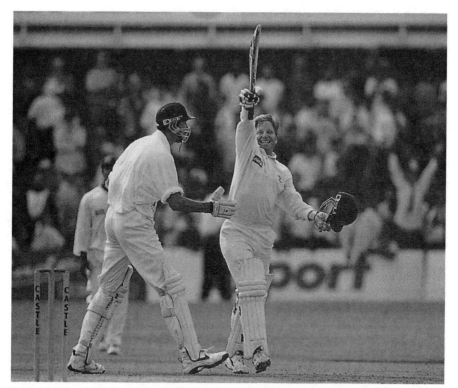

I've just hit the single most important shot of my life, to beat South Africa in the second Test, in Port Elizabeth. Jason Gillespie is moving in to give me a Dizzy hug, while I'm aiming my bat straight at my mates in the Australian dressing room.

First ball of Kallis' new over, Warney was lbw. Now Jason Gillespie was in, just Glenn McGrath to come, and I was stuck at the bowler's end with five balls still to come. Fortunately, Dizzy was calmness personified, the complete antithesis of Warney and me. If blocking out the rest of the over is what you want, Heals, then that's what I'll do. Kallis was bang on line, but Dizzy kept him out comfortably. Now it was Cronje's turn. And mine.

Before the first ball of the new over, the South African captain took out his second slip and moved him to deep on the leg side, in front of square. There was no way I was going to hit one out there, maybe behind square, but not there. The new field placing suggested he was going to bowl a middle-to-leg stump line, the intention, I assumed, being to limit me to a single so they could have another go at Dizzy. If Cronje had known how anxious I was, he might not have been quite so conservative. I looked down at the vacant third-man boundary, and thought, 'If he pitches outside off stump, I'll be aiming down there.' Bob Simpson had always bagged me for trying to late cut the first ball I faced in an innings; here was my chance to demonstrate the true value of that shot.

'Just watch the ball,' I told myself as Cronje moved in, 'and play the moment.' First ball, I defended, same with the second. The band played on, the schoolkids

Two happy tourists!

kept singing, and then, third ball, Cronje drifted into my pads ...

I didn't mean to hit it for six. When I saw the ball pitching short of a length on leg stump I reacted instinctively: 'I'll go with that.' The ball came off the bat sweetly and I looked up and thought, 'Gee, that's gone.'

The moments straight after remain a blur. Arms raised, I turned to the Aussie dressing room, where I could see that pandemonium had broken out. Dizzy ran up for an exuberant mid-pitch embrace that almost broke my back. The South Africans were disconsolate, then some fans were on the pitch and we were running for our lives to join the dressing room party. I've never had a feeling like it. I was exhilarated, numb, wobbly, all at the same time. Steve Waugh grabbed me and shouted, 'Karachi's gone, mate!' I was glad it was over and so proud, satisfied and vindicated that I'd come through the way I did. Back at our hotel, I interrupted the celebrations to ring Helen, and Mum and Dad, before heading back to revel in the victory some more. It was a special day.

The backpage headlines the following morning were all about my six, which was more than little unfair because it meant that Junior was pushed into the background somewhat, despite playing the innings of his life. Not that he cared — he was as happy for me as he was proud of himself, which typifies the bloke. His nonchalance is legendary, but it disguises a tough and caring inner self that has been scrutinised at cricket's highest level and rarely found wanting. As he showed so superbly in Port Elizabeth, Junior is a batsman who can make even the toughest conditions look easy and make the best bowlers look off their game on wickets that should be suiting them. His only major fault in cricket has been not turning hundreds into big hundreds — which, when you think about it, isn't a bad fault to have. And because he rarely gets over-animated, he has been unable to convince many outside the team that he is as committed to and learned about the game as some of his colleagues. Take it from me, Junior understands the game better than most and has a desire that burns fiercely.

He was one of my all-time favourite teammates. I recall an umpire in Sri Lanka in 1996 being so confused by Junior's easygoing approach that when he looked up at the keeper's end and saw him leaning on his bat he suddenly announced, 'That's two legs.' Two years earlier, again in Sri Lanka, as we were leaving a casino, he tossed a chip on the roulette table and said to the croupier, 'Wherever it lands, mate.' It landed on number 20, which, of course, immediately came up. Only Junior could have done that, or so it seemed as he calmly collected his chips and strolled, with no fuss, towards the cashier's window.

Junior was as aware as any of us that we'd been fortunate to win that second Test. We couldn't continue to give a strong side such as South Africa that sort of start and expect to keep succeeding. Within the team, there was a strong suspicion that the home authorities had produced a pitch at Port Elizabeth that suited their predominantly pace attack better than our two spinners, and we expected they would try this tactic again for the third Test at Centurion Park. Consequently, the make-up of our side became the subject of some quiet discussions among many of the players, and as vice-captain and a tour selector I became something of a sounding board for the disgruntled members of the squad. More than once a teammate would insinuate that the tour selectors weren't choosing our strongest side for the sake of the captain, while one or two even complained that some players' careers were being jeopardised by our selection strategy. I responded with the selection committee's argument that because the team was going well there was no reason to change things, but in my heart I knew I didn't agree with that. I wouldn't have dropped Tubby, but on these seaming decks we really did need the third quick more than Bevo's wrist spinners, which meant Tubby's batting would have to stand up without another batsman at No. 7 to protect it. But my fellow selectors, Tubby and Geoff Marsh, couldn't be swayed.

Tubby, meanwhile, bolstered by the team's victories and messages of goodwill from back home, had convinced himself that he'd soon come good and was either ignoring or not hearing the surreptitious whispers from his troops. Tubby was keeping a very positive face about his slump, which in so many ways was admirable, but it did create a problem in that it prevented other team members from talking to the captain about their own troubles. 'How can I speak to him about my form when he won't face up to his own problems?' I was asked by one teammate. I had great sympathy for Tubby's plight, and as vice-captain I was committed to being 100 per cent loyal, but more and more I hated being caught in the middle of this conundrum. I like Tubby a lot as a bloke, respect him enormously as a cricketer and leader, and knew he was suffering big time, but my patience was starting to wear thin. I just felt we couldn't keep going on like this. Then, to make things worse, during the Test it was announced that Justin Langer, Matthew Hayden and Matthew Elliott would not be staying for the one-dayers that followed straight after the Test. To say this was unexpected was an understatement, and did nothing for morale, especially as the two Matthews were at that moment playing in a Test match. I knew, too, that Tubby wasn't going to play in the one-dayers, but *was* going to stick around. Trevor Hohns, by now chairman of the Australian selection committee, had come to South Africa to discuss the future with Tubby and other senior players, and that was the decision that had been arrived at. As far as we all knew, Tubby's position as captain for the upcoming Ashes tour was rock solid.

Sure enough, the third Test pitch was one of the greenest, wettest wickets I'd ever seen. We lost the toss, were sent in, and struggled all day against their pacemen for 227. When we bowled, McGrath took six wickets (including Gary Kirsten, caught behind, my 300th Test dismissal) and Gillespie three, but our slow bowlers couldn't finish what the two quicks had started and South Africa totalled 384. This time we couldn't fight back, not least because the umpiring was atrocious, and we ended up losing by eight wickets. All up, 28 wickets fell to the quicker bowlers during the match, only four to the spinners.

On the first day I'd received a real insight into our captain's troubled state of mind. Although Steve Waugh topscored for us with 67, Tubs actually faced the most deliveries — 138 balls for 38 runs. He was scratchy, but he bravely stayed out there, until he became the fourth wicket to fall, caught behind off Klusener, with the score on 110. When he arrived back in the dressing room I was getting padded up, and I was disappointed to see that he wasn't dirty about having been dismissed, but relieved to have made so many. 'I nearly got there today,' he commented. As I prepared to bat, I couldn't help thinking that everything was out of kilter.

By the time I went out to bat in our second innings the cause was almost lost, but after Port Elizabeth I believed in miracles and was ready to have a red-hot go. Stephen was up the other end and going well, and we took the score from 108 to 131 without too many dramas, but then I was given out, caught behind down the leg side, when I didn't go close to hitting the ball. There'd been plenty of poor decisions in the Test, and both teams had suffered, but this, for me, was the worst (because it was me!). The South Africans only half-appealed, and were joking and chuckling when I eventually hustled off, after standing my ground incredulously for a second or two. Then, as I disappeared off the ground, I copped a mouthful from a big, fat bloke in the crowd, which was the spark that finally lit the fuse. All my stress and simmering anger of the previous week took over and near the top of the steps to our dressing room, I lost it unforgivably, underarming my bat up five steps onto a small landing in front of our viewing room. The one cameraman who remained focused on me during my trek off the ground must have thought it was Christmas when I gave him such a great present as a 'reward' for his persistence.

Once inside, I stayed angry for a long time. Angry with the impending loss, the dismissal, the thrown bat, the world. Between the end of the Test and a disciplinary hearing to which I'd been summoned, we farewelled Langer, Hayden and Elliott, and then it was up to see the ICC match referee, Mr Raman Subba Row of England. I wasn't too concerned, expecting no more than a reprimand, maybe a fine, worst case a suspended sentence. After all, in the overall scheme of

In Cape Town, I captained Australia in a one-day international for the first time since Sri Lanka in August-September 1996.

things what I'd done was minor — I hadn't hurt anyone or sworn at anyone, and the bat-throwing, for which I was very remorseful, had occurred all but out of view, near the door to our dressing room. Certainly, I'd seen much worse incidents go unchecked, so I went to the hearing ready to take my medicine and get on with life.

Besides Mr Subba Row, also in the meeting were umpires Mervyn Kitchen, Cyril Mitchley and the video-replay official, Rudi Koertzen, our manager, Col Egar, and Mark Taylor. I didn't have to say too much because the umps' report accurately described what went on. I just admitted my mistake and offered an apology. The fact that I'd received a poor decision and then been sledged by a bloke in the crowd was not relevant. I should have worn those provocations on the proverbial chin. Col Egar did make a positive statement, and I was thinking, this'll be sweet. Mr Subba Row then began his summing up with a comment that, while I was guilty of showing dissent to an umpire's decision, umpires around the world had been impressed with the way I played my cricket in recent years, that my record was excellent, that I played 'hard but fair'. They were his words. I thought, this is going well, and then he finished …

'… And because of these factors, I'm only going to suspend you for two one-day internationals.'

'Whaaaatttt?!?!'

No Australian Test cricketer had been suspended since Dennis Lillee missed two one-day matches after clashing with Pakistan's Javed Miandad at the WACA in 1981–82. If there had been another Test in the series, I probably would have been banned for a Test. There was no avenue for an appeal, no chance to question the severity of the sentence, nothing but stunned silence. Since then, I've seen one international captain destroy the umpires' room door at the Adelaide Oval and not get suspended and another get away with arguing angrily and publicly with the umpires and threatening to take his team off the field. I thought about blokes who'd been fined for spitting, swearing, pushing and shoving. But I'd got two matches. I couldn't help thinking, 'People are sure to start thinking that there was more to the incident than what actually occurred.'

When I eventually calmed down, a day or two later, we took the view that, rather than overdo the chopping and changing of the captaincy, Tubby would play in the first two one-dayers and then I'd take over as skipper. Luckily, Gilly made it to South Africa in time for the first match, which was handy because our back-up keeper for the Test tour, Justin Langer, was already on a plane going in the opposite direction. We won the series 4-3, winning the second, fourth, fifth and sixth games, all without Glenn McGrath, who was given a rest after bowling so many overs in the Tests, and the middle two wins without an injured Mark Waugh as well. Those last two victories were thrillers, and I was in at the death for both of them, which was very enjoyable, especially in game six at Centurion Park, where our target was 285 and we made it with an over to spare. Series won, I sat out the last game, to rest a number of niggling injuries, which meant Steve Waugh led his country in a limited-overs international for the first time.

I arrived home from South Africa to be greeted by Laura (far left), and Emma, and seven-month-old Tom Healy (below).

Throughout that one-day series, I kept coming back to that suspension and how severe that ban was. While a number of the other lads had headed out for a beer after the final day of that third Test, I had decided to go no further than the team room at our hotel. However, I couldn't get myself involved in any conversations, so I opted to head back up to my own room. As I stewed over the suspension, the phone rang and I picked it up to hear the familiar voice of Cracker Hohns.

'Mate, can I come up for a beer?' he asked. He was in South Africa to see Tubby, but was an old mate, a stalwart of the Queensland team during my early days in first-class cricket, Australian teammate on the 1989 Ashes tour, an excellent Queensland captain in the early '90s. We talked about a whole range of things, nothing too serious, just two old mates having a yarn. When he departed an hour or so later I felt a little better about life.

When I next received a phone call from Cracker, three and a half weeks later in Australia, I was stunned by what he told me. 'Heals,' he started, 'Congratulations on South Africa, a fantastic win in the one-dayers ... unfortunately, though, mate, I'm ringing to tell you we've decided to make a change for the England tour. You won't be vice-captain. Tugga will be.'

'What? Who else has missed out?'

'Sorry, I can't tell you, the team's still embargoed.'

He wouldn't even tell me who was in and out of the team. When I think back now, it still annoys the hell out of me that he wouldn't trust me with that information. But at the time it probably wouldn't have mattered, because I wasn't really listening. I was totally stunned. The way I felt about playing cricket for Australia changed as soon as I heard that decision. And my relationship with Cracker would never be the same.

CHAPTER 19

Sacked as Vice-Captain

I HAD BEEN VICE-CAPTAIN for nearly three years and in that time I thought I'd done a pretty fair job. We'd won Test series in the West Indies and South Africa, beaten England, Pakistan, Sri Lanka and the West Indies in series at home, and reached the final of a World Cup. The only negatives on our report card were our sometimes dismal one-day record and our lack of success in Test matches on the Indian Subcontinent. This record suggested that, at the very worst, the vice-captain wasn't hurting the team. My reputation had been tarnished somewhat by the two-match suspension, but ACB chairman Denis Rogers had assured me when he was in South Africa that the Board wasn't interested in taking the matter further, so long as it didn't happen again.

As I have said before, I always saw the vice-captaincy as being a totally separate role from the captaincy, a specific job in itself, and I thought I'd done a good job. I was very proud that I was Australian vice-captain. And now it was gone. Cracker justified the change by explaining that Tugga was their preferred choice as Tubby's replacement and because of this and the fact that a captaincy change could easily occur on the upcoming tour, they wanted the heir apparent in the deputy's chair. If I'd been able to argue my case, I would have countered by saying that I'd have had no problem with Stephen leap-frogging me if such a situation arose, and I had absolutely no problems with him becoming the next Australian captain because I knew he'd do a sensational job. All that would have been needed in such circumstances was for the senior players on tour to receive an instruction from the selectors. Instead, they had suddenly decided that the vice-captaincy was now a stepping stone to the captaincy.

By doing it this way they had created a situation where they'd be making three changes instead of one. They could have kept the vice-captain and simply changed the captain if that was necessary. Instead, they were sacking the vice-captain and appointing a new vice-captain in case they had to sack the captain, at which point the new vice-captain became the captain and then they'd also have to appoint a new vice-captain, who I assumed wouldn't be the old vice-captain.

I believe I was shown scant respect by all responsible. I felt like a rookie being spanked after misbehaving, not a senior player with 88 Tests under my belt. Cracker was the only selector who rang, and not to discuss the situation with me but to deliver the news of a fait accompli that was to be made public two or three hours later. Not one ACB member called, even though they continued to insist they were committed to improving communications with their elite players. The coach didn't call. I was very disappointed that these people either didn't recognise that I'd be hurting or didn't care. The captain did ring, unfortunately while I was out, and he left a message on our answering machine. It wasn't until the team arrived in England and Tubby and I, as captain and player, sat down for a one-on-one chat to discuss the tour that I had a talk with him about my demotion. Tubby conceded that his poor form had cost me my job, and I accepted his word that he'd had no input into the decision. I never thought he had.

One person who did call on that miserable morning was Steve Waugh. Tugga wasn't sure what to say, neither was I, but for me the important thing was that he made the call. He had my support and I knew he'd do a good job. Minutes later, the media was on the line.

'The players will love playing under Steve,' I told the *Sydney Morning Herald's* John Lingard, when he asked me about what kind of leader Tugga might be.

When asked if there was anything positive to come out of the change, I answered, 'Mate, I will never have to answer any of the speculation about the captain again. It's been a year now we've been answering the same questions. And I was a bit worried about the matches the day after the English Tests, where the vice-captain has to captain a side that isn't particularly well-motivated. Now, I'm out of that as well.'

I tried to say all the politically correct things, and pointed out that the calls made to people such as Matthew Hayden, Paul Reiffel and Stuart Law who had been left out of the team would have been tougher than the one made to me. These guys would have been shattered. I was grateful to Lawey — when he was approached to talk about his omission, he had time to support me. 'There is obviously something wrong with what has been done and the way it has been done,' he said. 'I'm sure Heals would be shattered. He held the vice-captaincy close to his heart. To have it taken away from him, he would be wondering what is going on. It's a shame to see that happen.'

— ◻ —

THE FIRST FEW WEEKS of the Ashes tour were dominated by our captain's continued poor form, while I struggled to come to grips with my new role within the team. I found myself battling to find enthusiasm for off-field team activities, and was missing my family much, much more than I had early on previous Ashes tours. But I was still committed to my on-field performance, and worked hard at the nets and on the park. One day, just before the start of the Texaco Trophy one-day matches, I heard a TV golf commentator say, 'What ego wants you to do, experience tells you to do and nerves allow you to do,' which struck a chord with me and went straight into my diary, opposite a simple line, 'Be happy and chirpy, whether going well or not.' My attitude was that I was a senior player, and it was important that I shared my vast experience with everyone in our squad. Let's get out there and enjoy it!

Mark Ealham, caught behind off Glenn McGrath, as England tumbles to defeat on the last day of the third Test, at Old Trafford.

We lost the one-dayers 3-0, and approached the first Test, at Edgbaston, down on confidence. The tabloids were having a field day at Tubby's expense, and he'd left himself out of the third limited-overs international, after failing in the first two. A ray of light, though, appeared in our game at Derby, the final hit-out before the start of the Test series, when Tubby managed to make 63 in the second innings. The Test, however, started disastrously, as we crashed to 8-54 after being sent in. Warney belted 47 to get us into three figures, but when England batted, Nasser Hussain made 207 and Graham Thorpe 138. Our first innings deficit was 360.

I think almost everyone believed that if Mark failed in our second innings then Tugga would be leading us in the second Test, at Lord's. Tubby later admitted that himself. I looked over at him as he prepared to leave the dressing room, and I could see in his eyes that he was intending to go out, damn the consequences, and hit the ball. Shades of 1989. I'll never forget that look.

Out in the middle, he scratched around a little and played and missed occasionally, as all but the very finest batsman do. But gradually he worked himself into a skerrick of form, and managed to get that most productive shot of his, where he works the ball off his legs, working again. He reached 50 in 66 balls, and then, from there to his hundred, appeared to do it pretty easily. I really believe getting that leg-side shot back was the key; without it over the previous nine months he'd kept putting pressure on every other part of his technique, his feet started to go in all the wrong directions, and he was forcing things, playing the wrong shot to the wrong ball. He might have been lucky that the Poms bowled too much at his pads, but he was entitled to a bit of good luck after everything that had happened to him.

I remember how positive we all were watching Tubby's dig. We all knew that he'd gone through a personal hell, so it was a big relief for everyone that his slump was over. Greg Blewett, who batted with Tubs for most of his hundred, later told us it was amazing watching Tubs' persona change as the runs began to pile up. Mentally, he was back to his best, enthused by the way he was hitting them, revving Blewey up between overs, setting goals and reaching them.

Despite the captain's 129 and a century by Blewey we lost the match by nine wickets, but in one sense it was a victory for us. At a team post-mortem immediately after the game, Tubs was extremely assertive. 'I hope you blokes realise the Test series has started,' he roared. 'We bowled badly and batted badly.' Geoff Marsh followed with, 'Don't take your coffins home tonight, we're back here at 9 o'clock for practice.' Our captain was back, our tour had begun.

June 18, 1997: Lord's preparation: Feeling strong, ready to concentrate well. Huge challenge for us to bounce back. This last month: Had to re-establish work standards.

Become best ever!

After the one-dayers, the UK papers were crowing as if the Ashes had already been won. On the balcony after their Test win at Edgbaston we thought the English players were a bit too arrogant. After all, there were still five Tests to go. I don't think any of us forgot the way the English carried on after that first Test win, and I think that was the catalyst for Shane Warne's over-the-top celebrations on the balcony at Trent Bridge after we won the fifth Test to go 3-1 up with one game to play.

After Edgbaston, the mood of the series changed quickly. Although the Lord's Test was severely interrupted by rain, we kicked some important psychological goals as Glenn McGrath took 8-38 and we bowled the Poms out for just 77 in their first innings. In the third Test, Tugga made a hundred in each innings after Tubby surprised us all by deciding (very shrewdly as it turned out) to bat first on a moist but 'patchy' pitch, and Warney bowled beautifully on a track that spun more and more as the game went on. We won decisively in the end by 268 runs. The fourth Test was secured by a whopping innings and 61 runs, and then at Trent Bridge we won by 264 runs, which prompted Warney's victory dance.

A personal highlight for me was my stumping of their left-handed opener Mark Butcher in the third Test. Michael Bevan played in the first three games of the series, batting No. 6 and bowling occasionally, and he had his longest spells in this game, on a pitch which Tubby had correctly and uniquely recognised

My stumping of England's opener, Mark Butcher, off Michael Bevan at Old Trafford in 1997. From a keeper's perspective (and a batsman's, too!), 'Bevo' is as quick and awkward a left-hand wrist spinner as you could find. In the photograph at right, the left-handed Butcher has tried to hit a full-pitched Bevo delivery through the legside, but missed and is about to overbalance slightly. This was a dismissal based on good instincts — I ignored what might happen if the ball hit a rough spot on the pitch, just kept my hands low, moved appropriately, and when the ball went into my gloves I was in position to take the bails off at exactly the right moment.

would spin a great deal. Against Butcher, Bevo speared one down the leg side, and I had my view of the ball impaired by the batsman right in front of me. It came through, quick and wide outside the leg stump, almost on the half volley; I grabbed it and took the bails off as Butcher stumbled forward. It was one of the best stumpings of my Test career.

Earlier, I'd been involved in an incident at Lord's that had the commentators saying what a good and honest sport I was. I'd never heard that before! Graham Thorpe nicked one off Glenn McGrath and I dived forward and might have caught it. But I wasn't certain it carried. As the umpires, England's David Shepherd and Srini Venkataraghavan of India, walked to each other for a consultation, I ran over and said, 'Shep, I'm not sure.' So they gave the batsman the benefit of the doubt, which they might well have done anyway. Mr Shepherd made a point of applauding my honesty, which I appreciated but wasn't necessary, and because play was washed out soon after with England 3-38, the event received more exposure in the press than it would have if there had been a full day's play. I think my actions showed that I'd learned from the Lara incident, in that this time I made sure the umpires knew what I was thinking. Some of the fieldsmen standing near me and bowler McGrath reckoned that I did catch it — but I wasn't sure. The TV replays didn't prove a thing.

The day we retained the Ashes was a big one for me. We began leading by 281 with six wickets in hand in our second innings, but Stephen was out almost immediately. I then came out and hit 63 off 78 balls and we were able to set them 451 to win in a day and a session. Forget that, we bowled them out in 48.5 overs, taking the extra half hour allowed under the tour conditions to snare the last two wickets before the sun set. My catch of Dean Headley off Pigeon near the end, diving in front of the slip cordon, was special, and the day was sealed when I was named man of the match.

Like 1993, we lost the final Test, at The Oval, although this time I don't think it was a mediocre, lazy match-performance so much as one ordinary batting effort. Our preparation was good, and we were determined not to fall to the 'dead' Test jinx again. But in some ways, I guess, we did. The Test was played on an ordinary surface, but by lunch on the third day we'd done pretty well to be on the verge of a fourth straight win. We only needed 124, but fell 20 runs short, because, I reckon, we got ahead of ourselves and thought the match was won. By the time we realised we were in trouble, the Test was gone.

You could argue that, cricket-wise, this was the best of the three Ashes tours I was a part of, because this time the team had to recover from early setbacks rather than lead from the jump as we had in 1989 and 1993. When the pressure was in the middle stages of the tour we played some outstanding cricket. My wicketkeeping was good, sometimes excellent (25 catches and two stumpings in all), while my batting was reasonable throughout and very good at Trent Bridge.

—✠—

The front cover of
the sixth Test souvenir
program featured a
photograph of me
batting earlier in
the series.

THE LONG-RUNNING SAGA of the cricketers' push for a better, more formalised relationship between themselves and the ACB gathered momentum during the 1997 Ashes tour. As I've explained, Geoff Lawson had been campaigning for a better deal back in the late '80s, and the new breed of senior players had been trying to work directly with the Board since before our 1995 Caribbean campaign. Both Greg Chappell and Allan Border had attempted to facilitate this process, but by 1997 we still felt we were a fair way from first base. Through 1995 and 1996, our meetings were with the ACB chief executive, Graham Halbish, but then Halbish's contract with the Board was terminated somewhat mysteriously.

Tim May, by now retired from first-class cricket, had taken on the role of president of the fledgling Australian Cricketers' Association, a body whose birth the ACB had helped fund but which had struggled to get itself noticed in the corridors of cricket power. By late on the Ashes tour, the players as a group decided to make some moves that we hoped would attract the immediate attention of the Board. At a meeting in Canterbury, on the Sunday night of our game against Kent, we voted that Halbish and James Erskine, a slick, no-

nonsense marketing executive who'd first come to prominence in Australian sports business with the IMG sports management group, be brought on board as consultants. We knew that employing Halbish, who as a former ACB chief executive knew the workings of the Board better than most, would be seen as provocative, but we'd reached the point where we wanted to spur the Board into taking our claims seriously.

The players were concerned about a number of issues, and had been for a number of seasons. In my diary in mid-1995, I had listed some of them, in no particular order:

- Were players' rights and responsibilities being adequately considered in the Board's sponsorship and official supplier negotiations?
- What percentage of turnover was paid to players?
- Were players and the game being marketed effectively?
- Were players adequately insured against injury?
- Did the Board appreciate the impact increased playing time was having on players' working lives?
- Why were elite footballers earning so much more than elite cricketers?
- Were Sheffield Shield players adequately recompensed for the time they were being asked to put in?
- Did the Board feel that the existing superannuation arrangements were adequate?
- Were global TV rights being sold effectively?
- Were the right people getting the tour manager positions?

In the ensuing two years, the ACB had addressed some of these issues to varying degrees but it would be wrong to suggest that we were happy with their overall response. In the lead-up to negotiations between the ACA and the Board that were scheduled for after the Ashes tour, we'd come to the conclusion that they expected us to merely come in, ask for single rooms on tour and a bit more money and they'd go, tick, tick, okay boys, see you later. There was still no appreciation by the Board that our concerns went way beyond that. That was why we brought Halbish and Erskine on board, to negotiate with the Board on our behalf.

As Geoff Lawson had found in 1989, it's only the senior players who care about these issues. The young blokes, such as me in '89, are delighted with whatever they can get. In this regard, we were in an almost unique position in 1997, in that the team had a nucleus of six or seven established, high-profile senior guys who believed changes needed to be made. Thus, we had to make things happen there and then. And if there was one key issue on which we wanted to see progress it was to get a better deal for the Shield guys — who were being asked to put in more and more time in pre-season camps, second XI games, extended training sessions, extra fitness work, coaching clinics and the like without receiving large enough incomes to be able to save anything after the rent was paid at home. When this situation had been raised in the past, the Board had always countered with the small attendance figures at Shield matches, to which we'd argue that the Shield was the training ground for Test matches. Many of these poor Shield players were the future of the Australian game. To me, it seemed that if the Board wasn't prepared to pay these guys a fair wage, then surely the only alternative was for the game to go back to the days when pure Shield players were almost amateurs, appearing in eight first-class matches, training two afternoons a week and otherwise being club cricketers. We were sure, with the game flourishing at international level, that the Board could afford to pay the Shield players more money.

Matters came to a head during the 1997–98 Australian summer, when we came close to going on strike. Most of us were pretty militant, though Tubby was keen to try to find some middle ground with the Board. We had received strong advice from industrial relations experts that if we did threaten to withdraw our labour, the dispute would be settled in a week — because by issuing such a threat in accordance with the Workplace Relations Act, under which our dispute fell, we would force the Board to the negotiating table. Consequently, before the second Test of our series against New Zealand, in Perth, the ACA had circulated an 'intention to strike' form to Shield cricketers across the country. The response was almost unanimously in favour. The ACA's intention, which had been kept among its members to this stage, was to threaten to withdraw their players from three early-season one-day internationals. However, the senior Test players had discussed the situation before the game at the WACA and we'd decided that, in our view, it would be preferable if matches later in the summer could be targeted for possible strike action. We asked Tim May to give the ACB another month to come to the table, even if it was only to talk. Because of this, when the Test began in Perth, ACA secretary Steve Waugh still had the Test guys' forms in his bag, and was waiting until the Test concluded before distributing them.

Then, on the opening day of the Test, 12th man Andy Bichel came running out at the fall of a wicket and announced that news of the proposed strike had been leaked. The Channel Nine commentators had got hold of a copy of the form, and had shown it to their viewers. At the same time, unbeknown to us, Tubby was involved in some one-on-one discussions with Denis Rogers, chairman of the Board, after which Tubby came back to us with what he thought was a solution to the impasse. At a Test players' meeting the following night to discuss Rogers' offer, the debate was going around in circles for an hour or two, when one of the younger blokes suddenly said, 'Why has the Board come to us like this? If they are sure of their position, why won't they negotiate with Maysie?' It was an excellent point, which turned the debate. A vote was conducted — a secret ballot, with pieces of paper going into a baggy green — and the offer was soundly rejected. Instead of accepting the Board's offer, we asked them to take their offer to the ACA's negotiators. The strike threat remained, with a one-dayer in January the likely target unless some real progress could be achieved.

No one wanted to hurt the game in this way, but we could see no alternative other than the course of action we'd taken. A critical moment came for us when Channel Nine took four members of the team — Tubs, Tugga, Warney and me, all of whom were doing work for the network — to dinner, to find out exactly what was going on. Their concern, we discovered, was that a rebel cricket competition of some kind was being developed in secret and they didn't like the idea of the team going on strike, but we soon set their minds at rest as to our true motives, which was significant because, as a consequence, Nine was able to put both sides of the story to air. Until this point, the ACA had been losing the public relations war — ACB sympathisers had been successfully portraying the Test men as cricket mercenaries chasing mega-dollars. We had been unable to get our message across that what we wanted was a fairer deal for *all* first-class Australian cricketers. The next day, Warney was interviewed on Nine before play, and gradually the tide of public opinion began to even out.

Negotiations continued through the early part of 1998, and the ACA and the ACB finally reached an agreement to the effect that a set percentage of all cricket revenue would go into a players' payment pool. More significant, in my eyes, was the fact that the Board had now experienced dealing with Tim May and the ACA. This was something I'm sure they would rather have avoided, but the development of this chain of communication can only alleviate many of the concerns players and the Board have had in previous years, when the lack of quality contact between the two groups has been a major negative. I, for one, hope the link between the ACB and ACA continues to grow. There are still a number of issues that need to be addressed, but I believe they will be in a way that can only benefit the game, the players and the officials in the seasons ahead.

CHAPTER 20

BOWLED WARNEY

THE TEST IS MAYBE 90 minutes old, but now a game within the game is about to begin. 'C'mon Shane, into 'im,' I shout down the pitch. One last tinker of the field, a start from the bowler, then a halt as the batsman, a right-hander, eyes wide open, settles into his stance. Down I go into my crouch, early enough so I can succinctly study Shane's run-up and delivery, not too long or my legs will complain. I've positioned myself outside the line of the off stump so the batsman can't obscure my view, and now, with Shane about to come in, I go through my cues. Every ball, for every slow bowler, I'd tell myself, 'Watch the ball ... move ... stay down.'

I've seen Shane's slow, deliberate walk-in a million times. Here's the energy through the crease ... and the release. Had it been the flipper I would have detected it two paces earlier. This, though, is the leg spinner, rolled out of the hand, not ripped ... but how much will it turn?

Almost immediately, I see the ball drifting down the leg side, heading for scuffed up footmarks left by Glenn McGrath's first spell. They won't affect the ball now, but later, three or four days away, Warney'll be spinning hard out of there. Now, though, I must ignore the batsman as I strive to isolate the ball. It should slide down, outside the line of the batsman's legs ...

I must wait for the ball, don't grab for it, eyes always on the ball, my feet taking me to the leg side, low and strong. The gloves stay relaxed, to give with the ball, and in it goes cleanly. I take a deep breath, underarm the ball to short leg, and settle in for the second ball of what could be a long spell. The next ball pitches perfectly, middle-and-off, and buzzes past the outside edge into my gloves. The fieldsmen throw up their hands, the crowd lets out an admiring groan, the batsman a sigh of relief ...

'Bowled Warney!'

—¤—

SHANE WARNE CAME INTO the Australian team at just the right time, as far as my career was concerned, in that I was by then confident of my position in the team and confident, too, that I understood my wicketkeeping technique. Thus Warney's bowling became a challenge to meet and enjoy, rather than one that might have had me questioning my talents. Mistakes didn't worry me, so long as the mind and body were relaxed, the gloves soft and the feet moving as I knew they had to. I found I was able to read his deliveries just about all the time, certainly much better than any batsman. How I did this I'm not quite sure, but

Shane Warne at Old Trafford in 1997, giving the ball a real rip as he bowls to England's Graham Thorpe. At this point, I haven't been in my crouch for too long. A keeper's legs and back can begin to bark if he or she constantly crouches too early.

it became instinctive, a product, I imagine, of the many hundreds of hours out in the middle and at practice that we shared. The golf ball drill helped as well, by giving me the chance to rehearse the movement of my feet and gloves, as well as getting the mind ready for stresses that would invariably arise.

In the seasons that followed I was lucky to have the best seat in the house, as the man who would become Australia's greatest wicket-taker and one of *Wisden's* five cricketers of the 20th century decimated opposition batting line-ups the world over and changed the way international cricket looked at its spin bowlers. If Shane bowled well, we'd win. In my view, three things set him apart: he rarely bowled a bad ball; he had bag of tricks as deep as any magician; and could change plans effectively in the middle of a game, a spell, even an over. Having to bowl differently to two batsmen never worried him, so a single was never going to upset his rhythm too badly. As well, he was tough, could bowl all day, every day, and had a paceman's aggression.

Vital to his success was the fact that in his delivery he was technically magnificent. Back-leg drive was the key to him achieving energy on the ball, and the perfect timing of the shoulder rotation ensured good follow-through patterns, ball flight and pace. This also allowed him to give the ball that healthy flick out of the hand, which meant the ball would drift and drop, often savagely.

Facing Warney's bowling was a rare experience for me, but I did so when I played for Australia A against Australia in 1997–98, the season I was dropped from the Australian one-day team. Adam Gilchrist is the keeper.

Having Warney meant that we were capable of performing on all wickets. With quicks such as McDermott, Hughes and McGrath we were always competitive on seaming decks, and Warney gave us an advantage over everyone on the turners. Our Test loss in India in 1996 was probably the best example of this — Shane was out, injured, and without him the home team destroyed us on a fragile, dusty track. Having Warney also meant that our attack was beautifully balanced. On a flat wicket he could bowl nice and tight, always at the stumps, and as the wicket deteriorated you could see the opposition starting to sweat, because they knew they'd be facing him on his terms before the match was out.

Wicketkeeping to him was challenging but batting to him is much harder, which I found out first-hand in 1995–96 when I faced him for the only time in a Shield match. Not only do you have to concentrate fiercely for every ball, but you're required to score runs as well, which I think I would have found impossible on a spinning deck. I recall a poor bloke in Bermuda in 1995 who turned to me, exasperated, and said of Warney, 'This fellow's a lot easier on spin vision.' He'd been watching the West Indies series on the television, when they focused on Warney's delivery, slow motion, spinning out of the hand. Other batsmen tried all sorts of ways to defeat him. Batting normally might have worked on a good pitch if your luck was in, but history suggests that unless you are very, very good, Warney will work you out in the end. The drift Shane gets on his leg break can be so pronounced that it keeps batsmen pinned to the crease — only the most daring dance down the wicket to him — and the bounce he gets on his top-spinner has a similar effect, making batsmen reluctant to stretch too far forward, for fear of popping a catch to the close-in fieldsmen.

I always thought batsmen needed to be adaptable against Warney. One set plan was never enough. Some batsmen tried to pad him away, working on the theory that if you could survive facing Shane then the runs could be scored at the other end. But in would hustle the close-in fieldsmen — Mark Waugh to silly mid-off, Stephen in the gully, Boonie or Justin Langer already at short leg, Tubsy at slip — and Shane might change his line, more at the stumps, to make the batsman use his bat. And don't forget that bowling at the other end might be Glenn McGrath or Craig McDermott or Merv Hughes or Tim May. So getting up there might not be an escape at all.

Plan C: sweep at everything. The South Africans are keen on this, and Hansie Cronje and Jonty Rhodes had some success using it (as did New Zealand's Adam Parore), but it was more a way of getting off strike than hurting us by scoring heaps of runs. I always thought it was a very risky strategy that didn't bring a high return. The prospect of a top-edged catch to short fine leg or deep square leg always loomed. Some batsmen resorted to slogging, but that was never going to last. I remember South Africa's excellent bowler and ordinary batsman, Fanie de Villiers, turning around one day before he faced Warney and saying, 'What'll it be today, Ian, six or stumped?' It was stumped.

One group that did have some success were the left-handed batsmen, who had an advantage because Shane's wrong 'un wasn't as effective as his other deliveries. The lefties could play straight to all but the big-turning leg-breaks, and hit with the spin through and over the leg-side field. Arjuna Ranatunga played Warney as well as anyone, especially on the small grounds in Sri Lanka, while another leftie, Brian Lara, was superb in the West Indies in 1999, when, admittedly, Shane was slightly below his best. Sachin Tendulkar, a right-hander, dominated in 1998 in India, but again Warney was struggling and after the tour he needed major surgery on his shoulder. Probably the best players of Shane's bowling, apart from those three, were Graham Gooch, whose patience helped him, and Pakistan's Salim Malik, who in Pakistan in 1994 probably handled him best of all. The worst, undoubtedly, was South Africa's Daryll Cullinan, who never had a clue.

The thing about Shane that makes him unique in leg-spinning history is that he was so great so young. When he spun through England in 1993 he was 23 years old. Wrist-spinners, the wise old sages in the members stands told us, weren't at their best until after they turned 30. What Shane did was revolutionise the game, make leg-spinning trendy and turn a whole generation of potential fast bowlers into Warney lookalikes. And his control is astonishing. Other leggies bowl loose deliveries and are forgiven because they're leggies, but Shane is on the money all the time. I reckon he's had maybe five really bad days in his Test bowling life.

I could nearly write a book just about Shane's greatest deliveries. Some I've already talked about in this one, such as the famous 'Gatting' ball earlier in the 1993 Ashes series. There was another from that series that I remember fondly:

Gooch bowled around his legs in the fifth Test. Warney had predicted that one in the bar the night before, that he'd come round the wicket and turn one a mile out of the bowler's footmarks. My main memory of that dismissal, however, is of the panic I felt as I saw that the ball was going to pitch so wide of the leg stump. I struggled for a clear view, but then it spun sideways in extraordinary fashion and shattered the stumps. A similar spinning ball cleaned up the West Indian left-hander Shivnarine Chanderpaul at the SCG in 1996–97. Chanderpaul didn't even play a shot at a delivery that, out of the hand, looked like it might have been a wide, but was actually one of Shane's best-ever balls. It landed in the footmarks and snapped back to bowl, via the pads, a good player who was 71 and going extremely well. My two favourite flippers are the ones that knocked over Richie Richardson at the MCG in 1992–93 and England's Alec Stewart at the Gabba two seasons later. The first was a breakthrough ball for Shane, who was still trying to establish himself in the side, and thus gained great confidence when he saw it get through a player as good as Richardson. From that moment, I reckon, batsmen all over the world were looking warily for it. The Stewart one was important because it came in the first Test of the series, and bowled him so comprehensively that all the Englishmen's nightmares of 1993 came flooding back.

My favourite dismissals off him? For best stumping I'd vote for the Graham Thorpe stumping at Edgbaston in 1993, when I had to get the ball back a long way from outside off stump after Thorpe swung rashly at a wide one. My best catch off him was probably the one I took to dismiss New Zealand's Ken Rutherford in 1993, from a ball that pitched well outside leg stump, spun across the batsman and took a healthy deflection. I did well to get a sight of the ball, and then to move my gloves still further after the nick. I was also pleased with my catch of Darren Gough that was the middle dismissal in Shane's hat-trick at the MCG in 1994–95. This wasn't as difficult as some of the others, but it was a thick edge that needed grabbing and in the context of history it was very important.

As a bloke Shane is very highly strung, either very high or very low. He likes the limelight and then it can get him down, never finding that happy medium for extended periods, which is why he sometimes finds himself in trouble. Everywhere he goes he gets talked about — either shouts or whispers, insults or compliments — so it's no wonder that every now and then he blows up. The sad part is that when he does lose his composure, he is the only loser, which is unfair but a fact of public life. This said, I believe that, in the main, he has handled himself very well; most of his mistakes have come after a build-up of scrutiny and stress made his life temporarily intolerable. I think we all need to understand this, rather than quickly condemn him.

Warney's eating habits are legendary — suffice to say that there are many more things he won't eat than he will. He'd much prefer a margherita pizza to a five-star hotel's finest cuisine, cheese and crackers to a business-class meal. Consequently, he can suffer on some tours, especially to Pakistan, where not every hotel can cater for his limited tastes. In 1994, I can remember him going without food for two days when we were in Multan, staying at a hotel that wasn't yet completely built. But despite these and other hurdles, in my years in the side Shane was always extremely generous with his time, working as hard as anyone to encourage others and build morale. Not all champions are like that. Friendships mean a lot to him, and he revels in seeing his mates go well. Because he was far and away the biggest thing in Australian cricket he shouldered a lot of the team's media profile and was responsible for much of the team's media hype. Warney has had to face more pressure and exposure than any other Australian player in my experience, which was great for us, not so good for him. While he was being pestered, we were just playing our natural games and focusing on what we were trying to achieve. We owe him plenty.

— ¤ —

WARNEY HAD A SENSATIONAL season in 1997–98, taking 39 Test wickets for the summer — 19 in a three-Test series against New Zealand and 20 in three matches against South Africa. With such a potent force leading the way, it was inevitable that the team would also go well, and it was only in the final Test of the summer, against South Africa in Adelaide, that we were in any real danger of defeat. Mark Taylor also had a productive time, scoring a century in the first Test against New Zealand and then batting right through our first innings of the third South African Test, finishing with 169 not out. We eventually won the New Zealand series 2-0 and beat the South Africans 1-0, but unfortunately my season had been tarnished when I was dropped from the one-day team.

I must confess I didn't see this one coming. In the early weeks of the season there had been much speculation as to Mark Taylor's future in limited-overs cricket. I was aware the selectors were keen to look at the two sides as separate entities, agreed with such a strategy, and presumed when Tubs was left out of a one-day exhibition game between an Australian XI and a Cricket Academy side in Adelaide that he was to be omitted from the Australian one-day team. But it had never occurred to me that my head was on the block as well. I thought my one-day form had been good — I'd led the team to a rare series win in South Africa and had a career strike rate of 84 runs per 100 balls. Adam Gilchrist had done well in South Africa, first as my replacement when I was suspended and then as a specialist batsman, and appeared locked in as my eventual successor. At least I knew, when I was dropped, that I was losing my spot to an outstanding talent, but I was sure that I still had much to offer the one-day team and, just as had happened earlier in the year, was angered by the way my sacking was handled.

I had made 25, run out, in that Academy game, while Gilly hit 45. In the first two Tests against New Zealand, both of which we won, I'd had three digs, for 68, 25 (batting as a nightwatchman), and 85. During that last innings I became the highest-scoring Australian wicketkeeper in the history of Test cricket, breaking Rod Marsh's record. When the new one-day side was announced in Hobart during the third match of the Kiwi series, I was playing in my 97th Test match.

The only inkling I had was when I was watching the TV coverage of the Test in our dressing room and they started putting up the commentators' selections for the one-day team. Gilly was in all of them — which made sense, he'd have been in mine — but my name was missing from one or two. That was cheeky of them, I thought.

Steve Waugh had been trying to get me for a couple of nights, just the two of us, for a meal, but I unknowingly kept thwarting what he really needed to do. 'What are you doing tonight, Heals?' he'd ask, and I'd reply, 'Nothing much, why?'

'Let's go for a pizza.'

'Righto,' I replied, looking around the room. 'Hey guys, anyone else for a feed.'

And off we'd go, six or eight of us. Next night it was the same, and I was thinking, 'Gee, Tugga's being sociable this trip.'

After the group split up following dinner that second night, I got a call from Stephen. 'Mate,' he said quietly, 'can I come up to your room?'

That's when he told me I'd been left out. I remember staring blankly straight ahead at the TV and muttering something like, 'If I'd known averages meant something in this one day game, imagine the number of times I'd have been not out in my career.'

Then I got up and grabbed the remote while Stephen sat on the couch. There was a long, huge silence, which he finally broke, saying that he knew how disappointed I must have been. I think he did, too. We talked for a little while, and then he left. I was shattered.

Steve Bernard, the only selector in Hobart for the Test, had wanted to tell me himself, on the basis that it was the selectors' job to inform dropped players, not one for the new one-day captain. But the Test team hierarchy, Tubby and Swamp, ruled that out, knowing how disappointed I'd be and knowing, too, that there was a Test match still to be won. But I had to be told, because the one-day team was being announced during the last day of the Test. Why they couldn't have waited another 24 hours to release the team publicly I don't know. As it was, it wasn't announced until late in the day. Tubs and Swamp thought it best that Tugga got the gig, which he later described as 'probably the hardest thing I've ever had to do'.

I had to keep through most of that last day, and was determined not to make an error, and I managed to go all right even though we couldn't break a stubborn last-wicket partnership between Simon Doull and Shayne O'Connor. I can remember Ricky Ponting and Greg Blewett being into me, asking 'What's wrong with you?' But I kept to myself, told them I was okay, and tried to concentrate on the game. They found out after stumps.

That night I took a very brief call from Trevor Hohns, who was in Brisbane. Again, I told him, I felt I'd been treated like a bloke who'd been playing for five minutes, not 10 years. Why couldn't he have called me a week before, a month before, and had a chat about the fact that my future in the side was in jeopardy?

At the presentation after the third Test against New Zealand, in Hobart, in December 1997, I couldn't put on a happy face. I'd just been sacked from the Australian one-day side, and was still coming to terms with the disappointment.

I couldn't accept, given that Australia's previous one-dayer had been in May and my omission seemed to reflect a major shift in selection culture towards a two-team policy, that the decision to drop me had only been reached in the previous couple of nights. Forget the fact that he was once a mate; I felt this was an ordinary performance by the chairman of selectors.

> *December 16, 1997: Can't play selfishly or differently. Will play best naturally and if selectors want something else, I can't do anything but perform.*

> *December 17, 1997: Ian Healy is Ian Healy. Battle against changing for others and second-guessing what others think and want.*

> *Don't worry. Just do and enjoy.*

One major bonus of being left out of the one-dayers was that I was able to spend a lot more time with my father, at a time when his life was slowly ebbing away. Dad had been diagnosed with cancer on the day before the first New Zealand Test, and I actually went from the hospital after hearing the sad news to the team's hotel in Brisbane for our team meeting. I went into that match determined to make a hundred for him, but missed out after doing all the hard yards, and then the same thing happened in Perth when I was dismissed for 85.

With Emma (far left), Mum, Laura and Dad, April 1996.

There were three and a half weeks between the second and third South African Tests, and I fondly recall spending a fair chunk with my dad, often watching the one-day internationals. For a long while he was coping with the chemotherapy well, but just before I had to go to Adelaide for the third Test, the family was beckoned to the hospital, where Dad had taken a severe turn for the worse. He wasn't in too much pain, but he couldn't speak, and then Mum said something along the lines of, 'I'm sorry Ian, but I won't be able to come to Adelaide now.' To be honest, that was the last thing on my mind at that moment; then I heard Dad give out a groan, as if he was trying to say something. And then he passed away. I was standing behind him, my hand on his shoulder and one second there was a breath but then there wasn't another one. It was very sad, the saddest I've ever been, but at the same time it was so worthwhile being there when he left us. I'll always believe he heard Mum say she wasn't going to my 100th Test and decided that he wasn't going to let her miss it. I'm sure he was happy when he died, surrounded by his family who meant the world to him. As I've said, I owe my father so much.

I was a fraction distracted during that Test, a mixture of very proud and very sad. At the presentation before the game, I got pretty emotional thinking about how this one was so different from the first 99. I had a good game with the gloves, but in the viewing area during our innings and even when I batted I was a bit off with the fairies, thinking about other times. In the second innings, when we were fighting to save the game and Mark Waugh was playing extremely well, I rushed out, hit two fours and then was caught behind playing at one I could have left alone. Fortunately, Mark stayed right to the end, his second superb hundred against South Africa in 12 months, despite a controversial moment just before the close when he knocked the bails off the stumps with his bat after being hit on the elbow. The umpires ruled, correctly in my opinion, that he hadn't broken the stumps while playing the shot, and he definitely wasn't setting off for a run either — they were the only circumstances in which he could have been given out.

So ended my 100th Test. I was proud of the achievement, especially as no wicketkeeper had got there before, but I couldn't quite explain how I'd made it. It had all gone so quickly. I could hardly believe that I'd played for so long and so often. I was aware that my knowledge of the game had increased dramatically; it was almost scary when I thought about how little I knew when I first played first-class cricket. By my 100th Test, if something was going wrong I knew how to identify and then fix the problem. Off the field, I was a much more confident and worldly person, less naive and unassuming. This was something Helen made mention of all the time. She often told others how much I'd grown up, and we both agreed that our relationship had matured at the same time.

As for cricket, the game had changed at an astonishing speed. The demands on the players' time, on and off the field, had ballooned. So had the money in the game. The Australian team, of course, was much more confident, as were all the young players in the game. The sport was moving too quickly for them to be anything else. And the conditions in which the elite cricketers were playing had improved, too, with the traditionally tough tours, such as India and Pakistan, no longer being so daunting. This was something that I recognised more than most of my teammates, especially when I recalled some of the reluctant tourists who were my teammates on my first international tour back 100 Tests ago.

— ✠ —

THREE WEEKS AFTER the end of the Australian international summer, the Australian Test team was travelling to India, for the first multi-Test series between the two countries since 1991–92. I was on the plane after two weeks of soul-searching, after which I'd changed my mindset. I realised that barring some miracle I was never going to play one-day cricket again, and that not even a miracle was going to get the vice-captaincy back. I assumed that some sceptics were watching me, looking for any indication that I was slowing down. My objective now was to prove the doubters wrong. Further than that, I didn't want people to question my right to the Australian Test wicketkeeper's position. I also set my sights on Rod Marsh's world keeping record of 355 dismissals. At the start of the India series I was eight behind.

We went into the Test series with our bowling stocks undermanned. Glenn McGrath was missing, owing to severely strained abdominal muscles, and Shane Warne's shoulder was hurting, but even so we started the series okay, knocking the Indians over for just 257 on a good wicket in Chennai. Warney and Gavin Robertson both took four wickets. In reply we garnered a lead of 71, and I played a leading role by making 90, one of my best Test innings. 'Robbo', who

My 100th Test, in Adelaide in January 1998, was a very proud occasion, tempered by the knowledge that my father wasn't there to see it.

was having quite a Test debut, and I added 96 for the ninth wicket in 37 overs under a very hot sun, before I was out trying to play a sweep at their left-arm spinner, Venkatapathy Raju. I had fought my natural instincts for over four hours until, as my brain started to melt in the heat, I tried a shot that I'd managed to avoid for so long.

> *March 8, 1998: Played beautifully. Forty-seven singles, worked as hard as possible. Hundred felt a long way off when on 90. That's a sign I was losing concentration. Raju, [Anil] Kumble round the wicket — sweep wasn't on. Should have kicked them away for a few overs and they'd have changed back because they needed to get us out.*

> *Impatience cost me, but no regrets. The extra hurdle would have been unbelievable though.*

I paid for that innings 24 hours later, when I had an ordinary day, especially during the first session. I felt listless and nauseous during warm-ups, and couldn't switch on until around two or three o'clock, when I think I was revived by the realisation that stumps, the light at the end of my tunnel, was not too far away. In fact, Sachin Tendulkar smashed us so completely, making 155 not out off 191 balls, that they were able to declare in time to have us 3-31 by stumps. 'Toughest day of cricket I've had,' I wrote with feeble hand in my diary that night. The way I felt had nothing to do with my age, because I would have felt the same in those oppressive conditions if I'd been 17. As I looked at my distressed colleagues around the Aussie dressing room, I could see that at least most of them felt just as totally stuffed as I did.

I found my legs and focus on the final day, and batted for an hour and a half for 32 not out while we crashed to a 179-run defeat. I was happy with the way I fought to the end, having based my batting plan on how Steve Waugh had gone about things when he played a long defensive innings in our Test at Delhi in 1996. Turn the strike over, try to hit the bad balls for four, defend the good balls, but more than anything else stay patient. Tugga's innings in Delhi had been the subject of a wonderful analysis by the cricket journalist, Greg Baum, and I had made sure Greg's article was close at hand throughout this tour.

Throughout this tour I could tell Warney was struggling, even though when any of us asked he'd just reply, 'Nah, mate, everything's fine.' But he wasn't spinning it and Tendulkar took to him, dancing down the pitch in a manner he would never have been able to do if Warney was ripping the ball. Unfortunately, Shane and all our bowlers copped more of the same in the second Test at the colossal Eden Gardens in Calcutta, when India replied to our ordinary total of 233 with 5-633, and we eventually lost by an innings and 219 runs.

There was one amusing moment amid the gloom. Greg Blewett had failed to score in the first innings, and was a little anxious as he waited to go in the second time around. 'I'm not sure what you're worried about,' said Mark Waugh, who himself had made four ducks in a row in Sri Lanka in 1992. 'I don't reckon you can call yourself a cricketer until you've bagged a pair.' Blewey then went out and made 25, defending grimly for an hour and a half, until he was trapped lbw. In the next over, Mark Waugh was out ... for a duck!

As we stumbled to that crushing loss, we didn't look capable of beating anyone, but at a team meeting afterwards we gave a commitment to each other to fight back. And that we did, despite Tendulkar making another big hundred on the opening day. Mark Waugh hit his highest Test score, 153 not out in more than six hours, Michael Kasprowicz took 5-28 in the Indians' second innings, and then Tubsy made an unbeaten 102 as we won by eight wickets.

Perhaps India suffered from the 'dead' Test syndrome, but even if they did it was still a brave comeback for us to win, especially after they made 400-plus in their first innings. Personally, I was very pleased with my performances throughout the tour. Even in Calcutta, when we were being slaughtered, my concentration levels were high and I stayed positive, kept in the present and fought hard throughout. I'd come to accept my omission from the one-day team, and when I looked at their upcoming itinerary, which had them crisscrossing the country to play matches at some obscure, upcountry venues, I felt home in Brisbane with my wife and kids was where I was meant to be. I certainly wouldn't have felt that way in 1993, but times had changed. As I followed Tubsy onto the plane home, I was content again with my cricket life and felt confident that, despite what some people thought, I was going to be around for a little while yet.

CHAPTER 21

A NEW WORLD
RECORD

WHEN ROD MARSH BROKE the world record for wicketkeeping dismissals in 1981, England's Alan Knott, the man whose aggregate he'd just surpassed, was quick to send him a bottle of champagne to mark the occasion. This was a marvellous gesture, but it was made a little easier by the fact that Rod took the record-breaking catch at Leeds, so the bubbly didn't have far to go once Knotty ordered it from his local bottle shop. When I finally took the record from Rod, I was at Rawalpindi, in north-east Pakistan, but that didn't stop the great West Australian, and that night, while I was savouring my new status, an expensive bottle of Australian champagne was put in front of me. How he got it there I'm still not sure, but it was magnificent of him, and I said right there and then that when my record is broken I'll be getting a bottle of champagne to the new record holder no matter where or when the new mark is established.

The record doesn't mean I was the greatest wicketkeeper of all time; it simply reflects the fact that I played a lot of Test cricket, which is something I'm very proud of. I was making my 104th Test-match appearance, whereas Rod played in 96 Tests. To be honest, I was never a big one for worrying about records — I remember when it was announced that I'd made my 200th Test dismissal, in Adelaide in early 1994, I didn't have a clue I'd taken anywhere near that many. For me, the team records are the ones that stick in my mind, and are the ones I always craved, because of the celebrations and the atmosphere they generate. It's a funny thing about keeping stats — the one that in my view best measures a keeper's worth is chances missed, and that's not even recorded. And if someone did try to tally such errors imagine the arguments there would be over whether a miss was actually a chance or not!

The record came on the afternoon of October 4, 1998, when an offie from Test debutant Colin 'Funky' Miller spun and jumped a bit and brushed the glove of Wasim Akram. Instead of a chorus of 'Howzats' from my teammates, I heard, 'That's it!' as soon as the ball was safely in my gloves, and within seconds I was surrounded by a group of Australian cricketers who seemed even happier than I was. Gavin Robertson and the rest of our reserves up on the team balcony hung a 'Congratulations Heals' sign over the railing. Likewise, the spectators at Rawalpindi were very kind, giving me a lengthy ovation ... then it was back to business, trying to seal an Australian victory. Wasim was the seventh wicket to fall in Pakistan's second innings, leaving us on the brink of an outstanding and

That's it! Wasim Akram is caught in Rawalpindi, my 356th Test dismissal.

historic triumph. Unfortunately, the light was fading — Wasim had actually complained about the gloom before his dismissal — and eventually we were left needing to come back the following morning to take the one last wicket that would complete an innings and 99-run victory.

As I was corralled by reporters after stumps to talk about the record, one recurring theme was 'so where to now for Ian Healy?' 'I'd like to get to 400 definitely,' I told the journos. 'But I don't want to think just about that because I'd be playing for the wrong reasons … I'd like to get out on my own terms and I'd like to get out not stale, still pretty enthusiastic.

'And then,' I continued, 'it would be time to move on and get good at something else.'

The celebrations after I broke my record took place at the British Embassy club, but they were muted somewhat by the fact that we had to return the next morning to get that last wicket. After the win, though, we partied with gusto, joined by many expat supporters who enjoyed the win as much as we did. It was a far cry from my first tour, when every day was one day closer to coming home. This was the first Australian Test win in Pakistan since November 1959, and was achieved despite the fact we were without Shane Warne, who'd had major shoulder surgery after our tour of India. His replacement, Stuart MacGill, filled in superbly, taking nine wickets for the match, while in our innings Steve Waugh scored another hundred, Michael Slater hit his first in Test matches for nearly three years, Darren Lehmann made 98 and I chipped in with a last-out 82. We relived all these achievements and reminded each other of plenty more at that bar throughout the day after our victory. The Australian Embassy had a Down Under Bar to which we were invited at 7pm, and we took the place by storm. The atmosphere was spirited, to say the least, as the chanting and shenanigans continued through the night.

Slats had made it back into the Test XI for the India tour, but had not scored too many there and was probably on shaky selection ground when he arrived in Pakistan. However, he followed up this first-Test century with a 96 in the third Test, in Karachi, then made three more hundreds in the home Ashes series that followed, and then another in the first Test of our 1999 tour of the Caribbean.

Slats was one of my closest buddies in the Australian team and remains a close friend, a very funny and very polite man who really enjoys a good time off the field. He just loves the team and being a part of it, and is a little dynamo who does everything in life at one speed — flat out! He hits the ball hard, goes hard at the ball in the field, practises very hard — on his body shape and stamina as well as in the nets — but is also an emotional bloke whose performances are occasionally spoiled by the fact that he can get too intense and start thinking a bit much. Slats is at his best when he's carefree and happy, and not trying to complicate things.

In my view, Slats is one of the finest players in Australian cricket at present, and has been for a while. He's similar to Mark Waugh in the way he can sometimes make the toughest conditions look ridiculously easy. A classic example of this would come after this Pakistan series, back in Australia, when he made a century against the Poms in Sydney on a turning deck where no other Australian could get any at all. One of his great values is that opponents shudder when they have to face him, because they know that if he does get on top of them he's going to score a lot of runs in a short space of time. I'm not sure the selectors were right to leave Slats out of the team when they did for two seasons from November 1996 to April 1998. His was a talent and a mindset that always needed to be nurtured, but by dropping him they cut at his confidence and it took a long while for him to recover.

In between Slats' two career-boosting scores at Rawalpindi and Karachi, his opening partner did something much, much bigger. Mark Taylor had been struggling a little going into the second Test, in Peshawar, but after he won the toss there on an absolute road of a pitch, he soon settled in for a long stay. How long, I don't think even he could believe. At stumps on day one, which was restricted by bad light to 69 overs, he was 112 not out. At stumps on day two, he was undefeated on 334. It was an astonishing performance of skill, endurance and concentration.

The mood in our dressing room that second evening was buoyant, as we savoured Tubs' achievement. There was much talk about whether we should or shouldn't bat on, and I could see plusses and minuses in both arguments. We were 4-599 at stumps. Batting on for the world record of 375 wasn't so much the issue, as whether there was an advantage to us in making the Pakistanis labour in the field a bit longer. If we did that, and Tubby went past Brian Lara's record,

Right: In the dressing room at Rawalpindi, with the world record now mine and Robbo's superbly crafted sign stuck above my spot.

Below: We had to come back on the fifth morning of the first Test in Pakistan to get the final wicket. Afterwards, I was quick to grab a stump and the ball as souvenirs of what was a very special match for me. The other Australians here are (left to right): Justin Langer (obscured behind me), Steve Waugh, Michael Slater, Glenn McGrath and Colin Miller.

fantastic. By reaching 334, Tubsy had, of course, equalled Sir Donald Bradman's Australian Test record score, but I don't think that had any bearing on his eventual decision to declare. All he had to do was decide in his own mind what was right for the side, and he'd demonstrated plenty of times in the past that he was a good judge of that. And he was also very good, as he had shown through his batting slump, at not worrying about what others thought, so long as he was contented and comfortable himself. He did declare, but the wicket was so flat that we couldn't bowl the home team out twice and the match ended in a draw.

— ✠ —

AT THE START OF my diary for 1998-99, before the Pakistan tour, I'd included two quotes, neither sourced unfortunately:

> *July 1998: 'The most important thing in my life at the*
> *moment is liking who I am and not feeling like I have to be a*
> *certain way for someone else.'*
>
> *July 1998: 'Champions don't insist that we believe in them,*
> *but inspire us to believe in ourselves.'*

I also included a magazine cutting, sticky-taped in to the front, which told the story of a cartoon that featured three men — one who lives in the past and is constantly feeling guilty, one who lives for the future and suffers from fear and a third man who lives in the present and looks mighty pleased with himself. I knew I needed to focus on what I was doing, rather than going back over past disappointments or worrying about impending challenges from Adam Gilchrist or others, and because I did this effectively in Pakistan, I came away very pleased with my keeping and batting, and my general persona on tour. I thought my glovework was as good as ever, and I followed up my 82 in the first Test with a 47 in the first innings in Karachi. That Test was drawn after we failed to bowl out the home team on the final day, but that was enough to get us the series win, 1-0, the first time that I'd been part of a series-winning team on the Indian Subcontinent.

However, despite these positive messages that I continued to drum into myself throughout the Australian summer, when Mark Taylor announced his retirement in late January, following our 3-1 Ashes series win, I couldn't help thinking he was a bit lucky to be not going on tour *yet* again. Throughout the Tests against the Poms I tried everything I could to keep my eagerness up, but as the series went on my spark wasn't quite there. The cricket was fine. As well, I kept reminding myself how lucky I was to be playing cricket for Australia, that there were any number of young people who'd love to be in my place. I'd look at my baggy green and still get that unique shot of pride that came with knowing I was an Australian Test cricketer. And I still relished the camaraderie — the simple pleasure of being with a tremendous bunch of blokes who wanted to win, wanted to be good and wanted everyone else on their side to be winning and good as well. However, it was everything that went with this — media spotlight,

Right: I always enjoyed batting with Steve Waugh, but never more so than in the First Test against England, at the Gabba, in 1998–99.

Below: Tugga and I walk off the Gabba at lunch on the second day of the First Test. We had both reached our centuries just before the interval.

pressure to perform, hotel rooms, time pressures, not seeing family, training, airports, functions — that began, drip by drip, to gnaw at me. I remembered back again to David Boon's last season, when I got a bit dirty on him for not trying harder to get his enthusiasm back — now I was wondering whether Boonie did try everything but the buzz just wouldn't return. The pros weren't thrashing the cons any more. I felt my form was still good, and hoped I wasn't dragging anyone down, but off the field I wasn't the same bundle of verve I'd been in the past.

The media scrutiny reached fever pitch in Adelaide before and during the third Test, after the fact that Shane Warne and Mark Waugh had been fined in 1995 for being paid in exchange for information finally became public. As part of the ACB's response to this, an inquiry into all aspects of gambling, supplying of information and match-fixing involving Australian cricket was established. Headed by Rob O'Regan QC, with support from a number of legal people, it was a wide-ranging probe that eventually made a series of recommendations to the Board but as far as I know didn't find any evidence of Australian involvement in bribery, betting on cricket matches or match-fixing. My experience before the O'Regan inquiry came after the Test series, when I was interviewed at the Quay West hotel in Brisbane. It was a very formal affair, and I was asked many questions about events that had occurred some years before. Personally, I felt I had nothing to tell them. As far as I knew, I'd never been approached by a bookie and certainly had never been offered cash in exchange for information. And I'd always tried my hardest every time I ventured onto the cricket field, from the good old days in Biloela to the 1998–99 Ashes Tests and beyond.

I'd certainly started the Ashes series on a high, scoring my fourth Test hundred in the opening Test, at the Gabba. Again, Steve Waugh was my partner for most of it. I always enjoyed batting with him, and I think I helped him sometimes because we had so much confidence in each other. We're roughly the same age, both uncompromising on the cricket field, and have shared plenty of cricket experiences, so there were no surprises when we batted together. There's nothing flamboyant or 'touchy-feely' about the relationship; we're just good mates.

Strangely, I outscored Tugga nearly two to one — 117 runs to 69 — during our 187-run partnership. 'Not that that's too hard,' I joked to him later. I faced 303 balls for my 134, while Steve saw 330 deliveries during his 112. In reality, I was just doing the same sorts of things at the batting crease that I'd been learning more and more about in the previous three or four seasons — being aggressive but sensible, playing to my strengths rather than worrying about my opponent's talents, playing the moment. The confidence I'd taken from my big hundred against the West Indies had helped enormously. Someone pointed out to me that my Test batting average was now almost 30, and had risen nearly four runs a dismissal — a run a year — since where it was on my 30th birthday. Following this innings, I needed just 204 runs to pass Alan Knott as the world's highest-scoring Test wicketkeeper. It's crazy to think I wouldn't get there.

With Mark Taylor and Steve Waugh after we'd retained the Ashes in Adelaide. This was the sixth straight Ashes series triumph for the three of us.

Despite the fact I was no longer in the one-day team, this was still a testing summer physically for me. The ACB had restructured the Australian international season, scheduling the five Tests from November 20 to January 6, and then the World Series through January to mid-February. For me, there was no respite after the Tests, as I went straight to three Shield games in three weeks. I enjoyed captaining and playing for Queensland, but coming straight after the Tests they took a bit more out of me than I needed, with a West Indies tour coming up.

Even during the Tests I felt a bit fatigued at times, as they came so quickly one after the other. However, the team thrived — after a colossal thunderstorm saved England on the final day in Brisbane, we retained the Ashes by winning decisively in Perth and Adelaide to go 2-0 up with two to play. The only disappointment came after that, in the fourth Test, in Melbourne, when we failed in a small run-chase after playing really well until that final innings. This was the third time we'd mucked one of these up, after Sydney against South Africa in 1993–94 and England at The Oval in 1997, and this one was probably the worst of the three, in the sense that the conditions were excellent. In the first two, I think we underestimated chinks in the pitch; at the MCG in the last week of 1998, however, we simply got a bit lazy and paid a heavy price. No doubt, though, we should have reached our targets on all three occasions, but we let ourselves down. This time, as we'd done against South Africa in '94, we came right back to win the next Test decisively, with Stuey MacGill taking a truckload of wickets and Warney making a successful return to Test cricket.

One controversy that came out of that Melbourne collapse was the reaction in Sydney to Steve Waugh's policy of not protecting tailenders late in an innings. I reckon if you took a poll of everyone in the team it would turn out that the majority of us disagreed with him, but that's his way and it has worked well on many occasions. Take the first innings of this Test, for example, when Tugga gave Stuart MacGill free reign and Stuey made 43 while Tugga went on to one of his best centuries and Australia finished with a 70-run first innings lead. But in the second, when we needed 14 to win when Stuey came to the crease, Stephen took a single off the first ball of a Darren Gough over, and two wickets fell straightaway and the Test was over. Stephen reckons that by taking every run available he's giving the tailenders confidence, but I wonder in real pressure circumstances whether he might be better keeping the strike for at least a couple of deliveries. What angered all of us was the suggestion in some quarters that he was being selfish and playing purely for the not out to help his batting average. The critics who said that just don't know the bloke, and what the team means to him.

— ✡ —

MARK TAYLOR HAD REACHED the 100-Test landmark at the beginning of the series, becoming — after AB, Boonie, Tugga and me — the fifth Australian to reach this milestone. By the final Test in Sydney, however, talk was mounting that he was about to give it away, and about three weeks later, his minders called the press conference where he made his retirement official. I'm not sure whether or not Tubby was 100 per cent certain that he was going to give it away immediately after the Ashes series ended, but I reckon the 'time off' he enjoyed straight afterwards, while the World Series went on without him, would have

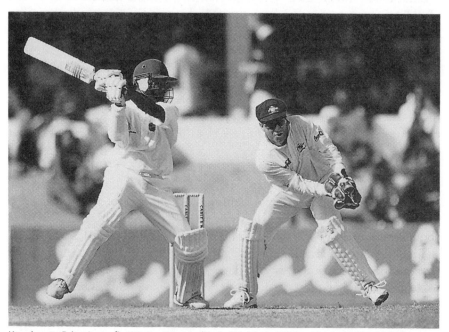

Keeping to Brian Lara, first Test v West Indies in Trinidad, 1999.

allowed him to think long and hard about it. During that break he may have discovered that the prospect of going on a West Indies tour wasn't quite as attractive as it had been in the past, and that there were plenty of other things to do back home.

My diary for the Windies tour reflects how I, too, had lost that crucial one per cent. There is little cricket written up in there, whereas on past tours I would have religiously kept the journal up to date. I was also not quite as zealous as I could have been treating injuries, which caught up with me near the end of the tour, and with hindsight I might not have been as much help to Steve Waugh, leading Australia in Tests for the first time, as I could have been. On the field, my keeping form stayed sound — in fact, once or twice I thought I was as good as I've ever been — but, frankly, I didn't enjoy the tour. The West Indies is not the easiest place to find your enthusiasm again if you're without it at the start, because the practice facilities are terrible and the grounds can be hard work. I found myself constantly fighting the grind.

Most days, when I opened my coffin I'd look inside at my gloves and think, 'Not again! I really don't want to put you guys on.' They never felt comfy, as they'd always done in the past; now they were sweaty and hard. Further dampening my mood was a calf muscle problem that I endured late in the tour. It came about, ironically, after I attempted to counter my negative attitude by working really hard at practice. But I did so on some ordinary fields, and initially tried to work through what were just some very minor strains. Looking back, I probably didn't get them rubbed out often enough —which is another indication that I was not totally switched on. I'll get by, was my attitude, whereas in the past I would have been queuing up for a massage whenever I felt the slightest niggle.

On the night before the last day of the third Test, in Barbados, it reached the stage where the tour management came to me and asked if I'd be right for the fourth Test, which was due to start in just four days time. 'If you're asking me now,' I responded, 'I'd have to say no.'

So a call went out to Gilly back in Perth, who was due in the Caribbean for the one-day series that followed the Tests, to come over early. Errol thought my calves would settle okay, but I wasn't so sure. We put some special cushioning inside my boots, and I wore a surgical stocking on each lower leg, to help the circulation during that third Test. However, the problem, I learned later, was that knots of fluid had collected in the calves, which meant that the impact of a natural lactic acid build-up during a long day in the field was accentuated many times over. This threw my nerves out, and it always felt as if the calf muscles were about to tear, even though they weren't. It made for some difficult sessions.

I had to motivate myself for a big effort in the final Test, knowing that there was a strong possibility that if I played poorly it could be my last. I was resigned to the fact that if I couldn't get myself up for what was such an important game, then my career was over. Having been down for much of the tour, now the thought that it might be all over got me going again, and I worked hard to get myself right. I kept well in the Test and the team won an important victory. I took my performance and the result to be indicators that I still wanted to be there. On the flight home, with my strong display in the final Test still fresh in my mind, I promised myself that I'd be keen and ready for the Sri Lanka tour in August. If I couldn't get myself up for that trip, I decided, I'd call it quits immediately, but if I was in the right frame of mind I'd go to Sri Lanka and Zimbabwe, and then, if my form held up, I hoped to enjoy one last Aussie season.

Alongside my fear that maybe I'd lost the desire to be Australia's wicketkeeper was a great concern that I'd lost the ability to score runs at the highest level. Throughout the tour, I felt that my keeping was okay. Perhaps, until the fourth Test, not quite at the standard I always set for myself, but acceptable. But my batting was terrible — just 53 runs in eight innings for the series, after scoring only 87 runs in the last four Ashes Tests of 1998-99. To try to get my runscoring back, I'd practise and practise, but in the Windies I found that too often the wrong messages were dominating my thought processes. Rather than treat every ball on its merits, I'd be waiting for a ball on my legs, or a short one, so I'd be able to sweetly hit one of my favourite shots. A few of those, my sub-conscious was saying, and you'll be right again. I needed to practise those shots separately, but in a regular net session you need to treat your time as if you're in a game. It was astonishing, even after I'd remind myself to keep a clear head, how I'd get in the nets, or out in the middle, and my mind would be crowded again with negative or confusing thoughts. Occasionally I'd have an excellent net and think I'd be right, but next time all the bad habits would return.

I just wasn't batting in my usual happy-go-lucky way. I didn't acknowledge it at the time, but I concede now that the combination of the slight blurring of my focus that came with thoughts of retirement, combined with the pressure I felt because the prime challenger for my spot, Adam Gilchrist, is a batsman capable of scoring Test hundreds as well as an excellent keeper, spoiled my batting mindset. Three years earlier, when I was in excellent batting form, Gilly's challenge wouldn't have been an issue; in fact, I'd have loved it and would have responded positively to it. But if your focus is just a little astray, and your batting form starts to go, it goes completely and quickly. Or it did for me.

—✠—

IRONICALLY, WHILE I BATTLED my lack of enthusiasm and injury off the field, on it the Test cricket was often fantastic, a pleasure to be a part of. We were hampered to some degree by the fact that Warney, still recovering from his shoulder reconstruction, was below his best, but to counter that Steve Waugh and Glenn McGrath were absolutely magnificent. For their part, the Windies were dreadful in the first Test, an uninspired shadow of the sides of the late '80s, and the criticism in the local media that followed that performance — which included being bowled out for just 51 in their second innings — was rancorous. The feeling we had then was that our opponents were divided and resigned to defeat, but rather than meekly lying down, they jumped up and bit us in

The scene straight after I'd dropped Lara in Barbados, when the Windies needed only six to win. Minutes later, the locals were celebrating an astonishing victory.

remarkable fashion, taking the next two matches in thrilling style. Critically, Brian Lara, Courtney Walsh and Curtly Ambrose led the way. Below their best in the first Test, the three of them were awesome for the rest of the series.

Lara's performances were brilliant, the best I've seen from him — which is not bad considering I was keeping when he made that famous 277 run out in Sydney in 1992–93. He did nothing in the first Test of this series, but then he peeled off three classic hundreds. The first of them was a double ton in Jamaica, when he batted all day with Jimmy Adams to set up a shock 10-wicket victory, and came at a time when most observers were predicting that Australia would win the series 4-blot and Lara was about to get the sack. The second was a stirring, unbeaten 153 in the second innings in Barbados that won the Windies a dramatic one-wicket victory. That was as pressure-packed a Test day as I ever played in, yet Lara seemed oblivious to it all, kept churning the runs out until he smashed one last four to give them the win. And the third century, maybe the most remarkable of all — an even 100 off just 84 balls — happened so fast that it didn't really hurt us. We were going well, with the Windies 2-20 in the 15th over, then Lara came out, smashed a hundred, was caught behind, 3-136 in the 39th over, and we then went on to have them all out for 222, a lead to us of 81 runs. It was almost as if his century hadn't happened.

That last day of cricket in the third Test had begun with the Windies 3-85 chasing 308, Lara 2 not out. Quickly they were 5-105, after Adrian Griffith and Carl Hooper were dismissed, but then Adams came in to stonewall while his captain attacked. The pair added 133 in a little under three hours, so when

Glenn McGrath finally broke the partnership the Test was very much back on an even keel. The wicket was a bit up and down — which adds to the lustre of Lara's great achievement. All day, I felt some pain every time I ran or moved sideways. Their keeper, Ridley Jacobs, had scored 68 against us in the first innings here, but this time he made only 5, and then Nehemiah Perry was lbw McGrath, first ball. The Windies, with just Ambrose and Walsh left to help Lara, still needed 60 to win. It was so quiet you'd have thought we were playing in a morgue.

Curtly's a strange man. When I'd rung him earlier in the tour, he answered the phone with a straight-to-the-point, 'Speak.' In the first two Tests of the series he'd scored the grand total of nine runs. But here in Barbados, having batted for over an hour in the first innings he batted for even longer in the second (though facing just 39 balls, so well did Lara shield him from the strike) defending stoically as the tension grew and the crowd became louder and more excited by the run. When he was finally dismissed, caught by Matty Elliott off Jason Gillespie, the home team needed just six to win.

Just before that dismissal, I'd dropped Lara. It was a sharp chance, high to my left, which might have made me a hero if I'd snared it. I didn't feel the same devastation as I did when I missed that stumping in Karachi, but I was still desperately disappointed and it ruined what had been to that point a good day for me, considering my crook legs. I made it through the day without a major hiccup ... almost.

One wicket to get, six to win, and Lara was not to be denied. In 14 minutes at the crease, Walsh only faced five deliveries, while Lara worked the scores level and then flayed Dizzy through the cover field to the boundary. With that, he dashed for the pavilion, to be met by a flood of fans and teammates, a reception he fully deserved. On the day, he was too good for us.

I have my problems with Lara and have never got to know him as a bloke, even though we've been rivals since 1991. Right from the first time I came into contact with him, back on that '91 tour, I thought it was strange that he seemed to spend more time in our dressing room with Mike Whitney and Greg Matthews than he did with his own team. He was 12th man throughout that series, and you would have expected him to be with his more experienced, highly gifted teammates, such as Viv Richards, Malcolm Marshall, Gordon Greenidge, Desmond Haynes and Jeffry Dujon. Maybe they didn't like him, or he them, or perhaps there was some sort of inter-island rivalry at work. I don't know.

Of the three great batsman of the late '90s — Steve Waugh, Tendulkar and Lara — the West Indian is the one with the 'loosest' technique. He'll often give you a chance early on, playing the flashy shots without the footwork. If he does offer you an opportunity, though, it'll take some catching and if you miss it you'll probably be in for a long, regretful day. Once his eye is in, he can be just as sure in defence and composed as Waugh or Tendulkar. In fact, with all three at their absolute best on a good batting track I'd put Lara up with Tendulkar as the No. 1, because both can make run-making look so easy, even against the very best bowlers. When they're on song, and the scoreboard's ticking over, there's not

Steve Waugh took this photo just before we got ready to go out for the final Test of our series in the West Indies in 1999. The surgical stockings and bandaging around my calves were the latest remedies for a muscle problem that had been frustrating me during the latter part of the tour.

too much you can do. Steve, on the other hand, is the most relentlessly determined cricketer in the world, the best concentrator in the game, and a man who loves batting when conditions are at their toughest. If I wanted someone to bat for my life, I'd choose him.

— ✠ —

AFTER OUR LOSS IN Barbados, something of a campaign was mounted in the Australian media for both Shane Warne and I to be dropped for the fourth Test, with some prominent former internationals leading the outcry.

My understanding was that my place in the Test XI wasn't in question, despite Gilly's early arrival, provided I could prove my fitness. Warney, unfortunately, wasn't so lucky, and I felt sorry for him while understanding the selectors' thinking. Still struggling a fraction with his shoulder, he couldn't quite get the rip on the ball that he can at his best. For three Tests, we played with both leggies, Warne and MacGill, but after neither could stop Lara on the last day of the third Test, in Barbados, it was clear that one of them had to go and the selectors opted to retain MacGill. It was a tough call, one of those ones I was glad I didn't have to make, and afterwards Shane was understandably disappointed and a little dirty. But he fought back superbly in the 12 months that followed, starring in the latter stages of the 1999 World Cup, winning the Australian one-day cricketer of the year award, and then, in March 2000, breaking Dennis Lillee's Australian Test wicket-taking record. It was always going to be impossible to keep him down for long.

There was no doubt at this point that Glenn McGrath was the team's bowling spearhead. He took six wickets in the fourth Test giving him 30 for the four-Test series, the most by an Australian in a Test series in the Caribbean. At series end, he was sixth in the Australian all-time wicket-taking list, and had come a long, long way from the raw, promising quick who'd made his debut back in 1993–94.

His achievement was tarnished somewhat when he was found guilty of bringing the game into disrepute after being seen on television spitting on the ground at the end of the fourth day's play of the fourth Test. It was not the first time, nor the last, that Pigeon would get himself into trouble for his on-field behaviour, but to us that was all part of the package. While we didn't condone one or two of his more exuberant outbursts, we understood they occurred because of the intensity he brought to his cricket — that same intensity that made him such a lethal strike bowler.

As his record shows, he is a tremendous bowler, very Curtly Ambrose-like in the way he can relentlessly deliver from a great height, ball after bouncing ball on the right line and length. He can bowl long spells, and if there's anything in the wicket he'll move it in and away off the seam. He has suffered a couple of significant injuries, but he's so good that he invariably walks straight back into the team.

I reckon when Pigeon's cricket career is over, he'll surprise a lot of people when they discover what a nice bloke he is. Today, everyone sees him as a cranky old sledger — and he is on the field; he'll tee off at any batsman who scores a run off him — but off the field he's a fantastic bloke with a vast knowledge of the game and a very positive, gentle approach to life. Away from cricket, he likes nothing more than to head off for a spot of hunting and fishing on his property out the back of Bourke. And — more than most international cricketers — he is a man with many and diverse interests outside the game.

One of Pigeon's most important contributions to the Australian team's success in the 1990s was the way he stood up to the Windies quicks despite the fact that he didn't really have the batting ability to counter the bumpers he knew he'd get in return. By doing so, he gave us all confidence; to not show similar courage ourselves would be to badly let him down. It was appropriate then that he ended this Caribbean campaign with a nasty lifter to their No. 10, paceman Corey Collymore, who was making his Test debut. I realised, as the ball lobbed from Collymore's bat to Stuey MacGill, that this was the last time I'd be out there when a West Indian wicket fell, and it was satisfying to know that I was finishing with an important victory.

CHAPTER 22

THE FINAL STRAIGHT

AT THE CONCLUSION OF THE Windies Test series, while the one-day team stayed to play a seven-match series, I headed for home. It would only be for a short break, however, until I left for the UK, to lead a tour group with Mark Taylor and do some commentary work during the 1999 World Cup. I loved the work, and was surprised how quickly the commentating bug took hold of me. It was something new to learn to be good at. On the field, the Cup tournament started poorly for the Australians, but gradually evolved into something of a personal triumph for Steve Waugh. First, Tugga scored a brilliant century to beat South Africa and get his team into the semi-finals; then he scored a half-century and led the side coolly and cleverly in a remarkable tied semi-final that got Australia through to the decider; finally he sat back and watched Shane Warne, Glenn McGrath, Adam Gilchrist and Mark Waugh dismantle Pakistan to win the tournament in rampaging style.

Stephen's catchcry is 'back yourself', which is perfect for the team of confident young men he's leading into the 21st century. While great champions such as Warne and McGrath need only to be fully fit to produce under any circumstances, brash young cricketers such as Slater, Ponting, Langer, Gillespie and Gilchrist need the team hierarchy to show absolute confidence in them at this stage of their careers, to tell them to get out there and play naturally. Because Stephen does this, these men are now enjoying the stresses and pressure of international cricket, and producing some magnificent efforts in Tests and one-day internationals. The team's astonishing winning streaks in both forms of the game in 1999-2000 is concrete proof of this.

He's got a sly sense of humour, has S. Waugh. He's a stay-in-the-background, throw-in-the-odd-one-liner type of bloke. He's worldly, has an unquenchable thirst for information and new experiences, but at the same time he can be somewhat reserved, preferring to do rather than explain. Perhaps because of this, and also because it wasn't easy to go from being a senior player who could afford to be self-focused to being the leader of a tired and injured Test team, Tugga struggled a little when he first became captain.

In 1999 in the West Indies, many of us weren't at our best after a long domestic summer. Warney, for example, was still on the comeback trail, I was below where I would have liked to have been and even brother Mark was not as productive as he had been in the past. On tour, the atmosphere at early team meetings was a little stiff, as Tugga attempted to stamp his mark on the team by imposing his team plans and goals. By doing this he unwittingly denied the ranks any ownership of those plans and goals, which reduced their value. In a team environment, the best way to achieve success is to get everyone involved in the development of objectives and the execution of battle plans.

After a drawn Test series, a 3-3 tie in the one-dayers that followed, and a slow start in the World Cup, there were strong rumours about that Stephen might lose the one-day captaincy. But he responded in superb, typically ruthless style. I think he learnt a lot from his early captaincy disappointments, and his leadership blossomed through the latter days of the World Cup and on into the 1999–2000 season. His team's style of play is attractive, and scares opponents because there are no let-ups — physically or psychologically. They're at you all the time, and always seem to know what they're doing and what they want. Stephen learnt quickly to lead through his actions and inspire with his words and is now able to fill his charges with pride and confidence. He does this with ideas such as the 'Victor Trumper' caps the team wore to celebrate the new millennium — he's a big one for recognising the game's great traditions — and bold statements about his players and their achievements.

Stephen puts great importance on the efforts of the Australian one-day team. Whereas Tubby would never have taken one-day slumps as seriously as Test-match setbacks, Stephen wants to win it all. He's one very hungry cricketer and captain, destined to be recognised as one of the giants in the game's history (if he's not already).

— ¤ —

I'D MADE TREVOR HOHNS aware of my cricket plans before the team was picked for our late-August to early October three-Test tour of Sri Lanka, and he seemed comfortable with my thinking. He stressed, though, that there was no guarantee I'd keep getting selected if my form didn't warrant it, which I accepted totally. I wouldn't have wanted it any other way. I also said that if I didn't get my enthusiasm back in Sri Lanka, I'd retire there and then; it wasn't as if I *had* to retire in Australia. As things turned out, that was a remark I wished I'd never made. Around the same time I spoke to Trevor, Wayne Bennett, the highly successful and highly respected coach of the Brisbane Broncos rugby league club commented to me, 'Heals, you're in the "tow-away zone" now, where you really need to be on top of your game every time you hit the field.' I backed myself to do that in Sri Lanka.

> *September 4, 1999: Sri Lanka Board XI 228 all out. Me —*
> *five dismissals. Good start, boy. Batting: out for a duck.*
> *Haven't lost my batting, just 1. Focus; 2. Concentration; 3.*
> *Intensity. Every practice, must get back to those three.*
>
> *Believe/trust that those three will get me there, like India and*
> *Pakistan '98. GET THOSE THREE!! Have a dash …*

This game ended in a comfortable win for us, but I failed again with the bat when sent in early in our second innings. Straight after, we were on the bus for a

Sri Lanka's Marvan Atapattu is caught by Justin Langer at short-leg off Funky Miller in Kandy, during the first Test of our rain-ruined tour, August–October 1999. As my enthusiastic appeal shows, even at this late stage of my career I had no problems getting excited on the field during a Test match.

three-and-a-half hour journey to Kandy, which was terrific — a couple of Foster's, cracking jokes, singing songs about the baggy green. Next morning, I was up at 7am for a cold, one-kilometre swim, then training, then another swim. I was determined to be ready and happy when the first Test started, and set myself a target of 150 runs and four dismissals a match for the series. 'Have a red-hot go every day' I wrote in my diary, but the Test was a disappointment as we crashed to a six-wicket defeat. My keeping was all right, my batting unproductive (11 and 3), and our performance badly hindered by a horrific collision between Steve Waugh's nose and Jason Gillespie's leg, which left Stephen looking less pretty than ever and Dizzy with a badly broken bone below the right knee.

The rest of the tour was ruined by bad weather, and in the last two Tests we never had a chance to get even. Stuck under an umbrella, in the dressing room or my hotel room, watching the rain come down, I had too much time to think, about cricket and other things. Gradually, I fell back into the same mindset I had fought in the West Indies. As far as my future was concerned, my mind was just about made up.

September 29, 1999 (day before third Test): Enjoy, Enjoy, Enjoy. Exactly like West Indies 1996-97. One good game will have media move on. No worries about outcomes, just enjoy making the effort.

Sadly, we lost the best part of three days in that game, and there was only time for Ricky Ponting to make a brilliant hundred as we totalled 342 and Sri Lanka to stumble to 4-61 in reply. I took two catches, both regulation nicks, but when I reflected on the tour immediately afterwards, as we prepared to fly to Harare for Australia's first Test match ever against Zimbabwe, I knew there was no way I'd be playing throughout the next Australian season. I kept telling myself to enjoy the experience, but it wasn't working — I wasn't enjoying it. The desire to prove myself and justify my place just wasn't there, at a time — near the end of my career — when I had to prove myself just as completely as I had needed to at the start.

I sat down first with Steve Waugh, then with other close comrades such as Michael Slater, Mark Waugh and Shane Warne, to let them know how I was feeling. I told them that I'd decided to retire, but asked them to keep the conversations private for the moment. Geoff Marsh had retired as Australian coach after the Sri Lankan tour, and Allan Border was taking over on a temporary basis; I would talk to him, too. AB was also a selector, and on October 12, two days before the Zimbabwe Test, I sat down with him to seriously discuss my options. I'd come to the conclusion that if the team and the selectors agreed, I'd play the Zimbabwe Test and then announce that the first Test of the Australian summer, against Pakistan at the Gabba, would be my last game. AB was happy with that, as were the senior guys I'd talked to. 'I'll talk to the other selectors about it,' AB said, 'and get back to you.' I knew it was important he talk to the rest of the panel, because if the selectors wanted me to finish up immediately, then I wanted to make an announcement before the Test. As I said to AB, if the selectors wanted to make a fresh start with Gilly in Australia, I'd fully understand, but I wanted to know where I stood before the start of the Zimbabwe game.

The next night AB came back to me and told me that he'd been in contact with the selectors and everything was sweet. I assumed he meant he'd spoken to the other selectors and they'd all agreed that my plan was okay, but in fact, as I learned later, he had only passed on my request and explained as part of that message that he was fully in favour of it. But he was only one vote out of four. This misunderstanding would later cause me a great deal of pain and grief. Thinking that this Harare Test would be the second-last of my life, I put off a retirement announcement, and started dreaming about my Gabba farewell. I knew I could get myself up for one last strong performance there, and was grateful that the powers-that-be had given me the chance. I was aware, too, that I needed seven dismissals for 400 in Tests, and 39 runs to break Alan Knott's run-scoring record for a keeper. I'd never been one for records, but wouldn't it be

The scene after our Test victory in Zimbabwe in October 1999. From left to right: Michael Slater, Matthew Nicholson, Justin Langer, Glenn McGrath, Steve Waugh, Greg Blewett, Mark Waugh (obscured), Shane Warne, Colin Miller, me, Simon Katich and Ricky Ponting.

terrific to set a couple of landmarks in my last game, in front of a crowd full of fellow Queenslanders? And wouldn't every bit of the occasion be good fun, too?

ACB chairman Denis Rogers and chief executive Malcolm Speed were in Harare, and I shared my retirement plans with them. Their responses were strangely muted; they merely commented that yes, it was a good idea, but no, they didn't want to get involved in selection procedures. I thought it strange that they weren't interested in the potential public relations opportunities that a long-serving Queensland cricketer ending his international career in a Test at the Gabba would create. I was determined, I told them, to emphasise my appreciation for being allowed to play one more game. That would have to be good for cricket and the image of the Board, and, I imagined with due modesty, for the size of the gate as well.

We won the Test against Zimbabwe by 10 wickets, and I sang *Under the Southern Cross* with added gusto afterwards, knowing that it might be the last chance I'd have to do it (there was no guarantee we'd beat Pakistan), and was certainly my final rendition on foreign soil. When I'd been left out of the one-day team two years earlier, I'd given the honour to Ricky Ponting and knew for sure that he was the man to take over for the Test team, too. But 'Punter' would have to wait until the Gabba, when, as Boonie had done for me at the Adelaide

Oval in 1996, I'd get him up on the dressing room table with me, we'd lead the team in song together, and then I'd hand over the mantle with style.

—✠—

I HAD A MUCH better time in Zimbabwe than I'd had in Sri Lanka or the West Indies. I was much more fun to be around, and was more relaxed about the cricket and the lifestyle. Looking back now, the fact that I'd resolved my cricket future played a huge part in that, as, I'm sure, was the fact that I no longer had to worry about losing my place, or being accountable to the selectors and the media. While AB and the one-day team stayed in Zimbabwe after the Test for a one-day tournament, I headed happily for home, and not long after we touched down, on Friday, October 22, I met with Trevor Hohns at the Gabba. His words left me stone cold.

'We've got to do what's best for the team,' he commented, a lead-in to him saying that, as far as he was concerned, I was no certainty to play the first Test.

In fact, from the tone of his voice, I was about a million to one.

'But what about what AB said in Harare?' I asked. 'He said it was okay ...'

'If AB said that, he had no right to,' Hohns cut me off, 'and, anyway, you said yourself before Sri Lanka that you didn't have to retire in Australia.'

That was true. I had said that. But since then, I'd come away from a conversation with Allan Border — who I had thought was speaking for all the selectors but I now knew wasn't — totally believing that I was going to end my career at home.

At this point I must stress that I have no problem with the logic behind the selectors' decision. Selectors are required to make tough decisions, and can never allow personal prejudices or bias to affect their decisions. If they thought Adam Gilchrist was a better candidate for the keeping job, I could accept that. Part of me conceded that myself, given how few runs I'd been scoring in recent Tests and Gilly's enormous batting talent. To play the first Test of a summer, knowing beforehand that you were going to retire straight afterwards, is just about unprecedented. And as Merv Hughes has said to me, 'You don't play testimonial Test matches, mate.' But the miscommunication between the selectors and me had ruined what could have been a great final hurrah for me, and meant that instead of going out on my own terms, I was dropped one Test before I had thought my career would end.

Hohns and I parted company that day with him promising to talk again to the other selectors and me agreeing to hold fire on any announcements until the Monday. By 5pm on that day, though, he hadn't called, so I rang him from my home, to have it confirmed that the selectors and the Board were going to give me the chance to retire immediately. Whether I did or not, I wasn't going to be picked for the first Test. I tried one last time to argue my case, but Hohns flatly stated again that AB had had no right to tell me I'd be right for the Gabba. That was it. I'd missed the chance to enjoy my last Test as a farewell game, and missed the chance to share the experience of my last Test with my family and my

Above: Colin Miller (in front, arms outstretched) calls for quiet in the Australian dressing room in Harare, as I prepare to lead the team in another rousing rendition of *Under the Southern Cross*. Though I didn't know it at the time, this would be the last time I'd have this privilege.

Left: With Michael Slater in the dressing room after the Zimbabwe Test.

teammates. I put the phone down, bitterly disappointed. Eventually, I looked up at Helen, and with a weak grin said, 'At least I don't have to go to training tomorrow.'

My first reaction was bucket the lot of them, but I soon realised that would only hurt me ... and maybe the game, too. I spoke to my manager, Paul Smith, who was as amazed at this turn of events as I was. Since the West Indies tour, he'd had more than one conversation with senior Board officials about getting my retirement — whenever it happened — right. Now we were hastily planning the press conference where I'd make my announcement, and needed to resolve issues such as what to say, and where and when to say it. I also spoke to Gary Burns, Director of Sport at Channel Nine. I had earlier told Gary of my plans for the summer, and he had confirmed that if I was available, then he wanted me to commentate. Now, I wanted his advice on how I might approach things.

—✠—

SO THAT WAS IT. I was now an ex-player. The press conference where my 'retirement' would be made official was eventually scheduled for the following Thursday, October 28, in Melbourne at the Board's request, with my announcement coinciding with the release of news of John Buchanan's appointment as the permanent replacement for Geoff Marsh as Australian coach. A few people connected with the team were concerned that I might go off the handle, but I'd calmed down sufficiently to make what I hope people saw as a dignified exit.

I was grateful for the tributes I received in the TV, radio and internet reports that day and night, and in the papers the following morning. Tugga's was a beauty. It appeared in News Limited papers across the country, and read in part:

… Heals and I have shared so many memorable moments. We were at the crease together when he scored his first Test century at Old Trafford in 1993. We've worn our baggy green caps together to the celebration party in Jamaica when Australia won the Frank Worrell Trophy and we drank together as he shed a tear at the British Embassy in Lahore after a heartbreaking defeat against Pakistan in 1994.

I've seen him in agony on the physio's bench after copping three blows in succession to the groin against the West Indies quicks and I have shared a cigar with him when his first child, Emma, was born when he was on the 1991 West Indies tour. I was with Heals on his first tour in Pakistan and can remember thinking 'we've got a beauty here' when he took a tumbling catch off Bruce Reid early in his first Test. Later I thought 'this bloke's a dud' when he put down Javed Miandad off my bowling.

But he was great for Australia right from the start. The rest of us couldn't believe that he would journey down to the hotel carpark at 6am in Pakistan and catch a golf ball with his inners. But by doing so he was showing us the type of commitment we all needed if our struggling side was going to surge to better days.

Keepers are the heartbeat of the side, the ones that set standards for the rest of the team to live up to …

We are, too, you know.

I must confess that in the wake of my retirement, I was concerned that people might start thinking: he's been dropped three times now, there must be more to this … what's wrong with him? However, the response from cricket fans across the country, and especially in Queensland, was fantastic. During the tea break on the first day of the Gabba Test, I jumped in the back of an open convertible with our three kids and was driven around the ground. I was stunned by the reception. Spectators cheered and clapped and threw green and gold streamers over us, while the entire Pakistan squad, led by captain Wasim Akram, came back out onto the field to acknowledge me as we drove past their room. I gave

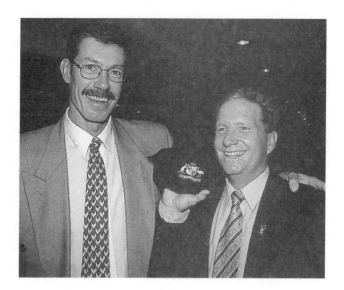

With John Buchanan on the day my cricket career officially ended and his new life as the Australian team coach began.

them a heartfelt thumbs-up for their tremendous gesture. The Australians, who'd been fielding, waved from the home dressing room. As well, when they came back out after the break, Slats dashed across the ground to shake my hand. I was choked up by all the fuss, and wondered whether I could have handled all the attention if I'd actually played in the game.

Straight after the Test, the Australian players had one more accolade for me, one I accepted with pleasure. Steve Waugh asked me to come down to the dressing room after the Australians had completed a 10-wicket victory, because the team wanted me down from the commentary box and up on the table one last time, to lead them in *Under the Southern Cross*. No way would I get up there; I wanted Ricky up there alone. I simply belted out my favourite song as part of the circle of players around him.

And with that, finally, my time with the Australian team was done.

CHAPTER 23

A GOOD LIFE

WHEN I SAT DOWN WITH my publishers to discuss a title for this book — as happens, I imagine, with many book projects — many potential names were thrown up until we settled on *Hands & Heals*. It's catchy, which is good for a wicketkeeper, and, of course, it brings together my nickname and my tools of trade. It's a racing term synonymous with winning, which, I'm happy and proud to say, was something the Queensland and Australian teams managed to do quite regularly for most of my career. And when I look beyond my cricket, to my childhood, my family and the many wonderful people I've met through the first 36 years of my life, I think I've been a big winner there, too.

The only negative with *Hands & Heals*, I thought, was that it might have suggested I achieved my success in cricket easily. When a racehorse breaks clear of the pack, and the jockey is riding 'hands and heels' it must appear to the punters that the horse and rider are winning effortlessly, while those horses behind, whipped and defeated, are vastly inferior. But those observers could not have seen all the hard work, planning, persistence, setbacks and doubts that went into that successful galloper's preparation. And while it might seem the horse won comfortably, the divide between its ability and the talents of the rest of the field might actually have been very small. As I learned through my cricket career, if you get your preparation right, do the hard yards, and have an excellent team working with you, you can gain an advantage on your opposition — and the confidence that you gain from knowing this can make the final size of your victory more substantial than you've expected.

So *Hands & Heals* it is.

Whenever I set out to do something, I just try to be good at it. That's what I did when I was a kid and it is still my attitude now. It's led to so many things that I never thought could happen, and left me very satisfied with what I've accomplished in my life to this point. When I started out, 18 months old with a plastic bat in my hand, I didn't know what would happen. I just did it. Today, I'm applying the same philosophy to my life in business and to my cricket commentary.

I'm fully aware, though, that in the whole great scheme of things what I've achieved in cricket hasn't changed the world. Elite cricketers get an extraordinary amount of publicity, travel the globe and get very well paid for doing what we love, without any of the enormous stresses that confront the real heroes in our community, who usually remain unsung. We've never fought in wars, suffered great hardship, or been confronted with natural disasters. Yet we get the headlines

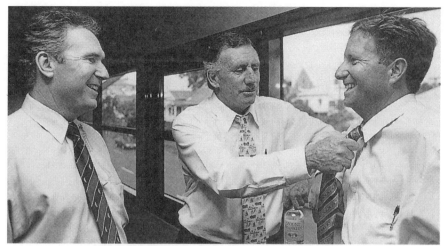
With Allan Border (left) and Ian Chappell, two of my new teammates in the commentary box. With blokes like these around, it's no wonder I'm enjoying myself.

and the rewards. Sometimes, as comfortable as we are in our world of sport, we forget there's a much tougher, much more brutal world beyond. Cricket is not *that* important. Sometimes, in this book, when I've written about being dropped, losing Tests and missing stumpings, it must seem as if I believe that cricket is all that matters. And when these things happened to me I probably felt that way. But it's not, and now that I'm retired from the game I'm becoming more and more aware of this. Take this into account and I really did do it easily; all elite cricketers do. Cricket is important and does matter to those who participate and watch and cheer, but no matter how hard we played on the field it is still a game. Some things in this world are not.

—✠—

WHILE MY PLAYING CAREER is now over, there is still so much to do. Fortunately, as part of the Nine cricket commentary team, I'm able to keep in close contact with the game in an exciting and incredibly interesting way, and I'm determined to do my new job well. It's fascinating watching my new teammates at work, learning from them, and realising that I've gone from one competitive line-up to another. I'm also lucky in that my work in the Nine commentary box has prevented me suffering any real heartbreak about no longer being out there on the field. Throughout 1999–2000 I was too pre-occupied with trying to learn more about the commentary craft to start thinking about what might have been. It's funny, in the same way that I used to record my cricket form in my diary, now the pages are full of comments on my new vocation:

> *November 26, 1999 (first day of third Australia–Pakistan*
> *Test, in Perth): Richie rushed for 10am start. I'm in with*
> *him. Looked okay, but 'staggered' a bit at start … feels good,*
> *don't get too repetitive when stressing a point …*

January 2, 2000 (first day of third Australia –India Test, at the SCG): Me to intro teams. Do it fine until I forget to throw to Richie. Go blank and hesitate over graphics, and in the end leave it badly open-ended when Richie takes over ...

January 14, 2000 (During Carlton & United World Series): Remember to stay on microphone when looking at monitor. Slow down — maybe say less in more depth. This will prevent rushing. You can still stay upbeat.

January 20, 2000 (Again, during the World Series): Rushed again yesterday with some comments and muddled some words — 'inningses' and 'recupering' — that I didn't know I'd said because I was thinking ahead and concentrating on how I was talking. Slow down and concentrate on what you're saying a little more. Don't overdo humour, especially at someone else's expense. Enjoy it!

Through my first season of retirement, I marvelled from the commentary box at the winning performances of Steve Waugh's Australian team, admiring especially the brilliant work of Adam Gilchrist. What I rated most about Gilly's cricket was his consistency — he never seemed to have a bad day — and the sensible way he went about his job. Quickly, he was touted as a possible successor to Stephen as captain, and I believe he is a potential leader. As you know, I've thought long and hard about the pros and cons of a wicketkeeper captaining a Test team; if Gilly thinks he can handle the captaincy of the team then I'd support him.

While I was no longer in the Test team I still managed to get selected in a couple of prestigious elevens. One, of course, was the Australian Team of the Century, but I also won a spot in the 'Queensland Team of the Century', which was named a few weeks later. Again, I was up against great keepers such as Wally Grout and Don Tallon, who starred for Queensland and Australia, and also John Maclean and Ray Phillips, men who received scant international recognition but who ran up impressive figures during long first-class careers. All chosen in the final XI received a commemorative maroon cap, with a 'Queensland Team of the Century' logo embroidered on the front, which immediately became one of my most prized possessions, along with two team photos, one of the living members of the side, and another of all the Queensland cricket captains who attended the function when the side was announced. I was so proud to be among them. The side chosen was: Bill Brown (captain), Sam Trimble, Greg Chappell, Peter Burge, Allan Border, Ken Mackay, Colin McCool, Ian Healy, Craig McDermott, Ray Lindwall, Jeff Thomson and Ron Archer (12th man)

Away from cricket I found myself as busy as I'd ever been, and relished the fact that much of this was in areas I was new to. I remember when I returned from the 1999 West Indies tour, and was trying to work out exactly what I wanted to do with my life and cricket career, I asked Paul Smith whether my sponsors had any long-term interest in me, or was it just my playing profile they were after?

Eight members of Queensland Cricket's team of the century, wearing their special commemorative caps. Back row, left to right: Ian Healy, Craig McDermott, Ron Archer, Sam Trimble. Front row: Greg Chappell, Allan Border, Bill Brown (captain), Peter Burge. The other members of the side are Ken Mackay, Ray Lindwall, Colin McCool and Jeff Thomson.

Paul was very confident that the future of the relationships we'd developed didn't depend on me remaining an active cricketer. 'It's your character they're after,' I remember him saying, 'and the fact you're proactive and want to help them.' I'd been with some of my sponsors — companies such as Puma, Kookaburra, Carlton & United Breweries, Toyota and Lexus — for 10 years and more, and wanted the associations to continue and grow. I had enjoyed my involvement in the corporate world to that point, but before my retirement it had in most cases only been at a peripheral level — mainly servicing sponsorships — because my cricket commitments had always been my No. 1 priority. Now, I wanted to take what I'd learnt in top-level sport and try to apply it in other fields. To that end, I had developed an association with Wizard Home Loans, which gave me the chance to do promotional work for them *and* become the principal in two of their financial offices. I also took a share in the Adrenalin Sports Bar in Brisbane and in the Greg Chappell Cricket Centre business, and was keen to learn as much as I could from these ownership roles.

The corporate world had plenty to offer me, but what could I, as a *former* international cricketer, offer them? Luckily, my commentary work meant that I was going to retain a reasonably high profile, but I wanted to be more than simply a public face for a product. I can be taught product knowledge and financial strategies, I thought, but teamwork, commitment, discipline and concentration, even patience and successfully combating stress — things you need to survive in the toughest of sporting schools — are harder to learn, and seemed to me to be often undervalued or misunderstood outside of sport. If I could take these traits with me as I moved into my business life, then I reckoned I had something. Through my cricket, I learnt that the return from effective team building can be enormous. When I was first picked for Australia, I was a very uncomplicated bloke. My talent was my glovework, allied to my enthusiasm, a very organised way of doing things — which I'd picked up from my parents — and an insatiable desire to be good. I had to perform better than I'd ever done, develop some nous and get a thicker hide, or I'd have been on the scrap heap very, very quickly. It's not so much a case of making your own luck, as being able to take advantage of any luck that comes your way. Fortunately, I was able to do that, and the ever-improving team environment I was in was a key factor in allowing me to do it as effectively as I did. In my first 12 months in the Australian team, as we went from that unhappy beaten side in Pakistan to a tight successful unit that regained the Ashes in England, I learnt that without faith in the people around you, you put yourself under too much pressure and trying to perform can become a very nerve-racking and unproductive experience.

From what I've seen, sports teams prepare for their battles more conscientiously than many businesses do, from a team perspective at least. That's not a sledge on business so much as a rap for the sporting sides, but my point is that business can learn from professional sport. The Australian cricket team today is very big on isolating everyone's responsibilities and making sure that every player knows exactly what's expected of him. There are very few surprises, to the point that if the captain decides that strategies need to change immediately everyone is on the same wavelength, adapting at the same speed, in the same way. The Aussie team is an organised, well-drilled unit, which is one of the main reasons it is so successful.

Of course, it's one thing to simply extol the value of teamwork. It's another to effectively communicate to others what I've learnt and experienced. It's an astonishing fact of sporting life that the most naturally gifted athletes rarely become the most effective coaches. Football codes are littered with classic examples of men who were the heroes of their playing days but later unsuccessful and frustrated coaches, while unsung journeymen have often proved to be the best tutors in the business. John Buchanan and World Cup-winning Wallaby coach Rod Macqueen are two examples of the latter. Not everyone is aware of what makes him or her different or special. Some naturally gifted champions can't explain what it was that made them special, while many lesser talents are actually keen observers and good communicators who are able to motivate and organise their charges with perceptive words and shrewd strategies.

I'd like to think of myself as being in that second category. The feedback I've received from sponsors is that they appreciate the fact that I can communicate on just about every level. I'm sure I can thank my sporting experiences for that — cricket took me to so many levels and introduced to me to a vast range of

With my successor, Adam Gilchrist, at the Gabba before his Test debut. Within a season, 'Gilly' would become, in my view, the best wicketkeeper on the world stage.

people, from prime ministers and corporate kings to all the battlers and working men and women who play and follow the game. It allowed me to keep my bush instincts and openness, while knocking many of the 'rough edges' away. These days, I've got my cricket reputation and contacts to get me through some corporate doors. From that point, I need to apply the lessons of my cricket experience and try to help and encourage others along the way.

In the future, cricket-wise, I don't see myself being a selector or an administrator — bar, perhaps, at club level — but I would like to do plenty of coaching. Not educating *teams*, though — I'd like to focus on tutoring wicketkeepers in Australia and around the world. I've already worked with the Queensland and South Australian keepers, and fielded approaches from Sri Lanka, New Zealand and Pakistan, so I think the opportunities are there. I've always felt that 'mainstream' coaches don't understand what goes into a keeper's job. As I've said, if your teammates don't understand and appreciate the effort and concentration that goes into effectively fulfilling your role, what hope do outsiders have? There's a void in the coaching of top keepers that I think I can help fill, and I'd like to try. On a different tangent, I have launched the 'Ian Healy Cricket Academy', which involves a series of camps staged in city and country Queensland. My main objective is to instil the right sporting values in the young cricketers who attend. The Academy is being supported by the Ian Healy Foundation, which is also distributing funds to a number of charities I believe in. It's very rewarding to be able to give something back, after receiving so much generosity from so many people throughout my cricket career.

What of cricket itself? In my view, it's desperately important that we don't start tampering with the game too much. Sure, spectators and viewers today want a result and they want to be entertained, but if you look at the way the Australian team played through most of the 1990s the paying public could hardly complain. And the buoyant crowd figures and massive TV advertising sales indicate that people are happy. My hope is that the aggressive style of Test cricket the Australians play will become a prototype for the rest of the world, and I think it will for the simple reason that it's proved to be a winning formula.

Played right, Test cricket is as good as any game around. It is absolutely unique in the way players from the two sides turn up on the first morning not knowing what they're going to do, and the fans don't know what they're going to see on that day. Thus, the atmosphere is expectant, and all players are very nervous and anxious at the toss. A match goes for 30 hours, five days, one team against another. A golf tournament goes for about the same amount of time, but involves individuals competing against each other, not two teams. All the while, as the match ebbs and flows, some blokes are going well, some are not, some might be injured, ill, confident or shattered. The conflicting emotions and changes in the two teams' fortunes, and the way the game tests your character, are what make cricket so special.

— ✠ —

OF COURSE THE BIGGEST blot on the game today is the match-fixing crisis that seems to get more ugly and damaging for the game by the day. I must confess I have no idea where it will end, because as I write these words in July 2000 it's already become much, much worse than I could ever have imagined. On the day in April 2000 when the allegations against Hansie Cronje were first raised, I was at Uluru, in central Australia; had I been at home, I would have been straight to my fax machine, to send a 'don't let your accusers get you down' type message to him. No way could Hansie, a seemingly single-minded, ambitious, driven leader of cricketers, be guilty of what he was being accused of. I had always got on really well with him, and found him to not be as dour and intense as his on-field manner implied. However, by the time I did get home a couple of days later, he'd admitted his crimes. The former South African captain's world, and the world of cricket, had changed dramatically.

To me, the first thing that stood out in the Hansie Cronje 'scandal' was that, yet again, it involved one-day cricket. But with the involvement of the South African captain confirmed, and the extent of the crisis widening by the day, I quickly realised that it would be naive to think there has never been contact between players and bookmakers in regard to Test matches. While I have no first-hand evidence, I would say there must be cases of illicit behaviour concerning Test matches that at present we just don't know about. Perhaps there have been times when players have withdrawn from Tests at the last minute, not because they've been injured but to take advantage of the odds which could then be offered. The stain is so big now, I cannot rule anything out.

My hope is that cricket's administrators go hard at the problem — even if it means the game has to go through some pain for the long-term good — and make sure that the penalties for players found guilty do fit the crime. Officials the world over can ensure players are contractually bound to avoid the temptation of quick money from illegal betting, perhaps even to the extent of making it against the rules of the game for cricketers to mix with illegal bookmakers. Certainly, if a player is found guilty of match-fixing, banning him from the game forever would seem to me to be an appropriate response.

The crooks involved have never approached me, but looking back, I think I have unknowingly given some of them information. Occasionally, on days before a match — more than likely a game on the Indian Subcontinent — I'd receive a phone call from someone whose name I didn't recognise but who claimed he knew me. It was rarely the same name but the conversation was usually similar. They'd claim they were from a newspaper, usually one from the local city, so I'd start answering the questions, but after a short period I'd cut them off, because their line of questioning was stupid, repetitive or naive. There was never a suggestion that I'd be paid for agreeing to talk. I guess these blokes were in the 'seeking information' game, and I wonder if I'd been more co-operative whether I might have heard from them more often. It does appear that their modus operandi is to start small, and gradually lure cricketers into their web. Once caught, as Hansie Cronje found, there's no escape.

It is absolutely astonishing that someone in a position such as Cronje's — captain of his country's cricket team — would throw it all away like this. Obviously, there must be something pretty powerful being offered for high-profile cricketers to do this and I guess that pretty powerful thing is money. I can't understand it. They say that everyone has his or her price, but having mixed with all of the world's top cricketers of the past decade I would have thought that for most of them there wasn't enough money in the world to get them to pervert the course of matches. And anyway, Cronje, for one, must have been on a huge earn as South African captain. How much money did he want?

One lesson of the affair, surely, is that we need to regulate the number of one-day internationals, so that each game retains value in the eyes of the cricketers playing and the spectators watching. The South Africans have clearly been unsettled and frustrated by the sheer volume of cricket they were asked to play, to the point where their captain, and maybe one or two of his teammates, decided that it wouldn't matter if they corrupted a game here and there.

I must confess, though, that it surprised me a little bit when people started to write about 'meaningless' one-day tournaments; I had always approached each competition, wherever it was held and at whatever time of year, as something to be looked forward to. Maybe there were a couple of tournaments in the second half of 1996, in Sri Lanka and then India, that we weren't too happy with, because they came after a gruelling period of cricket and before another tough stretch, but other than those I felt there was a solid justification for every other tour that we went on. And we definitely didn't deliberately place a lesser value on those contests in '96, though subconsciously we might have. We understood

Now just another face in the crowd ... with Tom at the Allan Border Field in Brisbane, for the Queensland v Pakistan match, October 31, 1999, the first missed game since my retirement three days earlier.

that the 'triangular' nature of the World Series played in Australia every summer meant that we had to reciprocate, and so long as we were in a position to perform at our best we were happy to do so.

For all the suspicion and concerns over how far this controversy might go, I do not believe people should automatically cast doubt over the integrity of *all* players in international cricket. I cannot and will not believe that anyone in the Australian team has ever given less than their absolute best in international matches. Throughout my career, we were always very close, probably closer than other teams, all of us dead-set mates. That's one of the main reasons we were so successful. We valued and respected what the baggy green represented, and were ultra-conscious of the traditions of the game in our country. And so many people in the Australian game — players, selectors, senior ACB officials — are readily accountable to the media and the paying public, probably more so than in many other parts of the cricket world. Under these circumstances, it would be highly unlikely that anyone would fall to the temptation of an ill-gained dollar, and even if they did it would be even more improbable that anyone could deliberately perform poorly without being detected by his comrades and those close to the team. This made us poor targets for the bookies involved in this scandal, who I'm convinced are very clever at selecting the 'right' players to approach, and don't go near blokes they know won't be of any use to them.

The worst part of this crisis is that any significant error made during a big game can now be looked at suspiciously. People will believe what they want to believe, which might not be the truth at all. Personally, I'm not going to waste my time worrying about whether a game from the past, present or future is tainted. As far as I'm concerned, every ball of every match I played in was fair dinkum; that's how I always went about my game and how the opposition's approach appeared to me. It was never easy, always a challenge, and I was always very satisfied when I succeeded on the field. If that makes me naive, then that I am.

—◻—

BEING AN ELITE CRICKETER and a husband and father is very difficult. I think I got better at it as I matured as a person and mellowed as a bloke, but it took me a long while to learn that I could successfully manage all three without hurting my cricket. The catalyst for this change was seeing how the new guys in the side — men such as Slats, Blewey and Pigeon — wanted their wives or partners with them. It was almost as if they were challenging an existing order. At first, I sledged them for being 'under the thumb', but while they didn't change I did, from our tours in 1993, to New Zealand and then England, when I was grateful for the time I had with Helen and Emma. As I've explained, their presence did soften my cricket, but rather than simply turning them away for the sake of my sport — as I would have done in the past — I looked at what I needed to do to keep a hard edge on my on-field performances without losing the pleasure and satisfaction of having my wife and child at my side. In the last few years of my career, having Helen and the kids around actually helped my cricket, because it gave me an outlet to relax and have fun away from the game.

The time I spent away from my children became increasingly difficult, though I was lucky in that they didn't know any other way. They just assumed that all dads were missing for weeks on end. Plus, when I was away, at least the kids could see their dad on the television, so they knew I was still alive. I was the one with the gloves on, so I was really easy for them to find. And though we were separated for many days at a time, there were other times when we were together for long periods at a time, so in that sense I was lucky. I've never done the arithmetic, but I wonder whether a parent working long hours five or six days a week, leaving for work early and getting home late, would see any more of his or her children over a 12-month period than an international cricketer gets to enjoy with his children. And cricketers are not the only people required to be away for huge stretches at a time — service men and women are one other example — so it's not *that* bad, though often less than perfect. We always remembered, too, that the rewards from my cricket career were exceptional. And, personally, the kids and I were lucky that Helen had the love, confidence, patience and ability to so often be two parents in one while I was away.

I'd like to think my cricket achievements are such that the sacrifices we've made as a family have been worth it. Similarly, I take great satisfaction from the fact that through my achievements I've been able to repay my parents, brothers and sister in a small way for everything they did to help and support me. It's not corny to say that I couldn't have made it without them. It's true. I think again of the time and money Mum and Dad spent umpiring and fund raising and

and assisting in the administration of the local cricket and getting other parents involved and getting their and other kids to games, whether they were at Biloela or Bundaberg or Gladstone or Rockhampton, often at the same time. One of the simple joys of my cricket career was the annual Gabba Test, walking out onto the ground, knowing my parents were in the crowd, and knowing they were proud of me.

The first 36 years of my life have flown by. I can't believe I've played more than 100 Tests, been an international cricketer for 11 years, made 395 Test dismissals, experienced so much, seen so much, met so many brilliant people, and despite the occasional setback had such a good time. I can still vividly picture myself in the primary school nets at Biloela, practising hard, having fun, trying to be good at the game. What will I want written on my tombstone when I'm gone, hopefully many years from now? 'Here lies a bloke,' it might read, 'to whom loyalty, respect and a sense of fun were what really mattered.' I remember when I was at teachers' college in the early 1980s, we did an exercise where we were asked to write down what we wanted to be remembered for. I thought for a while and then wrote, 'Good bloke, good cricketer.' In that order. I still want to be a good bloke, and I think I achieved my ambition to be a good cricketer. But the difference now is that what most others think of Ian Healy doesn't matter nearly as much to me, so long as I, and the people close to me, are happy with who I am. So what really concerns me most about my tombstone is not what words appear but that they are penned by someone who's been close to me and knows me well. They'll be on the money with what they write, and it'll sound fine.

And that'll do me.

IAN ANDREW HEALY

Born Spring Hill, Brisbane, Queensland, April 30, 1964
All statistics as at June 12, 2000

1. FIRST-CLASS CAREER

Debut: Queensland v. West Indians, Townsville, January 11-12-13, 1987,
scoring 21 and taking one catch.
Last match: Australia v. Zimbabwe, Harare, October 14-15-16-17, 1999,
scoring 5 and taking two catches.

Career batting and wicketkeeping

Season	Matches	Innings	N.O.	Runs	Highest	100	50	Average	Ct	St
1986-87	2	2	-	61	40	-	-	30.50	1	-
1987-88	4	8	2	176	58*	-	1	29.33	15	2
1988 (Pak)	6	8	2	117	29*	-	-	19.50	10	2
1988-89	13	19	5	407	90	-	2	29.07	35	3
1989 (Eng)	14	19	4	442	73*	-	1	29.46	35	2
1989-90	11	15	4	454	81*	-	2	41.27	41	2
1990 (NZ)	1	2	-	10	10	-	-	5.00	4	-
1990-91	10	15	1	320	69	-	2	22.85	47	-
1991 (WI)	7	10	-	177	53	-	1	17.70	15	-
1991-92	11	15	2	485	87*	-	3	37.30	43	1
1992 (SL)	5	9	3	326	78*	-	3	54.33	9	1
1992-93	10	17	2	340	53*	-	1	22.66	33	5
1993 (NZ)	4	5	1	173	87*	-	2	43.25	13	1
1993 (Eng)	16	20	7	499	102*	1	3	38.38	42	11
1993-94	10	14	4	368	113*	1	1	36.80	31	4
1994 (SA)	6	10	3	277	61	-	2	39.57	20	2
1994 (Pak)	3	5	1	183	58	-	2	45.75	14	1
1994-95	7	13	3	260	74	-	2	26.00	28	2
1995 (WI)	7	9	2	202	74*	-	1	28.85	13	2
1995-96	9	12	1	357	70	-	1	32.45	29	3
1996 (Ind)	2	3	-	78	49	-	-	26.00	2	-
1996-97	7	11	3	452	161*	1	1	56.50	23	-
1997 (SA)	6	9	2	146	41*	-	-	20.85	24	1
1997 (Eng)	12	16	4	407	63	-	1	33.91	39	4
1997-98	13	19	3	507	85	-	3	31.68	37	4
1998 (Ind)	6	9	1	208	90	-	1	26.00	10	2
1998 (Pak)	5	8	2	236	82	-	1	39.33	13	3
1998-99	10	17	2	399	134	1	2	26.60	36	4
1999 (WI)	7	12	-	150	42	-	-	12.50	16	5
1999 (SL)	5	8	1	74	32	-	-	10.57	13	2
1999 (Zim)	2	3	1	50	24*	-	-	25.00	7	-
Total	**231**	**342**	**66**	**8341**	**161***	**4**	**39**	**30.22**	**698**	**69**

* indicates 'not out'

Batting and wicketkeeping by country

IA Healy in	Matches	Innings	N.O.	Runs	Highest	100	50	Average	Ct	St
Australia	117	177	32	4586	161*	3	21	31.62	399	30
Pakistan	14	21	5	536	82	-	3	33.50	37	6
England	42	55	15	1348	102*	1	5	33.70	116	17
New Zealand	5	7	1	183	87*	-	2	20.50	17	1
West Indies	21	31	2	529	74*	-	2	18.24	44	7
Sri Lanka	10	17	4	400	78*	-	3	30.76	22	3
South Africa	12	19	5	423	61	-	2	30.21	44	3
India	8	12	1	286	90	-	1	26.00	12	2
Zimbabwe	2	3	1	50	24*	-	-	25.00	7	-
Total	**231**	**342**	**66**	**8341**	**161***	**4**	**39**	**30.22**	**698**	**69**

Note: 'England' indicates matches played in England and Wales.

Batting and wicketkeeping in Australia, by ground

IA Healy at	Matches	Innings	N.O.	Runs	Highest	100	50	Average	Ct	St
Townsville	1	1	-	21	21	-	-	21.00	1	-
Launceston	2	3	2	120	58*	-	1	120.00	2	1
Brisbane	37	53	10	1611	161*	2	5	37.46	133	10
Melbourne	14	25	2	484	60	-	1	21.04	52	4
Perth	17	24	4	730	113*	1	4	36.50	70	1
St Kilda	2	3	-	19	16	-	-	6.33	6	1
Sydney	13	21	7	411	69	-	1	29.35	31	4
Adelaide	13	22	3	531	90	-	4	27.94	54	3
Hobart	11	14	3	342	87*	-	2	31.09	30	4
Newcastle	2	4	1	146	66	-	1	48.66	6	-
Carrara	1	2	-	93	56	-	1	46.50	4	-
Toowoomba	1	1	-	8	8	-	-	8.00	2	-
Bankstown	1	1	-	8	8	-	-	8.00	4	-
Cairns	2	3	-	62	57	-	1	20.66	4	2
Total	**117**	**177**	**32**	**4586**	**161***	**3**	**21**	**31.62**	**399**	**30**

Batting and wicketkeeping in Australia, by team

IA Healy for	Matches	Innings	N.O.	Runs	Highest	100	50	Average	Ct	St
Queensland v. touring teams	10	14	1	340	57	-	2	26.15	25	5
Sheffield Shield	45	67	18	1859	90	-	11	37.93	158	7
Test matches	59	92	13	2317	161*	3	8	29.32	205	17
Australian XI v. touring teams	3	4	-	70	44	-	-	17.50	11	1
Total	**117**	**177**	**32**	**4586**	**161***	**3**	**21**	**31.62**	**399**	**30**

Note: Most dismissals in first-class matches for Queensland is 346 (317ct, 29 st) by JA Maclean, 96 matches, 1968-69~1978-79.

Batting and wicketkeeping in Sheffield Shield

IA Healy in	Matches	Innings	N.O.	Runs	Highest	100	50	Average	Ct	St
Tasmania	9	13	6	357	81*	-	3	51.00	22	1
South Australia	9	12	2	370	90	-	2	37.00	26	2
Victoria	8	12	1	237	50	-	1	21.54	31	1
Western Australia	8	13	2	360	87*	-	2	32.72	31	1
New South Wales	11	17	7	535	88	-	3	53.50	48	2
Total	**45**	**67**	**18**	**1859**	**90**	**-**	**11**	**37.93**	**158**	**7**

Keepers with 100 dismissals in a Sheffield Shield/Pura Milk Cup career for Queensland

No. of Dismissals	Keeper	Matches	Years
313 (289ct, 24st)	JA Maclean	86	1968-69~1978-79
276 (213ct, 63st)	ATW Grout	83	1946-47~1965-66
255 (246ct, 9st)	WA Seccombe	52	1993-94~
226 (214ct, 12st)	RB Phillips	68 +	1979-80~1985-86
207 (145ct, 61st)	D Tallon	67	1933-34~1953-54
165 (158ct, 7st)	**IA Healy**	**45**	**1986-87~1989-99**
136 (124ct, 12st)	PW Anderson	42 +	1986-87~1993-94

Notes:
1. Most dismissals in a Sheffield Shield/Pura Milk Cup career is 420 (383ct, 37st) by DS Berry (South Australia, Victoria), 105 matches, 1989-90~.
2. + indicates also played Sheffield Shield for other states: Phillips for NSW (three matches in 1978-79, 7ct) and Anderson for South Australia (11 matches in 1988-89, 28ct, 2st).

Batting and wicketkeeping overseas

	Matches	Innings	N.O.	Runs	Highest	100	50	Average	Ct	St
Tour matches	54	75	24	1716	90	-	4	33.64	138	27
Test matches	60	90	10	2039	102*	1	14	25.48	161	12
Total	**114**	**165**	**34**	**3755**	**102***	**1**	**18**	**28.66**	**299**	**39**

Note: 'Tour matches' are first-class matches played by touring Australian teams, excepting Test matches.

Highest scores

Score	Match	Venue	Season
161*	Australia v. West Indies (1st Test)	Brisbane	1996-97
134	Australia v. England (1st Test)	Brisbane	1998-99
113*	Australia v. New Zealand (1st Test)	Perth	1993-94
102*	Australia v. England (1st Test)	Manchester	1993
90	Queensland v. South Australia	Adelaide	1988-89
90	Australia v India (1st Test)	Chennai	1998
88	Queensland v. New South Wales	Brisbane	1996-97
87*	Queensland v. Western Australia	Perth	1991-92
87*	Australians v. NZ Board XI	New Plymouth	1993
85	Australia v. New Zealand (2nd Test)	Perth	1997-98
83*	Australia v. England (6th Test)	The Oval	1993
82	Australia v. Pakistan (1st Test)	Rawalpindi	1998
81*	Queensland v. Tasmania	Hobart	1989-90
80	Australia v. England (5th Test)	Birmingham	1993

Most dismissals in an innings

No.	How Out	Match	Venue	Season
6	(6ct)	Queensland v. Victoria	Brisbane	1990-91
6	(5ct, 1st)	Australian XI v. West Indians	Hobart	1991-92
6	(5ct, 1st)	Australians v. Northern Transvaal[2]	Centurion	1994
6	(6ct)	Australia v. England (1st Test)	Birmingham	1997
5	(5ct)	Queensland v. Victoria	Melbourne	1987-88
5	(4ct, 1st)	Queensland v. Pakistanis	Brisbane	1989-90
5	(5ct)	Australia v. Pakistan (2nd Test)	Adelaide	1989-90
5	(5ct)	Australia v. England (2nd Test)	Melbourne	1990-91
5	(5ct)	Australia v. England (4th Test)	Adelaide	1990-91
5	(5ct)	Australia v. New Zealand (3rd Test)	Brisbane	1993-94
5	(5ct)	Australians v. Northern Transvaal[1]	Centurion	1994
5	(5ct)	Australia v. Pakistan (2nd Test)	Rawalpindi	1994
5	(5ct)	Australia v. England (1st Test)	Brisbane	1994-95
5	(5ct)	Australia v. England (2nd Test)	Melbourne	1994-95
5	(5ct)	Australia v. Sri Lanka (3rd Test)	Adelaide	1995-96
5	(5ct)	Australia v. South Africa (1st Test)	Johannesburg	1997

5	(5ct)	Australia v. England (2nd Test)	Perth	1998-99
5	(5ct)	Queensland v. Western Australia	Perth	1998-99
5	(3ct, 2st)	Australians v. SL Board XI	Colombo PS	1999

Notes:

1. [1] indicates first innings; [2] indicates second innings.

2. The world record for most dismissals in an innings in a first-class match is:

No.	Keeper	Match	Venue	Season
9 (8ct, 1st)	Tahir Rashid	Habib Bank v. PACO	Gujranwala (Pak)	1992-93
9 (7ct, 2st)	WR James	Matabeleland v. Mashonaland Central Districts	Bulawayo (Zim)	1995-96

3. The Australian record for most dismissals in an innings in a first-class match is:

No.	Keeper	Match	Venue	Season
8 (all ct)	ATW Grout	Queensland v. Western Australia	Brisbane	1959-60
8 (6ct, 2st)	TJ Zoehrer	Australians v. Surrey	The Oval	1993
8 (7ct, 1st)	DS Berry	Victoria v. South Australia	Melbourne	1996-97

Most dismissals in a match

No.	How Out	Match	Venue	Season
11	(10ct, 1st)	Australians v. Northern Transvaal	Centurion	1994
9	(9ct)	Australia v. England (1st Test)	Brisbane	1994-95

Notes:

1. The world record for most dismissals in a first-class match is 13 (11ct, 2st) by WR James, Matabeleland v. Mashonaland Central Districts, Bulawayo (Zimbabwe), 1995-96

2. IA Healy's best for Queensland is 8 (all caught), v. Victoria, Melbourne, 1987-88.

3. The Australian record is 12 (9ct, 3st) by D Tallon, Queensland v. NSW, Sydney, 1938-39 and HB Taber, NSW v South Australia, Adelaide, 1968-69.

4. The record for most dismissals in an Australian season is 67 (63ct, 4st) by RW Marsh (Western Australia and Australia) in 15 matches, 1975-76, and 67 (65ct, 2st) by WA Seccombe (Queensland) in 13 matches 1999-2000.

Most dismissals in a career by an Australian wicketkeeper

Wicketkeeper	Years	Matches	Ct	St	Total	Other Matches	Other Ct
RW Marsh (WAust)	1968-69~1983-84	241	788	66	854	16	15
IA Healy (Qld)	**1986-87~1999**	**231**	**698**	**69**	**767**	-	-
WAS Oldfield (NSW)	1919-20~1937-38	223	677	67	744	7	4
ATW Grout (Qld)	1946-47~1965-66	179	472	114	586	4	1
BN Jarman (SAust)	1955-56~1968-69	186	426	129	555	5	5
DS Berry (SAust, Vict)	1989-90~	118	431	41	472	-	-
SJ Rixon (NSW)	1974-75~1987-88	150	395	65	460	1	-
TJ Zoehrer (WAust)	1980-81~1993-94	143	411	38	449	2	12
JMcC Blackham (Vict)	1874-75~1894-95	250	259	181	440	25	15
D Tallon (Qld)	1933-34~1953-54	150	302	131	433	-	-

Notes:

1. 'other matches' are matches in which the player was not selected as wicketkeeper.

2. The world record for most dismissals in a career is 1649 (1473ct, 176st) in 639 matches by RW Taylor (Derbyshire and England), 1960~1988

Bowling

Season	Overs (Six-ball)	Maidens	Runs	Wickets
1989-90	1	-	1	-
1995-96	0.1	-	1	-
1998 (Pak)	1	-	6	-
1999 (Zim)	3	1	14	-
Total	**5.1**	**1**	**22**	**-**

Captaincy

Captain of	Years	Matches	Won	Drawn	Lost
Australian XI v. touring teams	1991-92–1992-93	2	1	1	-
Queensland (Sheffield Shield)	1992-93–1998-99	20	9	6	5
Queensland (v. touring teams)	1992-93–1998-99	6	2	1	3
Australians (on tour)	1997	1	1	-	-
Total		**29**	**13**	**8**	**8**

Notes:
1. The Australian XI matches were both v. West Indians at Hobart
2. IA Healy was MA Taylor's vice-captain on four Test-playing tours: to Pakistan in 1994, to West Indies in 1995, to India in 1996 and to South Africa in 1997. Taylor played – and captained – in every first-class match on these tours except one match in South Africa (v. Border at East London), which he missed because of a back injury.
3. In the seven seasons, 1992-93–1998-99, Queensland played 84 first-class matches, of which IA Healy was available for 27. He led Queensland in 26 of these matches. The exception was the last match of the 1995-96 season when, although Healy and his usual deputy SG Law were in the team (they had just returned from the World Cup Final in Lahore), AR Border led Queensland in what turned out to be his final first-class game.
4. Queensland captains in first-class matches, 1992-93–1998-99 were:

Season	Matches	Captains In Chronological Order
1992-93	13	**IA Healy (4)**, DM Wellham (9)
1993-94	11	**IA Healy (4)**, SG Law (7)
1994-95	13	SG Law (9), **IA Healy (2)**, AR Border (1), ML Hayden (1)
1995-96	12	**IA Healy (2)**, SG Law (5), ML Hayden (1), AR Border (4)
1996-97	12	ML Hayden (2), **IA Healy (2)**, SG Law (8)
1997-98	11	**IA Healy (7)**, SG Law (3), ML Hayden (1)
1998-99	12	SG Law (7), **IA Healy (5)**

5. Healy played 55 first-class matches for Queensland, and was captain for 26. The 29 matches as non-captain were under the captaincy of RB Kerr (two matches in 1986-87), AR Border (13 between 1987-88 and 1995-96), GM Ritchie (six between 1988-89 and 1989-90), TV Hohns (four in 1990-91), CG Rackemann (four in 1991-92).

— ✠ —

2. TEST CAREER

Debut: v. Pakistan, Karachi, September 15-16-17-19-20, 1988, scoring 26 and 21, and taking one catch.
Last match: v. Zimbabwe, Harare, October 14-15-16-17, 1999, scoring 5 and taking two catches.

Test career batting and wicketkeeping

Season	v.	Tests	Innings	N.O.	Runs	Highest	100	50	Average	Ct	St	Results
1988	Pak (A)	3	4	-	74	27	-	-	18.50	6	2	LDD
1988-89	WI	5	8	-	138	52	-	1	17.25	12	-	LLLWD
1989	Eng (A)	6	7	1	103	44	-	-	17.16	14	-	WWDWWD
1989-90	NZ	1	1	-	28	28	-	-	28.00	3	-	D
1989-90	SL	2	3	1	64	26*	-	-	32.00	4	-	DW
1989-90	Pak	3	4	-	112	48	-	-	28.00	12	-	WDD
1990	NZ (A)	1	2	-	10	10	-	-	5.00	4	-	L
1990-91	Eng	5	7	-	175	69	-	1	25.00	24	-	WWDDW
1991	WI (A)	5	8	-	155	53	-	1	19.37	10	-	DLDLW
1991-92	Ind	5	8	-	157	60	-	1	19.62	19	-	WWDWW
1992	SL (A)	3	6	2	202	71	-	2	50.50	7	-	WDD
1992-93	WI	5	9	1	130	36*	-	-	16.25	19	4	DWDLL
1993	NZ (A)	3	4	-	86	54	-	1	21.50	12	1	WDL
1993	Eng (A)	6	7	2	296	102*	1	2	59.20	21	5	WWDWWL
1993-94	NZ	3	3	1	129	113*	1	-	64.50	13	1	DWW
1993-94	SA	3	5	2	41	19	-	-	13.66	6	1	DLW
1994	SA (A)	3	4	-	157	61	-	2	39.25	5	-	LWD
1994	Pak (A)	2	3	-	123	58	-	2	41.00	8	-	LD

Season	v.	Tests	Innings	N.O.	Runs	Highest	100	50	Average	Ct	St	Results
1994-95	Eng	5	10	3	249	74	-	2	35.57	23	2	WWDLW
1995	WI (A)	4	6	1	128	74*	-	1	25.60	9	1	WDLW
1995-96	Pak	3	5	-	92	87	-	-	18.40	7	1	WWL
1995-96	SL	3	3	-	154	70	-	1	51.33	17	2	WWW
1996	Ind (A)	1	2	-	29	17	-	-	14.50	1	-	L
1996-97	WI	5	9	3	356	161*	1	-	59.33	15	-	WWLWL
1997	SA (A)	3	5	1	57	19	-	-	14.25	11	-	WWL
1997	Eng (A)	6	10	1	225	63	-	1	25.00	25	2	LDWWWL
1997-98	NZ	3	4	-	194	85	-	2	48.50	6	2	WWD
1997-98	SA	3	5	1	77	46*	-	-	19.25	9	1	DWD
1998	Ind (A)	3	5	1	165	90	-	1	41.25	6	-	LLW
1998	Pak (A)	3	4	1	146	82	-	1	48.66	9	-	WDD
1998-99	Eng	5	8	1	221	134	1	-	31.57	16	3	DWWLW
1999	WI (A)	4	8	-	53	16	-	-	6.62	7	1	WLLW
1999	SL (A)	3	4	-	25	11	-	-	6.25	4	-	LDD
1999	Zim (A)	1	1	-	5	5	-	-	5.00	2	-	W
Total		**119**	**182**	**23**	**4356**	**161***	**4**	**22**	**27.39**	**366**	**29**	

Notes:
1. *(A) indicates Tests played overseas*
2. *'results' column indicates result of each Test for Australia*
3. *IA Healy never bowled in Test cricket.*
4. *IA Healy missed the third Test against Pakistan in 1994 because of injury; he was replaced by PA Emery. The match was drawn.*

Results summary, by opponent

Australia v.	Tests	Won	Drawn	Lost
Pakistan	14	4	7	3
West Indies	28	10	6	12
England	33	20	8	5
New Zealand	11	5	4	2
Sri Lanka	11	5	5	1
India	9	5	1	3
South Africa	12	5	4	3
Zimbabwe	1	1	-	-
Total	**119**	**55**	**35**	**29**

Results summary, by venue

Australia in	Tests	Won	Drawn	Lost
Pakistan	8	1	5	2
Australia	59	31	17	11
England	18	11	4	3
New Zealand	4	1	1	2
West Indies	13	5	3	5
Sri Lanka	6	1	4	1
South Africa	6	3	1	2
India	4	1	-	3
Zimbabwe	1	1	-	-
Total	**119**	**55**	**35**	**29**

Results summary in Australia, by ground

Australia at	Tests	Won	Drawn	Lost
Brisbane	11	7	3	1
Perth	11	6	2	3
Melbourne	11	6	2	3
Sydney	11	4	5	2
Adelaide	11	5	4	2
Hobart	4	3	1	-
Total	**59**	**31**	**17**	**11**

Test career, by opponent

IA Healy v.	Tests	Innings	N.O.	Runs	Highest	100	50	Average	Ct	St
Pakistan	14	20	1	547	82	-	3	28.78	42	3
West Indies	28	48	5	960	161*	1	3	22.32	72	6
England	33	49	8	1269	134	2	6	30.95	123	12
New Zealand	11	14	1	447	113*	1	3	34.38	38	4
Sri Lanka	11	16	3	445	71	-	3	34.23	32	2
India	9	15	1	351	90	-	2	25.07	26	-
South Africa	12	19	4	332	61	-	2	22.13	31	2
Zimbabwe	1	1	-	5	5	-	-	5.00	2	-
Total	**119**	**182**	**23**	**4356**	**161***	**4**	**22**	**27.39**	**366**	**29**

Test Career, by venue

IA Healy in	Tests	Innings	N.O.	Runs	Highest	100	50	Average	Ct	St
Pakistan	8	11	1	343	82	-	3	34.30	23	2
Australia	59	92	13	2317	161*	3	8	29.32	205	17
England	18	24	4	624	102*	1	3	31.20	60	7
New Zealand	4	6	-	96	54	-	1	16.00	16	1
West Indies	13	22	1	336	74*	-	2	16.00	26	2
Sri Lanka	6	10	2	227	71	-	2	28.37	11	-
South Africa	6	9	1	214	61	-	2	26.75	16	-
India	4	7	1	194	90	-	1	32.33	7	-
Zimbabwe	1	1	-	5	5	-	-	5.00	2	-
Total	**119**	**182**	**23**	**4356**	**161***	**4**	**22**	**27.39**	**366**	**29**

Test Career in Australia, by ground

IA Healy at	Tests	Innings	N.O.	Runs	Highest	100	50	Average	Ct	St
Brisbane	11	17	4	689	161*	2	1	53.00	41	3
Perth	11	15	2	461	113*	1	2	35.46	47	1
Melbourne	11	19	1	357	60	-	1	19.83	39	4
Sydney	11	17	3	338	69	-	1	24.14	21	3
Adelaide	11	19	3	377	74	-	3	23.56	49	3
Hobart	4	5	-	95	37	-	-	19.00	8	3
Total	**59**	**92**	**13**	**2317**	**161***	**3**	**8**	**29.32**	**205**	**17**

Test Centuries

Score	Match, Innings	Minutes	Balls Faced	Fours
102*	v. England, Manchester (1st Test, 2nd innings), 1993	165	133	12
	added 180 (unbroken partnership) for sixth wicket with SR Waugh			
113*	v. New Zealand, Perth (1st Test, 1st innings), 1993-94	268	181	11
161*	v. West Indies, Brisbane (1st Test, 1st innings), 1996-97	356	250	20
	added 142 for sixth wicket with SR Waugh			
134	v. England, Brisbane (1st Test, 1st innings), 1998-99	303	229	14
	added 187 for sixth wicket with SR Waugh			

Notes:

1. All centuries were scored batting at No. 7.

2. The 161* is the highest score for Australia by a wicketkeeper.

3. The 102* was the third instance of an Australian scoring his maiden first-class century during a Test match, following C Bannerman (in 1877) and H Graham (in 1893).

4. IA Healy was the 100th Australian to score a Test century.

5. Of the 107 Australians to score a Test century, IA Healy is the only one who never scored a first-class century outside Test cricket.

6. IA Healy's highest score as a nightwatchman was 69 v. England, Sydney (3rd Test, 2nd innings). He began that innings late on the 4th day at 1-21, and after being 9* overnight was the seventh batsman dismissed, at 166. In all, Healy was a nightwatchman five times in Test cricket, all in Australia's second innings, four times at no.3 and once at no.5. He survived until stumps on four of these five occasions.

Players with 100 appearances in Test cricket

Tests	Player (Team)	Years
156	AR Border (Australia)	1978-79~1994
131	Kapil Dev (India)	1978~1993-94
128	SR Waugh (Australia)	1985-86~
125	SM Gavaskar (India)	1971~1986-87
124	Javed Miandad (Pakistan)	1976~1993
121	IVA Richards (West Indies)	1974-75~1991
119	**IA Healy (Australia)**	**1988~1999**
118	GA Gooch (England)	1975~1994-95
117	DI Gower (England)	1978~1992
117	CA Walsh (West Indies)	1984-85~
116	DB Vengsarkar (India)	1976~1991-92
116	DL Haynes (West Indies)	1978~1994
114	MC Cowdrey (England)	1954-55~1974-75
110	CH Lloyd (West Indies)	1966-67~1984-85
108	G Boycott (England)	1964~1981-82
108	CG Greenidge (West Indies)	1974-75~1991
107	DC Boon (Australia)	1984-85~1995-96
104	MA Taylor (Australia)	1988-89~1998-99
103	Salim Malik (Pakistan)	1982~1999
103	ME Waugh (Australia)	1990-91~
102	IT Botham (England)	1977~1992

Note: Players with most Test appearances for countries not featured above are:

Team	Tests	Player	Years
South Africa	68	WJ Cronje	1992~2000
New Zealand	86	RJ Hadlee	1973~1990
Sri Lanka	87	A Ranatunga	1982~
Zimbabwe	43	A Flower	1992~
	43	ADR Campbell	1992~

Most Test appearances for Australia

Tests	Player	Years	Eng	SA	WI	NZ	Ind	Pak	SL	Zim
156	AR Border (NSW, Qld)	1978-79~1994	47	6	31	23	20	22	7	-
128	SR Waugh (NSW)	1985-86~	37	10	24	20	11	17	8	1
119	**IA Healy (Qld)**	**1988~1999**	**33**	**12**	**28**	**11**	**9**	**14**	**11**	**1**
107	DC Boon (Tas)	1984-85~1995-96	31	6	22	17	11	11	9	-
104	MA Taylor (NSW)	1988-89~1998-99	33	11	20	11	9	12	8	-
103	ME Waugh (NSW)	1990-91~	24	12	23	11	11	12	9	1
96	RW Marsh (WAust)	1970-71~1983-84	42	-	17	14	3	20	-	-
87	GS Chappell (SAust, Qld)	1970-71~1983-84	35	-	17	14	3	17	1	-
84	SK Warne (Vict)	1991-92~	18	12	16	12	8	9	8	1
79	RN Harvey (Vict, NSW)	1947-48~1962-63	37	14	14	-	10	4	-	-
75	IM Chappell (SAust)	1964-65~1979-80	30	9	17	6	9	4	-	-
74	KD Walters (NSW)	1965-66~1980-81	36	4	9	11	10	4	-	-
71	CJ McDermott (Qld)	1984-85~1995-96	17	6	14	13	9	5	7	-
70	DK Lillee (WAust)	1970-71~1983-84	29	-	12	8	3	17	1	-
70	KJ Hughes (WAust)	1977~1984-85	22	-	15	6	11	16	-	-
67	WM Lawry (Vict)	1961~1970-71	29	14	10	-	12	2	-	-
66	IR Redpath (Vict)	1963-64~1975-76	23	10	16	3	10	4	-	-

Notes:
1. The above table does not include the Third Test v. England, Melbourne, 1970-71, which was abandoned without a ball being bowled.
2. A total of 383 players have played Test cricket for Australia. IA Healy was the 344th.

Most consecutive Test appearances for Australia

No.	Player	Seasons
153	AR Border	1979-1994
80	ME Waugh	1993-
71	IM Chappell	1965-66-1975-76
64	**IA Healy**	**1988-1994**
60	DC Boon	1990-1995-96

Test colleagues (55)

Tests	Colleague	Tests	Colleague
103	MA Taylor	14	MS Kasprowicz, JN Gillespie
101	SR Waugh	13	DW Fleming
93	ME Waugh	12	BA Reid, GRJ Matthews, SCG MacGill
78	DC Boon	11	CR Miller
74	SK Warne	10	PL Taylor
62	AR Border	9	GF Lawson, MR Whitney
52	MJ Slater, GD McGrath	8	TM Moody
48	CJ McDermott	7	AIC Dodemaide, TV Hohns,
46	MG Hughes		CG Rackemann, DR Martyn, BP Julian,
38	GS Blewett		ML Hayden
37	DM Jones	6	GM Wood
35	PR Reiffel	5	DS Lehmann
31	GR Marsh	4	GD Campbell, J Angel, GR Robertson
28	RT Ponting	3	PR Sleep, MRJ Veletta, AJ Bichel
23	JL Langer	2	PE McIntyre, SH Cook, AC Dale
22	TBA May	1	CD Matthews, WN Phillips, SG Law,
20	MTG Elliott		GB Hogg, S Young, P Wilson,
19	TM Alderman		MJ Nicholson
17	MG Bevan		

Notes:
1. 'Tests' indicates the number of Test matches IA Healy played with each colleague.
2. The 103 Tests with MA Taylor (1988-89~1998-99) are a record for two Australian Test players playing together in Test cricket. It is exceeded only by the 104 Tests which DB Vengsarkar and Kapil Dev played together for India (1978~1991-92).

Bowlers off whom catches were taken (35)

Catches	Bowler	Catches	Bowler
58	GD McGrath	7	CG Rackemann
55	CJ McDermott	6	MG Bevan
46	MG Hughes	5	TBA May, SCG MacGill
34	SK Warne	4	GF Lawson, CR Miller
22	BA Reid	3	PL Taylor, GD Campbell, J Angel,
19	PR Reiffel		GR Robertson
14	SR Waugh	2	AIC Dodemaide, RT Ponting
13	ME Waugh	1	TV Hohns, PR Sleep, AR Border,
11	TM Alderman, DW Fleming		GRJ Matthews, BP Julian, SH Cook,
9	MR Whitney, MS Kasprowicz		GS Blewett, DS Lehmann,
8	JN Gillespie		MJ Nicholson, AC Dale

Bowlers off whom stumpings were made (7)

Stumpings	Bowler
15	SK Warne
7	TBA May
3	SCG MacGill
1	PL Taylor, GRJ Matthews, MG Bevan, CR Miller

Bowlers off whom most dismissals were made

Dismissals	Bowler
58	GD McGrath
55	CJ McDermott
49	SK Warne
46	MG Hughes

Batsmen dismissed most often

No.	Ct	St	Batsman	Team	No.	Ct	St	Batsman	Team
17	16	1	MA Atherton	England	6	6	-	GA Hick	England
12	11	1	GA Gooch	England	6	6	-	D Gough	England
11	10	1	BC Lara	West Indies	6	6	-	CL Hooper	West Indies
10	9	1	DL Haynes	West Indies	6	5	1	KR Rutherford	New Zealand
8	7	1	AJ Stewart	England	6	5	1	RA Smith	England
7	7	-	RB Richardson	West Indies	6	4	2	MA Butcher	England
6	6	-	MJ Greatbatch	New Zealand	6	4	2	GP Thorpe	England

Note: IA Healy dismissed 149 different batsmen in Test cricket.

Most dismissals in a Test innings for Australia

No.	How Out	Keeper	Match	Venue	Season
6	(6ct)	ATW Grout	v. South Africa	Johannesburg	1957-58
6	(6ct)	RW Marsh	v. England	Brisbane	1982-83
6	**(6ct)**	**IA Healy**	**v. England**	**Birmingham**	**1997**

Note: The world record for most dismissals in a Test innings is 7, by Wasim Bari (7ct) for Pakistan v. New Zealand, Auckland,1979; by RW Taylor (7ct) for England v. India, Bombay, 1980; and by IDS Smith (7ct) for New Zealand v. Sri Lanka, Hamilton, 1991.

Most dismissals in a Test for Australia

No.	Keeper	Match	Venue	Season
10 (all ct)	AC Gilchrist	v. New Zealand	Hamilton	2000
9 (8ct, 1st)	GRA Langley	v. England	Lord's	1956
9 (all ct)	RW Marsh	v. England	Brisbane	1982-83
9 (9ct)	**IA Healy**	**v. England**	**Brisbane**	**1994-95**
8 (all ct)	JJ Kelly	v. England	Sydney	1901-02
8 (all ct)	GRA Langley	v. West Indies	Kingston	1955
8 (6ct, 2st)	ATW Grout	v. Pakistan	Lahore	1959-60
8 (all ct)	ATW Grout	v. England	Lord's	1961
8 (7ct, 1st)	HB Taber	v. South Africa	Johannesburg	1966-67
8 (all ct)	RW Marsh	v. West Indies	Melbourne	1975-76
8 (all ct)	RW Marsh	v. New Zealand	Christchurch	1977
8 (7ct, 1st)	RW Marsh	v. India	Sydney	1980-81
8 (all ct)	RW Marsh	v. England	Adelaide	1982-83
8 (6ct, 2st)	**IA Healy**	**v. West Indies**	**Adelaide**	**1992-93**
8 (7ct, 1st)	**IA Healy**	**v. England**	**Melbourne**	**1994-95**
8 (all ct)	**IA Healy**	**v. Sri Lanka**	**Adelaide**	**1995-96**

Note: The Test record is 11 (11ct) by RC Russell for England v. South Africa, Johannesburg, 1995-96.

Most dismissals in a Test series (five Tests unless otherwise stated)

No.	Keeper	Series	Season
28 (all ct)	RW Marsh	Australia v. England	1982-83
27 (25ct, 2st)	RC Russell	England v. South Africa	1995-96
27 (25ct, 2st)	**IA Healy**	**Australia v. England (6 Tests)**	**1997**
26 (23ct, 3st)	JHB Waite	South Africa v. New Zealand	1961-62
26 (all ct)	RW Marsh	Australia v. West Indies (6 Tests)	1975-76
26 (21ct, 5st)	**IA Healy**	**Australia v. England (6 Tests)**	**1993**
26 (25ct, 1st)	MV Boucher	South Africa v. England	1998
25 (23ct, 2st)	**IA Healy**	**Australia v. England**	**1994-95**
24 (22ct, 2st)	DL Murray	West Indies v. England	1963

No.	Keeper	Series	Season
24 (all ct)	DT Lindsay	South Africa v. Australia	1966-67
24 (21 ct, 3st)	APE Knott	England v. Australia (6 Tests)	1970-71
24 (all ct)	IA Healy	Australia v. England	1990-91

Australian Test wicketkeepers (28)

Keeper	State	Career	Tests	Ct	St	Total	5/Inn	8/Match	100s As Wk
JM Blackham	Vict	1877-1894-95	32+	36	24	60	-	-	-
WL Murdoch	NSW	1881-82	1+	1	1	2	-	-	-
AH Jarvis	SAust	1884-85-1894-95	8+	7	9	16	-	-	-
FJ Burton	NSW	1886-87	1+	-	1	1	-	-	-
JJ Kelly	NSW	1896-1905	36	43	20	63	-	1	-
H Carter	NSW	1907-08-1921	28	44	21	65	-	-	-
W Carkeek	Vict	1912	6	6	-	6	-	-	-
WAS Oldfield	NSW	1920-21-1936-37	54	78	52	130	1	-	-
HSB Love	NSW	1932-33	1	3	-	3	-	-	-
BA Barnett	Vict	1938	4	3	2	5	-	-	-
D Tallon	Qld	1946-1953	21	50	8	58	-	-	-
RA Saggers	NSW	1948-1949-50	6	16	8	24	-	-	-
GRA Langley	SAust	1951-52-1956	26	83	15	98	3	2	-
LV Maddocks	Vict	1954-55-1956	7	18	1	19	-	-	-
ATW Grout	Qld	1957-58-1965-66	51	163	24	187	6	2	-
BN Jarman	SAust	1959-60-1968-69	19	50	4	54	-	-	-
HB Taber	NSW	1966-67-1969-70	16	56	4	60	3	1	-
RW Marsh	WAust	1970-71-1983-84	96	343	12	355	12	5	3
SJ Rixon	NSW	1977-78-1984-85	13	42	5	47	-	-	-
JA Maclean	Qld	1978-79	4	18	-	18	1	-	-
KJ Wright	WAust	1978-79-1979	10	31	4	35	1	-	-
RD Woolley	Tas	1983-1984	2	7	-	7	-	-	-
WB Phillips	SAust	1984-1985-86	18+	43	-	43	1	-	1
TJ Zoehrer	WAust	1986-1986-87	10	18	1	19	-	-	-
GC Dyer	NSW	1986-87-1987-88	6	22	2	24	-	-	-
IA Healy	**Qld**	**1988-1999**	**119**	**366**	**29**	**395**	**11**	**4**	**4**
PA Emery	NSW	1994	1	5	1	6	1	-	-
AC Gilchrist	WAust	1999-2000-	9	38	3	41	2	1	1

Notes:

1. '5/Inn' indicates instances of five or more dismissals in an innings
2. '8/Match' indicates instances of eight or more dismissals in a Test
3. + Indicates also played Tests for Australia as non-wicketkeeper: Blackham three Tests (taking one catch), Murdoch 17 Tests (12 catches), Jarvis three Tests (two catches), Burton one Test (one catch), Phillips nine Tests (nine catches).
4. Murdoch also played one Test as wicketkeeper for England (v. South Africa in 1892) making one stumping.

Most dismissals by a wicketkeeper in a Test career

No.	Keeper	Ct	St	Tests	Career	Runs	High	100	Average
395	IA Healy (Aust)	366	29	119	1988-1999	4356	161*	4	27.39
355	RW Marsh (Aust)	343	12	96	1970-71-1983-84	3633	132	3	26.51
270	PJL Dujon (WI)	265	5	79	1981-82-1991	3146	139	5	31.46
269	APE Knott (Eng)	250	19	95	1967-1981	4389	135	5	32.75
228	Wasim Bari (Pak)	201	27	81	1967-1983-84	1366	85	-	15.88
217	TG Evans (Eng)	173	46	91	1946-1959	2439	104	2	20.49
198	SMH Kirmani (Ind)	160	38	88	1976-1985-86	2759	102	2	27.04
189	DL Murray (WI)	181	8	62	1963-1980	1993	91	-	22.90
187	ATW Grout (Aust)	163	24	51	1957-58-1965-66	890	74	-	15.08
176	IDS Smith (NZ)	168	8	63	1980-81-1992	1815	173	2	25.56
174	RW Taylor (Eng)	167	7	57	1971-1984	1156	97	-	16.28
165	RC Russell (Eng)	153	12	54	1988-1998	1897	128*	2	27.10
152	DJ Richardson (SA)	150	2	42	1992-1997-98	1359	109	1	24.26

Notes:

1. Dujon also played two Tests as a non-wicketkeeper, taking two catches. All other keepers listed in this table played

every Test of career as a specialist keeper. Only performances by players in matches in which they were selected as keeper are included in the following notes.

2. Most dismissals for countries not listed above are for Sri Lanka: 83 dismissals (64ct, 19st) by RS Kaluwitharana in 36 Tests, 1992~; and for Zimbabwe: 112 (107ct, 5st) by A Flower in 39 Tests, 1992~.

3. Wicketkeepers to make 100 Test dismissals against one opponent are:

No.	Keeper	Opponent	Ct	St	Tests	Years
148	RW Marsh (Aust)	England	141	7	42	1970-71~1982-83
135	**IA Healy (Aust)**	**England**	**123**	**12**	**33**	**1989~1998-99**
105	APE Knott (Eng)	Australia	97	8	34	1968~1981

4. The most stumpings completed in Test cricket is 52, by WAS Oldfield, as above.

5. The most runs scored by a wicketkeeper in Test cricket are 4389, by APE Knott, as above.

6. The most centuries hit by a wicketkeeper in Test cricket are five, by APE Knott and PJL Dujon. The highest Test scores by a wicketkeeper are:

Score	Keeper	Match	Venue	Season
210*	Taslim Arif	Pakistan v. Australia	Faisalabad	1980
209	Imtiaz Ahmed	Pakistan v. New Zealand	Lahore	1955
201*	DSBP Kuruppu	Sri Lanka v. New Zealand	Colombo CCC	1987
192	BK Kunderan	India v. England	Madras	1964

Test 'milestones' for IA Healy

Dismissal No.	Test No.	Batsman	How Out, Bowler	Venue	Season
1	1	Ramiz Raja (Pak)	ct, BA Reid	Karachi	1988
50	19	Mushtaq Ahmed (Pak)	ct, CG Rackemann	Adelaide	1989-90
100	33	Kapil Dev (Ind)	ct, BA Reid	Melbourne	1991-92
150	47	AH Jones (NZ)	ct, MG Hughes	Auckland	1993
200	59	DJ Cullinan (SA)	ct, CJ McDermott	Adelaide	1993-94
250	74	Salim Elahi (Pak)	ct, GD McGrath	Brisbane	1995-96
300	88	G Kirsten (SA)	ct, GD McGrath	Centurion	1997
350	101	R Dravid (Ind)	ct, SK Warne	Chennai	1998
355	104	Mohammad Wasim (Pak)	ct, DW Fleming	Rawalpindi	1998
356 ®	104	Wasim Akram (Pak)	ct, CR Miller	Rawalpindi	1998
395	119	A Flower (Zim)	ct, GD McGrath	Harare	1999

® set new World record aggregate, passing RW Marsh

After Test No.	Ct	St	Total	DpT	Runs	Average
20 (v. Pakistan, Sydney, 1989-90)	51	2	53	2.65	519	20.76
40 (v. West Indies, Brisbane, 1992-93)	118	3	121	3.02	1253	22.37
60 (v. South Africa, Johannesburg, 1994)	188	14	202	3.36	1941	24.88
80 (v. India, Delhi, 1996)	256	20	276	3.45	2832	26.97
100 (v. South Africa, Adelaide, 1997-98)	322	25	347	3.47	3741	28.34
119 (v. Zimbabwe, Harare, 1999)	366	29	395	3.31	4356	27.39

Note: DpT indicates dismissals per Test

Evolution of the Australian Test wicketkeeping record aggregate

Record	New Record	Record-holder	Test No.	Final Record	Tests	Ct	St	Total
4	19 Mar, 1877	JM Blackham	1	1894-95	32	36	24	60
61	29 May, 1905	JJ Kelly	34	1905	36	43	20	63
64	29 Nov, 1921	H Carter	28	1921	28	44	21	65
66	19 Jan, 1931	WAS Oldfield	28	1936-37	54	78	52	130
131	25 Jan, 1964	ATW Grout	33	1965-66	51	163	24	187
188	13 Mar, 1977	RW Marsh	47	1983-84	96	343	12	355
356	4 Oct, 1998	IA Healy	104	1999	119	366	29	395

Notes about this table and the next:

1. Blackham completed four dismissals in the first-ever Test, making his fourth dismissal on 19 March, 1877. He increased the record aggregate until his last Test (his 32nd as a wicketkeeper) in 1894-95. The record aggregate remained at 60 until 29 May, 1905, when Kelly made his 61st dismissal during his 34th Test.

2. 'Test no.' indicates the number of Tests in each wicketkeeper's career when they first became the Australian record holder.

3. 'Final record' indicates the season in which the Australian record holder's career ended.

Evolution of the World Test wicketkeeping record aggregate

Test Record	New Record	Record-holder	Test No.	Final Record	Tests	Ct	St	Total
4	19 Mar, 1877	JM Blackham (Aust)	1	1894-95	32	36	24	60
61	3 Mar, 1904	AFA Lilley (Eng)	23	1909	35	70	22	92
93	27 Feb, 1933	WAS Oldfield (Aust)	39	1936-37	54	78	52	130
131	12 Aug, 1954	TG Evans (Eng)	57	1959	91	173	46	219
220	12 Aug, 1976	APE Knott (Eng)	78	1980+	93	244	19	263
264	18 Jul, 1981	RW Marsh (Aust)	72	1983-84	96	343	12	355
356	4 Oct, 1998	IA Healy (Aust)	104	1999	119	366	29	395

Note
+ indicates Knott played two more Tests in 1981, after Marsh had set the new record.

Most dismissals by wicketkeeper/bowler combinations

No.	Keeper, Bowler	Tests	Years
95	RW Marsh, DK Lillee (Aust)	69	1970-71~1983-84
71	PJL Dujon, MD Marshall (WI)	67	1983~1991
60	RW Taylor, IT Botham (Eng)	60	1978~1984
58	**IA Healy, GD McGrath (Aust)**	**52**	**1993-94~1999**
55	**IA Healy, CJ McDermott (Aust)**	**48**	**1988-89~1995-96**
51	SMH Kirmani, Kapil Dev (Ind)	67	1978~1985-86
49 (34ct, 15st)	**IA Healy, SK Warne (Aust)**	**74**	**1991-92~1999**
47	DJ Richardson, AA Donald (SA)	37	1992~1997-98
46	**IA Healy, MG Hughes (Aust)**	**46**	**1988-89~1994**
45 (44ct, 1st)	ATW Grout, AK Davidson (Aust)	28	1957-58~1962-63

Notes:
1. All dismissals in this list are catches, unless otherwise stated.
2. The most stumpings by a wicketkeeper/bowler combination are 28, by WAS Oldfield off CV Grimmett (Aust) in 37 Tests, 1924-45~1935-36.

No byes allowed in a large innings

The following Australians permitted no byes during innings totals over 500:

Keeper	Match	Venue	Season
JJ Kelly	v. England (551)	Sydney	1897-98
WAS Oldfield	v. England (521)	Brisbane	1928-29
WB Phillips	v. West Indies (509)	Bridgetown	1984
IA Healy	**v. West Indies (536, 9 wkts)**	**Bridgetown**	**1991**
IA Healy	**v. South Africa (517)**	**Adelaide**	**1997-98**

Notes:
1. Highest total in which no bye was permitted is 4-671 by HP Tillakaratne for Sri Lanka v. New Zealand, Wellington, 1991.
2. RC Russell (England) permitted no byes in innings totals over 500 on four occasions between 1989 and 1998.

— ✠ —

3. LIMITED-OVERS DOMESTIC CAREER

Debut: v. NSW, Brisbane, February 21, 1988, scoring 8 and taking one catch.
Last match: v.Victoria, Melbourne, January 30, 1999, not batting and making no dismissals.

Limited-overs domestic career batting and wicketkeeping

Season	Matches	Innings	N.O.	Runs	Highest	Average	Ct	St
1987-88	2	2	-	15	8	7.50	1	-
1988-89	4	2	-	13	7	6.50	5	-
1990-91	3	3	1	73	48	36.50	2	2
1991-92	3	1	-	33	33	33.00	2	2
1992-93	3	1	-	2	2	2.00	4	2
1993-94	3	2	1	6	6*	6.00	3	1
1995-96	2	1	-	48	48	48.00	8	-
1997-98	5	4	1	31	15	10.33	14	-
1998-99	4	-					8	-
Total	**29**	**16**	**3**	**221**	**48**	**17.00**	**47**	**7**

Notes
1. IA Healy's highest score in domestic limited-overs cricket was 48 v. Tasmania, Brisbane, 1990-91 and 48 v. Tasmania, Hobart, 1995-96.
2. The most dismissals he completed in one innings was five (all caught), v. Tasmania, Hobart, 1995-96.
3. He never bowled in domestic limited-overs cricket.

Limited-overs domestic career, by opponent

Opponent	Matches	Innings	N.O.	Runs	Highest	Average	Ct	St
New South Wales	6	6	1	65	33	13.00	8	2
Tasmania	5	5	1	121	48	30.25	9	2
Victoria	6	1	-	6	9	6.00	8	1
South Australia	5	1	1	4	4*	-	9	-
Western Australia	6	3	-	25	18	8.33	10	2
Canberra	1	-					3	-
Total	**29**	**16**	**3**	**221**	**48**	**17.00**	**47**	**7**

—¤—

4. LIMITED-OVERS INTERNATIONAL CAREER

Debut: v. Pakistan, Lahore, October 14, 1988, scoring 1 and making no dismissals.
Last match: v. England, Lord's, May 25, 1997, scoring 27 and making no dismissals.

Limited-overs international career batting and wicketkeeping

Season	In	Matches	Innings	N.O.	Runs	Highest	100	50	Average	Ct	St
1988	Pak	1	1	-	1	1	-	-	1.00	-	-
1988-89	Aust	11	6	2	53	23*	-	-	13.25	10	2
1989	Eng	2	2	1	36	26*	-	-	18.00	1	1
1989	Ind	5	4	1	26	14*	-	-	8.66	2	-
1989-90	Aust	10	5	1	89	33	-	-	22.25	17	2
1990	NZ	5	3	1	67	36*	-	-	33.50	8	-
1990	UAE	4	2	1	46	34	-	-	46.00	8	1
1990-91	Aust	10	5	3	92	50*	-	1	46.00	8	2
1991	WI	5	3	3	52	33*	-	-	-	7	-
1991-92	Aust	10	5	1	47	17*	-	-	11.75	11	-
1992 WC	NZ, Aust	7	6	2	51	16	-	-	12.75	9	-
1992	SL	3	1	-	6	6	-	-	6.00	1	-
1992-93	Aust	10	9	1	154	41	-	-	19.25	13	-
1993	NZ	5	4	-	34	17	-	-	8.50	6	3
1993	Eng	3	2	1	32	20	-	-	32.00	4	1
1993-94	Aust	10	8	3	122	48	-	-	24.40	16	3

Season	In	Matches	Innings	N.O.	Runs	Highest	100	50	Average	Ct	St
1994	SA	8	7	3	81	41*	-	-	20.25	6	4
1994	SL	3	3	1	73	30*	-	-	36.50	3	2
1994	Pak	4	3	1	38	18*	-	-	19.00	5	3
1994-95	Aust	4 †	2	-	96	56	-	1	48.00	8	-
1995	NZ	4	3	2	43	21*	-	-	43.00	7	2
1995	WI	5	5	-	102	51	-	1	20.40	5	1
1995-96	Aust	10	7	4	155	50	-	1	51.66	13	2
1996 WC	Ind, Pak	7	5	-	59	31	-	-	11.80	9	3
1996	SL (c)	4	4	-	37	20	-	-	9.25	4	-
1996	Ind	3	3	-	21	11	-	-	7.00	1	1
1996-97	Aust	8	5	2	44	22*	-	-	14.66	10	5
1997	SA (c)	4	4	2	56	25	-	-	28.00	2	1
1997	Eng	3	3	-	51	27	-	-	17.00	1	-
Total		**168**	**120**	**36**	**1764**	**56**	**-**	**4**	**21.00**	**195**	**39**

Notes:
1. *WC indicates World Cup*
2. *(c) indicates captain*
3. † *These four matches in 1994-95 were v. England (2) and v. Zimbabwe (2). Matches between Australia and Australia 'A' that were played in the same tournament are not recognised by ICC as limited-overs internationals*
4. *IA Healy never bowled in limited-overs international cricket.*
5. *UAE = Sharjah, United Arab Emirates*

Results summary, by opponent

Australia v.	Matches	Won	Tied	No Result	Lost
Pakistan	25	13	2	-	10
West Indies	39	20	-	1	18
England	16	8	1	-	7
Sri Lanka	20	12	-	-	8
India	15	9	-	-	6
New Zealand	23	17	-	-	6
Bangladesh	1	1	-	-	-
South Africa	23	14	-	-	9
Zimbabwe	5	5	-	-	-
Kenya	1	1	-	-	-
Total	**168**	**100**	**3**	**1**	**64**

Results summary, by venue

Australia in	Matches	Won	Tied	No Result	Lost
Pakistan	6	3	1	-	2
Australia	89	58	1	1	29
England	8	3	1	-	4
India	14	7	-	-	7
New Zealand	15	10	-	-	5
UAE	4	3	-	-	1
West Indies	10	5	-	-	5
Sri Lanka	10	4	-	-	6
South Africa	12	7	-	-	5
Total	**168**	**100**	**3**	**1**	**64**

Results summary in Australia, by ground

Australia at	Matches	Won	Tied	No Result	Lost
Adelaide	9	8	-	-	1
Sydney	28	18	-	-	10
Melbourne	29	21	-	1	7
Perth	9	4	-	-	5
Brisbane	8	4	-	-	4
Hobart	6	3	1	-	2
Total	**89**	**58**	**1**	**1**	**29**

Limited-overs international career, by opponent

IA Healy v.	Matches	Innings	N.O.	Runs	Highest	100	50	Average	Ct	St
Pakistan	25	18	4	201	30*	-	-	14.35	32	7
West Indies	39	31	11	479	51	-	1	23.95	45	4
England	16	11	3	238	56	-	2	29.75	14	4
Sri Lanka	20	10	2	190	50*	-	1	23.75	22	4
India	15	10	2	109	25	-	-	13.62	17	2
New Zealand	23	13	6	178	48	-	-	25.42	30	6
Bangladesh	1	1	-	34	34	-	-	34.00	3	-
South Africa	23	22	8	273	41*	-	-	19.50	22	10
Zimbabwe	5	3	-	45	40	-	-	15.00	9	1
Kenya	1	1	-	17	17	-	-	17.00	1	1
Total	**168**	**120**	**36**	**1764**	**56**	**-**	**4**	**21.00**	**195**	**39**

Limited-overs international career, by venue

IA Healy in	Matches	Innings	N.o.	Runs	Highest	100	50	Average	Ct	St
Pakistan	6	5	1	41	18*	-	-	10.25	5	3
Australia	89	57	18	896	56	-	3	22.97	113	16
England	8	7	2	119	27	-	-	23.80	6	2
India	14	11	1	104	31	-	-	10.40	12	4
New Zealand	15	11	4	151	36*	-	-	21.57	23	5
UAE	4	2	1	46	34	-	-	46.00	8	1
West Indies	10	8	3	154	51	-	1	30.80	12	1
Sri Lanka	10	8	1	116	30*	-	-	16.57	8	2
South Africa	12	11	5	137	41*	-	-	22.83	8	5
Total	**168**	**120**	**36**	**1764**	**56**	**-**	**4**	**21.00**	**195**	**39**

Highest scores

Score	Match	Season	Position in Batting Order	Balls Faced	Fours	Sixes
56	v England, Melbourne	1994-95	7	63	1	-
51	v. West Indies, Port-of-Spain	1995	7	45	3	1
50*	v. England, Melbourne	1990-91	8	37	2	-
50*	v. Sri Lanka, Melbourne	1995-96	7	55	-	-

Note: During 50* in 1990-91 (above) added 95 (unbroken partnership) for seventh wicket with SR Waugh

Most dismissals in a match

No.	How Out	Match	Venue	Season
4	(4ct)	v. New Zealand	Auckland	1990
4	(4ct)	v. Pakistan	Sharjah	1990
4	(1ct, 3st)	v. South Africa	East London	1994
4	(4ct)	v. Zimbabwe	Hobart	1994-95

Note: The Australian record for most dismissals in a limited-overs international is six (all caught) by AC Gilchrist v. South Africa, Cape Town, 2000.

Australian limited-overs international wicketkeepers (15)

Keeper	State	Career	Matches as Wk	Ct	St	Total
RW Marsh	WAust	1970-71-1983-84	92	120	4	124
RD Robinson	Vict	1977	1	3	1	4
SJ Rixon	NSW	1978-1984-85	6	9	2	11
JA Maclean	Qld	1978-79	2	-	-	-
KJ Wright	WAust	1978-79-1979	5	8	-	8
RD Woolley	Tas	1983	4	1	1	2
WB Phillips	SAust	1983-84-1985-86	42	42	7	49
TJ Zoehrer	WAust	1985-86-1993-94	22	21	2	23
GC Dyer	NSW	1986-1987-88	23	24	4	28
IA Healy	**Qld**	**1988-1997**	**168**	**195**	**39**	**234**

Keeper	State	Career	Matches as Wk	Ct	St	Total
MRJ Veletta	WAust	1989	1	1	-	1
DC Boon	Tas	1992	1	-	-	-
JL Langer	WAust	1994	4	1	1	2
PA Emery	NSW	1994	1	3	-	3
AC Gilchrist	WAust	1996~	90	124	18	142

Note: Six of the keepers listed above played additional matches as a non-wicketkeeper: Robinson one match, Phillips six matches, Veletta 19 matches (taking seven catches), Boon 180 matches (45 catches), Langer four matches (one catch) and Gilchrist five matches.

Australian limited-overs international captains (14)

Captain	State	Years As Capt	Matches As Capt	Won	Tied	No Result	Lost
WM Lawry	Vict	1970-71	1	1	-	-	-
IM Chappell	SAust	1972~1975	11	6	-	-	5
GS Chappell	Qld	1975-76~1983	49	21	-	3	25
RB Simpson	NSW	1978	2	1	-	-	1
GN Yallop	Vict	1978-79	4	2	-	1	1
KJ Hughes	WAust	1979~1984	49	21	1	4	23
DW Hookes	SAust	1983	1	-	-	-	1
AR Border	Qld	1984-85~1994	179	108	1	3	67
RJ Bright	Vict	1986	1	-	-	-	1
GR Marsh	WAust	1987~1990-91	4	3	-	-	1
MA Taylor	NSW	1992-93~1997	67	36	1	-	30
IA Healy	**Qld**	**1996~1997**	**8 (listed below)**	**5**	**-**	**-**	**3**
SR Waugh	NSW	1997~	76	47	2	1	26
SK Warne	Vict	1997-98~1998-99	11	10	-	-	1

Note: IA Healy was captain in eight limited-overs internationals, and won the toss in the first seven of them. These matches were as follows:

1996 in Sri Lanka

Aug 26	v. Zimbabwe, Colombo RPS	Australia won by 125 runs
Aug 30	v. Sri Lanka, Colombo RPS	Australia lost by four wickets
Sep 6	v. India, Colombo SSC	Australia won by three wickets
Sep 7	v. Sri Lanka, Colombo SSC	Australia lost by 50 runs

1997 in South Africa

Apr 3	v. South Africa, Cape Town	Australia lost by 46 runs
Apr 5	v. South Africa, Durban	Australia won by 15 runs
Apr 8	v. South Africa, Johannesburg	Australia won by 8 runs
Apr 10	v. South Africa, Centurion	Australia won by five wickets

A

ABC (Australian Broadcasting
  Commission) 13, 146–47
Abdul Qadir 36, 41
ACB *see* Australian Cricket
  Board
Adams, Bryan 200
Adams, Jimmy 157, 162,
  241–42
African National Congress 125
Alcott, Errol 42, 43, 56–57, 78,
  114, 136–37
Alderman, Terry 49, 53, 58,
  64–65, 74
Ambrose, Curtly
  Australia: 1988–89 42,
    45; 1992–93 106, 107;
    1996–97 188, 193, 195
  awesome in 1999 241–42
  Barbados: 1995 157–58
  Trinidad: 1995 155, 159,
    160
  World Cup 1996 175
Anderson, Peter 19–20, 22–23,
  28, 30–31, 32
Angel, Jo 107, 133
Antigua 158
appeals 73–74, 83
Archer, Ron 1, 4, 256
Arthurton, Keith 103–4
Ashes series
  1970–71 7–8
  1989 53–66
  1990–91 74–77
  1993 109–19
  1994–95 137, 141–45
  1997 209–13
  1998–99 236–38
Ashes urn 59–60, 73
Ashgrove Primary School 6–7
Atherton, Mike 142
Austral-Asia Cup 71
Australia A team 141
Australian Broadcasting
  Commission (ABC) 146–47
Australian Cricket Board (ACB)
  Border 128–29
  bribery offer 135

death threats 170–71
dinner in Bermuda 163
enquiry into match-fixing
  236
fines 125–26
Lara stumping 102
players' contracts 67, 154,
  214–17
Playing for Keeps 178
relationship with players
  153–54
selectors 208–9
Australian Cricketers'
  Association 150, 214–17
Australian (newspaper) 187
Azharuddin, Mohammad 92

B

Bacher, Adam 198, 200
ball-tampering 164, 166
'Banana' Shire (Qld) 5
Bangalore (India) 67, 68, 185
Barbados 82, 152, 156, 239,
  241
Barbados Sunday Sun 84
Barsby, Trevor 151
Base, Simon 57
bashing incident 146–47
bat throwing 12, 179, 197,
  204–6
Battersby, Dr Cam 125, 182
Baum, Greg 229
Bell, John 184
Benjamin, Kenny 158, 162
Benjamin, Winston 157
Bennett, Wayne 246
Bermuda 163
Bernard, Steve 224
Berry, Darren 109
betting 82, 129, 236
Bevan, Michael 23, 132,
  193–94, 197, 200, 211–13
Bichel, Andy 216
Bidgood, Merv 10–11
Biloela (Qld)
  High School 6
  Junior Cricket Association
    9, 13, 16

men's cricket 10
Primary School 8
Bishop, Ian 57, 106
Blackham, Jack 1
Blewett, Greg
  Ashes: 1997 211
  bowling changes 193
  Healy dropped 224
  Queensland Shield 148
  second Test century 145
  South Africa: 1997 197,
    198, 200
  West Indies: 1995 161
Bombay (India) 68, 173
bookmakers 82, 236, 260, 261,
  262
Boon, David
  Ashes: 1989 53, 62;
    1990–91 74; 1993 111–12
  Pakistan: 1988 35, 44;
    1994 132
  retirement 171–72, 196,
    236
  South Africa: 1994 90
Border, Allan
  Ashes: 1989 53, 55, 58,
    62–63, 66; 1993 114,
    116, 117
  bribery offer 130
  captain 25–27, 89–91
  Healy 52, 248–50
  Healy and 90–91
  last Test 128–29
  Madras: 1986 140
  Marsh, Geoff 91–92
  Nehru Cup: 1989 68
  New Zealand: 1993 109
  Pakistan: 1988 32, 33, 34,
    38, 40, 41
  players' contracts 214
  Queensland Team of the
    Century 256
  Sheffield Shield 152
  sledging 127
  South Africa: 1994 126
  spin bowlers 94
  Sri Lanka: 1992 96
  West Indies: 1988–89 42,

43, 51; 1991 83; 1992–93
    105, 106–7
Botham, Ian 24, 26–27, 59, 62
bowling
    leg-spin 93, 94, 219
    reverse swing 166
Bracewell, John 69
Bradley, Craig 18
Bradman, Sir Donald 3, 234
bribery 131, 133–35, 154, 164,
    236 see also match-fixing
Brisbane Broncos 246
Brisbane State High 17
British Sportsman's Club 112
Broad, Chris 59
Brown, Bill 256
Browne, Courtney 162
Buchanan, John 26, 52, 71,
    148–50, 252, 258
Burge, Peter 256
Burns, Gary 251–52
Butcher, Mark 211–13

C
Callide-Dawson Under 11s 9
Campbell, Sherwin 157, 189
Cape Town (South Africa) 126
caps
    baggy green 1, 2, 102,
        172, 234, 247
    'Victor Trumper' 246
Carlton & United Breweries 257
Carr, Donald 125
Centrebet 129
Centurion Park (Pretoria) 203,
    204, 206
Chanderpaul, Shivnarine 222
Chandigarh (India) 104, 175
Channel Nine 51, 85, 120, 151,
    195, 216–17, 251–52, 255
Channel Seven 128
Chappell, Greg
    approachability 24
    Biloela 15
    concentration skills 60–61
    country kids 8
    Healy 21, 31
    players' contracts 214
    Queensland Team of the
        Century 256
    Successful Cricket 14
Chappell, Ian 14, 56
cheating 98
Chennai (India) 227
chucking 164, 166–67
coaches 258
Collymore, Corey 244
Colombo (Sri Lanka) 170–71

Colts 148
contracts (players') 67, 154
Cornell, John 66
Courier-Mail 87, 104
Coward, Mike 187, 190
Craddock, Robert 11, 151–52
Cricket Academy 223
Cricket the Australian Way
    (Pollard) 14
Cronje, Hansie 200, 201, 221,
    260, 261
Crowe, Martin 95
Cullinan, Daryll 122, 123, 200,
    221

D
death threats 170–71
debut, first-class 23
DeFreitas, Phil 55, 111, 141
de Klerk, FW 125
Department of Foreign Affairs
    171
Derbyshire (England) 57–58
de Silva, Aravinda 96, 171, 177,
    183
de Villiers, Fanie 122, 221
Dimattina, Michael 31
'disco syndrome' 179–80
Djura, Bronko 17, 18
Dodemaide, Tony 18, 32, 46
Donald, Allan 122, 197
Doull, Simon 224
dressing rooms 118
Dujon, Jeffrey 51–52
Dunne, Steve 167
Durban (South Africa) 127
Dyer, Greg 31, 49, 101

E
Easts grade club 19
Edgbaston (England) 62, 119,
    210–11
Egar, Col 37, 71–72, 135, 206
Elliott, Matthew 200, 203, 242
Emery, Phil 109, 137, 141
Erskine, James 214
Evans, Grantley 28

F
Faisalabad (Pakistan) 38, 136
filling in 10–11
firsts
    Ashes tour 53
    bat 12
    contract 67
    controversy 48–49
    first-grade century 19
    'five-for' 68

season of commentary 50
Shield game 1987-88 24
Test catch 36
Test century 111
Fleming, Damien 148, 173, 175
Flower, Andy 140
Foreign Affairs, Department of
    171
Fourex (brewery) 66
Francis, KT 183
Francke, Malcolm 15
Frank Worrell Trophy 194

G
Gabba (Brisbane) 188, 248
gambling see bookmakers; match-
    fixing
gamesmanship 98, 195–96
Gateway to India 68
Gatting, Mike 33, 112, 113, 146
Gesler, Mr 13
Gibbs, Herschelle 135
Gilchrist, Adam
    challenge 234, 250, 256
    Emery's deputy 109
    international debut
        185–86
    one-day team 223–24
    Sheffield Shield 187
    Test understudy 23
    West Indies: 1999 239–40
    World Cup: 1999 245
Gillespie, Jason
    one-day debut 183
    South Africa: 1997 198,
        200, 201, 202, 204, 206
    Sri Lanka: 1999 247
    West Indies: 1999 242
    World Cup: 1999 245
gloves 16, 239
golf ball drill 22, 40–41, 176,
    219
Gooch, Graham 59, 64, 66, 118,
    146, 221–22
Gough, Darren 142, 222, 238
Gower, David 54–55, 59, 64, 66
Greenidge, Gordon 42
Grout, Wally 1, 16, 256
Gurusinha, Asanka 99
Guyana 81, 82

H
Hair, Darrell 104, 123, 124,
    166–67
Halbish, Graham 170, 185–86,
    214–15
Hammelmann, Harley 18
Harare (Zimbabwe) 248

Harper, Roger 48
Hayat, Khizar 166
Hayden, Matthew 33, 203, 209
Haynes, Desmond 51, 82–85
Headingley (England) 53
Headley, Dean 213
Healy, Emma Kate (IH's daughter) 87, 117, 263
Healy, George (IH's grandfather) 120
Healy, Greg (IH's brother) 6, 11–12, 14, 61
Healy, Helen (née Perkins) 19–20, 30, 86–88, 117, 130, 144, 147, 150–52, 171, 263
Healy, Ian
　Ashes: 1989 53, 54–56; 1990–91 75; 1993 110–11, 130; 1994–95 141–42; 1997 211–13
　Barbados 82
　batting 39–40, 45, 61, 82, 109
　Butcher stumping 211–13
　captaincy 177, 178, 181–82, 183, 198–200
　commentator 245, 252, 253, 255, 257
　diaries 140
　dropped from one-day team 223–25
　England tour in Under 19s 17–19
　enthusiasm 234–36
　firsts (see firsts)
　100th Test 226–27
　India: 1996 184; 1998 227–29
　injuries (see injuries)
　leader tour group 245
　man-of-the-match 76, 189, 213
　marriage 32
　missed stumping 133–35
　New Zealand: 1997–98 223
　nightwatchman 74–75
　one-day cricket 47–48, 184
　organisation 12–13
　Pakistan: 1988 28; 1994 132; 1998 231
　Playing for Keeps 178
　practice 8–9
　psychological edge 85–86
　radio interview 63
　relaxation 60–61
　retirement 248–50, 252
　selected for Australia 28
　self-doubts 108–9
　sledging 43, 195–96
　South Africa: 1997 200–202; 1997–98 226
　Sri Lanka: 1992 95; 1995–96 167–70; 1999 246
　suspension 206–7
　tarred with the cheat brush 102–4
　teammates as opponents 70–71
　Test career statistics 53
　Test catches 68
　Test century 188
　thinking ahead 73
　24 dismissals 77
　vice-captaincy 129, 130, 186, 187, 207, 208–9
　walkout vote 37–38
　West Indies: 1988–89 45; 1991 86; 1995 157; 1999 239–40, 240
　World Cup: 1996 175–76
　Zimbabwe: 1994 140
Healy, Ken (IH'S brother) 6, 12, 14
Healy, Kim (IH's sister) 6
Healy, Laura (IH's daughter) 88, 130
Healy, Neville (IH's father) 5, 11–12, 139, 225–26
Healy, Rae (IH's mother) 4, 5, 6, 12–13, 139
Healy, Tom (IH's son) 88, 196
Heath, Sir Edward 112
Hick, Graeme 112, 142
Hogg, Brad 183
Hohns, Trevor 30, 49, 57, 204, 207, 224–25, 246, 250
hook shot 139
Hooper, Carl 104, 157
Hudson, Andrew 125
Hughes, Merv
　Ashes: 1989 53, 65; 1990–91 74; 1993 111, 112–14, 119
　quick 220
　South Africa: 1994 125–26
　West Indies: 1988–89 42, 51
Hussain, Nasser 117, 210
Hyderabad (India) 68

I
'Ian Healy Cricket Academy' 259
Ijaz Ahmed 41

IMG (group) 215
Imran Khan 71
India, Gateway to 68
India tours
　1996 184–186
　1998 227–29
injuries
　ankle 116–17, 123, 130
　calf muscle 146, 239
　face 64
　finger 69, 78–80
　hamstring 164, 185
　head 75
　knee 54–58
　thumb 114–16, 136–37
International Cricket Conference (ICC) 38, 125, 135, 167, 171
Inwood, Brad 22, 24, 29
Inzamam-ul-Haq 133

J
Jacobs, Ridley 242
Jamaica 155, 241
Javed Miandad 34, 36, 37, 41
Jayasuriya, Sanath 169, 177, 183
Johannesburg (South Africa) 123
Jones, Dean
　Ashes: 1989 53, 54–55
　'Legend' 105
　New York: 1990 72
　Pakistan: 1989 44
　Sri Lanka: 1992 96
　West Indies: 1988–89 51
Julian, Brendon 157

K
Kallis, Jacques 200, 201
Kaluwitharana, Romesh 177
Kandy (Sri Lanka) 96, 247
Karachi (Pakistan) 35, 131, 232, 234
Kasprowicz, Michael 188, 229
Kelvin Grove College of Advanced Education 20
Kingston High School 20
Kirsten, Gary 122, 125, 198, 200, 204
Kirsten, Peter 123
Kitchen, Mervyn 206
Klusener, Lance 197
Knott, Alan 22, 230, 236, 248
Knox, Malcolm 191
Koertzen, Rudi 206
Kookaburra (company) 257
Kumble, Anil 184

L

Lahore (Pakistan) 34, 41, 131, 136, 176
Lamb, Allan 59
Langer, Justin 105, 137, 172, 203, 245
Lara, Brian
    Australia: 1992–93 102; 1996–97 194–95
    Barbados 157
    double century 241–42
    Healy and 99–101, 194–95
    Kingston 160
    stumping 99–101
    Warne 221
    World Cup 1996 175
Law, Stuart 183, 209
Lawson, Geoff
    Ashes: 1989 53, 65
    players' contracts 67, 214, 215
    West Indies: 1988–89 42, 43, 46
leg-spin bowling 93, 94, 219
Lehmann, Darren 231
Lexus (company) 257
Lillee, Dennis 26, 94
Lindwall, Ray 1, 2, 3, 4, 45, 256
Lingard, John 209
Logie, Gus 45
Los Angeles (USA) 71
Love, Martin 151

M

McCool, Colin 256
McDermott, Craig
    Ashes: 1990–91 77; 1993 113; 1994–95 142, 145
    bowel surgery 116
    death threats 170–71
    Healy and 26, 30
    Pakistan: 1988 32
    Queensland Team of the Century 256
    quick 220
    Sheffield Shield 149
    South Africa: 1993–94 122
    Under 19 tour 1983 18
    West Indies: 1988–89 48; 1991 80; 1992–93 106
    World Series Cup: 1986–87 23
McDermott, Jodie 30
McDonald, Ian 43, 89–90, 101, 142, 147
MacGill, Stuart 231, 237–38, 243–44
McGrath, Glenn

Ashes: 1997 211, 213
death threats 170–71
India: 1996 186
Pakistan: 1994 133
quick 220
South Africa: 1997 198, 201, 204
Sri Lanka: 1995–96 169
West Indies: 1995 154, 156, 157–58, 159; 1996–97 194; 1999 240, 242, 244
World Cup: 1996 173, 175
Mackay, Ken 256
McKnee, Dr John 78, 79
Maclean, John 3, 15–16, 22, 256
McMillan, Brian 127, 198
Macqueen, Rod 258
McSweeney, Kevin 9
Mahanama, Roshan 169
Mahboob Shah 37
Malcolm, Devon 57, 147
Mandela, Nelson 125
Manoj Prabhakar 92
Marsh, Geoff
    Ashes: 1989 53, 56, 64; 1990–91 74
    coach 177, 178, 181, 211
    dropping of 91–92
    Healy and 77
    retirement 248
    selector 203
    vice-captaincy 130–31
    West Indies: 1996–97 195
Marsh, Rod 1, 15, 22, 40, 46–47, 172, 223, 227, 230
Marshall, Charlee 10
Marshall, Malcolm 45, 46, 48, 51, 81
Martyn, Damien 105, 122
match-fixing 165, 236, 260, 261
Matthews, Chris 45–46
Matthews, Greg 69–70, 75, 96, 99
May, Tim
    Ashes: 1989 55
    Australian Cricketers' Association 214, 216, 217
    bribery 164
    Healy and 35
    New Zealand: 1993–94 120–21
    Pakistan: 1994 133–35
    West Indies: 1988–89 46; 1992–93 106
    Zimbabwe: 1994 140
Miller, Colin 230
Mitchley, Cyril 206

Mongia, Nayan 184
Moody, Tom 58, 91
Morris, Arthur 3
Mortensen, Ole 57
Mudassar Nazar 36, 40
Mulder, Brett 18
Multan (Pakistan) 136, 223
Munro, Mike 38–39
Muralitharan, Muttiah 96, 166–67, 183
Murray, Junior 157
Mushtaq Ahmed 133, 165, 166
My World of Cricket (Ian Chappell) 14
Myers, Dr Peter 79, 80, 137

N

Negus, George 51
Nehru Cup 1989 67, 68
New York (USA) 71, 72
New Zealand
    1990 69, 77
    1993 108–9
    1993–94 120–21
    1997–98 223–25
Norths 2, 14, 17, 19, 22

O

O'Connor, Shayne 224
O'Donnell, Simon 48, 71
Old Trafford (England) 59–60, 62–63, 112, 139
Oldfield, Bert 1
one-day cricket 108, 125, 141, 155–56, 184, 190–91, 203–4, 260, 261
O'Regan QC, Rob 236

P

painkillers 80
Pakistan
    1988 32–41
    1989–90 33–41
    1994 131–37
    1995–96 164–66
    1998 230–34
Pakistan Cricket Board 38
Park Lane (London) 65
Parore, Adam 221
Patterson, Patrick 42–43, 45, 106
Perkins, Ian 29, 30
Perry, Nehemiah 242
Peshawar (Pakistan) 232–34
Phelan, Bryan 17, 19
Phillips, Ray 22, 30, 73, 256
Phillips, Wayne 91, 92
players' contracts 67, 154, 214–17

Playing for Keeps (Healy) 178
Pocock, Blair 120–21
Pollard, Jack 14
Pollock, Shaun 197
Ponsford, Bill 3
Ponting, Ricky 193, 224, 245, 248, 249–50
Port Elizabeth (South Africa) 198, 203
Porteous, Gregg 87
Powers (brewery) 73
Prue, Terry 101–2, 103, 104, 123
Puma (company) 257

Q

Queensland
    Under 19s 17
    Colts 19, 20–21
    Cricket Association 16, 28
    Norths 2, 14, 17, 19, 22
    primary school team 16
    Sheffield Shield 20–27, 21, 26, 44, 104, 147–52
    Team of the Century 256
Quetta (Pakistan) 34

R

Rackemann, Carl 75, 149, 152
Raju, Venkatapathy 228
Ramiz Raja 36
Ranatunga, Arjuna 96, 167, 169, 170, 176–77, 178, 183, 221
Randell, Steve 107
Rashid Latif 133
Rawalpindi (Pakistan) 135–36, 230, 232
Reid, Bruce 36, 41, 74, 75
Reiffel, Paul
    Ashes: 1993 117
    Australia A 141
    bat throwing 179
    dropped 209
    one-day cricket 47
    Test debut 92
    West Indies: 1995 157, 161, 162
Rhodes, Jonty 122, 221
Richards, Viv 45, 46, 48, 51, 59, 81
Richardson, Richie 23, 81, 105, 157, 158–59, 160, 162, 175–76, 222
Ritchie, Greg 70
Robertson, Austin 66
Robertson, Gavin 227–28, 230
Rogers, Denis 170, 208, 216, 249

Rothmans coaching manuals 14
Royal Perth Hospital 146
Rundle, Des 170
Russell, Jack 62
Rutherford, Ken 120–21, 222

S

Sabina Park, Kingston (Jamaica) 80, 160
Saeed Anwar 131
St Johns Wood (Brisbane) 5
St Lucia (West Indies) 150–52
Saleem Jaffer 40
Salim Malik 36, 41, 131, 133–35, 164–65, 221
Samuels, Robert 189, 195
Saqlain Mushtaq 166
Sawle, Laurie 31, 92
Seccombe, Wade 23
Shakoor Rana 33
Sharjah (Dubai) 71, 108, 130
Sharma, Chetan 68
Shastri, Ravi 94
Sheffield Shield 15–16, 20–27, 44, 71, 104, 105, 147–52, 187, 215–16, 237
Shepherd, David 101, 213
'siege mentality' 128–29
Simmons, Phil 83
Simpson, Bob
    Ashes: 1989 58
    bribery offer 135
    coach 178–81, 201
    Healy 31, 46–47, 48, 52, 97
    Marsh 91–92
    Pakistan: 1988 35, 37, 40
    players' contracts 67–68
    West Indies: 1991 81, 84; 1995 156
    World Cup: 1996 171
Singer Trophy 184
Sixty Minutes (TV program) 38–39
Slater, Michael 141, 147, 158, 231–32, 245, 248, 253
sledging 43, 98–99, 118, 127, 195–96
Sleep, Peter 25, 34
Smith, Ian 124
Smith, Paul 147, 251, 256
Smith, Robin 59, 116
Soule, Richard 31
South Africa
    1993–94 121–24
    1994 108, 124–27
    1997–98 197–207, 223–27
    rebel tours 64, 67
Speed, Malcolm 249

Sri Lanka
    1992 95–97, 99
    1994 131
    1995–96 166–71
    1996 178, 182–83
    1999 246–48
Stackpole, Keith 8
statistics 230
Stewart, Alec 222
strike 216
Subba Row, Raman 204–6
Successful Cricket (Greg Chappell) 14
Sunday Mail 101
Sunday Telegraph 178
Sydney Morning Herald 191, 209
Symonds, Andrew 148

T

Tallon, Don 1, 256
Tausef Ahmed 40
Taylor, Bob 22
Taylor, Mark
    Ashes: 1989 58–59, 62
    Australia A 141
    batting 48, 191, 192, 197, 203–4
    bribery offer 135
    captaincy 129, 131, 154, 163, 177, 198–200, 208–9
    Edgbaston 209–11
    Healy and 206
    India: 1998 229
    Lara and 100–102
    one-day cricket 155–56, 191–93
    Pakistan: 1994 132
    Peshawar 232–34
    retirement 234, 238–39
    Sheffield Shield 70, 152
    sledging 127
    South Africa: 1997–98 223
    Sri Lanka: 1995–96 169, 170
    West Indies: 1991 86; 1992–93 107; 1995 157–58, 162; 1996–97 187
Taylor, Peter 40, 43, 48, 49, 69
Tazelaar, Dirk 45
team building 257–58
Team of the Century 2–4, 256
Tendulkar, Sachin 94, 173, 221, 228–29, 242
Texaco Trophy 209
Thomson, Jeff 15, 256
Thorpe, Graham 117, 119, 210, 213, 222
throwing 164, 166–67

Titan Cup 184
Today (TV program) 51
Toovey, Ernie 21
Toyota (company) 257
Trent Bridge (England) 54, 211
Trimble, Glenn 31
Trimble, Sam 256
Trinidad 155, 158
Tucker, Jim 151–52

U

Under the Southern Cross 4, 158,
    171, 194, 249, 253

V

Veletta, Linda 86
Veletta, Mike 18, 32, 86
Venkataraghavan, Srini 213
'Victor Trumper' caps 246
video-replay umpire 116, 183
Visakhapatnam (India) 173

W

Walsh, Courtney
    Australia: 1988–89 45;
        1992–93 106; 1996–97
        188, 195
    awesome in 1999 241–42
    Barbados: 1995 157–58
    Jamaica: 1991 80
    Trinidad: 1991 81; 1995
        160
Walters, Max 98
Waltzing Matilda 106, 188
Wanderers Ground, Jo'burg
    (South Africa) 125
Waqar Younis 132, 133, 165, 166
Warne, Shane
    Ashes: 1993 112–13;
        1994–95 141, 142; 1997
        210, 211; 1998-99 237
    bat throwing 179
    batting to 220
    bribery offer 164
    dismissals off 222
    dropped 243–44
    eating habits 222–23
    fines 154, 236
    Healy and 248
    India: 1998 227, 229

international debut 93–94
Miss India 175
New Zealand: 1993–94
    121; 1997–98 223
Pakistan: 1994 133–35;
    1995–96 164–65
players' contracts 216–17
South Africa: 1993–94 122;
    1994 125–26; 1997 197, 200,
    201; 1997–98 223
Sri Lanka: 1992 96
Taylor and 192, 193
West Indies: 1992–93 102,
    105; 1995 157, 160, 162
wicketkeeping to 218–20
wicket-taker 218–23
World Cup: 1996 173,
    175
Wasim Akram 72, 132, 166,
    230–31, 252
Waugh, Mark
    Ashes: 1993 119
    bribery offer 136
    fines 154, 236
    Healy and 248
    India: 1998 229
    South Africa: 1997 200,
        202–3; 1997–98 226–27
    Test debut 140
    Test debut hundred 76
    West Indies: 1991 83, 86;
        1992–93 105; 1995 161
    World Cup: 1996 173
Waugh, Steve
    Ashes: 1989 59, 62; 1993
        110–11, 117, 119; 1997
        211; 1998–99 236,
        237–38
    batsman 242–43
    captaincy 198, 208,
        245–46
    Chaplin 163
    Chennai: 1996 229
    dropped 76
    Healy and 54, 224, 248, 252
    maiden Test hundred 62
    Pakistan: 1988 37, 44;
        1995–96 165; 1998 231
    players' contracts 216
    radio interview 63

Simpson and 181
sledging 99
South Africa: 1994 127;
    1997 197, 200, 202, 204
Sri Lanka: 1996 183; 1999
    247
West Indies: 1988–89 42,
    43, 48; 1992–93 104, 105;
    1995 155, 157, 159, 161;
    1996–97 188; 1999 240
World Cup: 1999 245
Wellington (NZ) 69
Welsh, Pat 128
West Indies
    1987 23
    1988–89 42–52
    1991 78–88
    1992–93 99–101, 102–7
    1995 153–63
    1996–97 187–90, 193–95
    1999 240–44
West Indies Cricket Board 171
Whatmore, Dav 169
Whitney, Lorraine 28
Whitney, Mike 51, 92
Whitsunday Islands 73
Whyte, Graham 98
wicketkeeping 9–10, 14, 22,
    123–24, 131, 213, 218–20,
    259
Williams, Stuart 157, 161
Wisden 219
Woolmer, Bob 200
Workplace Relations Act 216
World Cup
    1992 95, 121
    1996 164, 170–71, 173–77
    1999 244, 245, 246
World Series Cup
    1986–87 23
    1988–89 43
Wright, John 69

Z

Zia, General 33
Zimbabwe
    1994 140
    1999 248–51
Zoehrer, Tim 46, 53, 56, 102,
    109, 111, 114

WATCH OUT FOR
IAN HEALY

COMING SOON TO VIDEO

This video represents a very detailed history not only of Ian's career in cricket, but also his childhood years and how his family contributed to his success.

When talking about cricket specifically, Ian covers the highs and lows of his career, the controversies and his outstanding achievements. We talk to both current and ex-international players, including Steve & Mark Waugh, Shane Warne, Ricky Ponting, Allan Border, Craig McDermott and Greg Chappell, to name a few.

We also talk to Ian about his 'forced retirement' and his disappointmen associated with the way it was handled. We talk about sledging and in particular the 'Arjuna incident'.

This video is yet to be classified at time of printing and will be available from all good video retailers.